AGROPOLIS

AGROPOLIS

The Social, Political and Environmental Dimensions of Urban Agriculture

Edited by Luc J. A. Mougeot

International Development Research Centre
Ottawa · Cairo · Dakar · Montevideo · Nairobi · New Delhi · Singapore

publishing for a sustainable future

London • Washington, DC

First published in the UK, USA and Canada in 2005
by Earthscan and the International Development Research Centre (IDRC)
Reprinted 2008
Moved to digital printing 2010

Copyright © IDRC, 2005

ISBN: 978-1-84407-232-3

Typeset by MapSet Ltd, Gateshead, UK
Cover design by Danny Gillespie

For a full list of publications please contact:

Earthscan Ltd, Dunstan House, 14a St Cross Street, London EC1N 8XA, UK
Earthscan LLC, 1616 P Street, NW, Washington, DC 20036, USA
Earthscan publishes in association with the International Institute for Environment
and Development

For more information on Earthscan publications, see www.earthscan.co.uk or write to
earthinfo@earthscan.co.uk

IDRC publishes an e-book edition of AGROPOLIS (ISBN 1-55250-186-8)
For further information, please contact:
International Development Research Centre
PO Box 8500
Ottawa, ON
Canada K1G 3H9
Email: pub@idrc.ca
Web: www.idrc.ca

IDRC is a Canadian public corporation that works in close collaboration with
researchers from the developing world with the aim of building healthier, more
equitable and more prosperous societies

A catalogue record for this book is available from the British Library

Library of Congress Cataloging-in-Publication Data

Agropolis : the social, political, and environmental dimensions of urban agriculture /
Edited by Luc J. A. Mougeot.
     p. cm.
 Includes bibliographical references and index.
 ISBN 1-84407-232-0 — ISBN 1-84407-231-2
 1. Urban agriculture. I. Mougeot, Luc J. A.
 S494.5.U72A44 2005
 630'.9173'2—dc22

                                                                    2005015725

At Earthscan we strive to minimize our environmental impacts and carbon footprint
through reducing waste, recycling and offsetting our CO_2 emissions, including those
created through publication of this book. For more details of our environmental
policy, see www.earthscan.co.uk.

FSC
Mixed Sources
Product group from well-managed
forests and other controlled sources
Cert no. SGS-COC-2953
www.fsc.org
© 1996 Forest Stewardship Council

Printed and bound in the UK by
CPI Antony Rowe.
The paper used is FSC certified.

Contents

List of Boxes, Figures and Tables

BOXES

FIGURES

TABLES

Foreword

In the array of published work on urban agriculture, AGROPOLIS is like a beam of light showing us a way forward in a new area of research that is not yet fully illuminated. The concept of urban agriculture is indeed highly contested – an oxymoron for some, despite its obvious presence as an activity pursued by many people. For there is no doubt that enormous numbers of urban farmers, mostly very poor and usually women, produce food in urban areas, with insufficient policy support. In trying to develop it as an area of research, students and academics approach it from a variety of disciplines, attempting to answer diverse research questions built upon a variety of underlying theoretical constructs.

It is to the credit of the International Development Research Centre (IDRC) that it has designed and run this programme of awards for a period of five years with an open mind. Despite the clear points of focus in its own programmatic work on Cities Feeding People, IDRC permits masters, doctoral and, since autumn 2002, post-doctoral students to apply for AGROPOLIS awards on urban agriculture subjects that are important to them. The collection of work presented in this book reflects the range of concerns that have come to light; concerns that are worth taking seriously.

What we can learn from this collection are not only the circumstances in which people farm in urban areas but, much more importantly, the reasons they have for how and why they do so. The fact that these reasons and methods are so diverse around the world should not deter scholars and readers from asking themselves the fundamental question about urban agriculture: what role does it play in people's strategies for having a decent life in urban areas?

We can reflect, with Amartya Sen, that people need the freedom to pursue their development with the resources they can obtain entitlements to use. As portrayed in this book, the ways in which people try to improve their lives through the production of food are extraordinarily diverse. Moreover, they produce food for extraordinarily different reasons. Policy makers in particular may find this volume helpful in understanding some of their fellow citizens' needs for engaging in urban agriculture.

Diana Lee-Smith
Sub-Saharan Africa Coordinator
Strategic Initiative on Urban and Peri-urban Agriculture
May 2005

Preface

This book presents the first harvest of graduate research on urban agriculture supported by the AGROPOLIS small-grant facility of Canada's International Development Research Centre (IDRC). Over the years, IDRC has been encouraging the establishment of new scientific expertise to tackle emerging development issues. One enduring way in which the centre has been doing this is through facilities that provide small grants, on a competitive basis, for graduate students from Canada and Southern countries to do their field research on neglected aspects of development. One such facility is the International Graduate Research Awards for Research in Urban Agriculture, better known as AGROPOLIS.

THE AGROPOLIS FACILITY

The word AGROPOLIS combines the Latin word 'ager' (field) with the Greek word 'polis' (city), to suggest a city of fields or agricultural city. The choice of this word for the naming of the IDRC small-grant facility for research in a new development reality was fittingly inspired by a daring Southern undertaking: Brazil's National Integration Programme. Launched in the 1970s, this federal programme aimed to integrate the Brazilian Amazon region into the national space economy through exploiting its natural riches and developing an urban system with three orders of settlements: from simple village-like 'agrovilas' to more complex economic centres called 'agropoles' and 'ruropoles'. The mid-range 'agropolis' order refers to mid-sized cities with a considerable measure of food self-reliance. The planned system has been building upon the historical pattern of settlement. It has evolved considerably since its introduction 30 years ago, but continues to organize human settlement in the Brazilian Amazon. There is a parallel to be drawn between Brazil's bold enterprise on its resource frontier and IDRC's daring initiative to populate a new area of scientific expertise with a young generation of researchers.

The AGROPOLIS facility responds to several needs identified over the years, both externally and internally to IDRC. Since 1993, as IDRC increased funding of institutional research on urban agriculture, project leaders had been asking for more systematic assistance for methodological and conceptual training in this new field of inquiry. While recognizing the need to support young researchers in this new field, IDRC, through its Cities Feeding People Programme Initiative (CFP), which was launched in 1997, looked at ways to:

- reduce transaction costs associated with processing individual grant requests;
- compare and assess more systematically such applications;
- network young researchers among themselves; and
- generally articulate synergies between training and other related and concomitant CFP activities (institutional research, information dissemination, result utilization and evaluation).

Therefore, since inception, the central objective of AGROPOLIS has been to heighten the quality and impact of Southern urban agriculture expertise through issue-focused, participatory applied, internationally selected and networked, efficiently managed and strategically disseminated graduate research.

The AGROPOLIS facility is financially supported, hosted and coordinated by IDRC. It is a project for which funding is periodically renewed and administered by the CFP and the Special Initiatives Programme (SIP) of IDRC. The concept for the facility was drafted in 1997 by CFP in consultation with SIP, then funded and launched in mid-1998. The first annual distribution of awards took place in early 1999. AGROPOLIS constitutes IDRC's own contribution to the research training component of the Global Initiative of the Support Group on Urban Agriculture (SGUA) formalized in Ottawa in 1996 (other components include information, led by ETC International; policy, led by the Urban Management Programme (UMP) of United Nations Human Settlements Programme (UN-HABITAT); technical assistance, led by the Urban Harvest initiative of the Consortium Group for International Agricultural Research (CGIAR) at the International Potato Centre; and credit and financing, also currently led by UMP).

IDRC's AGROPOLIS facility should be distinguished from the Agropolis complex of agricultural research institutions in Montpellier, France. However, it should be noted that the two are not operating in isolation. IDRC has collaborated over the years with several institutions of the Agropolis complex and its AGROPOLIS facility is no exception. Since its inception, AGROPOLIS has been weaving a multi-faceted collaboration with the French complex, as well as with other agricultural research systems (for example CGIAR). In early 1999, on the occasion of an AGROPOLIS project officer's visit to the director of the Agropolis Museum in Montpellier, both institutions agreed to collaborate with each other in the context of AGROPOLIS. AGROPOLIS has involved senior researchers from the French complex on its international Advisory Committee and made developing-country students in France eligible for AGROPOLIS field research awards, while Agropolis institutions have participated in the joint organization and delivery (with IDRC) of a training course on urban agriculture for francophone West Africa in mid-2000 and the joint editing and publication of a training manual (available at http://web.idrc.ca/en/ev-52181-201-1-DO_TOPIC.html). This collaboration is expected to continue on new fronts in the coming years.

A MORE ENABLING RESEARCH ENVIRONMENT FOR AWARDEES

Over a period of four years (1999–2003) AGROPOLIS has awarded 39 small grants, shared almost equally between women and men, and between masters and doctoral/post-doctoral projects. Awardees from 21 countries have conducted or are currently conducting research in some 26 countries in Central and South America, the Middle East, Southeast Asia and throughout Africa. These awardees include four Canada-born students and three from Southern countries who did their fieldwork in a country other than that of their citizenship. The 39 grants were awarded to the best of 104 applications that reached the final review stage, these making up about 54 per cent of all applications submitted to the facility. The remainder were rejected due to submissions being unfit and/or incomplete. By early 2003, 22 of the 39 awardees had completed their field. More information on the awardees and their research, findings and outcomes is available on individual fact sheets posted on the AGROPOLIS section of the CFP website (www.idrc.ca/cfp).

The awardees' research environment has improved considerably over this short period of time, partly due to the fact that the AGROPOLIS facility is managed by and interacts with CFP, which itself provides support to a range of activities, resources and institutions involved in urban agriculture research and policy.

The papers included in this book testify to synergies that have become more common in more recent cohorts of applicants. More proposals make use of literature generated by IDRC partners in this field, more applicants are being recommended for awards, and more awardees are being hosted by Southern institutions actively engaged in urban agricultural research and supported by IDRC and other agencies. There is greater communication among awardees, interaction with regional and global networks, and more projects aim to pursue research beyond the findings made by earlier awardees. Some have published in *Urban Agriculture Magazine* and other media even prior to completing their research. A few have already served on international advisory boards and/or taken faculty positions at universities, where they pursue their research on urban agriculture.

Awardees are encouraged to secure additional funding from other agencies and a partial survey of awardees in late 2001 indicated that eight had secured as much funding from other sources for their research programme in urban agriculture as they had received from AGROPOLIS for their fieldwork alone.

Luc J. A. Mougeot
Senior Programme Specialist
International Development Research Centre

Acknowledgements

The AGROPOLIS programme wishes to express its sincere appreciation to several individuals who helped with the production of this book. My colleagues Dr Ola Smith and Mr Naser Faruqui assisted me with selecting, commissioning and reviewing the papers presented in Ottawa in 2002. Ms Kristina Taboulchanas advised awardees on their oral presentations. Ms Wendy Storey, the Awards Administrator, is to be thanked warmly for her long-standing commitment to AGROPOLIS and support of the awardees. In addition to her involvement in some of the aforementioned tasks leading to the Ottawa event, Ms Storey effectively publicized and organized the event. Ms Linda MacWillie diligently handled all event-related multiple financial matters. During Ms Storey's maternity leave after the event, Liliane Castets-Poupart filled her position and ensured smooth communication with the external reviewers of the papers, allowing the publication project to keep moving forward.

The members of the 2002 Advisory Committee reviewed the research published in this book: Dr Diana Lee-Smith (International Potato Centre), Dr Chris Furedy (University of York), Dr Juan Izquierdo (Food and Agriculture Organization), Dr Paule Moustier and Professor Godfrey Mudimu. Also, the following specialists made additional suggestions that contributed greatly to the final versions of the papers: Dr Manon Bouliane (University of Laval, Canada), Dr Yves Cabannes (UN-HABITAT, Ecuador), Dr Axel Drescher (University of Freiburg, Germany), Dr Kathleen Flynn-Dapaah (Policy and Planning Unit, IDRC), Dr Mustafa Koc (Ryerson University, Canada), Dr David J. Midmore (Central Queensland University, Australia), Mr Alain Santandreu (UN-HABITAT, Ecuador) and Dr Steve Staal (International Livestock Research Institute, Kenya). Finally, my thanks are also extended to the academics who supervised the research of the AGROPOLIS awardees: Dr Jonathan Crush (Queen's University, for Bruce Frayne), Dr Kwame Gbesemete (Sveriges Lantbruks Universite, for Komla Tallaki), Dr Arthur Stoecker (Oklahoma State University, for Mody Bakar Barry), Dr Leonora C. Angeles (University of British Columbia, for Stephanie Gabel), Professor Dianne Rocheleau and Associate Professor Susan Hanson (Clark University, for Alice Hovorka), Professor Margaret C. Rodman (York University, for Adriana Premat), Mr Antonio Lattuca (Universidad Nacional de Rosario, for Eduardo Spiaggi), Dr Pierre Donadieu (École nationale supérieure du paysage, for Moez Bouraoui) and Dr Simon Anderson (Wye College, University of London, for Arturo Perez Vazquez).

List of Acronyms and Abbreviations

AEV	Agence des espaces verts (agency for green spaces – France)
ARSD	Agricultural Research and Statistics Directorate (Togo)
CAEFO	Casa de Altos Estudios Don Fernando Ortiz (Cuba)
CAP	countryside action plan (France)
CDR	Committees for the Defence of the Revolution (Cuba)
CFA	Communauté Financière Africaine – African Financial Community (Côte d'Ivoire)
CFP	Cities Feeding People Programme Initiative
CGIAR	Consortium Group for International Agricultural Research
CIP	Canadian Institute of Planners
CIRAD	Centre de Coopération Internationale en Recherché Agronomique pour le Développement
COOPEMA	Coopérative de Maraîchers d'Agoènyivé (Agèonyivé market gardeners' cooperative)
CVM	contingent valuation method
DDT	dichlorodiphenyltrichloroethane
DTRP	Department of Town and Regional Planning
ESA	Empresa de Suministros Agropecuarios (agricultural supplies enterprise)
FANJ	Fundación Antonio Nuñez Jiménez (Antonio Nuñez Jiménez Foundation)
FAO	Food and Agriculture Organisation (of the UN)
GDIC	Grupo para el Desarrollo Integral de La Capital (Group for the Holistic Development of the Capital – Cuba)
GDPD	General Directorate of Planning and Development (Togo)
GGPA	Greater Gaborone Planning Area (Botswana)
HHI	household income
IAES	Institute for Agricultural Extension and Support (Togo)
IDRC	International Development Research Centre
IDSP	Intercommunal District of the Saclay Plateau (France)
IOA	Institute of Agronomy (University of Lomé, Togo)
MARP	méthode accélérée de recherche participative (accelerated participatory research method)
MAVEL	Magasin de vente de légumes (vegetable shop)
MDGs	Millennium Development Goals
MDP–ESA	Municipal Development Program for Eastern and Southern Africa
MINAGRI	Ministry of Agriculture (Cuba)

MoA	Ministry of Agriculture (Botswana)
MoW	Municipality of Windhoek (Namibia)
NAD	Namibia dollars
NGO	non-governmental organization
NRI	Natural Resources Institute
NSALG	National Society of Allotment and Leisure Gardens Ltd (England)
PAIA	Priority Area for Interdisciplinary Action
PRA	participatory rapid appraisal; participatory rural appraisal
RALF	Regional Directorate of Agriculture, Livestock and Fishing (Togo)
RUAF	Resource Centre on Urban Agriculture and Forestry
SAFER	Société d'aménagement foncier et d'établissement rural (land-use and rural-settlement corporation – France)
SGUA	Support Group on Urban Agriculture
SIP	Special Initiatives Programme
SOTOCO	Société togolaise de coton (Togolese national cotton corporation)
TCA	Tiendas Consultorios Agropecuarios (agricultural goods and services store – Cuba)
TEV	total economic value
TIAR	Togolese Institute for Agronomic Research
UA	urban agriculture
UAA	useful agricultural area
UASPS	Union des associations de sauvegarde du plateau de Saclay (union of associations for the preservation of the Saclay Plateau – France)
UMP	Urban Management Programme
UNEP	United Nations Environment Programme
UN-HABITAT	United Nations Human Settlements Programme
USD	United States dollar
WHO	World Health Organisation
WTA	willingness to accept
WTP	willingness to pay

Introduction

Luc J. A. Mougeot

URBAN AGRICULTURE AND THE MILLENNIUM DEVELOPMENT GOALS

Governments across the world have entered the 21st century with a growing recognition that cities should be given much more attention in development strategies than has been the case in most regions and countries so far. In 2000, 2001 and 2002 respectively, the UN Millennium Declaration, the Declaration on Cities and Other Human Settlements in the New Millennium and outcomes of the World Summit on Sustainable Development reinforced the international commitment to sustainable urban development and poverty reduction (UN-HABITAT, 2004a). The conversion of the UN Centre for Human Settlements into a fully-fledged programme for cities, now called the United Nations Human Settlements Programme (UN-HABITAT); the merging of global advisory fora on various urban issues into a single bi-annual summit (the World Urban Forum); the UN system's growing statistical scrutiny of urban indicators through its Global Urban Observatory and other UN annual reports; all of these developments translate into more widespread and marked changes at national and local levels. Policy makers are coming to admit that better resourced and informed, more inclusive and comprehensive approaches to urban development are needed.

Clearly, the likelihood of meeting the current Millennium Development Goals (MDGs)[1] will depend greatly on how much progress is made in the cities of the developing world. By 2015–2020 well over half of the world's population will be living in urban and peri-urban areas, the majority of them in developing country cities. If present trends hold, the vast majority of these people will be living in irregular settlements, without access to decent food, shelter, water and sanitation (UN-HABITAT, 2004b). The slum population, currently estimated at 1 billion, could rise to 1.5 billion by 2020 (UN-HABITAT, 2004c).[2] Percentages of urban populations living in slums in 2001 ranged from 24 per cent in Oceania to 32 per cent in Latin America and the Caribbean, 42 per cent in Asia and the Pacific, and 61 per cent in Africa.

We can debate the political and technical capacity of agencies and governments to achieve the MDG targets over the next generation or so, but few will challenge their significance and urgency. The numbers quoted above will continue to rise if reforms do not reshape institutions and governance systems so that governments can stimulate pro-poor and socially inclusive development. This does not need to be an uphill battle. While more urban dwellers may suffer from low living standards, cities are centres of information, ingenuity and collaboration, where new approaches to housing, employment and service provision (such as water, transportation, education and health care) are introducing and, increasingly, mainstreaming new forms of building, working and living in the city. Meeting MDGs in cities does require in a large measure to recognize, support and empower on an unprecedented scale the urban poor's own livelihood strategies. The so-called informal urban sector used to be dismissed as a transient, minority phenomenon; it is now becoming the norm in a growing number of cities. Urban populations are setting new standards and cities must reinvent themselves with new references.

Informal urban agriculture (UA) is one livelihood strategy that the urban poor use in combination with other strategies. It has been defined in various ways over the years and across disciplines. A review of definitions commissioned by International Development Research Centre (IDRC) (Quon, 1999) led Mougeot to propose the following:

> Urban agriculture is an industry located within (intra-urban) or on the fringe (peri-urban) of a town, a city or a metropolis, which grows and raises, processes and distributes a diversity of food and non-food products, (re-)using largely human and material resources, products and services found in and around that urban area, and in turn supplying human and material resources, products and services largely to that urban area. (Mougeot, 2000, p10)

This definition has been used in technical and training publications by UN-HABITAT's Urban Management Programme (Cabannes and Dubbeling, 2001; Dubbeling and Santandreu, 2003), the Special Programme for Food Security of the UN's Food and Agriculture Organisation (FAO) (Drescher, 2001), and international agricultural research centres such as the Centre de Coopération Internationale en Recherche Agronomique pour le Développement (CIRAD) (Moustier and Salam Fall, 2004). Definitions of UA will continue to evolve, as they are applied to an ever-diverse range of contexts and purposes.

There always has been a formal UA sector in and around cities, but what is new is the dramatic expansion of its informal counterpart over the last 30 years. There are two major forces driving people from all walks of life, particularly those on low incomes and the poor, to cultivate the city: food security and income generation.

URBAN AGRICULTURE AND FOOD SECURITY

MDG 1 calls for halving, between 1990 and 2015, the proportion of people whose income is less than one dollar a day, as well as 'the proportion of people who suffer from hunger', particularly the prevalence of underweight children and the proportion of the population who have a below minimum level of dietary energy consumption. More than 30 per cent of the population in South Asia and sub-Saharan Africa suffers from undernourishment and the prevalence has been rising in the Middle East and North Africa.

In the majority of countries for which World Bank and World Health Organisation (WHO) data are available and comparable, the number of poor is increasing and the urban share of all poor is rising; the number of malnourished young children in urban areas is increasing and so is the urban share of all malnourished young children; the rich–poor gap in stunting is greater in urban than in rural areas; it is also greater than the overall gap between rural and urban areas (Lawrence et al, 1999).

Cities obtain their food from a variety of sources, domestic and foreign, rural and urban. IDRC research in the 1980s found that the urban poor experience difficulties in tapping into the formal food supply system of the city, regardless of how efficient such systems may be. Instead, the urban poor resort to various informal food procurement strategies, the mix of which will vary according to context. In urban settings where rural–urban migration is short-distance, where a majority of the urban poor retain access to rural food through land ownership or reciprocity exchanges (transportation is affordable), rural–urban food transfers play a more important role in feeding the urban poor and self-provisioning is more limited. This type of context is exemplified by Bruce Frayne's study of Windhoek, Namibia, in this volume. In contexts where long-distance rural–urban migration grows, where more of the urban poor have less access to rural assets, self-provisioning becomes more important. UA has spread to become a critical source of food for urban populations in countries affected by natural disasters (Honduras), economic crises (Togo), civil wars (Armenia) and disease epidemics (Malawi). Several such factors have endured for many years in Zimbabwe (Stephanie Gabel in this volume), where UA on public land in Harare grew from 267 ha in 1995, to 4822 ha in 1990 and 9288 ha in 1994 (data from Maseva, 2003, p21).

The difficulties that the urban poor face in acquiring sufficient and healthy food from traditional rural agriculture are compounded by policies that either neglect or discourage – when they do not repress – the informal food systems on which the poor depend. Policies often respond to globalization forces that may dictate both the supply and demand options for UA.

On the supply side, policy factors buttressing UA include: monetary or economic crises at home or abroad may restrict a country's ability to import food that is critical to urban supplies (Togo, Côte d'Ivoire, Cuba in this volume). Programmes to reduce dependency on food imports (Botswana in this volume) may spur market oriented UA. Civil strife, land redistribution reforms, extreme climatic events (Zimbabwe in this volume) may all concur to reduce rural food production and supplies to cities. Even without such stressors, agricultural policies that are largely export-oriented may promote rural crop choices and distribution networks that leave urban markets under-supplied. High transaction costs may discourage rural producers from supplying critical urban markets. Smaller cities may lose part of their surrounding food shed to larger urban markets. Where high-quality food is produced, it may be marketed locally only briefly in any given year. Some Southern countries import staple surpluses from the North which are lower-quality sources of protein and calories than their own domestic production, freeing the latter for export to strong-currency consumer markets.

On the demand side, policy factors that encourage the growth of UA include: currency devaluations, job cuts and the elimination of subsidies for basic needs, which reduce the urban poor's and the middle class's ability to obtain healthy food (see Togo and Côte d'Ivoire in this volume). Trade liberalization and other macro-economic adjustments may force the removal of price subsidies, which in turn may exacerbate the seasonality of food prices to urban consumers. Low-income households spend more than 50–80 per cent of their disposable income on food and still do not meet their daily dietary needs. Women retain a critical role in food procurement, preparation and distribution inside and outside their household. Poor female-led households are becoming more numerous in developing cities and these are especially at risk of food insecurity, given that they have less access to rural and urban land. Women's ability to perform their multiple roles in relation to food security may be enhanced by their participation in UA.

There is evidence to suggest that UA's contribution to urban food supply and household urban food security is significant and in many instances is growing. In 1996 UNDP estimated that some 800 million people were engaged in UA worldwide in the early 1990s, or one third of urban families supplying roughly one third of all food consumed in cities. Surveys conducted in some 24 cities and four countries (urban areas) across the world in the late 1990s suggest several recent trends in UA's contribution to urban food supply and household food security (Table 1).

Most cities for which data are available in English and French literature are located in Africa, Europe and Asia, with a few in Latin America. Most data are still drawn from non-official surveys, but a growing number of governments and international agencies are beginning to collect data themselves. In fact, several food policy programmes, councils, departments and offices, mostly at the municipal level, were created in the 1990s; this should contribute to improving the supply and demand for official statistics on local urban and peri-urban production. Countries like Nigeria, Tanzania and Uganda have been collecting official statistics on UA systems for one or two decades now.

Quantities supplied by intra-urban and peri-urban production are considerable, amounting to thousands of metric tons and millions of litres. This production provides the bulk of all fresh and perishable food consumed

Table 1 *Contribution of urban food production to urban food supply (city and households) in selected cities and countries, 1990s*

City	Weight supplied (per year)	% total supply (city or households)	Source
ACCRA, Ghana 1997	211,000 t vegs (1996) 66,500 t vegs (1992)	90% fresh vegs, city (7.5–66% total food value for producers)	Armar-Klemesu, 2000: 104; Dreschel et al, 1999: 28; Armar-Klemesu & Maxwell, 2000:194
ADDIS ABABA, Ethiopia 1999	34.6 m l/a milk	79% milk, city	Tegegne et al, 2000: 24
ANTANANARIVO, Madagascar		90% leafy vegs, city (grown by 50% households)	Moustier, 1999: 47
BANDIM, Guinea Bissau		31–68% vendors sell vegs self-grown, city	Lourenço-Lindell, 1995: 8
BANGUI, C.A.R.		100% leafy vegs, city	Moustier, 1999: 47
BISSAU, Guinea Bissau		90% leafy vegs, city (grown by 30% households)	Moustier, 1999: 47
BRAZZAVILLE, Congo		80% leafy vegs, city (grown by 25% households)	Moustier 1999: 47
CAGAYAN DE ORO, Philippines (0.5 m) 1995		70% fish (marine), city	Potutan et al, 2000: 419
DAKAR, Senegal (4.5 m) 1997	64,000 t vegs	60+% vegs, city 65–70% poultry (national) 10% total food consumption by households	Mbaye & Moustier, 2000: 243–4
DAR ES SALAAM, Tanzania 1996		90% leafy vegs, city 60% milk (16% intra, 44% peri-urban), city 20–30% of food consumption in 50% of households	Stevenson et al, 1996; Jacobi et al, 2000: 268; Sawio, 1993
HANOI, Vietnam		50% meat demand, city (forecast: 80% by 2010)	Peters, 2000: 37
HARARE, Zimbabwe		60% of food consumption in 25% of poor city households	Armar-Klemesu, 2000: 104

City	Weight supplied (per year)	% total supply (city or households)	Source
JAKARTA, Indonesia Aug 1999	5671 t produce (grown on vacant lands)		Purnomohadi, 2000: 453
KAMPALA, Uganda		20% of staple food consumption, households 40+% of food for 55% of households 60+% of food for 32% of households 70% of all poultry products consumed in city	Maxwell, 1994: 49 Maxwell & Zziwa, 1992 Idem Maxwell, 1995: 1672
KUMASI, Ghana	150 t/day of fish from farms	13,000 street food kiosks supplied with urban cattle meat, city	Brooks & Davila, 2000: 101; Dreschel et al., 2000: 25
LA HABANA, Cuba 2000 1996	150–300gr/p/d vegs-herbs 160,000 t foodstuff (44,243 t in 1995) 3650 t meat 7.5 m eggs 4 m cut flowers		FUNAT, 2001: 4 Gonzalez Novo & Murphy, 2000: 338 Altieri et al, 1999: 139
LONDON, United Kingdom	27 t honey (worth BRP 15.7 m) 232,000 t fruits/vegs (est.)	10% honey, city	Garnett, 2000: 488 Armar-Klemesu, 2000: 104
NEW YORK, U.S.A. (0.5 m) 1849	49,000 l/d milk		Tremante, 2000: 6
NOUAKCHOTT, Mauritania 1997	11,700 t fruits/vegs	18% vegs/fruits, city	Gueye & Sy, 2001: 30
SHANGHAI, China	1.3 m t vegs (4000 t/d)	60% vegs (100 before) 90% eggs, city	Yi-Zhang & Zhangen, 2000: 471
SOFIA, Bulgaria 1996 1997	15,400 t market vegs 17,155 l milk 5920 t pig/beef meat	100% milk, city	Yoveva et al, 2000: 507–8
ST PETERSBURG, Russia (5 m) 1998	23,812,000 eggs 15,800 t potatoes 47,400 t apples, pears, 38,500 t vegs 7,900 t strawberries 23 m cut flowers		Moldakov, 2000: 24
URBAN BULGARIA (WHO) 1998		47% vegs/fruits, city	Pederson & Robertson, 2001: 10

City	Weight supplied (per year)	% total supply (city or households)	Source
URBAN POLAND (WHO) 1997	500,000 t vegs/fruits (from 8000 council gardens)		Pederson & Robertson, 2001: 10
URBAN ROMANIA (WHO) 1994 1989		37% of household food supply – 1994 25% of household food supply 1989	Pederson & Robertson, 2001: 10
URBAN RUSSIA (WHO)		88% potatoes, city	Pederson & Robertson, 2001: 10

Source: Luc J. A. Mougeot (from official census and field samples reported in references quoted in the table)

by the cities (leafy vegetables, milk, fish, poultry, some starch such as potatoes). These foods are important sources of micronutrients, critical to citywide and household-level food security strategies.

The number of households involved in growing some food varies from city to city and from product to product, but their share tends to represent something between an important minority and a large majority of all households.

Their production contributes a non-negligible percentage of all food consumed by urban households; a percentage that is even higher for poorer households. Some data also suggest that there is, in many cities, an important association between urban food (and non-food) production and street and market vending of fresh and processed food. In some cities, UA production has been deemed critical to sustaining urban food fairs (Jacobi et al, 2000). Proper urban planning, micro-credit and food-safe practices can help these production and marketing components of the urban food supply system to increase their contribution to food security. UA production and street vending can make fresh and nutritious food more readily accessible to residents of sprawling cities, where they spend more and more time away from home and have less and less time to prepare their own meals.

Finally, where records for previous years and projections for the future are available, the figures suggest that the relative importance of UA production in total food supply increases over time, at city and/or at household levels. However, data are few and far between. A more systematic effort is needed to improve the breadth, periodicity and consistency of statistical monitoring on UA production.

In countries such as Zimbabwe, Kenya, Uganda and Haiti, where poor households practising UA have been compared with poor non-practising households, the former have been found to have lower food insecurity, eat more meals, maintain a more balanced diet year-round, and use their savings to buy other food items that would otherwise be unaffordable; their children have better health and nutritional status (women practising UA also give more maternal care time to young children) (Maxwell, 1995; ENDA-ZW, 1997; Foeken and Mwangi, 2000; Régis et al, 2000).

URBAN AGRICULTURE FOR MORE DECENT AND PRODUCTIVE URBAN LIVELIHOODS

The second major force driving UA is income (and savings) generation. Data from surveys conducted in the late 1990s for 24 cities and one country (urban areas) around the world indicate that UA represents a sizeable source of employment and income (Table 2).

Thousands of farmers and tens of thousands of workers may be engaged in a particular type of UA production at any given time. The Lomé case study in this volume illustrates the capacity of market-oriented systems to absorb workers from other urban activities, when urban demand justifies it. Since the late 1980s, employment in Lomé's market vegetable-growing business multiplied several times (from 620 in 1987 to 3000 in 1994), in response to population growth, reduced food imports and rising local unemployment. Only 6 per cent of the growers in Tallaki's sample had previous primary-sector work experience and the great majority of them, both men and women, were now occupied full time in vegetable growing. The Gabarone case study shows that a category of small entrepreneurs in UA can emerge, in which women participate, where financing programmes are made accessible to this occupational category. UA production is an even more important second or third source of income for poor urban households who try to reduce economic insecurity.

Another finding from Table 2 is that, generally, the higher the market value of the produce, the larger is its contribution to household income (eg maize versus ornamentals or milk). This indicates the difference that urban producers' access to certain production systems can make to their living standards.

Incomes and wages from UA tend to compare favourably with those of unskilled construction workers. They are often larger than those of mid-level civil servants (Tanzania, Cuba). By growing their food, producers can save considerable money because they have to purchase less food. Annual savings in food purchases may equate to several months of a minimal wage. Selling some of the harvest generates income that can subsequently be used to meet other basic needs, such as schooling for children. Particularly in less consolidated poor settlements, savings or incomes from home-based UA allow women to invest in other home-based income-generating activities that contribute to improved household well-being (see, for example, Gough and Kellett, 2001). This can be especially useful in cultures that do not allow adult and married women to work away from home. With fair access to resources and services, UA can be an integral component of income and employment strategies, while also building more self-reliant local food supply systems.

Table 2 *Contribution of urban agricultural production to urban employment, income and food expense savings in selected cities and countries, 1990s*

City	Producers (self-provision market)	Economic return (income, savings)	Source
ACCRA, Ghana 1997	13.6% of households in 16 city areas 700 market farmers	income of 20–100s USD/month (seasonal)	Sonou, 2001: 33; Armar-Klemesu & Maxwell, 2000: 184, 193
ADDIS ABABA, Ethiopia 1999	5167 dairy units	76% of secondary city and 54% of inner Addis dairy units owned by women	Tegegne et al, 2000: 24
BAMAKO, Mali 1994		wages equivalent or higher than for senior civil servants	Zallé, 1999: 9
CAGAYAN DE ORO, Philippines 1995 1997	13,000 jobs (farmers and tenants) 40% households 96% public elementary schools 1397 fishermen		Potutan et al, 2000: 419
CAIRO, Egypt 1995	16% households (livestock) – 59% of whom are poor	livestock assets exceed 2–3 times monthly capita income	Gertel & Samir, 2000: 215
CALCUTTA, India 2000	17,000 jobs in wetland fisheries		Edwards 2001: 20
DAKAR, Senegal 1996	15,000 + jobs 3000 family veg farms (14,000 jobs) ca 1250 commercial vegetable farms (9000 jobs) 250 poultry units		Mbaye & Moustier, 2000: 246
DAR ES SALAAM, Tanzania 1997	15–20% families home garden (2 areas) (full-time production)	30% of average salary 35,000 households depend on fruit/veg production for income	Nugent, 2000: 76 Jacobi et al, 2000: 264
HARARE, Zimbabwe 1996	42 of HD households in off-plot	2 weeks–7 months minimum industrial wage (savings)	Mbiba, 1995: 61 ENDA-ZW, 1997
JAKARTA, Indonesia 1999	100,234 owners & workers	wage higher than for unskilled construction work	Purnomohadi, 2000: 454, 457
KUMASI, Ghana (0.7 m)	1470 registered farms (+ 30,000 unregist) 500 ft cattle owners (+ 200 pt) 100 registered poultry farms (+ 200 unregis)	14% of cattle owners drew 50%+ of income from cattle	Dreschel et al, 2000: 25; Poynter & Fielding, 2000: 28

City	Producers (self-provision market)	Economic return (income, savings)	Source
LA HABANA, Cuba 1998	117,000 direct and 26,000 indirect jobs		Gonzalez & Murphy, 2000: 334, 344
LOME, Togo		net wage from market vegetable production equivalent to mid-level manager in civil service	Kouvonou et al, 1999: 98
LONDON, United Kingdom	3,000 jobs 1000 bee-keepers 30,000 allotment holders 77 community gardens 50% population home gardens	BRP 3 m fruits/vegs	Garnett, 2000: 478
LUSAKA, Zambia		savings equivalent to 3 months worker's wage (very seasonal)	Drescher, 1999
MEXICO CITY, Mexico 1990–96	1.3–19% EAP in some Delegaciones	10–40% income (swine) up to 100% income (milk) 10–30% income (maize) 80% income (veg) 80% + income (ornamentals) 100% income (nopal, tuna, HS)	Torres Lima et al, 2000
MOSCOW, Russia 1999	65% families (20% in 1970)		Deelstra & Girardet, 1999: 46
NAIROBI, Kenya 1994	150,000 households (30% population)		Foeken & Mwangi, 2000: 307, 314
NAKURU, Kenya (0.24 m) 1999	20% households (livestock) (14% LI – 38% HI) majority women		Foeken & Owuor, 2000: 20
PORT SUDAN, Sudan (0.8 m) 1999	23% households (goats) – Beja		Pantuliano, 2000: 15
SANTIAGO, Dominican Republic (0.5 m) 1997		40% + minimum salary	del Rosario et al, 2000: 99
SHANGHAI, China (13 m)	2.7 m farmers (31.8% workers) 13,400 workers	2% of city GDP 28% households get some income	Yi-Zhang & Zhangen, 2000: 467, 468
SOFIA, Bulgaria 1997	(official)		Yoveva et al, 2000: 509

City	Producers (self-provision market)	Economic return (income, savings)	Source
THIES, Senegal 1998	70,000 poultry market farmers		Touré Fall et al, 2001: 19
URBAN RUSSIA	55 million dasha producers	12% of income (3 capital cities) 10.6% of income (smaller cities)	

Source: Luc J. A. Mougeot (from official census and field samples reported in references contained in the table)

The UN website on MDGs reports that youth unemployment now represents 41 per cent of global unemployment. Rates have worsened in most developing regions since the mid-1990s, particularly in Latin America and the Caribbean and Asia. Youth underemployment is probably even more widespread. For a growing number, in the face of rising school costs and shrinking formal employment, market-oriented UA provides a relatively accessible entry into the urban job market. They can earn an income, save on food, learn another trade and, perhaps later, set up a small business.

The practice of UA is expanding to many social groups and competition for resources is growing. First, rising unemployment has forced men to enter UA trades formerly dominated by women, as in Zimbabwe. A second group of competitors are impoverished middle-class households and property owners who are increasingly competing with the landless poor and tenants to cultivate public open spaces next to their homes. Poor UA producers' lack of organization – or more pertinently the lack of recognition for their informal organizations – is seen by many analysts as a major impediment to this occupational group reaping greater benefits from their trade (see the Zimbabwe and Cuba case studies in this volume). When growing or raising produce on land that is not their own (often on public rights-of-way), poor urban producers are often denied the right to formally organize, to make claims on public resources and any entitlement to compensation in case of eviction. It almost goes without saying that these producers are allowed no participation in policy decisions that impact on them.

Urban Agriculture as a Tool for Sustainable Urbanization

MDG 7 calls for 'ensuring environmental sustainability', particularly through integrating principles of sustainable development into policies and programmes, reversing the loss of environmental resources, and significantly improving the lives of at least 100 million slum dwellers (improved sanitation and secure tenure). Lack of access to improved sanitation is more severe in the crowded cities of South and East Asia but progress in sub-Saharan Africa was stalled in the 1990s.

Because UA links cities and their environment, it can be an increasingly acceptable, affordable and effective tool for sustainable urbanization (Deelstra and Girardet, 1999). Poor sanitation, unsafe water supply, uncollected garbage and polluted rivers, all create environmental health hazards, reduce living standards, increase costs, reduce productivity and inhibit socio-economic development. The production of trees, shrubs, flowers and ornamental plants and food crops can beautify the city, cool its climate, curb erosion and absorb air pollution and odours. In Argentina, the Municipality of Rosario's Parks and Gardens Department is now implementing the multifunctional use of the city's green areas, combining recreation, education and food production (Dubbeling, 2004). Cities in Ecuador and Peru have made similar arrangements with organized groups of urban producers.

A most significant link between UA and environmental and public health is waste management. Millions of children, mostly in cities, die every year from diseases caused by the improper disposal of wastewater and solid waste. Urban waste production is constantly on the rise and large-scale conventional collection and disposal systems are inappropriate for the pace and nature of the growth in urban populations and urban waste in developing countries. This is particularly true for water and sanitation provision in poor urban neighbourhoods (UN-HABITAT, 2004d). Not only does the use of vacant land for crops and grazing livestock reduce municipal maintenance of green spaces, it also discourages garbage dumping and squatting (del Rosario et al, 2000). In residential areas, replacing wild-grass fields with low-height crops eliminates hideouts for thieves and other delinquents. Some UA systems can safely decontaminate polluted waters and soils while others can safely reuse organic and liquid wastes of varying quality. Human waste can be turned into compost (Esrey and Andersson, 2001), domestic wastewater can safely irrigate many crops and aquiculture can stabilize animal manure. As managers of household resources in urban contexts, women's participation in UA plays a pivotal role in improving human health and urban environments (Argentina case study in this volume).

In order to make urbanization more sustainable, UA can be planned as a separate land-use or one that can be combined with other land-uses, either on a temporary or permanent basis. The diversity of production systems and the degree to which UA can be practised makes it compatible with a wide range of urban activities, meshing with the urban fabric at different scales (lot, city block, ward, district, zone, in urban and peri-urban areas) (see for instance, Viljoen, 2005). Dynamic planning must also provide for UA land-uses to evolve as the city expands and transforms itself. Capital intensive forms of UA requiring relatively small areas of land (fruit trees, medicinal and ornamentals, silk worms, mushrooms, catfish, small stall-fed livestock) can thrive in city cores, while more land-intensive and waste-generating forms should relocate to less central and less populated locations.

The challenge for much of the UA practised by the urban poor and others is for it to become an environmental benefit rather than a liability, and to be seen in this light by the authorities. Because poor urban producers frequently operate illegally, on marginal and often hazardous sites, with limited means and assistance, their practices are often unsustainable, posing risks to their own health, that of their family and consumers. This is particularly true of producers engaged in market-oriented systems. Komla Tallaki's study of market gardeners in Lomé, Togo, in this volume, demonstrates the need for policy makers to turn their attention to UA systems that can play a critical role in self-reliant urban food systems. Rather more is needed than simply an awareness of by-law; slashing crops or seizing livestock have proven ineffective. The poor continue to work perilously, not simply because of their ignorance of the risks and alternatives, but because they are often deprived of a safer or healthier way to make their living.

LINKING RESEARCH WITH POLICY DEVELOPMENT

In different regions of the world a growing number of local and national governments and international agencies are including UA in their development strategies to eradicate extreme poverty and hunger and ensure environmental sustainability. Over 50 municipalities of Latin America and the Caribbean have now signed the Quito Declaration, in which they commit greater support to UA through improved policies; similar commitments were signed by the Association of Urban Councils of Zimbabwe and by six Ministers of Local Government from Southern and Eastern Africa in 2003. City consultations, action plans, pilot projects, new institutional, normative and legal frameworks have been introduced in Latin America and West Africa in recent years. Some cities have created municipal programmes in partnership with other local actors, including UA in participatory municipal budgets, in development and land management plans. Cities have issued new regulatory provisions and fiscal measures to support UA. In many instances such developments have been assisted by UN agencies: FAO and UN-HABITAT are increasingly responsive to the particular aspects of UA that fall under their respective mandates. Recent editions of FAO's State of Food and Agriculture reports, of UN-HABITAT's Global Reports on Human Settlements and State of the World's Cities Reports, as well as the United Nations Environment Programme's (UNEP) Global Environment Outlook reports have highlighted the practice of UA, its significance, constraints and potential.

Canada's International Development Research Centre (IDRC) has been a major supporter of the aforementioned initiatives at both the municipal, national and international levels. The following are specific activities that IDRC has assisted. In the late 1990s and early in this decade UN-HABITAT and FAO progressed toward mainstreaming UA as a legitimate and effective tool to further urban food security, urban poverty reduction and sustainable urbanization. UN-HABITAT's Sustainable Cities Programme implemented the Sustainable Dar es Salaam project. This included a UA component and led to the rehabilitation of agricultural stations within the urban perimeter of Dar es Salaam with National Income and Employment Generation funds. Since then,

UN-HABITAT has clarified its own mandate on UA, created a sub-programme on UA in Latin America and the Caribbean, surveyed good public practices in UA and developed municipal policy briefs on UA, as well as manuals and city demonstrations on UA.

Recognizing the significant potential of UA in the fight against urban hunger at its 1996 Food Summit, FAO moved in 1999 to adopt a resolution to coordinate the agency's programme delivery on UA. Since then FAO programmes involved in the agency's new Priority Area for Interdisciplinary Action (PAIA) 'Food for the Cities' have published guidelines on UA as well as supported the inclusion of UA interventions in several national food security programmes. Furthermore, FAO and UN-HABITAT have jointly sponsored and participated in summit sessions and regional workshops of officials on UA, food security and urban management. Experiences in financing for UA have been debated for further action at the Second World Urban Forum in Barcelona (2004), thanks to collaboration between IDRC, UN-HABITAT and their Southern and Northern partners. In 2004 the urban agriculture programme of the city of Rosario in Argentina, supported by IDRC and UN-HABITAT, was granted a Dubai Award for Best Practices to Improve the Living Environment, one of ten winners out of 680 submissions. Several actions flowing from international declarations mentioned earlier have been implemented and more should follow. The number of cities creating special offices for UA and food security grew in the 1990s. Increasingly, cities with good practices in support of UA are being called upon to assist their peers, working within networks to promote socially more inclusive, economically more productive and environmentally more habitable cities.

THE ORIGIN OF THIS BOOK

The studies collected in this book have been designed, carried out and selected against the background just discussed. They clearly link UA with urban development concerns targeted by the MDGs highlighted. They do so in a wide range of developing country contexts, with the full awareness that research needs to assist local actors, particularly governmental actors, in working out creative strategies to more effectively tackle urban food insecurity, poverty and environmental degradation.

The authors of the studies all received grants from IDRC's AGROPOLIS to carry out the required fieldwork. Since its inception in 1998 the AGROPOLIS facility has operated with an international Advisory Committee (AC). This Committee is composed of specialists representing different regions of the world and different areas of expertise in urban agriculture. The Committee meets annually to: (a) review directions, norms and procedures of the facility, coordinated and administered by IDRC; and (b) review applications and select award recipients. In early 2001 an IDRC proposal to the AGROPOLIS Advisory Committee accepted that a first group of awardees, those more advanced in their research, be invited to the 2002 AC meeting in Ottawa, to present and debate publicly their findings and outcomes. This suggestion was heartily endorsed by both the AC and the awardees and it is expected that this experience will be repeated with a second cohort of award recipients in 2–3 years time.

Nine papers were delivered via PowerPoint presentations and later edited for publication in this book. All the papers were rigorously debated before a full auditorium that included foreign embassy officials, the press, as well as researchers and managers of non-governmental organizations (NGOs) and higher learning institutions in Eastern Ontario and Western Quebec. The AC then discussed the papers with the awardees in a closed session. Finally, the papers were submitted to a final review process, involving Advisory members and IDRC personnel, plus one external expert for each of the papers.

The papers were commissioned, following specific terms of reference. The authors were asked to discuss their working definitions of key concepts, their original and revised objectives and hypotheses. Similarly, any change to their original methodology was to be signalled. Most pointed to additional needs for research that could overcome constraints imposed by the limitations of their own data. The core of the paper was to highlight research findings and also any initial outcomes of their interactions with local actors during their field research. Outcomes could pertain to one or more of the following categories: human resource development; gender-sensitive analysis; institutional capacity building; effectiveness of partnerships; methodological and scientific advances; utilization of research results; or additional financial support secured by the awardee for his or her research.

Even though AGROPOLIS is a global awards project, this first selection does not include papers from North America, Eastern Europe or Asia. The set is representative of the actual geographical reach of AGROPOLIS in its early years (1999–2001). Field research at developed country sites is largely confined to comparative studies including developing country sites. The limited participation of Asian graduates is partly explained by the relatively quieter presence of IDRC's own programming in that region during the period. However, applications from Asia are expected to grow, thanks to the recent establishment of regional partners in China and India for the global Resource Centre on Urban Agriculture and Forestry, coordinated by ETC International and funded by several agencies, including IDRC. In 2003–4 there was a notable increase in the number of applications received from Asia, which bodes well for Asian contributions to future volumes of AGROPOLIS.

THE CONTRIBUTIONS TO THIS BOOK

This final section of this chapter discusses the main features of the case studies assembled in this book. It reviews the key questions raised by the different pieces of research. It highlights the field adjustments that the authors have brought to their planned methodology in a responsive and creative way. It explains the varying function of the different studies, positioning them at different stages in the research cycle (baseline-oriented versus action-oriented).

The collection encompasses a wide range of country situations, in terms of the relative significance of UA and the relative importance of public policy for UA. The series of papers also shows how particular public policy systems and practices may affect or benefit different groups of small and poor UA practitioners. This series also illustrates how gendered approaches to studying different UA issues do enrich both process and findings. It points to the many instances where fieldwork affiliations have enabled researchers to facilitate greater local public attention to urban producers. Finally it underlines the various ways in which some of the young authors have already started to improve institutional awareness and support for research and training on UA in their working environment, both in the North and the South.

Key research questions

The case studies are concerned with very pressing challenges facing the future of UA in developing countries (Table 3): for how long can the urban poor go on reducing their food insecurity without resorting to UA, and when this is not possible, what else is left? When governments do decide to support UA through various policies, what impact can a neglect of certain categories of producers have on their well-being, contribution to food supply, management of resources and general environmental and human health? How can the multiple benefits that certain UA systems bring to practitioners and others be assessed and accounted for in deciding on the nature and measure of public support to such systems? What are the conditions needed for agriculture and the city to be reconciled with one another on the urban fringe? What is the role and responsibility of different actors in redressing the risks and improving the sustainability of certain UA practices? These are critical questions confronting the fair, viable and sustainable development of UA in a growing number of developing country cities. The studies assembled here raise important considerations for resolving such challenges.

Field adjustments to planned methodology

In almost all cases, field conditions led the authors to modify their original methodology. This was in order to address cultural concerns, overcome time constraints, or respond to opportunities afforded by new information. In Namibia, Bruce Frayne added interviews with rural relatives of migrants interviewed in urban centres to explore extended household or family-level coping strategies. In Zimbabwe, Stephanie Gabel did not carry out interviews with non-cultivating households due to concerns expressed by local women farmers about the exact focus of her study. In Togo, Tallaki re-focused his field research as a result of interacting with two other ongoing projects that he discovered in the same study zone; he also allowed for local women's reluctance to be interviewed individually by male field researchers by interviewing women in groups. Aid fatigue also biased the composition of attendants to his project sessions and information gathered at those meetings

Table 3 *Study locations, research issues and key research questions of the case studies*

Study Locations	Research Issues	Key Research Questions
Windhoek (240,000), Namibia	Estimating and explaining the contribution of rural–urban food transfers and urban agriculture (self-provisioning) to the urban poor's food security	In a context of rapid rural–urban migration and rising urban poverty: • how do the urban poor secure adequate food supplies? • how are solidarity linkages, including food security, embedded in household migratory behaviour? • under which macro conditions may particular food security strategies work or not for the urban poor?
Lomé (850,000), Togo	Estimating, explaining and correcting chemical pesticide misuse in market vegetable gardening	• can chemical pesticide misuse be solely or largely attributed to the growers' faulty knowledge? • what are the long-term effects of chemical pesticide misuse on the growers' trade and public health? • what are the possible corrective interventions?
Korhogo (285,000), Côte d'Ivoire	Explaining small-ruminant husbandry adoption by urban households	• what household characteristics are more associated with the adoption of small-ruminant husbandry?
Harare (2 million), Zimbabwe	Analysing poor women's strategies and assessing the actions needed for them to gain better access to urban open space for cultivation	• how do land-poor women access urban open spaces for cultivation? • what relationships, interactions, differences and/or similarities exist between women with access to urban cultivation and local departments and decision-makers? • which action strategies can be identified to promote more accommodating planning initiatives or practices for land-poor women cultivators?
Gabarone, Botswana	Understanding the relationship between a gendered commercial UA sector and the nature of urban food supply	• what constraints and opportunities are faced by different (gender-specific) groups in creating, shaping and sustaining commercial UA systems?

Study Locations	Research Issues	Key Research Questions
		• how and why does gender influence the net outcomes of commercial UA systems?
		• what are the key factors (socio-economic, locational, environmental) affecting agricultural productivity?
La Habana (2.2 million), Cuba	Identifying and explaining differences between small-scale producers and official experts in how they perceive small-scale UA for self-provisioning, its proper domain and benefits	• how is urban farming described or practised by various differently positioned actors within La Habana? • what might differing perspectives imply for the future of UA in this city?
Rosario (1.1 million), Argentina	Testing and monitoring the multiple functionality of local urban agriculture (social, economical, technical, environmental) within broader strategies for sustainable development	In urban sectors suffering from extreme poverty: • is large-scale vermiculture technology viable in urban agriculture to recycle organic waste and derive fertilizer? • can urban agriculture projects work as local development tools for such urban sectors? • can urban agriculture projects increase local urban biodiversity?
Paris, France and Tunis, Tunisia	Comparing policy options for resolving the *agricultural problematique* on the urban fringe	• what is the sociopolitical process whereby agriculture gets assigned a new role in local and regional land-use policy? • what are the various strategies developed by farmers to adapt to changes in their social and spatial environment? • what are the key principles of the French experience that could inspire new policy strategies in the Tunisian context?
London, Ashford, Wye, England	Assessing non-monetary benefits from allotments as a component of UA	• what are the benefits derived by allotment holders and residents from their allotment gardens? • how can the differences between settings be explained in terms of perceived benefits? • what monetary value can be assigned to the benefits perceived by allotment holders and residents to be derived from the allotment gardens?

had to be cross-checked for reliability. Despite the urbanization of West African livestock (reported as early as 1995 by FAO), this activity remains largely invisible in the official statistics of many countries. Even when it is recorded, urban livestock keeping is usually grossly under-reported, as noted by Frayne in Namibia; in most cases livestock keeping is subject to particularly stringent regulations – when it is not prohibited – and owners are aware of this. In Khorogo, Côte d'Ivoire, Mody Bakar Barry had to resort to transect surveys to establish livestock density patterns and define his sampling framework, then visit heads of households very early or late in the day, to gain access, observe and secure accurate figures. When they exist, even official data on UA enterprises may be hard to come by. In Botswana, Hovorka had to painstakingly assemble a complete list of the statistical population of formal UA enterprises in the survey area. Her sampling was modified based on initial field information: she did not pursue crop-related ecological sampling as proposed. When she realized that space-confined livestock operations (poultry) dominated the UA commercial sector; crop-related ecological conditions became secondary. In any event, standardizing ecological sampling across various agricultural activities would have posed problems.

In countries where public UA programmes do exist, some systems or categories of producers can be left out and data on these will not be readily available. In Cuba for instance, Premat had to resort to snowball-sampling to identify and interview producers associated with a UA system that remains marginal to the official Cuban programme. Also, when she realized how extensive multi-disciplinary teamwork was in Cuba, Premat went on to consider the experts' institutional affiliation as a potentially more useful factor to explain differences in their discourses and practices regarding UA. City residents with no connection to UA had to be excluded from the study due to time restrictions. Also, producers were not asked to draw counter-maps to gather information on local land use, as interviewees felt uncomfortable with recording private neighbourhood land-use. In Argentina, Spiaggi added to his original hypotheses the role played by UA in increasing the biodiversity of the urban ecosystem. In Tunisia, given the lack of literature on the subject for comparison with the French case study, Bouraoui found it appropriate to add a survey of Greater Tunis inhabitants' relationships with the peri-urban area.

As can be seen, in all cases where statistical sampling was proposed, estimating the statistical population was a painstaking task. This required the researcher to consult a multitude of sources, as in most cases those UA systems of interest lacked public recognition and statistical monitoring. This remains a challenge facing students of the urban informal sector in general and those interested in UA in particular.

Baselines and action research: Different stages in the research cycle

Most studies used participatory methodologies to engage researchers bilaterally with different categories of actors, and in some cases with several categories at the same time. Also, development researchers often go through a research cycle during their career, focusing on a particular development problem or region of the world. Particular pieces of research are conditioned by the stage at which the researcher may find him or herself, along this research cycle. This is why in some studies methodologies were less participatory than in others: they exist largely to provide quantitative baselines from which action-oriented research can later be developed (as is the case of the Windhoek and Koghoro studies). Others were well positioned to build on baselines previously completed by the authors at the same locations. In these cases, the researcher's familiarity with local actors and institutions afforded a more complex set of interactions with different types of informants, thus enabling the research to engage more readily in some practical interventions locally (Lomé, Gabarone, La Habana). For instance, in Cuba, Premat has now been granted a post-doctoral award by AGROPOLIS, which will allow her to further advance her research cycle on UA in Cuba.

A wide range of country situations

The variety of case studies is also interesting on other fronts: they actually encompass a wide range of country situations. These countries illustrate different combinations of degree of importance of UA given to food security with degree of policy-making on UA. Cuba and Argentina represent countries where both UA is significant to food security and public policy on UA are important; in Zimbabwe, Côte d'Ivoire, Togo and Tunisia, although UA is very important to food security, public policy on UA is comparatively less developed. France and England illustrate countries where there are specific policies for UA, even though UA plays a much more limited role in food-security. Ironically, it is 'richer' countries that have developed policies to make the practice of UA easier. Finally, Botswana and Namibia are typical of situations where both UA's significance for food security and explicit policy on UA remain limited at the time of writing.

However, it should be noted that there has been a great deal of movement within this overall classification in recent years. Not surprisingly, some of the countries studied in this book could shift to another category in the future. Zimbabwe is not only developing more explicit public policy in support of UA but is leading an attitudinal shift at the ministerial level in the region. Also, UA could become more important to food security strategies as predominantly rural countries, such as Namibia, undergo rapid urbanization. England has witnessed a weakening of policy support for UA as a tool for food security in the post-Second World War period, but the safe-food agenda and the rising popularity of UA among youths and immigrants could revert this trend. After a similar decline in France, public pressure and resulting policies for preserving the landscaping value of agriculture in urban environments has motivated very recent developments.

Public policy influence on small-scaled urban agriculture

More interestingly, all the studies are preoccupied with higher-order (institutional) constraints or enabling conditions and their effect on the performance and benefits accruing to small (peri-) urban producers. Clearly in Windhoek, although UA for self-provisioning is still limited, it is significant to those practising it; the noteworthy contribution of rural–urban food transfers to the provisioning of poor urban migrants appears only to be workable on any significant scale where there are rural food surpluses in the first place, and then where transportation is both available and affordable. In countries where these latter conditions have deteriorated, UA has become an attractive substitute. The erosion of rural entitlements with each passing generation among the urban poor could be another aggravating factor. How can cities devise robust food supply systems for their growing poor populations, as urbanization proceeds and conditions change over which cities themselves exercise little control?

Studies in Lomé, Gabarone, Harare and La Habana highlight the impact that public policy (or a lack thereof) can have on the performance of particular categories of producers. In Lomé the misuse of agrochemical pesticides is sustained by a vicious circle of technical ignorance, institutional neglect and material deprivation; nurturing an increasingly self-defeating and unsafe production strategy among market vegetable growers. In Gabarone, public financing discriminates against small female entrepreneurs and thus deprives the local food supply industry from potential gains in both productivity and volume within niche subsectors. Among these, poultry production (a critical source of animal protein for urban workers) is one area where women are already very active and could be more so.

In Harare, discontinuity in local public support to agricultural cooperatives over time has instilled mistrust among women producers; the lack of NGOs offering credit facilities that cater to women producers' preference for individual rather than group loans has also probably curtailed local entrepreneurial potential. In La Habana government technocrats and an important category of small urban producers are found to hold contrasting views on what are acceptable types of UA production, their location and functions within the city. They also differ on what role each one should play in UA. As a result, certain production systems, city areas and urban producers – including women – have been disregarded by the official UA programme. However, at the time of writing, certain governmental agencies were seen to be making progress in trying to mend some of these differences.

The Rosario case study and the Tunis–Paris comparative study demonstrate the importance of national decentralization policies and participatory local governance to integrate UA into robust urban and peri-urban management frameworks. In Rosario, Argentina, an inclusive approach involved a national public programme for food production in urban and rural areas, various units of municipal government and several poor urban communities. It led to the inclusion of multifunctional UA in poor urban communities' development agendas. In late 2001, while the research was still going on, the Municipality launched an Urban Agriculture Programme within its Division for Social Promotion.

General public perceptions, social organization for policy change and decentralization of decision-making seem to be critical for improving policy toward peri-urban agriculture. In France, the view that peri-urban agricultural land is merely a reserve for urban development is now essentially obsolete. Moez Bouraoui's study quite unexpectedly suggests that, in a similar way to the dramatic shift in the dominant public perception in France between 1960 and 1980, a change in the same direction may now be taking place among the Tunis population. But a shift in public perception was just the first step in France. There, decentralization in 1983 facilitated the emergence of a wide range of actors at the peri-urban level, intercommunal collaboration became possible and structures became legitimate. This was crucial to establishing a genuine peri-urban land-use policy, including technical guidelines and indicators for action with clear benefits to farming and farmers. These principles are now framing several agreements between the State and local farmers.

In contrast, in Tunisia the constitution prescribes that land-use management falls under national jurisdiction. This was found to hinder or discourage local service coordination for the management of the urban perimeter, an otherwise effective response to local land speculation and degradation. In the Tunis region, there are still no collective land-use management plans specifically for the rural-agricultural parts of the peri-urban area, nor any pressure from local community organizations to promote such policy innovations.

The Paris–Tunis comparison points to three elements that could inspire changes in the Sijoumi context. First, institutional actors need to recognize the multifunctional character of urban or peri-urban farming and the advantages it brings to the urban community. Secondly, policy must move beyond simply promoting passive cohabitation of rural with urban environments: this would only fuel conflicts. Cohabitation must encourage limited and controlled visits from city dwellers to farming areas. Thirdly, on a more challenging level, an intercommunal approach must be fostered for the formulation and application of appropriate land management rules. Further cooperation between countries is a promising avenue for mutual learning on how to promote positive policy change in quite different sociocultural and legal-institutional settings.

A gendered approach to research on urban agriculture

This series breaks away from a literature that too often has disregarded women's role in UA. Frayne interviewed adult household members of both sexes to fully embrace the household's migrancy and reciprocity strategies and documented the high food insecurity of women-led poor urban households with little entitlement to rural resources. Barry's econometric model quantified the critical role played by women in the culturally innovative adoption of small ruminant keeping by urban households. Tallaki stressed women's multiple exposure to the risks posed by unsafe horticultural practices, while Gabel revealed landless women's strategies and struggles to overcome unreliable policies and gain access to land and credit for UA. Both Premat and Hovorka characterized women's relative invisibility or low priority in public programmes that support UA. Spiaggi underscored women's commitment to UA embedded in community development agendas, while Pérez-Vasquez documented clear differences between women's and men's conception and management of allotment gardens, again with implications for technical extension.

AGROPOLIS maintains at least one international gender expert on its Advisory Committee, which also functions as an award-adjudicating panel. The AC issues recommendations to awardees on particular issues deserving gender analysis and directs applicants and awardees to several gender analysis resources available online. It requires awardees to report on insights afforded by gender analysis in their research, whenever applicable. Also, the AC believes that university faculty and curriculi can currently be credited for instilling in a new generation of researchers a greater awareness of gender equity issues and better skills for gender analysis than afforded by previous generations of researchers.

Facilitating local public attention to urban producers

AGROPOLIS requires all its awardees to formally affiliate with a non-academic entity, seated or represented in the area where field research will be conducted and for the whole duration of the fieldwork. This is to promote greater public attention to the problems facing urban and peri-urban producers. The non-academic entity may be the local office of an international agency, a national or private technical institute, a governmental body, an NGO or a professional association. Awardees can even affiliate with private enterprises that meet certain requirements. Candidates for an AGROPOLIS award must, in their application, document this entity's interest in and support for the research, as well as its intended use of the research results. This requirement is to counter the 'hit and run' practice of researchers, which is detrimental to both local research uptake and to future researchers wishing to work in the same areas.

This is a demanding requirement, but one which most awardees have greatly appreciated. Many reported significant outcomes in their contributions to this book. Some have even maintained the relationship beyond their fieldwork and are serving as advisors on local processes. Tallaki organized a roundtable between producers, government officials and pesticide distributors on the health hazards of pesticide use. Hovorka facilitated a public workshop that addressed the effectiveness of public credit programmes in reaching male and women producers. Premat documented and discussed with officials the neglect of small producers by the national urban agriculture programme in Cuba. Gabel promoted urban producers' participation on the Harare UA stakeholder committee. Spiaggi explored several ways in which to integrate UA into the development agenda of a very poor urban community. Bouraoui made recommendations to a commune administration, much appreciated by the planning director (with a letter to the AGROPOLIS programme), on how to preserve agriculture in the commune's development plans.

Promoting institutional research and training on urban agriculture

The research assembled here suggests that their authors are already influencing changes in UA research and training capacities in universities. Bruce Frayne became a lecturer at Queen's Southern African Studies Centre, where he developed a regional research proposal with Canadian and Southern African institutions. He now works at the International Livestock Research Institute in Addis Ababa, Ethiopia. Alice Hovorka is an assistant professor in the Department of Geography of the University of Waterloo, from where she provides advisory services to several organizations and local students. Arturo Pérez-Vasquez's research has provided impetus for the Wye College in England to develop a specialist option in UA in their master's programme on Sustainable Agriculture and Rural Development. Stephanie Gabel's supervisor has developed a research interest in UA, having produced a paper on the Philippines experience. Other changes are in the making. Komla Tallaki has returned to Togo where the Ecole Supérieure d'Agronomie, to which he was affiliated, is developing a follow-up project to his research. Impressed with Mody Bakar Barry's research, the National Agency for Rural Development in Côte d'Ivoire, to which he was affiliated, is considering a policy network for urban animal husbandry systems.

CONCLUSION

UA remains a relatively new field of inquiry in mainstream academia. All of the authors were among the first, the very first in some cases, to conduct graduate research on this subject in their home institutions. They creatively combined methods developed by different disciplines into batteries which they applied to researching UA issues. In this way they have enriched the collection of tools available to future students. To cite only a couple of examples, Bruce Frayne used quantitative and qualitative methods to capture the fluidity (migration and reciprocity) of households, as units of analysis which extend across time and space, while Pérez-Vasquez experimented with monetary valuation methods to assess, in combination with other methods, the aggregate benefits that people derive from their allotment gardens. During the public debate of their papers in March 2002, the authors conveyed a genuine eagerness to work constructively with local actors, both individual and institutional, and to help all parties to advance public agendas for sustainable and equitable UA. Their field research, I believe, has afforded them a real measure of their capacity to connect with humanity beyond research and, in this way, reaffirm their social consciousness as development professionals. May they never compromise with it, whatever the country, institution or occupation in which they elect to pursue their career.

Urban agriculture is still viewed by many as the oxymoron par excellence. Yet, it is part of a larger set of trends that are transforming our living urban (and rural) space on a massive and unstoppable scale. At the beginning of the 21st century, more people from wildly different walks of life are engaging in forms of UA, either for therapy, recreation, self-provisioning or income – or a combination thereof. I am not aware of any piece of literature, scientific or other, which a generation ago would have predicted the growth of this trend to the point it has reached today. The Food Policy Council of the City of Vancouver in Canada now uses UA to strengthen the connections between its food and its sustainability policies, while a growing number of developing country cities link UA to their food security agenda. Together with less agrarian developments, as in information and communications technologies, urban agriculture is stalling, if not erasing, the compartmentalization of spaces and times that a Western generation has come to know. These developments are transforming the way in which our cities are laid out and, more immediately, the way in which they work. No doubt these transformations will profoundly affect the very meaning of urbanity and rurality in the future.

NOTES

1   See http://www.developmentgoals.org.
2   A slum household is defined as a group of individuals living under the same roof with one or more of these conditions: insecure residential status, inadequate access to safe water and/or to sanitation, structurally poor housing, overcrowding.

REFERENCES

Altieri, M. A., Companioni, N., Canizares, K., Murphy, C., Rosset, P., Bourque, M. and Nicholls, C. I. (1999) 'The greening of the "barrios": Urban agriculture for food security in Cuba', *Agriculture and Human Values*, vol 16, no 2, June 1999, pp131–140

Armar-Klemesu, M. (2000) 'Urban agriculture and food security, nutrition and health', in Bakker et al (2000), pp99–118

Armar-Klemesu, M. and Maxwell, D. (2000) 'Accra: Urban agriculture as an asset strategy, supplementing income and diets', in Bakker et al (2000), pp183–208

Bakker, N., Dubbeling, M., Gundel, S., Sabel-Koschella, U. and de Zeeuw, H. (eds) (2000) *Growing Cities, Growing Food: Urban Agriculture on the Policy Agenda. A Reader on Urban Agriculture*, German Foundation for International Development (DSE), Feldafing, Germany

Brooks, R. and Davila, J. (eds) (2000) *The Peri-urban Interface: A Tale of Two Cities.* School of Agricultural and Forest Sciences, University of Wales, and Development Planning Unit, UCL, London

Cabannes, Y. and Dubbeling, M. (2001) 'Urban agriculture, food security and urban management', in *Urban Agriculture in Cities of the 21st Century: Innovative Approaches by Local Governments from Latin America and the Caribbean*, working paper 84. Urban Management Programme – Latin America and the Caribbean, UN-HABITAT, Quito

Deelstra, T. and Girardet, H. (1999) 'Urban agriculture and sustainable cities' in Bakker et al (2000), pp43–65

del Rosario, P. J., Cornelio, Y., Jiménez Polanco, L., Russell, A., Lopez, H. and Escarraman, P. (2000) *Manejo de Residuos Solidos y Agricultura Urbana en la Ciudad de Santiago De Los Caballeros*, Centro de Estudios Urbanos y Regionales, Pontificia Universidad Catolica Madre y Maestra. Santiago de los Caballeros, Dominican Republic

Dreschel, P., Amoah, P., Cofie, O. O. and Abaidoo, R. C. (2000) 'Increasing use of poultry manure in Ghana', *Urban Agriculture Magazine*, vol 1, no 2, October, pp25–27

Dreschel, P., Quansah, C., and De Vries F. P. (1999) 'Urban and peri-urban agriculture in West Africa – Characteristics, challenges and need for action', in Smith (1999), pp19–40

Drescher, A. W. (1999) 'Urban microframing in Central Southern Africa: A case study of Lusaka, Zambia', *African Urban Quarterly*, vol 11, nos 2–3, May–August 1996, pp229–248

Drescher, A. W. (2001) 'Urban and peri-urban agriculture – A briefing guide for the successful implementation of urban and peri-urban agriculture in developing countries and countries of transition', Special Programme for Food Security SPFS/DOC/27.8 Revision 2, Handbook Series Volume III, Food and Agriculture Organization, Rome.

Dubbeling, M. (2004) 'Optimizing use of vacant space for urban agriculture through participatory planning processes', Paper presented at workshop on IDRC-supported initiatives on urban agriculture and food security, Ryerson University, Toronto, August–September 2004

Dubbeling, M. and Santandreu, A. (2003) 'Diagnosticos participativos de agricultura urbana. Lineamientos metodologicos y coneptuales', Cuaderno de trabajo 86, Programa de Gestion Urbana – América Latina y el Caribe, UN-HABITAT, Quito

ENDA-ZW (Environment and Development Activities – Zimbabwe) (1997) *Urban Agriculture in Harare: Household nutrition, economic costs and benefits*, ENDA-ZW, Harare

Edwards, P. (2001) 'Public health issues of wastewater-fed aquaculture', *Urban Agriculture Magazine*, vol 1, no 3, March, pp20–22

Esrey, S. A. and Andersson, I. (2001) 'Ecological sanitation. Closing the loop', *Urban Agriculture Magazine* vol 1, no 3, March pp35–37

Foeken, D. and Mwangi, A. (2000) 'Increasing food security through urban farming in Nairobi', in Bakker et al (2000), pp303–328

Foeken, D. and Owuor, S. O. (2000) 'Livestock in a middle-sized East-African town: Nakuru', *Urban Agriculture Magazine*, vol 1, no 2, October 2000, pp20–22

FUNAT (2001) *Agricultura y Ciudad: Una Clave para la Sustentabilidad*. Fundacion Antonio Nunez Jiménez de la Naturalez y el Hombre, Havana

Garnett, T. (2000) 'Urban agriculture in London: Rethinking our food economy', in Bakker et al (2000), pp477–500

Gertel, J. and Samir, S. (2000) 'Cairo: Urban agriculture and "visions" for a modern city', in Bakker et al (2000), pp209–234

Gonzalez Novo, M. and Murphy, C. (2000) 'Urban agriculture in the city of Havana: A popular response to crisis', in Bakker et al (2000), pp329–348

Gough, K. V. and Kellett, P. (2001) 'Housing consolidation and home-based income generation', *Cities*, vol 18, no 4, pp235–247

Gueye, N. F. D., and Sy, M. (2001) 'The use of wastewater for urban agriculture: The Example of Dakar, Nouakchott and Ouagadougou', *Urban Agriculture Magazine*, vol 1, no 3, March, pp30–32

Jacobi, P., Amend, J. and Kiango, S. (2000) 'Urban agriculture in Dar es Salaam: Providing for an indispensable part of the diet', in Bakker et al (2000), pp257–284

Kouvonou, F. M., Honfoga, B. G. and Debrah, S. K. (1998) 'Sécurité alimentaire et gestionintégrée de la fertilité des sols: contribution du maraîchage péri-urbain à Lomé', in Smith (1999), pp83–103

Lawrence H., Ruel, M. T. and Garrett, J. (1999) 'Are urban poverty and undernutrition growing? Some newly assembled evidence', Discussion paper 63, Food Consumption and Nutrition Division, International Food Policy Research Institute, Washington, DC

Lourenço-Lindell, I. (1995) 'Food for the poor, food for the city: The role of urban agriculture in Bissau', Delivered at Workshop on the Social and Environmental Implications of Urban Agriculture, University of Zimbabwe, Harare

Maseva, C. (2003) 'Urban agriculture and urban environmental challenges', in Mushamba, S., Mubvami, T., Marongwe, N. and Chatiza, K. (eds), *Report of the Ministers' Conference on Urban and Peri-Urban Agriculture: Prospects for Food Security and Growth in Eastern and Southern Africa*, Annex 7, Municipal Development Programme for Eastern and Southern Africa (MDP-ESA), Harare, pp21–27

Maxwell, D. (1994) 'The household logic of urban farming in Kampala', in Egziabher, A. G., Lee-Smith, D., Maxwell, D. G., Memon, P. A., Mougeot, L. J. A. and Sawio, C. J., *Cities Feeding People: An Examination of Urban Agriculture in East Africa*, International Development Research Centre, Ottawa, pp47–65

Maxwell, D. (1995) 'Alternative food security strategy: A household analysis of urban agriculture in Kampala', *World Development*, vol 23, no 10, pp1669–1681

Maxwell, D. G. and Zziwa, S. (1992) *Urban Agriculture in Africa: The Case of Kampala, Uganda*, African Centre for Technology Studies, Nairobi

Mbaye, A. and Moustier, P. (2000) 'Market-oriented urban agricultural production in Dakar', in Bakker et al (2000), pp235–256

Mbiba, B. (1995) *Urban Agriculture in Zimbabwe*, Ashgate Publishing Ltd, Avebury, Hants, England

Moldakov, O. (2000) 'The urban farmers of St Petersburg', *Urban Agriculture Magazine*, vol 1, no 1, June, pp24–26

Mougeot, L. J. A. (2000) 'Urban agriculture: Definition, presence, potential and risks', in Bakker et al (2000), pp1–42

Moustier, P. (1999) 'Complémentarité entre agriculture urbaine et agriculture rurale', in Smith (1999), pp41–55

Moustier, P. and Salam Fall, A. (2004) 'Les dynamiques de l'agriculture urbaine: caractérisation et evaluation', in Smith, O. B., Moustier, P., Mougeot, L. J. A. and Fall, A. (eds), *Développement durable de l'agriculture urbaine en Afrique francophone. Enjeux, concepts et méthodes*, Centre de coopération internationale en recherche agronomique pour le développement (CIRAD), Montpellier, and Centre de Recherches pour le Développement international (CRDI), Ottawa, pp23–43

Nugent, R. (2000) 'The impact of urban agriculture on the household and local economies' in Bakker et al (2000), pp67–98

Pantuliano, S. (2000) 'The Beja urban economy: Understanding and responding to an evolving reality', *Urban Agriculture Magazine*, vol 1, no 2, October, pp14–16

Pederson, R. M. and Robertson, A. (2001) 'Food policies are essential for healthy cities', *Urban Agriculture Magazine*, vol 1, no 3, March, pp9–11

Peters, D. (2000) 'Improved feed for pig raising in Vietnam', *Urban Agriculture Magazine*, vol 1, no 2, October, pp37–38

Potutan, G. E., Schnitzler, W. H., Arnado, J. M., Janubas L. G. and Holmer, R. J. (2000) 'Urban agriculture in Cagayan de Oro: A favourable response of city government and NGOs', in Bakker et al (2000), pp413–428

Poynter, G. and Fielding, D. (2000) 'Findings of a survey into urban livestock in Kumasi, Ghana', *Urban Agriculture Magazine*, vol 1, no 2, October, p28

Purnomohadi, N. (2000) 'Jakarta: Urban agriculture as an alternative strategy to face the economic crisis', in Bakker et al (2000), pp453–466

Régis, M. D., Bartels, G. and Philoctete, G. (2000) *Rapport Final. Projet Horticulture Urbaine*. CARE Haiti, Pétionville, Haiti

Quon, S. (1999) 'Planning for urban agriculture: A review of tools and strategies for urban planners', *Cities Feeding People Report 28*, International Development Research Centre, Ottawa

Sawio, C. (1993) 'Feeding the urban masses? Towards an understanding of the dynamics of urban agriculture and land use change in Dar es Salaam, Tanzania', Ph.D. Thesis, Graduate School of Geography, Clark University, Worcester, MA, USA

Smith, O. B. (ed.) (1999) *Agriculture Urbaine en Afrique de l'Ouest: Une Contribution à la Securité Alimentaire et à l'Assainissement des Villes – Urban Agriculture in West Africa: Contributing to Food Security and Urban Sanitation*, Technical Centre for Agricultural and Rural Cooperation, Wageningen, and International Development Research Centre, Ottawa

Sonou, M. (2001) 'Periurban irrigated agriculture and health risks in Ghana', *Urban Agriculture Magazine*, vol 1, no 3, March, pp33–34

Stevenson, C., assisted by Xavery, P. and Wendeline, A. (1996) 'Market production and vegetables in the peri-urban area of Dar es Salaam, Tanzania', *Urban Vegetable Promotion Project* (Ministry of Agriculture and Co-operatives – Deutsche Gesellschaft fur Technische Zusammenarbeit GTZ), UVPP, Dar es Salaam

Tegegne, A., Tadesse, M., Yami, A. and Mekasha, Y. (2000) 'Market-oriented urban and peri-urban dairy systems', *Urban Agriculture Magazine*, vol 1, no 2, October, pp23–24

Torres Lima, P., Rodriguez Sanchez, L. M. and Garcia Uriza, B. I. (2000) 'Mexico City: The integration of urban agriculture to contain urban sprawl', in Bakker et al (2000), pp363–390

Touré Fall, S., Cisse, I. and Salam Fall, A. (2001) 'Urban livestock systems in the Niayes zone in Senegal', *Urban Agriculture Magazine*, vol 1, no 2, October, pp17–19

Tremante, L. P. (2000) 'Livestock in nineteenth-century New York City', *Urban Agriculture Magazine*, vol 1, no 2, October, pp5–7

UN-HABITAT (United Nations Human Settlements Programme) (2004a) 'Dialogue on urban sustainability', working paper of the Committee of Permanent Representatives to UN-HABITAT for World Urban Forum 2004 (HSP/WUF/2/10, draft 17/03/04)

UN-HABITAT (2004b) 'Dialogue on urban realities', working paper of the Committee of Permanent Representatives to UN-HABITAT for World Urban Forum 2004 (HSP/WUF/2/5, draft 17/03/04)

UN-HABITAT (2004c) 'Dialogue on urban poor', working paper of the Committee of Permanent Representatives to UN-HABITAT for World Urban Forum 2004 (HSP/WUF/2/8, draft 17/03/04)

UN-HABITAT (2004d) 'Dialogue on urban services: Making the private sector work for the urban poor: Revisiting the privatization debate', working paper of the Committee of Permanent Representatives to UN-HABITAT, HSP/WUF/2/11 (17/03/04 draft)

Urban Agriculture Magazine (2001) Special issue on The Integration of Urban and Peri-urban Agriculture into Planning, no 4, July, Resource Centre on Urban Agriculture and Forestry (RUAF), Leusden

Viljoen, A. (2005) *Continuous Productive Urban landscapes: Designing Urban Agriculture for Sustainable Cities*. Architectural Press, imprint of Elsevier, Oxford

Yi-Zhang, C. and Zhangen, Z. (2000) 'Shanghai: Trends towards specialized and capital-intensive urban agriculture', in Bakker et al (2000), pp467–476

Yoveva, A., Gocheva, B., Voykova, G., Borissov, B. and Spassov, A. (2000) 'Sofia: Urban agriculture in an economy in transition', in Bakker et al (2000), pp501–518

Zallé, D. (1999) 'Stratégies politiques pour l'agriculture urbaine, rôle et responsabilité des autorités communales: le cas du Mali', in Smith (1999), pp1–18

1

Survival of the Poorest: Migration and Food Security in Namibia

Bruce Frayne[1]

INTRODUCTION

Namibia is a large, semi-arid country situated in southern Africa with a population of 1.6 million, two-thirds of which lives in rural areas. Windhoek, as the capital city of Namibia, is the predominant economic, service, manufacturing and political centre of the country. The population of Windhoek has been growing at an annual rate of 5.4 per cent in recent years, the largest annual growth rate in its history (MoW, 1996b). In 2000 the population of Windhoek was about 240,000,[2] a figure that represents almost half of all urban residents in the country.

Most of the population growth is taking place in Katutura, the large, previously designated African township located to the northwest of the city. Approximately 60 per cent of the urban area's population lives in Katutura, on about 20 per cent of the city's land (Pendleton, 1998). It is estimated that the population of Windhoek will have doubled over the decade 2000–2010 (MoW, 1996a). As a result of this projected growth and the limited formal housing stock available, it is estimated that in future 50 per cent of the city's housing may be shanties (MoW, 1996b).

The recent and projected population growth of Windhoek, fuelled by rural–urban migration and natural increase, represents a significant challenge to meeting the future demand for social and physical infrastructure, as well as employment, in the city. Although employment opportunities broadened with independence in 1990, the sheer volume of urban growth appears to negate the potential benefits for the urban poor (Pendleton, 1998; Hansohm, 2000). A survey undertaken in the informal areas of the city reports an unemployment rate of 46 per cent among household heads (Peyroux and Graefe, 1995). The growth in the informal economy is largely occurring in response to the real constraints to employment that exist in the formal sector (Norval and Namoya, 1992; Pendleton, 1996).

Table 1.1 *Changes in reported problems in Katutura, 1991–1996*

Issue	1991		1996	
	n	%	n	%
Food problems				
Not serious	65	18	242	47
Neutral	43	12	117	23
Serious	256	70	157	30
Health problems				
Not serious	196	54	329	63
Neutral	69	19	86	17
Serious	99	27	101	20
Debt problems				
Not serious	41	11	221	43
Neutral	28	8	101	20
Serious	295	81	190	37

Source: Adapted from Pendleton (1998)

This tension between migration, urbanization and urban poverty has often been described as an urban crisis and has been conceptualized as a transfer of rural poverty to the urban context (Devereux et al, 1993; Pomuti and Tvedten, 1998; Pile et al, 1999; Tvedten and Nangulah, 1999). Moreover, vulnerability and deprivation are increasingly viewed as an urban problem, which is more severe than the situation in the rural areas (Pomuti and Tvedten, 1998).

At face value, this line of argument appears to be supported by the data. For example, in 1991, some 67 per cent of migrants reported the lack of employment as a 'serious problem' they faced in Windhoek (Pendleton, 1991). In the same survey, 70 per cent of the sample reported food shortages as a serious problem.

However, although consistently high unemployment rates have been reported among households in Katutura and migrants face the highest levels of unemployment in the city (MoW, 1996a, 1996b; Pendleton, 1996; Pomuti and Tvedten, 1998), data also show that, on aggregate, poor urban residents are not as vulnerable as they were before independence. In a comparison of household data collected from Katutura between 1991 and 1996, Pendleton (1998) reported a decline from 70 per cent to 30 per cent in the proportion of households that considered food a serious problem. In addition, similar declines have been reported in the problems associated with debt and health (Table 1.1).

Looking further at health data, we find that UNICEF's work in Namibia throws an interesting light on the argument that levels of rural poverty are increasingly transferred to urban situations (Cogill and Kiugu, 1990). Malnutrition was reported as being three times lower in Katutura than it was in the rural north, and undernutrition, stunting and wasting were also less evident in Katutura (Cogill and Kiugu, 1990; Pendleton, 1996). Moreover, the majority of respondents in this research stated that hunger was not a serious problem in their households (Frayne, 2001).

How, then, is this apparent contradiction explained: unemployment is high, rural–urban migration is growing, and yet respondents report that levels of hunger are lower than only ten years ago? On the basis of the evidence, this chapter argues that an alternative source of income must have been introduced since independence and that it is one that is not generally reported in surveys (as they are not designed to retrieve this hidden income source). The stated improvement in the food situation from 1991 to 2000 leads one to the hypothesis that this hidden income is most likely in the form of food. In addition, the primary source of migrants is the rural north, where land continues to be used productively. Although food transfers from rural households to migrants during the colonial era have not been documented, this research and Pendleton's work (1991, 1996) confirm that this is a new factor among both migrant and non-migrant households.

During the colonial period, personal mobility was extremely limited for migrants, with typically only one visit home per year (Moorsom, 1995). Since independence migrants have become a highly mobile group, making frequent visits to the rural areas each year (Pendleton, 1996; Frayne and Pendleton, 2001; Frayne, 2001). Social linkages between the rural and urban areas thus appear to underpin the greater mobility and potential for the transport of goods between households. Therefore, this apparent contradiction might be best explained by the increasing fluidity of rural–urban links in Namibia. This, in turn, has been made possible by the deregulation of the labour market and the freedom of movement now possible under a new and independent government.

The research reported in this chapter is therefore concerned with how poor urban households in Namibia ensure adequate food supplies in the context of high rates of rural–urban migration and rising urban poverty. The project is the first of its kind in Namibia to systematically conduct research in both the places of origin and the destination of rural and urban migrants and their families. The research aims to develop a comprehensive understanding of how rural and urban households cooperate to survive under current economic hardship and poverty. In particular, the research identifies the contribution that food transfers from the rural areas to families living in Windhoek make to food security for poor urban households.

In addition to making a contribution to theories of migration, this research contributes to the recent shift in the theoretical debate away from aggregate measures of urban food security to household and individual measures of vulnerability and access to food sources (Moser, 1996, 1998). The results of this research are of critical importance to policy makers, planners and scholars in Namibia and, more broadly, in southern Africa, where similar socio-economic and demographic processes may be at work (see W. Smit, 1998 on South Africa; Morapedi, 1999 on Botswana; Potts, 2000 on Zimbabwe).

This chapter proceeds by situating the research within its scholarly context. The methodology is then outlined, and this is followed by a summary of the key research findings and reflections on future research.

LITERATURE OVERVIEW AND KEY CONCEPTS

Especially in the developing world, poverty and hunger have long been regarded as a rural problem. This is no longer so: between 1990 and 2025 the number of urban dwellers in the world is expected to double, reaching more than 5 billion, and 90 per cent of these people will be living in the South (UNCHS, 1996; WRI, 1996; UNFPA, 2000). In sub-Saharan Africa alone, the number of city dwellers is expected to triple over the same period (Smit et al, 1996). Precipitating factors include environmental stress, declining agricultural yields, structural adjustment and trade liberalization (including export-oriented agricultural policies and reductions in wage employment and in welfare), as well as war and natural disasters (Mougeot, 1994; IDRC, 1997; Potter and Lloyd-Evans, 1998). How do poor households survive these pressures and the effects of growing urban poverty?

The literature indicates that urban food security measures and strategies have generally been considered at the city scale, rather than at the level of the household. However, it is well documented that urban poverty is often most acutely felt at the household level (Moser, 1996, 1998; UNICEF, 1998, 2000; Devereux, 1999; Tvedten and Nangulah, 1999; Barrett and Carter, 2000). Moreover, the most direct and possibly most threatening consequences of poverty are limited or threatened food security and consequent hunger, despite adequate levels of food security being reported at the city scale. Urban poverty reduction strategies generally aim to increase productivity within the manufacturing and retail sectors (that is, increase employment opportunities). Yet with persistently high levels of urbanization and limited economic opportunity, vulnerability to hunger and the associated problems are not adequately addressed in the majority of the urban centres of the developing world (Drakakis-Smith, 1990, 1991, 1995, 1997; Moser, 1996, 1998; Todaro, 1997; UNICEF, 1998; Koc et al, 1999). Recognizing the failure of the formal economic and urban sectors to provide adequate services and employment to address the increasing poverty in much of the developing world, the international and local development and research communities have drawn into their ambit the question of how urban populations feed themselves under constrained and difficult conditions (IDRC, 1997).

Research on issues of food security has tended to focus on rural areas and communities, and a strong body of literature and theory has developed around the theme of economic entitlement (Dando, 1980; Sen, 1981; Rotberg and Rabb, 1983; Watts, 1983, 1987, 1991; Currey and Hugo, 1984; Bowbrick, 1986; Glantz, 1987; De Waal, 1990; Devereux, 1993, 1999; Devereux and Næraa, 1996; Young, 1996; Potts, 2000). However, little complementary work has been done on food security in urban areas, where hunger, malnutrition and other ailments associated with poverty are widespread and worsening as urbanization proceeds apace (Drakakis-Smith, 1990, 1997; Potter and Salau, 1990; Watts and Bohle, 1993; Moser, 1996, 1998; Todaro, 1997; UNICEF, 1998). The emphasis of urban studies has been on the informal sector and more recently on urban agriculture (UA) (De Soto, 1989; Drakakis-Smith,

1990; Egziabher et al, 1994; May and Rogerson, 1995; IDRC, 1997; Binns and Lynch, 1998; Koc et al, 1999). Much less attention has been paid to linkages and food chains between rural and urban areas and their embeddedness in systems of migrancy. In their research on the migration experience in Africa, Baker and Aina (1995, p25) asked what 'kinds of coping and survival mechanisms are employed and [whether] households [are] becoming more multi-active and multi-spatial in order to survive and/or maintain living standards.' Clearly, survival is a serious issue in the African context of poverty, and migration is one coping mechanism recognized as important (Stichter, 1985; Martin and Beittel, 1987; Baker, 1990; Crush et al, 1991; Stark, 1991; Baker and Pedersen, 1992; Adepoju, 1995; Amin, 1995; Baker and Aina, 1995; Oucho, 1996; Crush and Soutter, 1999; McDonald, 2000; Sharp, 2001).

The limited but current research on urban livelihoods indicates that urban households in sub-Saharan Africa do rely to varying degrees on a supply of food from the rural areas to survive within hostile urban environments (Murray, 1987; Baker, 1990; Stark, 1991; Baker and Pedersen, 1992; Weeks, 1994; Baker and Aina, 1995; Pendleton, 1996; Speigel et al, 1996; Weisner et al, 1997; Kamete, 1998; Krüger, 1998; Potts and Mutambirwa, 1998; Smit, 1998; Tacoli, 1998; Potts, 2000; Frayne and Pendleton, 2001). What is not known is the prevalence of these urban–rural linkages, their dynamics and their current or potential contribution to urban food security for poor urban households (IDRC, 1997).

This research is therefore situated at the intersection of three bodies of scholarship: urbanization and survival, migration and economic entitlement. It contributes to an emerging theory of urban entitlement and links into the growing body of theoretical and empirical work on migration and survival (Watts and Bohle, 1993; Drakakis-Smith, 1997; IDRC, 1997; Moser, 1998; Devereux, 1999; Potts, 2000).

METHODOLOGY

The methodology consisted of two data collection techniques: the standardized questionnaire survey and in-depth, semi-structured, case-study interviews. These two data collection methods complement each other by providing generalized information through the survey and more fine-grained information through the in-depth interviews. Given the importance of the migrant-sending areas in the research, the methodology was extended beyond the original proposal to include in-depth interviews in the rural areas.

The methodology is innovative for two reasons. First, by combining quantitative and qualitative approaches to the question of migration, it creates the methodological synergy needed to uncover the multidimensional nature of 'the household' as a unit of analysis (an important consideration in this context, where households are fluid and may extend across time and geographic space). Second, the rural homes (places of origin) of migrants interviewed in the urban centres are identified, and rural household members are selected for in-depth interviews in the rural areas. This approach helps to provide data and information on the migration and reciprocity process from both the urban and the rural perspectives. To evaluate possible changes over time, use was made of secondary survey data from a variety of sources available in Windhoek.

Given that Windhoek is almost 10 times the size of any other urban place in Namibia and that, as the capital, it provides a destination for all sectors of Namibian society, this city was selected as the research locale for the quantitative survey and urban-household case studies. Because most of the growth in the city occurs within the former African township of Katutura, the urban component of the research was undertaken there. Katutura is the primary destination of migrants to the city and appears to have the strongest urban–rural linkages evident in Windhoek. Furthermore, Katutura is home to more than half of the city's entire population and represents the poorest (and most vulnerable) sectors of society. It should be noted that the term *Katutura* is used to refer to both the formal area of the township and the informal areas to the northwest of the city.

Within each of the various residential areas of Katutura selected for the survey the number of housing sites (*erven*) was counted. The number of surveys allocated to a particular area was then divided into the number of dwelling sites to arrive at a sample interval. An arbitrary point within each residential section was selected as the starting point. Although the head of the household was considered the primary decision-maker, the need to gain insights on intricate dynamics within and between urban households and their rural components required interviews with other members of the household as well. For example, migration in recent years has achieved closer gender parity than under the contract-labour system, which was male dominated (Frayne, 2001). This change, together with the fact that social, political and economic conditions vary according to gender in Namibia, made it crucial that the methodology be designed to make a gender analysis of the data possible (Iipinge and LeBeau, 1997). Therefore, it was decided that adult respondents within each household would be selected in a systematic fashion (those 18 years of age and older).

A total of 305 interviews were conducted through a standardized survey, which included 95 mostly closed-ended questions. A systematic random sampling technique was used for sample selection. Questions were designed to collect information at the household and individual levels. The questions were divided into five categories, depending on the nature of the information sought: demography and socio-economic characteristics; migration and household arrangements; food and commodity transfers and remittances between rural and urban households; social linkages; and UA. Data were collected by local interviewers fluent in local languages.

Semi-structured in-depth interviews were conducted with 31 urban and 10 rural respondents. Convenience sampling, derived from introductions through the survey and community connections, was used to select the interviewees.

Local interviewers and languages were used to facilitate communication. Questions were grouped into five sections, covering socio-economic and demographic information, migration history, rural and urban assets, food security and commodity transfers.

RESEARCH FINDINGS

The research resulted in three major findings that help to explain the urban food security conundrum outlined in the introduction. Despite the conclusion that urban poverty is rising in Windhoek, the evidence from this research supports the proposition that urban households are increasingly reliant on transfers of food from the rural areas to supplement their urban food budgets. The results also demonstrate that it is impossible to understand this household-level coping mechanism in the urban areas without also understanding the complexity of rural–urban linkages and the high degree of social reciprocity that underpins the economic linkages evident between rural and urban households. A summary of each of these findings is presented after the contribution of UA to household food security is examined below.

Urban agriculture in Windhoek

It is well established that households in many cities in the world engage in UA to improve food security (Koc et al, 1999). Mass urbanization and a rise in urban poverty are central factors in the development of UA. It is therefore important to quantify the extent to which UA is used by households in Windhoek to contribute to their level of food security.

UA is undertaken in Windhoek, despite the climatic constraints. Five per cent of the sample was involved in some form of UA and a further 4 per cent knew of someone else in the city who grew some food themselves. General observation in the area supports the fact that, although it is limited in incidence and scale, UA is evident in Windhoek.

On average, the produce of UA saves households about 60 Namibia dollars (NAD) per month in groceries, which they would otherwise be required to purchase from a retail outlet (in 2003, 7.51 NAD = 1 United States dollar (USD)). Within the Namibian context, this is a significant amount of money and indicates the important contribution that improved conditions for UA in Namibia could make toward meeting the costs of food for poorer households.

Less than 1 per cent of respondents reported keeping urban livestock (within a 10km radius of the city), but this activity may be underreported. When asked whether they knew of any neighbours or friends who kept livestock in the city, a little more than 3 per cent said that they did. Also, goats were observed on numerous occasions within the city limits. However, the fact that the municipal and health by-laws are strict in this regard might explain the reluctance of people to identify themselves as having urban livestock.[3]

Nonetheless, the numbers are small, and these figures appear to correctly indicate the limited extent to which people are engaged in livestock production

Table 1.2 *Incidence of households receiving food from relatives and friends in the rural areas over the past year (2000)*

	Receiving food from relatives		Receiving food from friends	
	n	%	n	%
Yes	190	62	11	4
No	115	38	294	96

within the urban area of Windhoek. Even with more proactive policies, the strained water supply of the city, as well as the limited biomass available, suggests that keeping livestock in the city and its environs has limited potential under current systems of land-use and water allocation.

Despite the potential that might exist for expansion of this sector, the current low levels of production again point to the importance to poorer urban households of food sources beyond the urban boundary. The quantity of food being produced in the city suggests that UA does not play a significant role in ameliorating urban food insecurity at the household level in Windhoek.

Rural–urban food transfers and survival

The primary argument of this study is that migrants survive in the urban areas in part because of food they receive from the rural areas. Over the previous year, some 62 per cent of the Windhoek households sampled had received food from relatives in the rural areas; a further 4 per cent, from friends (Table 1.2). This represents two-thirds of all households surveyed, including those that did not have first-generation migrants living in them (that is, all members were born in Windhoek – 14 per cent of the sample).

Even more significant is the fact that about 58 per cent of the households reported being sent food two to six times a year. Respondents also indicated receipt of a wide range of products, some of which were seasonal; these included cultivated and wild foods, some meat, poultry and fish (Table 1.3).

Pearl millet (*mahangu*) is the staple cereal crop in Namibia, and when asked what quantity of particular food items were sent to the household the last time they received food, respondents reported a significant amount of

Table 1.3 *Types of food people report receiving from the rural areas (2000)*

	n	%
Pearl millet (*mahangu*)	150	42
Other cereals	13	4
Meat and fish	31	9
Commercial foods	14	4
Wild foods	147	41
Total	355	100

Note: multiple responses were possible, accounting for total exceeding number of respondents.

Table 1.4 *Amount of millet received the last time by people in households (2000)*

Amount (kg)	n	%
1–4	51	27
5–9	26	14
10–19	64	34
20–50	48	25

millet. Table 1.4 indicates that 48 per cent of the respondents claimed that they had received 5–19kg of millet the last time it was sent to them, with about one-quarter of the sample receiving 20–50kg.

In addition to millet, fish was important, as were wild foods. Commercial foods, which would be purchased in a store, were of little significance (N values ranged from 0 to 4). Given the generally low levels of rural cash income and widespread poverty, it is not surprising that the food the rural household had access to was available through farming or collection from the bush. The most common wild food to be sent to urban households was spinach, which is culturally important and provides micronutrients. When in season, fresh and dried fruit of various kinds was also sent. The following testimony illustrates this reliance on the productive capacity of the land for the type and volume of food sent to urban relatives:

> We send mahangu flour, beans and dried spinach, when someone is visiting them from here [Owamboland], or if they visit us. We don't send money, and the food is only sent a few times per year, perhaps five or six. This is partly because we have to rely on visitors to transport the goods to Windhoek, which is not a regular thing, and also because food is not as abundant here as we would like.[4]

The importance of these rural–urban transfers of food is a further indicator of the central role of migration and urban–rural links in urban food security at the household level. The survey shows that the most recent amount of millet received lasted nearly half of all households about one month, and a further 16 per cent of households between two and six months. Moreover, 81 per cent of respondents rated the food they received from the rural areas as 'important' or 'very important' to the household, with a further 11 per cent reporting that the food they received was 'critical to their survival' (Table 1.5).

The importance of this food to survival was further validated by the responses respondents gave when asked why food was sent to the household from the rural areas. Seventy-nine per cent of the rural respondents said that the food was sent to help the members of the urban households feed themselves. About 91 per cent of the urban respondents reported consuming by themselves all the food they received, with only 6 per cent using some of the food they received for business purposes; the other 3 per cent gave it away

Table 1.5 *Importance of food sent from the rural areas to
urban households (2000)*

	n	%
How important is this food to the household?		
Not important at all	1	1
Somewhat important	15	8
Important	50	26
Very important	104	55
Critical to our survival	20	10

to friends and relatives. Without these food transfers, food insecurity and malnutrition among migrant households would undoubtedly be significantly higher than current levels.

Demographic coping strategies and survival

Sen (1981) argued that when entitlement to food is threatened as a result of economic shock or stress, rural households employ various coping strategies to ameliorate those entitlement failures. One such strategy is to increase sharing between households. Sen recorded limited interhousehold reciprocity within the boundaries of the urban area (less than 5 per cent of the sample reported borrowing food with any regularity), in contrast to the rural situation.

Instead, my findings clearly demonstrate that strong linkages exist between rural and urban households and that coping strategies are based on these urban–rural relationships. Thus, although it is not possible to transpose Sen's (1981) analysis of interhousehold sharing to the urban context in Windhoek, it is plausible to argue that urban households reduce their food gap by invoking rural entitlements, theirs by virtue of their social links. This is an unexpected application of the entitlement approach in relation to household sharing, but it is valid nonetheless and emphasizes the dominance of urban–rural links in the urban survival equation.

Limited interhousehold reciprocity in urban areas is therefore closely related to the substantial connection and flow of food between urban and rural households. These very networks provide the 'social infrastructure' that promotes linkages between urban migrants and their places of origin. This social infrastructure (capital) is also responsible for a number of demographic activities that promote food security within urban areas (and vice versa, in that rural areas benefit, too, from the transfer of money and other commodities from the urban areas).

In cases in which urban households – migrant or non-migrant – experience economic stress and food scarcity, sending children and adults to live with rural relatives is a common practice. In the entitlement and coping literature, migration by rural households to urban areas in search of employment when

Table 1.6 *Why children are sent to live with relatives (2000)*

	n	%a
Not enough money to provide for them	81	35
No schools in Windhoek for them	29	12
Not enough time to look after them properly	44	19

Note: a Column percentage not equal to 100, as multiple responses possible.

rural sources of entitlement fail is called distress migration (Devereux, 1999). However, in this study, it is equally valid to talk about distress migration in relation to both children and adults within the urban area. Seventy per cent of the sample indicated that they had sent their children to stay with relatives elsewhere. The primary reason given by respondents (35 per cent) was that the household did not have enough money to support the children in Windhoek (Table 1.6). Of those children sent away, at least 90 per cent were living with relatives in the rural areas of Namibia, and about 70 per cent of them would stay away from their home in Windhoek for more than a year at a time.

Another demographic adjustment (distress migration) strategy of the struggling urban migrants or households is to send adult members to the rural areas, either as returnees or, in some instances, as new migrants to the rural homestead. The burden of providing the daily food requirements for an extended household where few are employed in any significant fashion is immense. This strategy of returning adults to the rural areas therefore helps to minimize the need to ration food, sell off assets, borrow food or money, or engage in crime to survive (all of which are coping and survival strategies invoked in response to failing entitlements).

Vulnerability to hunger in the rural context is determined in part by the variability and reliability of food sources (Sen, 1981; Devereux, 1993, 1999). The results of this research show that a loss of entitlement sources increases vulnerability and hunger in Windhoek. The most marginal and vulnerable urban households were those that had poor or non-existent relationships to kin in the rural areas and had few social or economic urban resources. In other words, the limitation of their social infrastructure directly curtailed their entitlement to both urban and rural resources. Typically, these households comprised young, single males who were often involved in piecework and crime, or they were female-headed households that relied on the informal sector for their income (see Frayne, 2001, for a detailed discussion of the gender aspects of vulnerability and urban food security). Although these cases represent a small proportion of the sample, they are significant as they illustrate the importance of urban–rural links in the survival equation and also help to identify the most vulnerable members of society. In most cases, however, returning to the rural areas permanently was not perceived as a solution to the household's current circumstances of deprivation, and the urban area remained the destination of first choice.

CIRCULAR AND RECIPROCAL URBANIZATION

Social networks have been described as important in understanding the demographic strategies used by rural and urban households to ameliorate economic stress and improve food security. In this regard, the survey showed that 85 per cent of the respondents were migrants to Windhoek, and only five households (1.6 per cent) sampled reported having no relatives in the rural areas of Namibia. That more than 98 per cent of the sample said they had relatives in the rural areas and 86 per cent said they visited their relatives and friends in the rural areas at least once a year confirms the strength of social ties between urban and rural households in the country. These strong and dynamic social connections underpin the reciprocal characteristics of the Namibian social economy.

In Namibia, sending remittances back to their rural households is a well-established tradition among migrants in urban centres (Pendleton, 1994, 1996; Moorsom, 1995; Pendleton and Frayne, 1998; Pomuti and Tvedten, 1998). The historical pattern of forced migration to meet the colonial labour needs of Namibia has given way to voluntary migration, precipitated by the increasing reliance of rural households on non-farm incomes (UNICEF–NISER, 1991; Pendleton, 1994). The recent decline in the formal urban economy in Namibia has reduced the income-earning opportunities of urban migrants, thereby diminishing their potential to send money back to rural households. Yet studies show the importance of urban earnings to the survival of rural households, especially during times of economic hardship (Devereux et al, 1995; Moorsom, 1995; Pendleton, 1996).

Given this tension between rising need and falling earning potential, it is not surprising that the percentage of households remitting money to rural households has not increased over the past 10 years. Sixty-three per cent of respondents in this study said that they sent no money to family elsewhere, which is the same proportion that responded to a similar question in a household survey carried out in Katutura in 1991 (Pendleton, 1991). However, given that the absolute number of migrants to Windhoek has doubled over the same period, the actual number of people remitting money from the urban area to the rural areas has increased substantially. This suggests that the number of rural households that receive urban remittances is continuing to rise and that this source of income is therefore increasingly important. A rural respondent described the role of remittances as follows:

> Hunger is not generally a problem. Even in years when there is not enough rain, we are able to get enough money to buy what we need. This comes from our relatives in town, who work and get money. Without them, there could be a serious food shortage here, especially when there is drought.[5]

The amount of money sent to rural relatives varies, although the median category is 101–150 NAD (sent 'every few months'). In comparison to the average household remittance of 156 NAD reported in 1991 (Pendleton, 1991), average amounts sent have not increased over the past decade. It is also significant that about 50 per cent of households remit money to rural relatives every month, or at least every 2 or 3 months. The amounts of money sent and the frequency of remittances support the argument that rural households continue to depend on their urban counterparts for income, although the actual value of remittances has remained static.

Placing a monetary value on food transfers from the rural areas to urban households is difficult, not least because of seasonal variance. However, it is noteworthy that during the year of the survey (2000), half of all households sampled reported that they had used millet sent from the rural areas. This food item alone would cost about 60 NAD a month for a household of four if substituted with commercial maize meal. This value compares favourably with that of money remitted to rural households every few months. However, the percentage of urban households receiving food regularly is greater than the percentage of those remitting cash to rural relatives. The economic balance appears to have moved in favour of urban households over the past decade.

The economic values associated with demographic reciprocity are complex, but the research did record the importance of urban incomes for the support of parents and children based in the rural areas. The largest proportion of remittances (85 per cent) is sent to parents or children living in the rural areas. This figure highlights the importance of the social and economic ties between extended families that straddle the rural and urban sectors.

These very networks are key to our understanding of the persistence of the cyclical migration in Namibia. The increase in urban poverty and the limitations of economic opportunities available to migrants make rural–urban interdependence an integral characteristic of the Namibian social economy.

In the past, migration to urban areas was largely temporary, in both legal status and practicality, serving the labour needs of the colonial system. A cyclical pattern of movement was typical (although more permanent migration with families to urban areas did occur simultaneously). In present times, this form of cyclical migration of labour per se is much less significant and is being replaced by the equally mobile but more complex phenomenon of reciprocal migration.

The conventional wisdom assumes that urbanization is both sustained and unilinear. However, the process of urbanization is seen as being slower in southern Africa than elsewhere and as having been hindered by the slow industrial growth and limited employment opportunities of the past decade. Although permanent urbanization certainly continues in the region, the persistence of non-commercial agricultural production and a rise in urban poverty have set in motion a complex system of cyclical or reciprocal migration between rural and urban areas. Pressures on rural systems of production are increasing as per capita economic opportunities in urban areas decrease, and it appears to be this interplay of factors that is increasing the interdependency of urban and rural systems, spawning a new form of urbanization within Namibia. This form of multilayered, complex, disorderly urbanization is described in this research as 'reciprocal urbanization'. This new form of urbanization appears to be enhanced by modern communications and transport technologies, which make the flow of information and people easier than ever before in the country's history.

This finding challenges current theory that relies on the unilinear model of migration and urbanization and suggests that the urban futures of countries like Namibia are likely to be intimately tied to rural systems and that the two will operate in direct symbiosis. This symbiosis will have political, social, economic and environmental dimensions.

REFLECTIONS FOR FURTHER RESEARCH

The findings of this research are sufficiently provocative to suggest a number of important research directions. Within Namibia, including both the rural and the urban sectors, a range of future research is indicated. At the rural end of the spectrum, the importance of rural agriculture suggests that protecting rural productivity at the household level is crucial, and this includes addressing issues around land tenure, technology and the environment.

The environmental impact of urbanization is typically researched within the urban context, with rural environmental inquiry being carried out as an unrelated endeavour. However, migration and urbanization might well have significant impacts on the rural environment in Namibia, as well as important consequences and policy implications for both rural and urban livelihoods.

This research raises a potentially important question about the extent to which rural–urban migration degrades the rural environment or contributes to the social and economic development of the rural population. The logic behind this question is that access to money by rural migrants in the urban areas results in return spending in the rural areas. This spending makes a range of modern goods and services for rural households affordable, which might well promote local development objectives. A good example of this is the recent rise in the number of brick houses built in the rural setting, which reduces reliance on local forest resources for construction materials.[6]

However, the number of vehicles is rising in the rural areas, with significant negative impacts on the environment (people drive on tracks in the bush between homesteads and from homesteads to town). Also, an important focus of investment for urban dwellers is rural herds of livestock. Numbers of livestock have risen over the last decade, and this may have important negative environmental consequences that may, in turn, reduce agricultural output in the rural areas, which this research demonstrates plays an important role in urban livelihoods.

At the urban end of the spectrum, it is likely that UA will provide a significant source of urban food in the future. Research is therefore needed in Namibia on intensive, small-scale, water-conserving agricultural irrigation systems applicable at the urban household level. In addition, ways of managing urban livestock are likely to become more relevant, so proactive research in this direction would be important. This work may also have relevance to other countries in the region.

It seems probable that the form of reciprocal urbanization described in this paper is not unique to Namibia. Similar conditions and processes are at work elsewhere in the region and beyond. In her work on Zimbabwe, Potts (2000) suggested that migrants in the urban areas depend directly on their rural land and that recent urban difficulties may have resulted in increased rural productivity. The migration and urbanization phenomenon is sufficiently complex in Namibia to challenge modernist views of unilinear urbanization. Potts (2000, p831) concurs for Zimbabwe:

> *Indeed, the nexus between rural production, migration and urbanization is too complex to comprehensively address through neoliberal assumptions about economic growth and private ownership of land.*

In addition to Zimbabwe, it is likely that similar dynamics are at work in other countries in the region that have similar social and economic histories. These countries would include Malawi, South Africa and Zambia. Although South Africa is often regarded as unique within the regional context, a similar situation might be observed in certain parts of the country. Smit (1998) argued that rural ties are important in the urbanization process for rural migrants to Durban.

Rural–urban linkages warrant further investigation within the Namibian context, given the failure of industrial growth to create employment. If reciprocal urbanization is the emerging reality in the region, research is urgently required to further uncover the dynamics at work, as these have direct implications for the ways development practitioners might shape policy and practice, with poverty alleviation as a central objective.

The general issue of coping (demographic and food transfers) raises another important question in relation to these findings: what happens when sources of rural food supply are interrupted? Because of their long histories of civil war, Angola and Mozambique would be good subjects for case studies of the consequences of disrupting rural productive systems and limiting rural–urban mobility. In both Angola and Mozambique, the urban boundary has been largely impermeable, as a result of the sustained conflict limiting the flow of people and food between rural and urban centres. These case studies would help us understand the coping strategies of urban households when access to rural food supplies is disrupted. UA, for example, might play a significant role in promoting urban food security, but further investigation is required. Now that the war is over in Mozambique, are people reclaiming rights to rural land and growing food there? If so, will the direction of urbanization conform to the emerging pattern of reciprocity evident in Namibia?

The research questions posed here aim to assess the degree to which the Namibian food-security situation is illustrative of that of other countries in the region. If the findings in Namibia are indicative of a new form of social and economic organization in southern Africa, the agenda of development policy and planning needs to be reshaped accordingly. Certainly UA would be at centre stage in that development paradigm.

ACKNOWLEDGEMENTS

This research was funded by the International Development Research Centre through an AGROPOLIS Research Award under the Cities Feeding People programme. The additional financial and in-kind contributions from Queen's University at Kingston (School of Graduate Studies, Department of Geography, Southern African Migration project, and the Southern African Research Centre), the Social Sciences Division of the Multi-Disciplinary Research Centre at the University of Namibia, and the international non-governmental organization Ibis (Wus-Denmark), Windhoek, are gratefully acknowledged.

NOTES

1   Bruce Frayne is Assistant Professor in the Southern African Research Centre and Department of Geography at Queen's University at Kingston. Dr Frayne has worked extensively in Namibia and South Africa as a social science researcher and land-use planner and has participated in numerous research projects on a range of rural and urban development issues in the region. His current research on rural–urban links examines the relationship between migration and household food security in southern Africa.
2   Interview with the Chief, Urban Policy, Strategy, Facilitation and Implementation Services, Department of Planning, Urbanization and Environment, City of Windhoek, Namibia, 1 September 1999.
3   Interview with the Chief, Urban Policy, Strategy, Facilitation and Implementation Services, Department of Planning, Urbanization and Environment, City of Windhoek, Namibia, 1 September 1999.
4   Rural case study 3, rural north, 22 June 2000.
5   Rural case study 2, rural north, 20 June 2000.
6   Many of these houses are used by people who are truly living between two worlds. Personal mobility makes it possible to have two 'homes', one in the urban area and one in the rural area; both houses serve equally important purposes.

REFERENCES

Adepoju, A. (1995) 'Migration in Africa: An overview', in Baker, J. and Aina, T. (eds), *The Migration Experience in Africa*, Nordiska Afrikainstitutet, Uppsala, Sweden, pp87–108
Amin, S. (1995) 'Migrations in contemporary Africa: A retrospective view', in Baker J. and Aina T. (eds), *The Migration Experience in Africa*, Nordiska Afrikainstitutet, Uppsala, Sweden, pp29–40

Baker, J. (ed.) (1990) *Small Town Africa: Studies in Rural–Urban Interaction*. Scandinavian Institute of African Studies, Solna, Sweden

Baker, J. and Aina, T. (eds) (1995) *The Migration Experience in Africa*, Nordiska Afrikainstitutet, Uppsala, Sweden

Baker, J. and Pedersen, P. O. (eds) (1992) *The Rural–Urban Interface in Africa: Expansion and adaptation*, Scandinavian Institute of African Studies, Solna, Sweden; Nordiska Afrikainstitutet, Uppsala, Sweden. Seminar Proceedings No. 27

Barrett, C. and Carter, M. (2000) 'Directions for development policy to escape poverty and relief traps', *Africa Notes*, February, pp1–5

Binns, T. and Lynch, K. (1998) 'Feeding Africa's growing cities into the 21st century: The potential of urban agriculture', *Journal of International Development*, vol 10, pp777–793

Bowbrick, P. (1986) 'The causes of famine: A refutation of Professor Sen's theory', *Food Policy*, vol 11, no 2, pp105–124

Cogill, B. and Kiugu, S. (1990) *Report on a Survey of Household Health and Nutrition in Katutura and Selected Northern Areas of Namibia*, UNICEF; Ministry of Health and Social Services, Government of the Republic of Namibia, Windhoek, Namibia

Crush, J., Jeeves, A. and Yudelman, D. (1991) *South Africa's Labor Empire: A History of Black Migrancy to the Gold Mines*, Westview Press, Boulder, CO

Crush, J. and Soutter, C. (1999) 'Natural family conditions: Narratives of stabilization and the South African coal mines, 1910–1970', *South African Geographical Journal*, vol 81, no 1, pp5–14

Currey, B. and Hugo, G. (eds) (1984) *Famine as a Geographical Phenomenon*, Reidel Publishing Co., Dordrecht, Netherlands

Dando, W. (1980) *The Geography of Famine*, Edward Arnold, London

De Soto, H. (1989) *The Other Path: The Invisible Revolution in the Third World*, Harper & Row, New York

Devereux, S. (1993) *Theories of Famine*, Harvester Wheatsheaf, New York

Devereux, S. (1999) *Making Less Last Longer: Informal Safety Nets in Malawi*, Institute of Development Studies, University of Sussex, Brighton, IDS Discussion Paper 373

Devereux, S., Fuller, B., Moorsom, R., Solomon, C. and Tapscott, C. (1995) *Namibia Poverty Profile*, Social Sciences Division, Multi-Disciplinary Research Centre, University of Namibia, Windhoek, Namibia. SSD Research Report 21

Devereux, S., Melaku-Tjirongo, E. and Næraa, T. (1993) *Urban Situation Analysis: A Study of Five Namibian Towns*, Social Sciences Division, Multi-Disciplinary Research Centre, University of Namibia, Windhoek, Namibia

Devereux, S. and Næraa, T. (1996) 'Drought and survival in rural Namibia', *Journal of Southern African Studies*, vol 22, pp421–440

De Waal, A. (1990) 'A reassessment of entitlement theory in the light of the recent famines in Africa', *Development and Change*, vol 21, pp469–490

Drakakis-Smith, D. (1990) 'Food for thought or thought about food: Urban food distribution systems in the Third World', in Potter, R. B. and Salau, A. T. (eds), *Cities and Development in the Third World*, Mansell, London, pp100–120

Drakakis-Smith, D. (1991) 'Urban food distributions systems in Asia and Africa', *Geographical Journal*, vol 157, pp51–61

Drakakis-Smith, D. (1995) 'Third World cities: Sustainable urban development. I', *Urban Studies*, vol 32, pp659–678

Drakakis-Smith, D. (1997) 'Third World cities: Sustainable urban development. III: Basic needs and human rights', *Urban Studies*, vol 34, pp797–823

Egziabher, A. G., Lee-Smith, D., Maxwell, D. G., Memon, P. A., Mougeot, L. J. A. and Sawio, C. J. (1994) *Cities Feeding People: An Examination of Urban Agriculture in East Africa*, International Development Research Centre, Ottawa

Frayne, B. (2001) 'Survival of the poorest: Migration and food security in Namibia', Department of Geography, Queen's University at Kingston, Kingston, ON, Canada. PhD thesis

Frayne, B. and Pendleton, W. (2001) 'Migration in Namibia: Combining macro and micro approaches to research design and analysis', *International Migration Review*, vol 35, no 4, pp1054–1085

Glantz, M. (ed.) (1987) *Drought and Hunger in Africa: Denying Famine a Future.* Cambridge University Press, Cambridge, UK. 457 pp.

Hansohm, D. (2000) 'Alternative paths of economic development in Namibia', in Fuller B. and Prommer, I. (eds), *Population–Development–Environment in Namibia: Background Readings*, International Institute for Applied Systems Analysis, Laxenburg, Austria, pp65–184

IDRC (International Development Research Centre) (1997) *Development Research in Urban Agriculture: An International Awards Program*, IDRC, Ottawa, ON, Canada.

Iipinge, E. and LeBeau, D. (1997) *Beyond Inequalities: Women in Namibia*, Southern African Resource and Documentation Centre, Harare

Kamete, A. (1998) 'Interlocking livelihoods: Farm and small town in Zimbabwe', *Environment and Urbanization*, vol 10, no 1, pp23–34

Koc, M., MacRae, R., Mougeot, L. and Welsh, J. (eds) (1999) *For Hunger-proof Cities: Sustainable Urban Food Systems*, International Development Research Centre, Ottawa

Krüger, F. (1998) 'Taking advantage of rural assets as a coping strategy', *Environment and Urbanization*, vol 10, no 1, pp119–134

Martin, W. and Beittel, M. (1987) 'The hidden abode of reproduction: Conceptualizing households in southern Africa', *Development and Change*, vol 18, pp215–234

May, J. and Rogerson, C. M. (1995) 'Poverty and sustainable cities in South Africa: The role of urban cultivation', *Habitat International*, vol 19, no 2, pp165–181

McDonald, D. (ed.) (2000) *On Borders: Perspectives on Cross-border Migration in Southern Africa*, St Martin's Press, New York

Moorsom, R. (1995) *Underdevelopment and Labour Migration: The Contract Labour System in Namibia*, Development Studies and Human Rights, Christian Michelsen Institute, Bergen, Norway

Morapedi, W. (1999) 'Migrant labour and the peasantry in the Bechuanaland Protectorate', *Journal of Southern African Studies*, vol 25, pp197–214

Moser, C. (1996) *Confronting Crisis: A Comparative Study of Household Responses to Poverty and Vulnerability in Four Poor Urban Communities*, World Bank, Washington, DC, Environmentally Sustainable Development Studies and Monograph Series, No. 8

Moser, C. (1998) 'The asset vulnerability framework: Reassessing urban poverty reduction strategies', *World Development*, vol 26, no 1, pp1–19

Mougeot, L. (1994) 'The rise of city farming must catch up with reality', *ILEIA Newsletter*, vol 10, no 4, pp4–5

Municipality of Windhoek (MoW) (1996a) *1995 Residents Survey Report*, vols 1–3, City of Windhoek, Windhoek, Namibia

Municipality of Windhoek (MoW) (1996b) *The Windhoek Structure Plan*, City of Windhoek, Windhoek, Namibia

Murray, C. (1987) 'Class, gender and the household: The developmental cycle in southern Africa', *Development and Change*, vol 18, pp235–249

Norval, D. and Namoya, R. (1992) *The Informal Sector Within Greater Windhoek*, First National Development Corporation, Windhoek, Namibia

Oucho, J. (1996) 'Migration, urbanization and development: New directions and issues', in Billsborrow, E. (ed.), *Migration, Urbanization, and Development: New Directions and Issues*, Kluwer, Dordrecht

Pendleton, W. (1991) *The 1991 Katutura Survey Report*, Namibian Institute for Social and Economic Research, University of Namibia, Windhoek, Namibia

Pendleton, W. (1994) *Katutura: A Place Where We Stay – Life in a Post-apartheid Township in Namibia*, Gamsberg Macmillan, Windhoek, Namibia

Pendleton, W. (1996) *Katutura: A Place Where we Stay*, Ohio University Centre for International Studies, Athens, OH

Pendleton, W. (1998) *Katutura in the 1990s*, Social Sciences Division, Multi-Disciplinary Research Centre, University of Namibia, Windhoek, Namibia. SSD Research Report 28

Pendleton, W. and Frayne, B. (1998) *Report of the Findings of the Namibian Migration Project*, Social Sciences Division, Multi-Disciplinary Research Centre, University of Namibia, Windhoek, Namibia. SSD Research Report 35

Peyroux, E. and Graefe, O. (1995) *Precarious Settlements at Windhoek's Periphery: Investigation into the Emergence of a New Urban Phenomenon*, Centre for Research Information and Action, Windhoek, Namibia.

Pile, S., Brook C. and Mooney, G. (eds) (1999) *Unruly Cities?* Routledge, London

Pomuti, A. and Tvedten, I. (1998) 'Namibia: Urbanization in the 1990s', in Pomuti, A. and Tvedten, I. (eds), *In Search of Research*, Namibian Economic Policy Research Unit, Windhoek, Namibia. Publication No. 6, pp103–133

Potter, R. and Lloyd-Evans, S. (1998) *The City in the Developing World*, Longman, Harlow, Essex

Potter, R. and Salau, A. (eds) (1990) *Cities and Development in the Third World*, Mansell, London

Potts, D. (2000) 'Worker–peasants and farmer–housewives in Africa: The debate about "committed" farmers, access to land and agricultural production', *Journal of Southern African Studies*, vol 26, pp807–832

Potts, D. and Mutambirwa, C. (1998) 'Basics are now a luxury: Perceptions of the impact of structural adjustment on rural and urban areas in Zimbabwe', *Environment and Urbanization*, vol 10, no 1, pp55–66

Rotberg, R. and Rabb, T. (eds) (1983) *Hunger and History*, Cambridge University Press, Cambridge

Sen, A. (1981) *Poverty and Famines: An Essay on Entitlement and Deprivation*, Clarendon Press, Oxford

Sharp, J. (2001) 'Copperbelt and Cape Town: Urban styles and rural connections in comparative perspective', *Journal of Contemporary African Studies*, vol 19, no 1, pp149–158

Smit, J., Ratta, A. and Bernstein, J. (1996) *Urban Agriculture: An Opportunity for Environmentally Sustainable Development in Sub-Saharan Africa*, Environmentally Sustainable Development Division, Africa Technical Department, World Bank, Washington, DC

Smit, W. (1998) 'The rural linkages of urban households in Durban', *Environment and Urbanization*, vol 10, no 1, pp77–88

Spiegel, A., Watson, V., Wilkinson, V. and Wilkinson, P. (1996) 'Domestic diversity and fluidity in some African households in greater Cape Town', *Social Dynamics*, vol 22, no 1, pp7–30

Stark, O. (1991) *The Migration of Labour*, Basil Blackwell, Cambridge, MA

Stichter, S. (1985) *Migrant Laborers*, Cambridge University Press, Cambridge

Tacoli, C. (1998) 'Rural–urban interactions: A guide to the literature', *Environment and Urbanization*, vol 10, no 1, pp147–166

Todaro, M. (1997) *Urbanization, Unemployment, and Migration in Africa: Theory and Policy*, Policy Research Division, Population Council, New York, NY. Working Paper 104

Tvedten, I. and Nangulah, S. (1999) 'Social relations of poverty: A case-study from Owambo, Namibia', Christian Michelsen Institute, Bergen, Norway. Draft research report

UNCHS (United Nations Human Settlements Programme) (1996) *An Urbanizing World: Global Report on Human Settlements 1996*, Oxford University Press, Oxford

UNFPA (United Nations Population Fund) (2000) *State of the World's Population*, UNFPA, New York, NY

UNICEF (United Nations Children's Fund) (1998) *The State of the World's Children, 1998*, Oxford University Press, Oxford

UNICEF (2000) *The State of the World's Children, 2000*, Oxford University Press, Oxford

UNICEF–NISER (United Nations Children's Fund; Namibia Institute for Scientific and Economic Research) (1991) *A Situation Analysis of Children and Women in Namibia*, NISER, University of Namibia, Windhoek, Namibia

Watts, M. (1983) *Silent Violence: Food, Famine and Peasantry in Northern Nigeria*, University of California Press, Berkeley, CA

Watts, M. (1987) 'Drought, environment and food security: Some reflections on peasants, pastoralists and commoditization in dryland West Africa', in Glantz, M. (ed.), *Drought and Hunger in Africa: Denying Famine a Future*, Cambridge University Press, Cambridge

Watts, M. (1991) 'Entitlements or empowerment? Famine and starvation in Africa', *Review of African Political Economy*, vol 51, pp9–26

Watts, M. J. and Bohle, H. G. (1993) 'Hunger, famine and the space of vulnerability', *GeoJournal*, vol 30, no 2, pp117–125

Weeks, J. (1994) 'Economic aspects of rural–urban migration', in Tarver, J. (ed.), *Urbanization in Africa: A Handbook*, Greenwood Press, Westport, CT

Weisner, T. J., Bradley, C. and Kilbride, P. (eds) (1997) *African Families and the Crisis of Social Change*, Bergin & Garvey, Westport, CT

WRI (World Resources Institute) (1996) *World Resources 1996–1997*, WRI, World Bank; Oxford University Press, New York

Young, L. (1996) 'World hunger: A framework for analysis', *Geography*, vol 81, no 351, Part 2, pp97–110

2

The Pest-control System in the Market Gardens of Lomé, Togo

Komla Tallaki

INTRODUCTION

This study belongs to an area of research dealing with agriculture in an urban setting – a concept that has developed a great deal in recent years. According to Mougeot (2000), urban agriculture (UA) is agriculture practised within or close to urban centres, using primarily urban-based resources to provide the urban population with certain services, not necessarily food. To a greater or lesser extent, UA in developing countries can and, in fact, does help reduce urban poverty and improve the food security of urban households. It also has great potential to use composted household waste and, as a result, is a sustainable means of managing the urban environment.

In certain cities around the world, urban and semiurban agricultural production meets an estimated 25–100 per cent of urban household needs for certain foodstuffs (Birley and Lock, 1999). For example, the cities of Bamako in Mali and Ouagadougou in Burkina Faso produce all the vegetables that their populations consume (Smit et al, 1996). Another example is Kampala, Uganda, where an estimated 70 per cent of the eggs and poultry consumed are locally produced (Smit et al, 1996). This pattern reccurs many times throughout the world, and not only in the poorest countries. However, in each case, a fairly high proportion of such production often appears to come from the most disadvantaged households, in which the women usually do the work, and is one way of meeting their family's food needs.

To be feasible, UA needs to be well integrated into the urban economy and to complement rural agriculture (FAO, 1998; Mougeot, 2000). For example, UA needs to make rational use of urban space that is intended for many other purposes. A system of extensive agriculture, based on an itinerant fallow system, is obviously not suitable for the urban environment. The type of intensive agriculture that is feasible is a danger to the local population and the environment because of the inputs it regularly requires. For example, pesticides and chemical fertilizers will always carry the risk of accumulating in the soil, water and air, thus polluting the environment. In addition, irrigation can erode and degrade the soil. Urban agriculture, therefore, needs to be well planned and monitored to take full advantage of all its potential. That is why a system needs to be developed to sustainably manage the dangers inherent in any effort to intensify UA. Any implementation of such a system begins with identifying all the constraints producers are subject to in a specific context. An example of this identification process is the primary focus of this study of a pest-control system used in the market gardens of Lomé, Togo. Analysis of the various producer interviews reveals a picture of the difficulties facing Lomé's market gardeners, which lead them to systematically misuse pesticides. Knowledge of these constraints makes it possible to propose a number of actions to raise awareness of the dangers of harmful pest-control practices and the need, for the common good, to find sustainable solutions to these challenges.

The Issue and Methodology

Urban agriculture in Togo

Agriculture is fairly common in most cities and towns in Togo. Many urban residents, especially in the interior, keep a few animals (poultry, rabbits, pigs, sheep and goats) in their houses or huts and work small gardens or fields, either just beside their dwellings or on the city outskirts. In reality, most towns in the Togo interior continue to be just big villages, in the sense that agriculture is still their inhabitants' primary economic activity.

In fact, in most cases, the way agriculture is practised in the cities and towns is only slightly different from the way it is practised in the countryside. In both contexts, rain-fed agriculture is the primary mode of farming. This system makes limited use of agricultural inputs (selected seeds, natural or chemical fertilizers, pesticides, etc.) but maximum use of the soil's natural productive capacities. In these traditional systems, vegetables are grown as secondary crops and animals (poultry, pigs and common small ruminants) are left to wander around the community. The animals are only shut up in enclosures in the evening. Only a few exceptions to this pattern are found. These are generally subsistence farming, with the livestock or crops used to feed the farm families. Despite the major contribution this type of production can make to the survival of these households, to date no study has focused on this type of agriculture in an urban environment.

Alongside these extensive agricultural systems are other more stable systems, such as horticulture, in general, and market gardening, in particular. In 1987, the Togolese government's Agricultural Research and Statistics Directorate (ARSD) conducted the first general census of market gardeners in Togo (ARSD, 1994). This census found that in 1987 Togo as a whole had 4218 market gardeners, 53 per cent of whom were women. These producers were mostly found within or around cities or large towns such as Lomé, Atakpamé, Sokodé, Kara and Dapaong. A 1995 survey revealed a marked increase in the number of market gardeners in Togo, especially in the maritime region, which accounted for 12,659 producers of the total 16,751 (ARSD, 1995). Lomé, which is part of this region, exhibited striking growth – from 620 market gardeners in 1987 to more than 3000 in 1995 (ARSD, 1994, 1995).

For most of these producers, except for those in Lomé, market gardening is an off-season activity, that is, something practised around bodies of water during the dry season. Among the market gardeners counted in 1987, for example, only 19 per cent of those in the national total were listed as full time, compared with 79 per cent for Lomé alone. Lomé is also distinguished by the fact that 94.4 per cent of its market gardeners use chemical fertilizers, compared with 29.2 per cent nationally. The number of market gardeners who use synthetic pesticides was also significantly higher in Lomé than in the rest of the country: 76 per cent versus 27.6 per cent. Because of the importance of market gardening in Togo, these disparities call for closer examination of the reasons for the differences between the interior and the capital in terms of fertilizer and pesticide use.

The simple explanation for the widespread use of chemical and mineral fertilizers in Lomé is that these inputs are required by the intensive system of agriculture in use and the soil's lack of fertility. A recent study by Kouvonou et al (1999) indicated that the rates of fertilizer use are below those recommended by the government's agricultural extension services. The study also pointed out that the growers prefer organic to chemical fertilizers. In these circumstances, there is no reason to worry about the impact of such practices on the system's sustainability. What is worrisome, however, is the misuse of pesticides, a concern shared by all the experts. In a 1986 study, Schilter (1991), for example, drew attention to the misuse of prohibited pesticides such as DDT (dichlorodiphenyltrichloroethane), lindane, aldrin and dieldrin. The use made of these products is not only reprehensible in its own right, but also illegal, because the pesticides are directly mixed in freshwater bodies or watering cans. Raymondo (1997) added that market gardeners use twice as much pesticide when they mix it directly into the irrigation water as when they apply it through sprayers. Why do they do this? Growers also generally fail to respect the time required between pesticide application and crop harvesting. Excessive use of the most toxic pesticides only aggravates the pest problem, because it helps the various bugs develop pesticide resistance. Such practices thus undermine the long-term feasibility of the system and jeopardize the health of both the farmers and the environment. Do the growers actually realize all the risks they are running? Do they know of methods less harmful to the environment? Urgent action is needed to regulate pesticide use. Before this can be done, it will be necessary to work with all the stakeholders concerned to identify the constraints preventing use of a sustainable and more environmentally sensitive pest-control system in Lomé.

Study objectives

The main aim of this study was to analyse the pest-control system in the market gardens of Lomé to identify factors that might explain the farmers' misuse of pesticides. In particular, one objective was to determine what the producers know about pest-control methods and what the suppliers know about the health risks of pesticides. An analysis was also made of the existing pesticide distribution networks to identify any difficulties in obtaining recommended products and what action might be taken to set up a more sustainable pest-control system in Lomé.

Conceptual framework

The study was based on the primary hypothesis that pesticide misuse in the market gardens of Lomé cannot be explained solely by the farmers' faulty knowledge, but by a combination of natural, economic, sociocultural and political factors in the urban ecosystem. In fact, according to Fernandes (1998), any form of environmental pollution indicates that the prevailing economic model is ineffective. That is why we need to look in the urban context for the root causes of the problems faced by urban farmers, which is in itself the expression of contradictory and complex forces.

The organization of human community life and the construction of artificial infrastructures designed for specific human needs automatically bring about the partial destruction of the natural ecosystem. However, each of the infrastructures that the local population installs (buildings, roads, drainage canals, etc.) constitutes an ecosystem favourable to other living species. For example, a building, regardless of whether it is used as a dwelling, service facility or factory, creates a microclimate that attracts a plethora of creatures (insects, lizards, cockroaches, mice, rats, squirrels, etc.). The same goes for sewers, latrines, parks, public gardens, garbage dumps and so on. Without regular maintenance, urban infrastructures can quickly become unliveable for the human occupants they are intended to serve.

From a technical standpoint, it has been estimated that external factors, such as site choice, construction plan and lack of green-space maintenance, exert considerable influence on the management and control of pests found in urban environments; in addition, the use of pesticides is implicit in the maintenance of many infrastructures and urban spaces developed in the immediate post-World War II period (IPMPA, 1996). However, McGranahan (1991) stated that pests, pesticides and other environmental problems (such as wastewater, household garbage, food contamination, lack of sanitation) that are felt to pose serious threats to human health are actually planning and design problems. For example, programmes related to maintenance of urban infrastructure were not even envisaged for most of the African cities that emerged in the early postcolonial period in the 1960s. As a result, in many cities, areas with shallow water, the sides of public highways, lakes, administrative property and public parks have either been left undeveloped or turned into little better than garbage dumps. These locations have thus become ecologically-ideal breeding grounds for a proliferation of pests. As it happens, these are precisely the sites that urban growers are usually confined to. In addition, the growers are also regularly forced to deal with new strains of pests brought into town by the frequent movement of people, animals and goods between the city and the rest of the world, in general, and the countryside, in particular. This is why an awareness of the market gardeners' working environment makes it easier to understand the pest problems these gardeners face.

From a socio-economic standpoint, Satterthwaite (1998) indicated that all the health problems caused by pollution of the urban environment are linked to social, economic and political factors. In his view, it is these factors that actually determine or explain what the risks are, why nothing is done to reduce them, which sectors of the population are most at risk, and why these people cannot obtain social assistance or adequate health care. McGranahan (1991) followed the same line of thinking when he maintained that lack of appropriate technology or failure to use it reflects a fundamental institutional problem: either people are not sufficiently motivated or the means used to motivate them are not appropriate. McGranahan considered ignorance, poverty and dishonesty as constraints that aggravate environmental problems and that these factors often cannot be dissociated from each other.

According to Kiss and Meerman (1991), the low level of education and almost total lack of regulatory mechanisms prevailing in sub-Saharan African countries make the risks of inadequate and dangerous pesticides more serious than anywhere else. This is all the more true because the local environmental-protection and public-health organizations are smaller and less influential than their counterparts in more industrialized countries. The low level of education in the sub-Saharan African countries is not only a problem of lack of means, but also one of lack of political will. In fact, the lack of information, stemming directly from the low level of education, suits the very people who are supposed to set up mechanisms to regulate the economic system. Such lax regulation works to the advantage of the better-off social classes, who are thus spared the obligation of paying into the public coffers (Satterthwaite, 1998). This is how dishonesty breeds ignorance and poverty, and vice versa.

Ignorance, however, is relative, as no one is totally ignorant and every human being possesses a certain amount of knowledge useful specifically to themselves. For example, certain producers sometimes do not treat all their crop inputs, such as fertilizer and pesticide, in the same way – in the same field, both fertilizers and pesticides may be used on the crops that are going to be sold, but great care may be taken to apply neither to the crops that the growers are going to use for their own consumption. This situation can be interpreted in various ways. One could argue on one hand that the producers concerned are aware of certain negative effects of agricultural chemicals on food quality; the reason why they make a discriminate use of them. On the other hand, it could be simply that they lack sufficient resources to treat all the cultivated land in the same way and therefore give priority to the crops destined for sale,

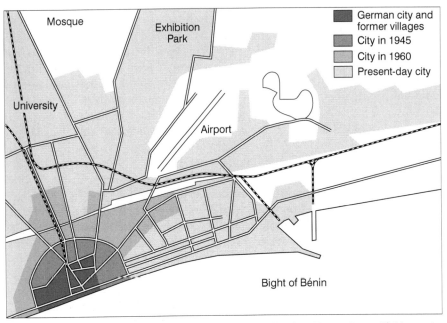

Source: ORSTOM (1992) quoted by Centre SYFED/REFER (Système Francophone d'édition et de Diffusion/Réseau Electronique Francophone)

Figure 2.1 *Map of Lomé, Togo*

which are certain to generate monetary income; or they could also do so to meet certain market requirements.

Whatever the reason, agricultural inputs cost money, and this factor should be a sufficient incentive to discourage their misuse. The reasons for overapplication need to be examined, not only at the grower level, but also throughout the whole production chain.

Study community

This study was conducted in and around the city of Lomé, Togo. As the country's political and economic capital, as well as its largest urban centre and main port, Lomé is bordered to the south by the Atlantic Ocean, to the west by Ghana, to the north by Agoé Township, and to the east by Baguida Township (Figure 2.1). The city covers an area of 333 km², 30 km² of which is a lagoon zone.

Natural characteristics

Lomé is in Togo's maritime region. It has a dry coastal climate, with two rainy seasons and two dry seasons. The main rainy season lasts from April to July, with May and June having the heaviest rainfall. The short September–October rainy season has been somewhat disrupted in recent years. December and January are the driest months. Owing to the orientation of the Togolese coast,

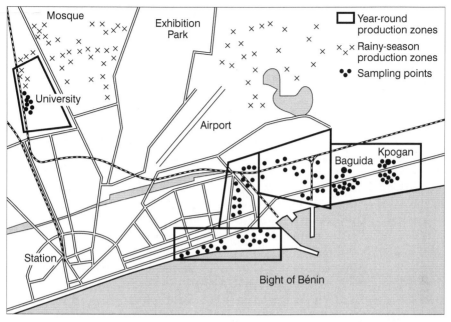

Source: Adapted from West African Economic and Monetary Union (WAEMU) and Central African Economic and Monetary Community (CAEMC) (1998)

Figure 2.2 *Lomé's market-garden zones and sampling points*

which is parallel to the southwesterly monsoon winds, annual rainfall is generally quite low (about 800 mm of rain spread over 86 days of the year). But relative humidity is quite high (70–90 per cent). The average minimum and maximum temperatures are fairly stable – about 23°C and 30°C, respectively.

Lomé is divided into two sections by a series of polluted lagoons that run parallel to the coast (Figure 2.2). The coastal ribbon to the south of these lagoons corresponds to the Lomé geological series, once planted with coconut trees that were devastated by lethal yellowing disease a long time ago. A sandy formation lying above a water table that is 2 m below, the coastal ribbon is the area preferred by Lomé's market gardeners. Market gardening has been practised there for more than a century, but it has really developed since 1980 (Schilter, 1991; ARSD, 1994). The main areas of intensive market gardening along this ribbon are the industry–port zone (9km from the city centre), Baguida (12km away), and Kpogan (20km away) (see Figure 2.2). Today, these zones contain more than 1000 full- or part-time market gardeners, who produce mainly exotic vegetables (carrots, cabbage, lettuce, beets, tomatoes, onions, peppers, basil, amaranth, etc.), as well as some tropical vegetables (spinach (*gboma*), kerria (*Corcorus* species, or *adémè* in the local language), green peppers, Guinea sorrel, and so on). According to ARSD, the total cultivated area in these main zones and the immediate surrounding area is more than 900 ha (ARSD, 1995).

North of the lagoon, the Tokoin plateau, with its many small depressions, gradually rises, reaching 120m above sea level. With a fairly impermeable sandy clay soil, rich in iron, the Tokoin plateau has better farming potential. It is more supportive of no-fallow cultivation, with corn and cassava being the main crops. This is where Lomé's seasonal urban farmers practise their rain-fed agriculture. The main drawback for these growers is that the water table is normally very low and drops much lower during the dry season (usually 12–20m below ground, receding to 33m below ground in the dry season).

Demographic characteristics

From a village of only several thousand fishers at the beginning of the last century, Lomé has become the largest urban, administrative, industrial and commercial centre in Togo, attracting thousands of migrants from all parts of the country. Lomé's population started to grow rapidly after World War II, with an influx of people looking for work (civil servants, shopkeepers, dockers and military personnel). Today it is a cosmopolitan city, having people from all of Togo's tribes and almost all foreign nationalities. The local people (the Evé, Mina and Ouatchi tribes) still constitute 66 per cent of the population. Even though Lomé's influence is felt across the country, it has greater impact on the southern part (ILO, 1985; Cornevin, 1988). Most of the in-country immigrants to Lomé from the southern regions are women, whereas most of the immigrants from the north are men. According to the 1981 census, the male–female ratio in Lomé is 93.4 per cent. The city's development has been facilitated by the progressive improvement of its social and sanitary infrastructure (Cornevin, 1988). From 86,000 inhabitants in 1960, Lomé's population grew to 170,000 by 1972 and to 370,000 by 1981, the year of the last census. According to the Togolese government's General Directorate of Planning and Development (GDPD), Lomé's population in 1996 was 850,000 (73 per cent of Togo's total urban population) (GDPD, 1996). According to the same source, even if this population only grows at a moderate pace, it should reach 2.92 million by 2020, thus constituting 40 per cent of Togo's projected total population for that year (United Nations, 2001).

Lomé's population is young. In fact, 38 per cent of the inhabitants are under 14 years old. The labour force constitutes 44 per cent of the total population. In 1982, the unemployed made up 20–25 per cent of this population (ILO, 1985), but this proportion was only 11.6 per cent in 1996, according to the country's statistics service (Statistics Directorate, 1999). More men than women were unemployed (11.4 per cent versus 7 per cent). An unemployed person spends an average of 4–5 years out of work before finding a job (Statistics Directorate, 1999). All this time, the unemployed person is supported by parents, relatives or friends, because the government provides no safety net for the unemployed. In Lomé, an employed person supports on average 2.6 persons, including him- or herself. With low wage levels (Harris et al, 1999), it is virtually impossible to make ends meet without an additional source of income.

Socio-economic characteristics

At the end of the 19th century, most of Lomé's inhabitants (about 2000) worked mainly in the primary sector (fishing, field crops and livestock production) (Rita, 1987; Schilter, 1991; ARSD, 1994). With the arrival of European merchant trading companies, primarily German, English and French, and then the Hausa traders from 1880 onwards, Lomé became an important commercial centre in West Africa, especially after the wharf was built in 1904. Three railroad lines were laid in 1910–1919, and these linked Lomé with the main inland regions producing coffee, cocoa beans and cotton, Togo's main agricultural exports. Lomé's status as a major West African trading centre was reaffirmed in 1968 with the enlargement of Lomé's free port (Decalo, 1977). Until the sociopolitical crisis of 1990, most of the merchandise for the landlocked Sahelian countries (Burkina Faso, Mali and Niger) transited through Lomé.

About 75,000 traders and 58,000 artisans are in Lomé (1999). These two occupational categories constitute 36.44 and 28.06 per cent, respectively, of the country's labour force. Other major occupational categories are banking and services (21.28 per cent), transportation (11 per cent), and urban agriculture (2.48 per cent). Most commercial units and handicrafts, as well as the farming production units, whether operated by individuals, families or groups, are often small and found only in the informal economy.

The country's trading activity at the wholesale, retail and micro-retail levels is primarily run by women, who constitute 90 per cent of this overall sector and are present at all levels (Rita, 1987; François, 1993). The goods available cover a wide range: fruit, vegetables, cereals, clothing, manufactured items, etc. However, Lomé's particular reputation is mainly based on the long-running era of the thriving commerce in printed cotton fabrics that was conducted by the *nana-benz* – wealthy women traders who reputedly all drove Mercedes-Benz automobiles (Rita, 1987; François, 1993). Unfortunately, the economic crisis brought an end to that era, and many of the large fabric-producing companies disappeared.

The craft and trades sector comprises a wide range of occupations, such as painting, shoemaking and repair, woodworking, carpentry, welding, mechanics, sewing, hairdressing and artisanal processing of agricultural products (for example, beer, juice, milled grist, soap and the local staple food, *gari*). Although men and women are almost equally represented in this sector, it has a certain gender-based specialization: men are generally found in occupations such as mechanics, welding, painting, woodworking and shoemaking, whereas women are concentrated in occupations such as hairdressing, sewing and farm-product processing.

The number of Lomé residents working in industry constitutes only a small proportion of the city's labour force, even though the city contains 90 per cent of the country's industries (ILO, 1985). In practice, the national industrial policy, implemented during the 1970s, was not successful, because the country, relying on phosphate-mining revenues, went heavily into debt to finance industrialization projects requiring heavy capital investment. Economic forecasts were based on rapidly rising phosphate prices in world markets, but the new industries scarcely had time to get going when prices plummeted in 1979, leaving the country with an enormous debt. Because a strict austerity programme was needed to get the country out of the crisis, Togo became one of the first countries in the subregion to implement a structural adjustment programme, supported by the World Bank and the International Monetary Fund. Hiring in the civil service and state-run companies has been reduced to a bare minimum since 1981, and wages have also been frozen since that time. During this period, many newly hired personnel were dismissed. Because most of the jobs were located in Lomé, the city suffered more than other Togolese cities. Today, most of the state-run companies have been privatized, and the whole country has been declared an industrial free zone for exports since 1989. The roughly 40 companies currently set up in this zone are all in Lomé. They have created nearly 7000 jobs (Togonews, 2001)

Besides being the place in Togo where people are most likely to find a wage-paying job, Lomé is home to most of Togo's sociocultural and educational institutions. With approximately 30 good-quality hotels, Lomé's hotel infrastructure is one of the most comprehensive in the subregion. For a time, the city's enormous accommodation capacity, its legendary hospitality, and the many international gatherings held there earned it the title of the 'city of international meetings'. Diplomatic missions and the representative offices of international organizations in Togo are all based in Lomé. The University of Lomé – previously Université du Bénin – with nearly 15,000 students, is Togo's only university. Several other institutions offering opportunities for higher education in general, technical or professional fields are also in Lomé. As a result, the city boasts of high enrolment and instruction rates, at 93 and 66.4 per cent, respectively.

With all these advantages, Lomé used to be the best place to succeed at market gardening. Unfortunately, since 1990 the city's economy has been seriously affected by Togo's sociopolitical crisis.

Sociopolitical crisis
Between 1990 and 1993, Togo underwent a major sociopolitical crisis that seriously affected Lomé. In 1990 a series of demonstrations were staged throughout the country, as the start of a process of democratization, to attempt to force the government to abandon its monoparty system for a multiparty one. The movement reached its peak on 5 October 1990 and the government had to give in to popular pressure. The political parties that were then officially authorized began a fierce struggle to overthrow the prevailing regime. The National Conference, held in 1991, set up a transitional government to prepare a new constitution and organize general elections within a year. Care was taken to ensure that this transitional government did not contain anyone closely connected with the regime that had been in power since 1967. Perhaps it was inevitable that the partisans of the former regime mobilized all their efforts to prevent the new government from functioning normally. As a result, the transitional government failed to organize the scheduled elections within the

specified timeframe, and the previous regime effectively regained power. At the same time, the new regime seemed determined to continue the ongoing democratic process and made every effort to organize the general elections called for in the new constitution. However, the opposition parties were not totally convinced of the transparency of such elections and resolutely committed themselves to blocking the process. As a result, they started a non-negotiable, unlimited general strike in November 1992 that paralysed the national economy for nine months.

The strike organizers' primary strategy for destabilizing the government was to encourage their supporters to leave the country. Thus, just two weeks after this line of action was announced, two-thirds of Lomé's inhabitants had left the city and mostly taken refuge in Benin and Ghana. In the process, everything in Lomé shut down – public and private services, businesses and the transportation system. Most of the people still remaining in the city were forced to turn to agriculture to survive. In view of the total paralysis of the economy and the political leaders' obstinate refusal to meet around the bargaining table, the international community had to intervene and exert pressure. This took the form of a total freeze, as of February 1993, on all economic cooperation with Togo. After some haggling, a presidential election was organized in August 1993, while many supporters of the opposition parties were still out of the country. These political parties naturally boycotted the election and rejected its result. This tense political climate deadlocked the efforts of the entire international community, which saw no other option but to continue the suspension of international cooperation, an action that continues to this day.

The political refugees gradually began to return to the country when the national currency, the CFA franc (Communauté Financière Africaine (African Financial Community)), was devalued at a meeting in Dakar, in January 1994. Lomé, more than other capitals, was paralysed by this development, because Togo did not benefit from the various alleviating measures approved at the same time as the devaluation, as the international community was still maintaining its freeze on economic cooperation. Prices skyrocketed, and all Lomé residents, regardless of social status, were forced to become much less dependent on the market for foodstuffs.

Methodology

The methodology for this study was based on the Participatory Rapid Appraisal (PRA) approach. According to Chambers and Guijt (1995, p5), the term 'PRA' can be described as a growing family of approaches and methods to enable local people to share, enhance and analyse their knowledge of life and conditions, to plan and take action. This approach is based on an awareness that the disadvantaged social classes are quite capable of analysing their circumstances and finding appropriate solutions to their problems, as long as they are given the opportunity to express themselves (Chambers, 1992; Mosse, 1994; Scoones and Thompson, 1994; Chambers and Guijt, 1995). In this sense, the term corresponds more to a change in the behaviour and attitudes of development practitioners in relation to the masses, rather than just a simple aggregate of methods. In other words, PRA derives its information from the same sources as any other form of research – that is, secondary sources, interviews, direct observation and so on. The difference is that in each context, PRA looks for what works, rather than for what is normal – that is, acceptable or desirable. As a result, this approach is flexible, thoughtful, pragmatic and participatory.

According to Mosse (1994, p499), 'information does not just exist "out there" waiting to be "collected"or "gathered", but it is constructed, or created, in specific social contexts for particular purposes'. In such circumstances, the researcher cannot be considered as a neutral agent, charged with describing an actual, objective situation, and the target population is not treated simply as an object of study observed from the outside. Along the same lines, Scoones and Thompson (1994) indicate that each actor in agricultural development operates within relations of power (gender, age, education ...), which determine his or her ability to respond to, and initiate, agricultural change. Mosse (1994) pointed out that despite any overriding concern for representative input, PRA sessions are unlikely to be equally accessible and open to every social level. PRA takes this into consideration by studying a range of views, rather than just the dominant ones. As a result, it provides an overall view of a situation, rather than making somewhat hasty generalizations on the basis of specialized data.

In this study, the women's views were particularly important because women are doubly concerned with the risks of pesticide misuse. First, when they are not themselves producing the crops, women act as intermediaries between growers and consumers; and, second, as nursing mothers, they have a vested interest in food quality.

It was on the basis of these principles that this study involved onsite visits and individual or group meetings, mainly with growers, but also with vegetable sellers and resellers, and pesticide retailers. The study also made use of small-group discussions and a questionnaire survey (interviews were conducted in several phases between June and November 2000).

Preparatory phase

The study project was prepared and presented during a seminar in the Department of Rural Development Studies at the Swedish University of Agricultural Sciences, as part of the work for a master's degree in research and development. The feedback on this presentation led to improvements in the project before the researcher's departure for Togo. After the first contacts were made and secondary data were collected in the field, the focus of the research was clarified and, as a result, reoriented. The research topic was discussed with the market gardeners during an exploratory tour of the city to identify the production areas. During this tour, the researcher discovered that two other research projects on UA were also taking place within the same study zone.

The first of these was a project in Guinea (Conakry), Senegal and Togo, funded by the European Union, to study the use of composted organic household waste for phytosanitary protection purposes in West African semi-urban agriculture (Kessler and Streiffeler, 2001). At the time, this research study was in the second of its three years. Piloted in Togo by the Togolese Institute for Agronomic Research (TIAR), the project operated a composting site within the study zone. The caretaker of this site was a local, well-known former market gardener. He played the role of in-field facilitator in the study of the outlying market garden zone.

The aim of the second project, conducted by a team of students of the International Centre for Development Oriented Research in Agriculture, was to study the sustainable intensification of urban and semi-urban agriculture in the market gardens of Lomé, Togo (Dossa et al, 2000). This project lasted from May to August 2000, and its fieldwork was supervised by the International Fertilizer Development Centre – Africa. As part of this project, a results-sharing workshop was organized in mid-July 2000. Attending this workshop made it possible for the present author to meet those involved in urban agriculture in Lomé and share the concerns of the new study with them before the field interviews began.

Exploratory phase in the market gardens

The three main market garden zones in Lomé – the industry–port zone, the Baguida zone and the Kpogan zone (see Figure 2.2) – were all identified during the exploratory tour of the preparatory phase. All the individual or group interviews with growers were held in these three main zones. These interviews focused particularly on the main crops grown: spinach (*gboma*), kerria (*adémè*), cabbage, carrots, lettuce, peppers, onions, tomatoes, cucumbers and beets.

The interviews took place in two stages: a questionnaire-survey stage and a small-group discussion stage.

Questionnaire survey – The questionnaire survey was carried out by a team of three agronomists plus the author. The survey consisted of a sample of 102 head market gardeners, broken down as follows:

- The industry–port zone – 79 growers, including 10 women;
- The Baguida zone – 16 growers, including 2 women;
- The Kpogan zone – 7 growers.

The number of growers surveyed in each zone was based on the proportion that that zone had of the overall total market growers. As a first step, the survey team walked through the plots and talked to the growers who were there and had a few minutes to spare. If, for one reason or another, a grower could not answer the researchers' questions, he or she was asked to point out another grower who knew about, for example, crop pests. Once suitable growers were identified, the survey team went to their plots to interview them if they were both present and available or to make an appointment if they were not. Most of the growers identified in this way were very experienced and were the main source of information on all the growers. This method made it possible to obtain representative data from a limited sample.

The questionnaire survey contained both general questions and more specific ones concerning pests and crop diseases. The general questions covered:

- type of grower: full-time, part-time, or temporary;
- number of years of experience in market gardening;
- initial training received;
- gender;
- how the plot was acquired: rent, purchase, gift, inheritance, etc.;
- size of overall operation and size of plot;
- the main crops grown and the farming practices followed: mixed-cropping, crop rotation, use of manure, crop-residue disposal, pest-control methods, etc.;
- occupancy status (reflects a certain insecurity in land tenure – in practice, insecure tenure often leads to loss of the plots and infrastructures, not to mention the possible need to relocate and so on).

Knowledge of these various parameters made it possible to understand the particular market garden system in Lomé and how it is affected by perpetual change. These same characteristics also affect pest population dynamics and thus the methods used to control them.

The specific questions about pests covered:

- the main types of disease and pest observed in each crop;
- the plant varieties resistant to, or tolerant of, the diseases and pests observed;
- preventive and remedial control methods;
- the main types of pesticide used: type, instructions for use, selection criteria, retail price, availability;
- the pesticides recommended for market garden crops: whether the grower was aware of them, efficiency, price, availability;
- application equipment and tools;
- the people who physically applied the pesticide;
- pesticide-related risks: types of risk, victims, precautions, etc.

Group interviews – one grower category was not sufficiently represented in the sample for the questionnaire survey. This was the women, who accounted for only 12 per cent of the survey sample, whereas, according to Kouvonou et al (1999), about 35 per cent of Lomé's market gardeners are female. In the field, the women were reluctant to talk with members of the survey team individually. This was possibly because the team comprised only men. The problem of reaching more of the women was solved by deciding to discuss the information collected during the previous survey in small groups, especially ones made up of women. As a result, 90 women – 20 growers and 70 vegetable sellers (producer–sellers or wives of producers) – were contacted. The questions covered in these discussions mainly dealt with pesticide misuse, the risks involved in this misuse, and decision-making power in existing market garden operations.

Analysis of Lomé's vegetable and pesticide distribution networks

After the market garden tours and a brief analysis of the data collected, the next step in the project was to analyse the city's vegetable and pesticide distribution network. Information on this network came from both primary and secondary sources. Most of the existing documentation on vegetable marketing in Lomé was consulted, and then this information was rounded out by interviews with grower organizations that also market their produce and with the women's vegetable-seller associations and the pesticide suppliers. The questions mainly focused on the sources of supply for vegetables, price-setting mechanisms, consumer preferences and the effects of pesticides on vegetable quality. The questions relating to the constraints affecting local distribution of agricultural inputs were discussed with three private distribution companies and the Société togolaise de coton (SOTOCO, Togolese national cotton corporation).

Information-sharing workshop

After the individual meetings with the various people surveyed (as described above), a joint meeting was organized with managers of pesticide suppliers, the market gardening extension staff at Togo's Institute for Agricultural Extension and Support (IAES), and researchers from the University of Lomé's Institute of Agronomy (IOA). The purpose of this meeting was to discuss the preliminary research findings. Although 10 people attended, it was particularly regrettable that no representatives of grower or consumer organizations were present. However, the purpose of the meeting was more to share information with the various actors than to confront them. In any event, an interesting discussion took place with those who were present. Feedback on the preliminary results was received from all sides, with the result that the interviewers were better prepared to return to the field and collect the missing data.

Study methods used

Despite all the explanations given to those involved in the project, the methods used continually raised people's hopes that they would get something out of it – like an international development grant, a loan or some kind of technical or organizational support. Simply bringing a few people together seemed to imply that a major initiative was in the offing. The reality is that the co-operative approach that had been promoted in the community was not well understood or at least not well explained to everyone involved. This was particularly so because of the burgeoning of non-governmental organizations (NGOs) in the community over the last 10 years, all scrambling for members. In this context, promises had become a popular commodity. The producers were told, 'If you form a group, you will qualify for inputs, motorized pumps, watering cans, loans, etc.' As a result, groups were forming in all areas, not so much out of the belief that cooperation is a better way of dealing with common problems, but out of the hope that once a group was formed, aid would follow. In fact, many of the market gardeners had even been exploited more than once by unscrupulous individuals asking for money and photos to make group membership cards. That is why some of the growers did not want to hear anything more about forming groups. Only those who continued to believe in promises came to the meetings. So the information provided in the group sessions could not be considered necessarily reliable and had to be cross-checked to guarantee a certain validity.

Participatory research methods are expected to lead to self-initiated community development. That is why these methods are especially relevant in preparing, monitoring and assessing development projects. In this case, where it was a question of preparing a completion-of-studies dissertation, there is no way that the researcher could monitor the action at the end of the process. Unfortunately, this left a feeling that the job had not been successfully completed.

RESULTS, ANALYSIS AND DISCUSSION

Market garden system

What is meant by the market garden system is the complete set of productive resources used by the growers and the way these resources are combined to achieve certain production objectives. The productive resources available vary from one grower to the next, as do their combinations. It is, therefore, not strictly correct to speak of only one market garden system in Lomé, but rather of several market garden systems. However, the intent of this study has not been to provide a detailed explanation of each system. Instead, it describes the main characteristics of the overall system – the main types of grower, the land-tenure arrangements, the work force, the production equipment, the cropping system, financing and the main combinations of these factors.

Types of grower

Several types of grower can be categorized in terms of the time spent in market garden production. Overall, two broad groups of growers were recognized: permanent and temporary.

Permanent growers – the group of permanent growers includes all growers who practise market gardening from one year to the next. This category comprises two subgroups: full-time and part-time growers. Full-time growers spend all their time on market gardening. This is the largest category of market gardener found in Lomé, constituting 77.5 per cent of the sample (79 per cent of the men and 67 per cent of the women). This proportion seems to be fairly stable, as a similar proportion appeared in the 1989 census of market gardeners (ARSD, 1994). For this type of producer, market gardening is the sole source of revenue. The activity thus becomes a question of survival, and any factor that threatens this survival (like pests) needs to be combated as vigorously as possible.

Part-time growers share their work time between market gardening and other activities that may or may not generate income. Even though market gardening may not necessarily constitute their main activity in terms of work time, most of these growers derive their main income from market gardening, and that is why it is important for them to continue operating in this sector. This category of grower constituted 13.7 per cent of the study sample and included a larger proportion of women than men – 33 per cent versus 11 per cent. Many of these women split their time between growing and selling market garden products and can be considered as totally dependent on market gardening in one way or another. In contrast, most of the men in this category were employees of either the port or the industries located in the port area where most market gardens in Lomé are located. This type of grower thus had much easier access to the land and a somewhat greater ability to hire production help. Their fairly flexible schedule of rotating shifts also allowed them to look after their plots from time to time. This is why the biggest producers were found in this group. Even though market gardening for them may have started out as simply a way of making some extra money, over time it became a major source of income. Thus, a major concern for all permanent growers was being able to continue this practice.

Temporary growers – temporary growers, working continuously for a certain period of the year but not necessarily from one year to the next, constituted only 8.8 per cent of the study sample. Essentially casual operators, the growers in this group were students, apprentices and workers (especially agricultural labourers) who at a given time of the year had little to do. They were often relatives of permanent growers. No women were found in this category. For these producers, market gardening was an important survival mechanism for a time, but they were not primarily concerned with continuing in it. Nonetheless, several of these growers would stay in this occupation, as had more or less been the case for all the full-time growers. In Lomé, it took an average of 3–5 years to learn market gardening and acquire control of a plot.

Most of the growers in the study had received no previous training in market gardening. On the contrary, they started out in other occupations: as artisans (23 per cent), technicians (21 per cent), drivers or apprentice drivers (14 per cent), high-school or university students (14 per cent), microretailers (10 per cent), and so on. Approximately 9 per cent of the growers had never been to school or learned an occupation before becoming market gardeners. Only 6 per cent of the sample consisted of people with previous experience in the primary sector as crop farmers, livestock producers or fishers.

Table 2.1 *Breakdown of growers by number of years of experience*

Years of experience	Entire group (%)	Gender Male (%)	Female (%)	Grower type Full-time (%)	Part-time (%)	Temporary (%)
1–5	32	29	42	27	50	44
5–10	23	27	16	29	7	23
10–20	45	44	42	44	43	33

Regardless of their previous training, most of the current market gardeners in Lomé are fairly experienced growers. The study found that 45 per cent of the respondents had 10–20 years of experience; 23 per cent, 5–10 years; 30 per cent, 2–5 years; and only 2 per cent, less than 2 years. Table 2.1 shows the breakdown by years of experience with respect to the gender and time-commitment status of the grower.

Practically no difference appeared between men and women in the number of years of experience. As might be expected, however, the full- and part-time permanent growers were more experienced than their temporary counterparts. Most of the growers were still young: 55 per cent of the respondents were 30–45 years old, whereas only 24.5 per cent were over 45 years of age. Women were generally older than the men: for example, 50 per cent of the women were over 45 years of age, whereas only 21.1 per cent of the men were. This difference can be explained by the fact that few women in the younger age groups work for their own account, and even when younger women work in the plots, they usually work under the direction of their husband. It is only when a husband dies that his wife takes over the operation.

Land-tenure arrangements

In 97 per cent of the cases, the market garden plots are located on land belonging to one level or another of government (The Free Port of Lomé; the Ministry of Agriculture; or the Commune of Lomé). However, to gain access to this land, 10 per cent of the respondents had to pay the previous occupants for the existing facilities. The cost of this change of ownership varied between 40,000 and 60,000 CFA francs (XOF) (in 2003, 579.4 XOF = 1 United States dollar (USD)). Some of the older landowners continued to claim user fees in the form of a gesture such as a few bottles of liquor. In addition, some few years ago the Lomé port authority had instituted, with the growers' consent, a system of user fees based on the size of the operation: 500 CFA francs per 1000m² per month (10,000m² = 1ha). The tenant agreement stipulated that growers would receive at least three months' notice if their plots had to be taken back for industry. Some growers, however, refused to pay these fees, on the grounds that they had only inherited land that previously belonged to their relatives. For example, only 41 of the 79 growers operating on port property said they paid user fees, and those who did not pay were not sanctioned in any way.

The individual size of grower operations varied from a fraction of a hectare to more than 2.5ha: 57 per cent of the respondents operated plots of less than 0.2ha (53 per cent of the men and 83 per cent of the women), and only 6 per cent of the growers (all men) operated plots of more than 1ha. Plot size increased proportionately the farther the site was from downtown Lomé.

Despite certain land-associated problems, the situation of individual growers was fairly stable. For example, 28 per cent of the respondents had operated the same plot for more than 10 years. However, this prolonged cultivation of the same plot of land every year encouraged the proliferation of soil pests, especially if growers did not practise crop rotation. In addition, if growers were forced to leave their plots because the land was needed for industry, they did not hesitate to move to other locations around the city. About 11 per cent of the growers surveyed fell into this category and were operating in at least their third location.

Work force

Market gardening is highly labour intensive. In Lomé, a market gardener's workday lasts an average of 10–12 hours. Even by working that hard, some respondents believed that one grower alone, regardless of equipment, could not tend more than a quarter of a hectare. Thus, to perform all the tasks required, most growers made use of relatives or paid workers.

The family work force consists of the grower and family members (spouse, children, cousins, etc.). The chief grower (usually a man) is the decision-maker. He alone decides what to do and who will do it. Women only take part in decision-making if they own the operation. In such cases, the man, that is, the husband, rarely does any physical work. Often, division of labour is gender based. For example, preparing the soil and the seedbeds and applying the plant protection products are men's work, whereas harvesting and selling the crops are mainly the women's responsibility. Although sowing, transplanting, weeding, hoeing, fertilizing and watering can be done by either men or women, it is usually the women and children who perform these tasks. If children go to school or are on practical training, they do their share of the market garden work in the evening, on weekends or during vacations.

Where the family work force is insufficient, growers use outside workers. This supplemental work force comprises rural migrants who have come to the city looking for paid work, as well as students and apprentices looking for some part-time employment. The rural migrants are often hired as permanent workers, whereas the second category is usually temporary help hired for specific tasks (watering, fertilizing, weeding, transplanting and so on). The monthly wage of permanent workers ranges from 10,000 to 15,000 XOF. Temporary workers, on the other hand, are paid on task. The availability of these temporary workers depends on the time of the year. For example, it is easier to hire temporary workers during the extended school vacation (June–August) than at other times of the year.

It was apparent that operations of less than a quarter of a hectare used only family labour, whereas larger ones used both types of worker. As might be expected, operations larger than a hectare made greater use than the others of paid help. Operations belonging to women were typically dependent more on family labour, whereas part-time growers made more use of paid help (see the remarks on permanent growers under 'Types of grower' above). Market garden operations in Lomé can thus be classified on the basis of their size and the type of labour they use.

Production equipment

Production equipment consists of all the equipment and tools used by market gardeners:

- tillage tools: hoes, rakes, machetes, etc.;
- irrigation and other hydroagricultural equipment and facilities: wells, drill-holes, water tanks, motorized pumps, sprayers, saws, pipes, ropes;
- plant-protection equipment: sprayers and protective clothing;
- harvesting and carrying equipment: baskets, basins, wheelbarrows, etc.

Production equipment determines the productive capacity of a market garden and capitalizes on the other productive factors, such as land and work force available. For market gardeners in Lomé, the most important piece of production equipment was the irrigation system.

All the market gardeners in the studied zones used the water table as their source of irrigation water. Depending on location, the water table is 2–5m below ground level. To reach the water table, growers made either a well or a drill-hole. The difference between the two is simply the diameter of the hole: a well is a fairly large hole, often lined with brick, whereas a drill-hole is a small hole only a few centimetres wide, through which a galvanized pipe can be inserted to reach the water table. A well can be dug by hand, whereas a drill is always needed for making a drill-hole.

In Lomé, it is cheaper to make a drill-hole (50,000 XOF) than to dig a well (100,000 XOF). However, with a drill-hole, a motorized pump is also needed to suck the water up, as the hole is too narrow for a bucket. A motorized pump costs about 300,000 XOF in Lomé. More than 85 per cent of the respondents owned a pump, but 35 per cent of the pump owners had a broken pump at the time of the study. That is why 80 per cent of the market gardeners surveyed preferred a well that lets them draw water manually when the pump is out of commission. It was usually the large producers who used drill-holes.

Water is drawn from a well by either manual dewatering (bucket attached to a rope) or mechanical dewatering (motorized pump). Workers need to have sufficient muscular strength for manual dewatering, because it is difficult. Growers who did not own a pump (15 per cent of the sample studied) used this method. In addition, the pump owners with broken pumps also had to manually draw water from a well. Once water is brought up, it is stored in water tanks arranged in various places on the plot. The water is transferred to watering cans for watering the plants. To water the entire plot, two or three times a day, operators have to make as many round trips as needed between the crop beds and the water tank. This is tedious. In fact, 40–75 per cent of a market gardener's time is spent on watering (40 per cent for those who own a pump and 75 per cent for those without one). To facilitate the task somewhat, the larger producers set up a watering system in which a long flexible hose directly links the water tank to a watering pump located in the plot to be irrigated. This device saves time because the workers no longer need to go back and forth between the water tank and the crop beds. Despite the fact that this is a simple system, most growers cannot afford to install it, because it requires a fairly powerful and thus expensive pump. The hosing is also expensive.

Cropping system

A cropping system consists of all the crops grown and all the cropping techniques used.

Crops grown – The market gardens of Lomé contain a wide range of crops – around 40, according to ARSD (1995). The most common crops in terms of cultivated land area are lettuce, cabbage, carrots, spinach (*gboma*), kerria (*adémè*), amaranth, onions, tomatoes, sorrel, eggplant, beets and chives. Often, more than 10 different crops can be found in a space of barely 100m². The crops are often placed in beds 2m by 12m (24m²) on average. These beds are separated by small central and secondary alleys 15–20cm wide. It is rare to find associations of crops within the same bed, but given the size of the plots and the number of plant species they contain, there is almost a de facto system of crop association. Nonetheless, 48 per cent of the growers surveyed said they did not practise crop association. This indicates that crops are not always combined on the basis of their agronomic characteristics. Contamination from one crop to another is actually quite frequent. The growers who acknowledged practising crop association said they did so because of the small size of their plots. Only 10 per cent of the growers surveyed thought that certain crop associations would favour or discourage certain types of pest infestations (such as the onion–lettuce combination that protects against nematodes). Crop rotation is also not widespread, although 58 per cent of the respondents recognized that it might help to break the pest cycle in the soil. Land scarcity is the main reason given to explain the impracticability of this technique.

Inputs – Seed, organic or chemical fertilizers, and pesticides are the main agricultural inputs the market gardeners use. Seed is of two types: local and imported. Local seeds (*adémè*, *gboma*, okra and peppers) are produced on the spot by either the market gardeners themselves or by producers from the surrounding villages. After being sorted and dried, these seeds are bottled or bagged and carefully sealed. All the market gardeners use these seeds. The imported seeds (cabbage, lettuce, onions, peppers, parsley, basil, cucumbers, beets, etc.) come from neighbouring countries, such as Ghana, Nigeria, Burkina Faso and Niger, as well as from Europe and the United States. These kinds of seed come from specialized seed-supply companies and itinerant peddlers. These seeds have no quality control system. Sometimes seed is sold that is no longer able to germinate. The growers prefer seed from neighbouring countries than from Europe or the United States because it is better suited to local conditions.

All the growers use both organic and chemical fertilizers. The sandy soil in the Lomé area is naturally low in plant-nutritional content and cannot produce crops without improving its physical and chemical composition. To improve the soil's physical qualities, the Lomé growers use poultry or cattle manure or cottonseed-processing waste. Poultry manure is the most common organic fertilizer; it is obtained from producers in the city or surrounding area. A 25-kg bag of poultry manure is sold for 500 XOF. The maximum single-application rate for poultry manure is 200kg per 100m^2, or 20t per ha. The growers often fertilize with poultry manure two or three times a year, which means a total application of 40–60t per ha per year. Some authors recommend larger applications (50–100t ha per year) (Messiaen, 1992). The cattle manure is collected at the Lomé slaughterhouse. Not enough cattle manure is available for everyone, but the growers feel it is ineffective as a fertilizer anyway. However, the application rates for both types of manure are more or less the same. The cottonseed-processing waste comes from the Noito (Togo's new oleaginous industry) plant located in the industry–port zone. This product is applied at a maximum rate of 30–50t per ha per year. All these upper-limit values have gradually become the standard rates that all the growers mechanically communicate to any investigator, but in practice many growers make do with chemical fertilizer supplemented by a few bags of poultry or cattle manure. In general, it is mainly the growers with smaller gardens who use organic fertilizer, because their plots require only small quantities of it.

The most common chemical fertilizers used are urea, NPK 15–15–15, and potassium sulphate (K_2SO_4). These are obtained from local firms or from the fertilizer sales outlets operated by the government's Regional Agriculture, Livestock, and Fishing (RALF) directorate. These kinds of fertilizer cost an average of 200 XOF per kg. Depending on the fertilizer, application rates vary from 200 to 400kg per ha and are sometimes even higher. These rates are more or less similar to the Ministry of Agriculture's recommended norms. However, we were not able to verify application rates in the field, so I cannot categorically state that these rates are used in practice. In fact, Kouvonou et al (1999) found that Lomé's market gardeners apply lower rates than normally recommended. That is why the crops can show signs of nutritional deficiency, which are sometimes confused with the symptoms of a pest infestation.

Cropping calendar – every crop has a growing cycle of a definite duration. In theory, the cropping periods are determined by the seasons. For Lomé's market gardens, irrigation allows the growers to crop year round. Nevertheless, because of each crop's particular climatic requirements (relative-humidity levels, average temperatures, day length, etc.), certain times of the year are more suitable for some crops than for others. Market demand also varies according to periods of the year. As a result, the growers have developed an

Table 2.2 *Crop calendar for certain market garden vegetables in Lomé*

	Growing cycle (months)	J	F	M	A	M	J	J	A	S	O	N	D
Adémè (spinach)		—	—	—	—	—	—	—	—	—	—	—	
Basil	4	—	—	—	—	—	—	—	—	—	—	—	
Beet	2.5							—	—	—	—		
Cabbage	3.5				—	—	—	—	—	—	—	—	
Carrot	3	—	—	—	—	—	—	—	—	—	—	—	
Gboma (kerria)	5.5						—	—	—	—	—	—	
Green pepper	4.5	-						—	—	—	—	—	
Lettuce	1.5	—	—	—	—	—	—	—	—	—	—	—	
Okra		—	—	—	—	—	—	—	—	—	—	—	
Onion	5						—	—	—	—			
Pepper	6	-						—	—	—	—	—	
Sweet potato leaf		—	—	—	—	—	—	—	—	—	—	—	
Sorrel		—	—	—	—	—	—	—	—	—	—	—	
Tomato	4								—	—	—	—	

annual cropping calendar (presented in Table 2.2) for each crop based on its most favourable growing periods of the year. This table shows that the period from April to October is the most favourable for most market-garden crops in Lomé, as well as for local vegetables in the countryside. This growing pattern is not without impacts (most of which are negative) on the marketing of the vegetables.

Marketing – all the vegetables grown are intended for sale in the city's markets. In fact, some of Lomé's market gardeners have never tasted some of the vegetables they produce. Marketing their produce is thus the primary concern of all the growers. Although the market for their products is basically local, certain products can be sold in neighbouring countries – for instance, carrots are sometimes exported to Accra (Ghana) and Cotonou (Benin). And amaranth, spinach, sorrel and sweet potato leaves are exported to Europe (Belgium, France and the Netherlands). Usually, a slump in sales occurs during the peak production period, which roughly corresponds to July through September. This slump is mainly caused by poor production planning. All the growers wait for the most suitable time of the year to start producing a given crop, although they could just as well produce during the off season. The result is that all the harvesting of the same crop takes place at the same time and floods the market.

The vegetables are sold to vegetable resellers either on foot, or at the edge of the plots, or around the Magasin de vente de légumes (MAVEL, vegetable store), the main vegetable outlet in Lomé's big central market. In this marketing system, each grower operates on the basis of an implicit wholesale contract with a certain number of women who actually retail the produce. These women sometimes even advance money to the growers to help them buy inputs. When the crop is ready, the women negotiate a price with the growers, based on the going market rates. In the meantime, the grower cannot sell produce to anyone else before these regular customers have made their choices. In most instances, the produce is sold on credit, and the vegetable women settle up with the grower only after they have sold the vegetables to consumers. After the grower and the vegetable resellers have agreed on a price in the field, the produce often does not sell easily at the retail level; in such circumstances, both parties bear the loss. Despite the dependency that develops between the growers and the resellers, the growers prefer this system because of its assurance of shared risk in the event the produce is not sold. Because of the perishability of vegetables, the growers are always vulnerable, which is to the advantage of the resellers, who effectively have the control in this business relationship.

Once these regular customers of the growers have made their choices, the growers' wives take the rest of the produce to the vegetable market around MAVEL. There again, the resellers hold the powerful position, because the growers, or their wives, do not have the time to remain seated at the market and retail their vegetables. Sometimes, when certain products have not been sold at the end of the day, they are just left on the spot. It was to address these marketing problems that the Togolese government initiated, in 1979, the construction of MAVEL, a central store equipped with a cold-storage room for the market garden produce. This was made possible by a financial contribution from the European Development Fund. The purpose of this facility was to stabilize vegetable prices through centralized distribution. As part of the process, the market gardeners were asked to gather themselves into producer co-operatives; the first – the Coopérative de Maraîchers d'Agoènyivé (COOPEMA, Agèonyivé market gardeners' co-operative) – was then set up in a northern suburb of Lomé. After a period of joint management between 1986 and 1989, MAVEL was turned over to COOPEMA. At the time, MAVEL was already experiencing difficulties because the cold-storage room had been in disrepair since 1986. During the sociopolitical crisis of 1990–1993, COOPEMA broke up, and MAVEL shut down in 1995. Today, the Fédération national des organizations maraîchères du Togo (national federation of market-garden organizations of Togo) is taking some initiative by attempting to repair the MAVEL cold-storage room, but the group's internal divisions are not helping matters.

The vegetable women are the real beneficiaries of the market gardening system in Lomé, and they are the ones who gain the most from the way vegetables are marketed. Akue-Adotevi (1995) estimated that the vegetable women earn an average monthly net income of between 251,500 and 396,936 XOF, in contrast to the 27,660 XOF that the growers earn. Despite the difficulties the sector is currently experiencing, this distribution of profits seems to have remained virtually the same to this day.

Financing

Financing is a big problem for most market gardeners, and they generally have difficulty in obtaining loans from financial institutions. Apart from the

Fédération des unions coopératives d'épargne et crédit (federation of credit and savings' co-operative associations), the Caisse d'épargne du Togo (Togo's savings bank), and a few NGOs that give loans to the larger producers and producer groups, it is practically impossible for market gardeners to obtain loans from banking institutions. Even in these cases, financing is mainly provided only for setting up. Otherwise, for operating capital, the growers are obliged to fall back on their own resources, their network of friends, or even the vegetable women and the local moneylenders. The drawback of resorting to the vegetable women for the money to finance market garden production has already been pointed out, and resorting to moneylenders can also be expensive. In practice, the interest moneylenders demand is sometimes more than 100 per cent of the loan. To escape the clutches of both moneylenders and the vegetable women, some market gardeners form tontine group-insurance schemes. However, the meagre contributions from the members are generally not sufficient to generate enough money to meet each member's needs, and they then sometimes resort to the vegetable women or the moneylenders.

Pest control

Pest control is a major concern of Lomé's market gardeners. However, implementation of an effective control programme for every pest depends on a good knowledge of the pest concerned and the damage it can do to the host crops. That is why it is important to take stock of what the market gardeners know about the pests that attack their crops, before describing their main pest control systems.

Main crop pests

Lomé's market gardeners generally agree that the number of pests that attack their crops is climbing steadily. The older growers recall that, until the 1970s, they did not have to treat crops against pests, but for the last 10 years or so, they have not been able to achieve good yields without plant-protection measures. Indeed, most pests apparently no longer attack just a single type of crop, but nearly all of the crops. This phenomenon probably indicates the onset of pesticide resistance.

Table 2.3 summarizes all the pests and crop diseases reported by the market gardeners during the interviews. The most common pests in Lomé's market gardens were caterpillars (reported by 90 per cent) and nematodes (66 per cent).

The term *caterpillars* is generally used to designate the larvae of several insects that feed on leaves. Some caterpillars are polyphagous and feed on several host plants. The damage can range from severe (the growth of the host plant completely stops) to moderate (a loss of both yield and quality). Most of Lomé's market gardeners do not differentiate between caterpillars causing the serious damage and those without economic repercussions.

As far as nematodes are concerned, the most well known is *Meloidogyne* (root-knot nematode). These creatures provoke the formation of galls (easily

Table 2.3 *Main pests and plant diseases in Lomé's market garden crops*

Pests and diseases[a]	Crops most affected
Nematodes (66)	Kerria, nightshade, tomato, cabbage, lettuce, carrot, sweet pepper, pepper
Caterpillars and ladybugs (90)	All crops
Midges (13)	Lettuce, chives, carrot, onion
Insects (9)	
Crickets	Carrot, tomato, zucchini
Ants	Carrot
Termites	Carrot, onion
Fireworms	Carrot, lettuce, young plant
White flies	Tomato, sweet pepper, pepper
Bugs, etc.	Tomato, pepper
Worms (7)	Lettuce, carrot, beet
Centipides, leeches (12)	Beet, carrot
Bacteria (2)	Tomato
Fungi (3)	Tomato, cabbage, lettuce
Rotting (40)	
Stems	Tomato, onion (bulb)
Leaves	Tomato, cabbage
Fruit	Tomato
Buds	Cabbage
Neck	Tomato
Smut (17)	
Leaves	Tomato, lettuce, carrot, pepper, chives
Leaf edges	Cabbage
Falling (20)	
Leaves	Pepper
Flowers	Pepper, tomato, sweet pepper
Fruits	Pepper
Yellowing (35)	Tomato, nightshade, kerria, pepper, carrot, cucumber, chives, sweet pepper
Leaf deformation (63)	
Rolled up	Onion, nightshade, pepper, tomato, chives, sweet pepper
Hardening	Nightshade, kerria
Bent over	Nightshade
Rusting (5)	Nightshade, kerria, lettuce
Browning of leaves (16)	Beet, sweet pepper
Black or brown spots on leaves (23)	Lettuce, kerria
Soft seeds (15)	All crops
Drop (5)	Onion, pepper

Note: a The values in parentheses represent the number of reported cases per 100 growers interviewed.

recognizable swellings) on the roots of infected plants. The consequent stunting of the root system and the metabolic damage caused by this pest reduce the plant's uptake of water and minerals. This inhibits plant growth (creating an emaciated appearance, with discoloured leaves, less foliage, insufficient flowering, and reduced fertility) and makes the plant more susceptible to drought.

A number of the market gardeners were unable to associate the pests infesting a plant with the disease symptoms evident on the same plant. Table 2.3 clearly indicates this, inasmuch as pests and disease symptoms were cited in a hodgepodge manner, without any connection between the two. It is evident that there is more than one type of causal factor leading to disease symptoms in plants (Messiaen, 1992). An effective pest-control programme therefore depends on knowing in every instance all possible causal factors leading to a disease symptom. Because of their poor understanding of these factors, the producers continue to treat symptoms long after the pests have been eliminated.

The presence of crops throughout the year in an area completely bare of other vegetation naturally encourages infestations. Because the natural vegetation cover is sparse on the Togolese coast at Lomé, certain pests that would normally feed on non-domesticated species turn to the crops. During the dry season, when the area has no natural cover at all, the pests depend almost solely on the crops, and as a result, infestations are more frequent. Year-round production and the natural characteristics of the growing sites are therefore factors in the high level of pests in the market gardens. But poor knowledge of these pests encourages the use of chemical methods of control.

Chemical control

Chemical control is the main means of combating pests in Lomé's market gardens. Growers regularly use pesticides either to protect the crops against potential attacks or to treat already damaged crops.

Types of pesticide – the list of pesticides currently used in Lomé's market gardens was basically drawn up on the basis of what was written on the packaging because the gardeners were not able to remember the names of all the pesticides they use. In fact the growers use a wide range of products. Although all the chemical families are represented, the list shows a predominance of both organophosphorus products (chlorpyrifos, dimethoate, azinphos-methyl, fenitrothion, mevinphos, Nemacur™, diazinon, triazophos, acephate, naleb, Malathion™ and parathion) and pyrethrinoids (cypermethrin, Karate™, fenvalerate, cyfluthrin and Decis™). The carbamates are also fairly well represented (Dithane™, Furadan™–carbofuran, carbaryl, methomyl, propoxur, aldicarb, zineb, ziram, maneb and mancozeb). It was observed that the most commonly used pesticides were of the wide-spectrum variety. Some of the respondents (5 per cent) also mentioned using a couple of organochlorine products (dicofol and endosulfan).

The use of neem-seed juice is popular (70 per cent of the growers use it), but it is mainly combined with other pesticides, or sometimes with soap powder or motor oil. Most of the pesticides are used in mixtures. Some biopesticides, such as *Bacillus thuringiensis* (Biobit™ and Dipel™), have started to appear, but they are always mixed in 'cocktails'. The types of products and blends were the same for all types of producer and sizes of operation. The differences between growers were mainly in their plant-protection equipment.

Phytosanitary equipment – according to van der Meijden (1998), the effectiveness of pesticides and the risks associated with their application are largely determined by the type and condition of the equipment used. The type of phytosanitary equipment varies according to size of operation. The growers with smaller gardens (less than 10 ares (1 are = $100m^2$)) use only watering cans to apply pesticides, and their only measuring tools are spoons, container caps and small tomato cans. This group constituted 53 per cent of the sample, but some of these people (23 per cent) borrowed sprayers from other growers, without giving anything directly in return. With this form of sharing, the number of growers owning or using a sprayer rises to 69 per cent of the sample. The measuring instruments were the same for all types of grower. Although most of the market gardeners were aware that protective clothing – such as gloves, nose masks and goggles – exist, none of them said that they owned any. In practice, cloths and handkerchiefs were used as face masks. The scarcity of protective clothing on the market and lack of money were the main reasons why growers did not use protective clothing.

Suppliers – the pesticides and the pesticide equipment are supplied by private distributors or itinerant peddlers. Lomé has more than 10 authorized distributors, which are responsible for importing agricultural inputs and distributing them throughout the region. Besides these, itinerant peddlers wander through the plots every day, offering products at unbeatable prices. This group is the growers' main supplier of pesticides. Most of these products are imported illegally from Ghana, but some also come from Benin, Côte d'Ivoire and Nigeria. According to the management of one distributor in Lomé, some itinerant peddlers buy expired products from local authorized distributors and then resell them at the microretail level. Also, the cotton-crop pesticides distributed on credit to cotton growers by SOTOCO are sometimes resold for a cheaper price to the market gardeners. Thus, a litre of cotton pesticide, selling for 4250 XOF at SOTOCO, can selling for 2500–3500 XOF in Lomé's market gardens. Some of the authorized distributors have tried to set up a form of mobile sales system, but they have not been able to compete with the 'independents'.

Pesticide application methods – The way pesticides are applied in Lomé's market gardens depends partly on the form the product comes in, but mainly on the type of application equipment available. Three main methods of application were observed: dusting, sprinkling and spraying. In dusting, the soil-treatment powders or granules are mixed with sand and then spread by hand without masks or gloves. All the market gardeners used this practice. Sprinkling methods varied according to the crop and the equipment available. For example, carrots were treated against soil-borne insects (ants, grasshoppers, mole crickets, etc.) at seeding time. In this case, a few drops of pesticide would be added directly to the water in the watering can. Sometimes, fertilizer (urea, for example) would be added as well. Growers who had no access to sprayers used this method for all crops (31 per cent of the growers). This method entails obvious waste, owing to the multiple operations involved. For instance, at least four fills were needed to cover a $24m^2$ bed, and each time a few drops would be lost in the process. Because the growers who use this method own only small plots (less than 10 ares), they do not realize the extent of the waste. Raymondo (1997), for example, estimated that sprinkling uses twice as much pesticide per unit than spraying. Indeed, 69 per cent of the growers spray, but the application rates are still universally high.

Rates and frequency of pesticide applications – the figures for application rates per hectare were extrapolated from the information provided for plant beds of various sizes. This information itself is only approximate because of the wide range of measuring tools used, as mentioned above. Also, only the liquid pesticides normally sprayed on cotton were considered in calculating the estimates. Instead of the six litres per hectare per year, broken down into six treatments, as recommended for cotton growers, the market gardeners used applications of one to six litres per hectare in a single treatment (that is, up to six times the recommended rate). Thirty-three per cent of the growers used more than three litres per hectare per treatment (three times the recommended rate). These rates are definitely high for fresh produce. The growers explained that the aridity of the growing zone was the reason for these repeated high application rates. The differences in application rates seem to depend more on factors such as the differences in measuring instruments, application methods and the operator's speed of coverage. However, the producers with smaller plots used the highest rates. No difference was noted between men and women in this regard.

Frequency of pesticide application depends on the crop concerned. Leafy vegetables, such as lettuce, cabbage, spinach (*gboma*) and kerria (*adémè*), require more frequent treatment. Lettuce and cabbage, for example, were treated every three days, right up to harvest. However, the various crops were planted in association, so they all regularly received more or less pesticide. The most serious concern is the time lapse before harvest, because 66 per cent of the respondents suspended pesticide applications for a period of only seven days (or less) before harvest, regardless of the pesticide, whereas the government's extension services recommend stopping pesticide applications on vegetables at least a month before harvest (ARSD, 1993). Here, too, the growers justified the practice on grounds of the need to water the plants frequently and regularly. Another concern is that the growers sprinkle the leaves, rather than the place where the stems meet the ground. As a result, a considerable portion of the pesticide is washed away by irrigation water and then constantly builds up in the water table.

Awareness of poisoning and pollution risks

In the opinion of 99 per cent of the respondents, pesticides were toxic products to be handled with care and kept out of the reach of children. In their view, pesticides threatened the operators and producers, consumers, local residents and the whole environment.

It is mainly males (including boys) who apply the pesticides. Boys are particularly exposed to pesticides, not only because they are not very skilled at applying them, but also because their skin is more sensitive than an adult's. Despite the reported cases of poisoning, 33 per cent of the respondents claimed that they were immune to them after using them for so long. Yet the growers were well aware of the various signs of poisoning. As many as 15 per cent of them acknowledged that pesticides caused harmful effects, such as skin problems (irritation, burning sensations, flaking, etc.), vision problems (8 per cent), heart and lung ailments (10 per cent), headaches and dizziness (8 per cent) and intestinal problems (23 per cent). The risks of environmental contamination were also well known. In fact, some of the growers wanted to combine market gardening with fish farming but were put off by the high mortality rate of the fingerlings because of contamination of the fish ponds. It is easy to imagine from this example how polluted the water table must be.

Most of the growers said that, to avoid being poisoned, they needed to wear protective clothing (masks, goggles, gloves and boots) and avoid working into the wind when applying pesticides. Despite this awareness, none of the producers were ever seen during the study wearing this kind of clothing. In their view, the protective equipment is too expensive and, in addition, needs to be replaced regularly to avoid becoming an additional source of contamination. Palm oil and milk are considered effective antidotes to pesticide poisoning. Although the respondents seldom put the guidelines into practice, they all acknowledged that strict observance of the timeframes for suspending pesticide applications before harvest would ensure that the produce was harmless. The vegetable women who buy the produce directly from the field are mostly held responsible for the contaminated vegetables seen on the market, because they do not consult the growers before harvesting. To deal with this risk, some growers now advocate putting up signs to warn the women not to harvest prematurely. Given what the growers know about the risks of poisoning and pollution, their apparently lax behaviour is difficult to understand. To get more insight, it is necessary to closely examine the constraints the growers operate under.

Constraints affecting the pest-control systems

Analysis of Lomé's market gardening and pest-control systems reveals why the growers systematically resort to chemical methods of control. The market gardeners face three major constraints in their efforts to control pests: difficulty in identifying the pests, high cost of pesticides and resistance to pesticides.

Identifying all the factors responsible for plant disease requires thorough study, which, in turn, often requires a certain expertise. Left to their own devices, the growers would attribute all plant diseases to insects and nematodes (Dossa et al, 2000). Messiaen (1992) indicated that it is important to know that more than one causal factor is associated with a particular disease symptom. As the growers have little knowledge of the causes of the plant diseases they observe and no access to any other source of help, they resort to the most toxic wide-spectrum pesticides. Regardless of their years of experience (45 per cent have been growing vegetables for between 10 and 20 years), the growers still need help identifying pests. The technical support provided by IAES and RALF covered only 17 per cent of the growers in the study sample and, furthermore, is only available to members of groups constituting 37 per cent of the growers. The primary source of advice on combating pests comes from the itinerant peddlers, who are totally untrained in this area. The authorized pesticide distributors play some role in providing advice, but they complain that the growers have their own strong views and are not prepared to listen. Anyway, it is evident that pesticide dealers cannot be expected to promote limited use of their products (Kiss, 1990).

In the view of 70 per cent of the respondents, price is the main criterion in choosing pesticides. For the other 30 per cent, the main criterion is the product's effectiveness. Thus, overall, price and effectiveness are the two main criteria. According to the importers and authorized distributors, agricultural inputs are theoretically exempt from duties, but the customs officials ignore this. The indirect taxes resulting from problems at customs and during overland transportation increase the free-on-board price of pesticides by about 50 per cent. When transportation, handling and a profit margin are added, the price of pesticides can easily reach 150 per cent of their free-on-board value. In such circumstances, the growers resort to the cheapest sources of supply and feel that the broader the product's pest spectrum, the better value it is. This situation has only been aggravated by the drop in vegetable prices in Lomé as a result of the decline in the population's purchasing power over roughly the last 10 years (ARSD, 1994; Akue-Adotevi, 1995; Raymondo, 1997; Dossa et al, 2000).

The regular use of pesticides leads to pesticide resistance. Studies have shown that pests that were host-specific in the past are now all polyphagous. This explains why, in the absence of more potent products, the growers resort to stronger concentrations and more frequent applications. This is actually a classic scenario (Carson, 1962; Kumar, 1984; Fenemore, 1984). In this situation, the only possible solution is to adopt an integrated approach to plant protection (Kiss, 1990; Kiss and Meerman, 1991; Birley and Lock, 1999). There is an urgent need to educate all the market gardeners and to co-ordinate the actions of everyone involved in the production chain.

ASSESSING THE STUDY'S IMPACT

Human resources development

During this study, four people benefited from training in participatory research methods: a TIAR field agent and the three agronomists who helped administer the survey's semi-structured questionnaire. The field agent, who acted as an assistant, benefited from training during all phases of the study, especially before and after each session. This training focused on teamwork, role-sharing, group discussions, note-taking and activity assessment. The three agronomists were trained during a three-day session on conducting a survey using a semi-structured questionnaire.

Gender-based analysis

The gender-based perspective primarily highlighted the division of labour that is still deeply rooted in the social and cultural mores of African societies. In Togo, women play a crucial role in agriculture, inasmuch as they are responsible for a major portion of the production activities (sowing, transplanting, weeding, harvesting and carrying), as well as being more or less solely responsible for selling the produce. Unlike other parts of the world where they play the leading role in urban agriculture, women in Lomé are more involved at the marketing end of the chain. In this capacity, they play an absolutely essential role in the market garden system because of the paramount importance of marketing in the overall scheme of things. However, in relation to the risks associated with pesticide misuse, women also have a doubly critical role to play: first, as 'middle women' between producers and consumers; and second, as homemakers. Although they may not be responsible for the harmful practices, they should at least be well informed on how to minimize the risks. Unfortunately, women are often ignored by the country's agricultural extension services. One proof of this is that a general meeting organized for the vegetable women at the Lomé market became solely a pesticide-awareness session because the women knew nothing at all about them.

Institutional impact

Although this is not the first time that the topic covered in this paper has been covered by a Department of Rural Development Studies student at the Swedish University of Agricultural Sciences, several colleagues in the department had never heard the term *urban agriculture* before. Thus, the researcher's presentation during the project's preparatory phase helped promote this new field of research, which deserves more attention. At the local level, the main effect of the study was to raise awareness of the problems of pesticide misuse, as previous research had been confined to just assessing the socio-economic impact of UA without paying too much attention to its repercussions. Because this study was limited to collecting qualitative data, physical research remains to be done in testing pesticide residues in vegetables at the retail level, as well as in the watertable, at the grower level, and in the general population. In this way, it would be possible to quantify the real dangers and the damage that pesticides cause to Togo's economy. Certain IOA and TIAR specialists have already taken serious note of the situation and expressed an interest in continuing the work in the field. A research project along these lines is being developed at IOA, but funding is still lacking.

Importance of local partners

The importance of local partners was reflected not only in the implementation of the study but also in the use of its results. Local partnerships guaranteed easy access to documentation, facilities and, especially, institutional support. The precarious situation of urban farmers because of their lack of secure land tenure led them to mistrust all strangers. Consequently, local partners played a crucial role in making this project successful. From another perspective, too frequently it has been standard practice not to refer to the results of research conducted in developing countries. With local partners, at least someone will make use of the findings. In addition to IOA and TIAR, which were actively involved in the study, IAES and the national association of consumers concerned with the environment have been interested in the results obtained.

Scientific and methodological impact

The participatory method as a research approach still fairly unknown in Togo. It is slowly gaining ground, but a lot of work needs to be done before it becomes common practice. In this sense, this study represents methodological progress. Most of the participants, especially the market gardeners, were keen to express their satisfaction with this new research approach. For once, they felt free to express themselves in their own terms and were treated as experts in their own right.

Use of the study's findings

An information-sharing meeting at IOA at the end of the project gave the author the opportunity to present the results of the study to senior staff from the agricultural extension and agronomic research services and to pesticide distributors. The scale and scope of the risks associated with using pesticides stimulated interest in looking for alternatives. In addition to this need for a search for alternatives to pesticides, the study's results underscore the need to reconsider the guidance that the extension services deliver, so as to make it relevant to vegetable distributors and consumers, as well as growers.

Additional material support

Apart from a grant, the study received logistical support from IOA and TIAR. Both these institutions facilitated access to meeting rooms and audio-visual equipment and sent out invitations for the workshop where the study's preliminary findings were shared. Their support imbued the meetings with a certain formality and implicitly communicated the importance of the research to the various stakeholder groups involved in Lomé's market garden sector.

Conclusions and Recommendations

Analysis of the various pest-control systems in the market gardens of Lomé shows that the growers face several major constraints that lead them to systematically resort to pesticides. In practice, they suffer from a lack of logistical support to help them identify pests and effective ways of controlling them. In addition, the proximity of the plots to each other facilitates the rapid spread of pests. Finally, the high cost of the recommended pesticides forces the growers to rely on the cheapest ones and the ones with the broadest coverage.

Suffering from these constraints, the growers have no other choice but to resort to prohibited pesticides and ignore the risks. Pesticide resistance then forces them to increase the concentrations and the frequency of applications, and this practice, in turn, jeopardizes not only their own health, but that of consumers and the environment as well. Not knowing who to turn to, they place their confidence in the pesticide peddlers, who have been known to offer unsuitable products, like fungicides against insects and insecticides against fungi, not to mention an array of strange mixtures.

In view of these dangers, it is imperative to inform producer and vegetable marketing organizations, as well as consumer groups, of the risks. Most important, steps must be taken to strengthen these organizations and support marketing initiatives through MAVEL, the only structure that can facilitate control of vegetable quality. Finally, it will be necessary, in the medium term, to set up a system for checking the quality of all foodstuffs. This would be the surest and least expensive way of ensuring the population's health at a time when food contamination continues to be a global concern.

Acknowledgements

I would first like to thank all those who, from near and far, have helped produce this study – above all, the International Development Research Centre, whose AGROPOLIS grant programme funded the field research. I would also like to thank the senior staff at IOA (University of Lomé) and TIAR, especially Koffi-Tessio Egnoton and Sedzro Kossi, who handled the project logistics brilliantly from start to finish. I would also like to express my appreciation and profound gratitude to Angelika Kessler, a doctoral student at Humboldt University, Berlin, and co-ordinator of a project on the use of composted organic urban household waste for phytosanitary protection in West African peri-urban agriculture. This project played a major role in reorienting the focus of my research and providing input for the grower manuals. Last but not least, I cannot forget the hundreds of coastal market gardeners in Lomé, who, to ensure their daily survival, have no choice but to gradually poison themselves, drop by drop, with toxic pesticides.

REFERENCES

Akue-Adotevi (1995) *Étude Socio-économique en Vue d'une Amélioration du Système de Commercialisation des Produits Maraîchers dans l'Agglomération Urbaine de Lomé*, Institute of Agronomy University of Lomé – previously Université du Bénin, Lomé. Agricultural Engineer's Dissertation

ARSD (Agricultural Research and Statistics Directorate) (1993) *Résultats Définitifs du Recensement National des Exploitations Maraîchères en Milieux Urbain et Péri-urbain (1987–1989)*, Ministry of Agriculture and Rural Development, Lomé

ARSD (1994) *Secteur Maraîcher: Une Alternative aux Problèmes de l'Emploi et à la Sécurité Alimentaire. Vu à Travers l'Analyse des Résultats du Recensement National des Exploitations Maraîchères en Milieux Urbains et Péri-urbains (1987–1989)*, Ministry of Agriculture and Rural Development, Lomé

ARSD (1995) *Recensement National des Exploitations Maraîchères, Togo 1995: Analyses des Résultats Préliminaires*, Ministry of Agriculture, Fisheries and Livestock, Lomé

Birley, M. H. and Lock, K. (1999) *The Health Impact of Peri-urban Natural Resource Development*, Department for International Development and Natural Resources Institute, London

Carson, R. (1962) *Silent Spring*, Hamish Hamilton Ltd, London

Centre SYFED-REFER de Lomé (Système Francophone d'édition et de Diffusion/Réseau Electronique Francophone pour l'Education et la Recherche). (no date) La ville de Lomé: Ville messagère de la paix. Available at http://www.tg.refer.org/togo_ct/tur/mairie/accueil.htm#sommaire. Francophone University Agency, Montréal, Canada

Chambers, R. (1992) 'Rural appraisal: Rapid, relaxed and participatory', Institute of Development Studies, University of Sussex, UK. Discussion Paper 311

Chambers, R. and Guijt, I. (1995) 'PRA – five years later: Where are we now?' *Forest, Trees and People Newsletter*, no 26/27, pp4–14

Cornevin, R. (1988) *Le Togo: des Origines à Nos Jours*, Académie des sciences d'Outre-Mer, Éditions Henry, Montreuil-sur-Mer, France

Decalo, S. (1977) *Historical Dictionary of Togo* (2nd edition), Scarecrow Press, Metuchen, NJ

Dossa, K., Guira, M., Loko, B., Traore, B. and Vigelandzoon, J. (2000) 'Intensification durable de l'agriculture urbaine et périurbaine à Lomé, Togo: Cas du maraîchage', International Centre for Development-Oriented Research in Agriculture, Montpellier, France. Working Document Series, No. 91

FAO (Food and Agriculture Organization of the United Nations) (1998) *Urban and Peri-urban Agriculture*, Committee on Agriculture, FAO, Rome

Fenemore, P. G. (1984) *Plant Pests and Their Control* (revised edition), Butterworth & Co. Ltd, London

Fernandes, E. (1998) 'Learning from the South', in Fernandes, E. (ed), *Environmental Strategies for Sustainable Development in Urban Areas: Lessons from Africa and Latin America*, Ashgate Publishing Ltd, Aldershot, UK. Studies in Green Research, pp1–15

François, Y. (1993) *Le Togo*, Éditions Karthala, Paris

GDPD (Directorate-General Planning and Development) (1996) *Politique Nationale de Population du Togo*. Document de base: dagnostic de la situation démo-économique, Ministry of Planning, Lomé, Togo. CP-TG 108

Harris, E., Doré, O., Ossié, W., Mathisen and Kabedi-Mbuyi, M. (1999) *Togo: Selected Issues*, International Monetary Fund, Washington, DC. Staff Country Report 99/54

ILO (International Labour Office) (1985) *Crise Économique et Perspectives de l'Emploi dans une Économie Ouverte: le Cas du Togo*, Vol. 1: Rapport principal. Programme des emplois et des compétences techniques pour l'Afrique, ILO, Addis Ababa, Ethiopia

IPMPA (IPM Practitioners' Association) (1996) *Introduction to Integrated Pest Management (IPM) for 'Urban' Landscapes*, IPM Associates, Inc. Eugene, Oregon

Kessler, A. and Streiffeler, F. (2001). *Composted Household Waste for Plant Protection in Peri-urban Agriculture in Five West-African Towns*, Votrag un Tagungsband des Seutschen Tropentags, Born

Kiss, A. (1990) 'Insect ecology and agricultural pest management: Theory and practice', in Goodland, R. (ed), *Race to Save the Tropics: Ecology and Economics for a Sustainable Future*, Island Press, Washington, DC, pp81–99

Kiss, A. and Meerman, F. (1991) *Integrated Pest Management and African Agriculture*, World Bank, Washington, DC. World Bank Technical Paper 142, African Technical Development Series

Kouvonou, F. M., Honfaga, B. G. and Debrah, S. K. (1999) 'Sécurité alimentaire et gestion intégrée de la fertilité des sols: Contribution du maraîchage périurbain à Lomé', in Smith, O. B. (ed), *Agriculture Urbaine en Afrique de l'Ouest: Une Contribution à la Sécurité et à l'Assainissement des Villes*, International Development Research Centre, Ottawa, ON, pp83–104

Kumar, R. (1984) *Insect Pest Control: With Special Reference to African Agriculture*, Edward Arnold Ltd, London

McGranahan, G. (1991) *Environmental Problems and the Urban Household in Third World Countries*, Stockholm Environmental Institute, Stockholm

Messiaen, C. M. (1992) *The Tropical Vegetable Garden: Principles for Improvement and Increased Production with Application to the Main Vegetable Types*, Cliff & CT Macmillan Press Ltd, London

Mosse, D. (1994) *Authority, Gender and Knowledge: Theoretical Reflections on the Practice of Participatory Rural Appraisal*, Institute of Social Studies; Blackwell Publishers, Oxford, *Development and Change*, vol 25, pp497–525

Mougeot, L. J. A. (2000) 'Urban agriculture: Definition, presence, potential and risks, main policy challenges', Cities Feeding People, International Development Research Centre, Ottawa, ON. Report Series, No. 31

Raymondo, T. K. (1997) *Contraintes Techniques et Socio-économiques du Secteur Maraîcher: Cas de l'Agglomération Urbaine de Lomé*, Institute of Agronomy, University of Lomé – previously Université du Bénin, Lomé, Togo. Agricultural Engineer's Dissertation

Rita, C. (1987) *Femmes Africaines et Commerce: Les Revendeuses de Tissu de la Ville de Lomé*, Éditions l'Harmattan, Paris,

Satterthwaite, D. (1998) 'Environmental problems in cities in the South: Sharing my confusions', in Fernandes, E. (ed), *Environmental Strategies for Sustainable Development in Urban Areas: Lessons from Africa and Latin America*, Ashgate Publishing Ltd, Aldershot, UK. Studies in Green Research, pp62–82

Schilter, C. (1991) *L'Agriculture Urbaine à Lomé: Approches Agronomique et Socio-économique*, Èditions Karthala, Paris, France; Institut universitaire d'étude du développement, Geneva

Scoones, I. and Thompson, J. (eds) (1994) *Beyond Farmer First: Rural People's Knowledge, Agricultural Research and Extension Practice*, Intermediate Technology Publications Ltd, London

Smit, J., Ratta, A. and Nasr, J. (1996) *Urban Agriculture: Food, Jobs and Sustainable Cities*, United Nations Development Programme, New York, NY Publication Series for Habitat II, Vol. 1.

Statistics Directorate (1999) *Enquête sur les Dépenses des Ménages à Lomé: Analyse des Résultats; Projet d'Harmonisation des Indices de Prix dans les Pays de l'UEMOA*, Ministry of Planning and Development, Lomé

Togonews (2001) 'Un contexte encore difficile', *All Africa Global Media*, Saint Louis, Mauritius.

United Nations (2001) *World Population Prospects: 2000 Revision*, United Nations Population Division, New York

van der Meijden, G. (1998) *Pesticides Application Technique in West Africa*, Food and Agriculture Organization of the United Nations, Rome

WAEMU (West African Economic and Monetary Union) and CAEMC (Central African Economic and Monetary Community) (1998) Plan de la ville de Lomé: available at www.izf.net/izf/documentation/Cartes/CentreVille/Lome.htm

3

Determinants of Urban Livestock Adoption in the 'Zone Dense' of Khorogo, Côte d'Ivoire: A Tobit Approach

Mody Bakar Barry

INTRODUCTION

Côte d'Ivoire is traditionally a meat importer. As in other coastal West African nations, the strong challenge of animal disease along the humid coastal areas has precluded the development of traditions of animal husbandry, especially in the case of cattle. As they have been for centuries, livestock and livestock products are imported from drier areas to the north. As a result, animal production is still a marginal activity, and the livestock sector constitutes less than 2 per cent of the gross domestic product of the country.

Agricultural activities dominate traditional production systems. However, despite the adoption and use of draft power in cotton plantations, livestock (especially cattle) are not integrated into the agricultural production system. Farmers do own cattle, but animals are collectively managed at the village level by a hired herder, and owners have no direct interaction with their animals in terms of labour allocation. In most cases, animals are kept during the cropping season to prevent them from destroying crops. During the dry season, they are left to scavenge around the villages without any supplement. Fodder crops are not grown, and even crop residues are burned after harvest, instead of being used as foodstuffs. Managing cattle is considered taboo in this society; it is a minor activity, in comparison to cropping.

Generally, cattle owners do not use animal products. Milk goes to the herders as part of their salary. Manure is not used because its ownership is undefined – the animals are collectively managed at the village level, and the draft animals have been bought somewhere else from extension agencies or outside the area, from the Fulani herds. In the traditional systems, farmers seldom sell their animals. Livestock are kept mostly for celebrations (funerals, weddings). In the production system, activities related to cropping and those related to cattle are technically separated, and the herd has a sociological rather than economic function.

Because of rapid urbanization and population growth, the protein deficit (especially beef) is getting wider and wider, with a negative impact on the balance of payments. The recent devaluation of the CFA (Communauté Financière Africaine – African Financial Community) franc and the emergence of new and more attractive markets (Ghana, Nigeria and North Africa) have undermined the regularity and stability of the traditional supply channels (European Community and the Sahelian countries).

Objectives, hypothesis and concepts

International comparisons of research on the agronomic, social and policy aspects of urban agriculture (UA) share the conclusion that urban food production is an important component of household survival strategies, especially among the poor. As in many regions of the world, UA is a growing activity in West Africa. It is often considered an alternative to conventional agriculture, in response to urbanization. It promotes food security and generates income for marginal classes. Because of land constraints, UA is often considered to be a women's activity. In their strategies for poverty alleviation, planners are interested in gaining a better understanding of the contours of urban livestock and its impacts on both households' food security and the environment.

Many studies (Due, 1986; Lele, 1986; Due and Magayanne, 1989; Gladwin and McMillan, 1989; Poats, 1991) have shown that a gender approach to economic development may be essential to households' nutritional status and overall welfare in developing countries. By the early 1980s, Henn (1983) had already argued that increased attention to the problems of women could help solve both rural and urban food supply issues. More recently, Dennery (1995), in her study on Kibira (Kenya), added a qualitative dimension to UA research by providing empirical evidence on gender relations, labour relations and the multiple use of produce at the individual, household and community levels. Emphasizing the role of women, Maxwell (1994) argued that farming in the cities is the deliberate effort of urban women to provide a source of food that does not depend on cash income and fluctuating markets. To understand how UA works, however, the activity should be analysed in the context of the household.

The concept of the household varies widely across cultures. It ranges from the Western nuclear household to the African extended family system, in which several generations can share the same residential compound and the same consumption unit. As Sadoulet and de Janvry (1995) mentioned, the key element in defining the household is to identify the decision-making unit, which sets the strategy for the generation of income and the use of this income for consumption and reproduction. Focusing on the concepts of 'household' and 'strategy', Rakodi (1991) pointed out that households and individuals formulate and adjust strategies according to their own circumstances, that is, the opportunities available to them. Strategies are linked to the decision-making of the household and may take the form of income generating activities.

Livestock is a major component of UA. It contributes directly or indirectly to food security and sustainable development (Ehui, 1997). Many studies (Barry, 1978, 1990, 1992) and technical reports (Sodepra, 1985, 1987, 1989) have described the traditional production systems in Côte d'Ivoire. Yapi-Gnaoré et al (1995) have studied peri-urban livestock in the Bouaké area. However, no work has addressed the mechanisms of the urban livestock system and the determinants of its adoption in northern Côte d'Ivoire, especially in the 'Zone dense' of Khorogo, where many poor urbanites tend to adopt small ruminants as a food security strategy.

One of the objectives of the Côte d'Ivoire government is poverty alleviation. A better understanding of how urban livestock develops in a big city like Khorogo will help meet the challenge. Cattle and other animals are not managed directly by the owner, and they play a minor role in the livelihood of the households. Because small ruminants are the only type of animals that are integrated into the production system in resource allocation, the objective of this study is to use a Tobit analysis to identify the determinants of small ruminant adoption and intensity of adoption in the city of Khorogo.

It was hypothesized that:

- Households headed by a man (or a woman) whose primary occupation is farming are likely to adopt livestock as a food security strategy.
- Low-income households are more likely than wealthier households to invest in small ruminants.
- People with an ethnic background in animal husbandry are more likely to adopt urban livestock.
- Young and educated people are less likely to have small ruminants among their assets.
- Due to labour constraints, large urban families are more likely than small ones to raise livestock.
- Women's labour supply is a determinant in urban livestock husbandry.

METHODOLOGY

Farm-household models integrate in a single institution the decisions regarding production, consumption and reproduction over time (Sadoulet and de Janvry, 1995). In economic theory, the problems of production decisions, consumption decisions and labour supply are usually analysed separately through the behaviour of three classes of agents:

1   producers, who maximize net revenues with respect to levels of products and factors, subject to constraints determined by market prices, fixed factors and technology;

2   consumers, who maximize utility with respect to the quantities of goods consumed, subject to constraints determined by market prices, disposable income, household characteristics and tastes;

3   workers, who maximize utility with respect to income and home time, subject to constraints determined by the market wage, total time available and worker characteristics.

In the case of the household, the decision-maker is engaged simultaneously in making decisions about production, consumption and work.

Following Sadoulet and de Janvry (1995), we can integrate the three problems into the single household problem as follows:

Max $u(c_a, c_m, c_l; z^h)$ utility function

subject to: $g(q_a, x, t; z^q) = 0$ production function

$p_x x + p_m c_m = p_a(q_a - c_a) + w(l^s - l)$ cash constraint

$c_l + l^s = E$ time constraint

where u is a utility function to be maximized; a is an agricultural good; m is a manufactured good; q_a is the quantity produced of good a; g is the function symbol; and p_a is the price of product a. Similarly, p_m is the price of m; c_l is home time; l^s is time worked; and E is total time endowment. z represents the household characteristics; h is the household number; t is the production technology; x is the vector input; l is labour; and w is the wage rate.

In the context of African economies, characterized by market failures and credit constraints, this typical household doesn't work. According to Sadoulet and de Janvry (1995), the household's problem is to maximize $u(c, z^h)$, subject to cash and credit constraints, production technology, exogenous effective market prices for tradables and equilibrium conditions for non-tradables.

In decision-making, farmers have to make a choice between many risky alternatives. Although the decisions they make are complex, they are typically modelled as a binary choice. They accept or reject a given technology or policy according to their own perceptions of the expected benefits and costs of the technology and the expected risks. The rationale for their decision (often a priori criticized by Western standards of thinking) is based on a myriad of factors and some complex social relationships, which can condition benefits and costs. In many African societies income maximization, for instance, is not a goal per se; income smoothing, or reducing variability in income, may be more important, for example, and this may be particularly true of food-insecure households.

The adoption of any technology can be modelled as an economic decision based on expected marginal benefits and costs. Most empirical specifications deal with a variety of models of farmer or household optimization: maximizing profits, expected utility of profits or expected utility of consumption and leisure subject to production function and time. The economic analysis of the behaviour of individual decision-makers often leads to models of a limited dependent variable or qualitative variable nature.

The decision will depend on each farmer's own characteristics, beliefs and objectives. The dichotomous nature of the response in that framework will require a specific econometric approach, namely, the use of qualitative response models.

Four types of model have been commonly used in the literature: the linear probabilistic, probit, logit and Tobit models. These models are discussed in Annex 1. The Tobit (or probit of Tobin) model used here is associated with the normal distribution. The resulting probability distribution is represented as

$$P_i = F(\alpha + \beta X) = F(Z)$$

where Z is an index determined by a vector of explanatory variables X; and $Z = \alpha + \beta X_i$ (where i stands for individuals).

Probit analysis solves the problem of how to estimate the parameters α and β while obtaining information about the underlying index Z (Greene, 1997, 1999).

FIELD DATA COLLECTION

The city of Khorogo is located in the savanna, 650km north of Abidjan. Despite the great potential of the region for livestock production, the local populations are farmers rather than herders. Although they own some livestock, the farmers do not have the skills for animal husbandry. In the culture of the Senoufo (the dominant ethnic of the region), keeping cattle is traditionally forbidden. Cattle are not part of the economic system. Usually, hired folk from neighbouring countries are in charge of cattle, and the first function of cattle is for social purposes (funerals and celebrations). These animals are a long way from the production and economic systems (cows are not milked; animals are not sold). However, small ruminants are kept by farmers themselves in the vicinity of their compounds. They are part of the production, economic and social systems. The entire household manages them, especially women who own part of the herd. In the city, goats and sheep are essentially fed human garbage. Animals are considered cash assets; they are also sold or consumed by households during celebrations.

The survey was based on proportional sampling, the aim being to survey approximately one-third of the area. The livestock density was first estimated by following transects (streets or alleys) through the 11 neighbourhoods of the city of Khorogo. The approach was to randomly select the first street to be surveyed and subsequently every third street. The surveyors walked, for example, streets 2, 5, 8, etc., and counted the number of livestock. Inventories were taken early in the morning and late in the afternoon, to maximize the probability of finding respondents at home and obtaining accurate estimates of livestock numbers. For greater accuracy, the method should have been based on secondary statistics from extension agencies, but those data unfortunately did not exist. The results of the inventory are presented in Annex 2 and show that 13,654 adult goats and sheep were found in one-third of the area, which suggests around 27,300 small ruminants in the city, or about one animal for every nine inhabitants. On the basis of this livestock density, 90 households were randomly selected and surveyed.

THE EMPIRICAL TOBIT MODEL

Definition of variables

The dependent variable (NRUM) is the number of small ruminants (goats and sheep) owned by a household. This small stock is considered a liquid asset (a food security strategy for some adopters), in the sense that it can generate cash income to buy food or fulfil other needs.

The explanatory variables are as follows:

- AGE = age of the respondent
- GEND = gender of the owner (0 = female; 1 = male)
- EDUC = education level of the respondent (in years of schooling)
- NATION = nationality of the respondent (1 = Ivorian; 0 = non-Ivorian) as a proxy of ethnic background
- FSIZE = number of members in the household
- NWIF = number of wives in the household
- WPROCC = wife's primary occupation (employment opportunity outside the home)
- INC = income of the household
- PROCC = primary occupation of the head of the household
- NYXP = head of household's number of years of experience in farming.

Access to land resources, although important in agriculture, is not a determinant in the case of urban livestock, which do not feed on a grazing area, but on human wastes and purchased feedstuffs.

The explanatory variables can be further described as follows:

- Age may affect the adoption of small ruminants. It is commonly assumed that young people do not have small ruminants because they do not have enough money to capitalize. Moreover, their labour supply is not sufficient for animal husbandry and crop production. Younger people are also assumed to have less farming experience. So it is expected that the coefficient of variable AGE will have a positive sign.
- Gender is often considered an important variable in livestock ownership and management in Africa, where animals play a major role in

matrimonial compensations. Women usually receive animals as presents in marriages, so they often own part of the household herd, especially the small stock. In the model, this variable is a dummy (1 = male; 0 = female). Therefore GEND is expected to have a negative sign, with small stock adoption.

- Level of education may affect investment decisions in many ways. Usually, education and income are positively correlated, although not linearly. High-income households are more likely to have incentives for profitable and innovative activities. So, in general, education will tend to have a positive effect on investment. However, in the case of investing in small ruminants in the city as a food security strategy, the problem looks different. In the area of the study, educated people usually have alternative sources of income (government salaries), so they are less exposed to food insecurity. As a result, they are less inclined to invest in small stock as a food security strategy. So a negative sign is expected for EDUC. In other words, educated people in the city are less likely to share their homes with livestock. This is not a matter of income but of a psychological or sociological conception of living conditions.

- In traditional society, activities are often differentiated by gender and ethnic background. Among the indigenous people of the region, farming is considered more prestigious than animal husbandry, even though farmers own animals. The daily care and management of the stock are considered activities best left to women, children and people from ethnic groups such as the Fulani, for whom livestock-keeping is a traditional practice. Cattle owners are often foreigners from countries to the north, many of whom work in Côte d'Ivoire. In the model, NATION is a dummy variable (1 = citizen of Côte d'Ivoire; 0 = foreigner). It is thus meant to capture the ethnic background and the ability of the respondent to raise animals. Because it is expected that more foreigners are involved in animal husbandry, a negative sign is expected for this variable.

- Family size refers to the total number of people living in the same compound, having their meals together, and being under the responsibility of the head of the household. The idea that large families will have greater labour resources and be more likely to invest in keeping small ruminants in cities is not always correct, as children go to school and it is usual for large urban families to rely on other sources of income, such as commerce. Thus, the sign for FSIZE could be either negative or positive.

- The number of wives in a household may have a positive influence on livestock adoption, as it is predominately a woman's role to keep small ruminants. However, sometimes in the cities, only wealthy people can afford several wives but, as they have other sources of income, they might not invest in livestock. So the sign could be positive or negative.

- Employment outside the home is another important element in the practice of animal husbandry in the cities. In the model, this variable is a dummy (1 = wife is available for animal husbandry; 0 = wife works regularly outside the household). If she works outside the household, time constraints might affect her livestock activities. As a result, WPROCC is expected to have a positive sign.

- Household income is also considered an important factor in the decision to adopt livestock. It is often assumed that small ruminants are mostly present in low-income households, for food security reasons, or as a way of saving money. However, some urbanites raise small ruminants for celebrations and social activities, regardless of their income levels. So the sign expected for INC is uncertain.
- Urban livestock owners are diverse in their occupations and motivations. However, those who rely on livestock for their livelihood are more likely to be farmers. In the model, PROCC is a dummy variable (1 = farmer; 0 = non-farmer). As a result, it is expected that having farming as a primary occupation will be positively correlated with having small ruminants as a food security strategy.
- Number of years of experience in farming might also have a positive effect on livestock management. However, in the study area, experienced farmers do not necessarily raise animals. So either sign is expected for NYXP.

RESULTS AND DISCUSSION

The interpretation of any fitted model requires our being able to draw practical inferences from the coefficients estimated in the model (Hosmer and Lemeshow, 1989). For linear models, in which the link function is the identity function, coefficients express a corresponding change in the dependent variable for a unit change in the independent variable. However, in the logit and Tobit models, these coefficients do not have a straightforward interpretation. The slope coefficients represent a change in the link function for a change of one unit in the independent variable. Proper interpretation of the coefficients depends on being able to give meaning to the difference between two values of the link function. One of the main problems encountered in cross-sectional analysis is heteroscedasticity. Table 3.1 shows that only income exhibits heteroscedasticity. Autocorrelation between factors was also checked.

Significant factors related to livestock adoption for the survey include AGE, age of the household head; GEND, head of household gender; NATION, the nationality of the household head; WPROCC, wife's primary occupation; and INC, the household income level. All these variables enter the model with the expected sign. As expected, AGE has a positive sign, meaning that on average, old people are more likely to adopt small ruminants than young people. GEND has a negative sign, as this variable was a dummy (1 = male; 0 = female). Women are more likely to be small ruminant adopters than men. EDUC exhibits a negative sign, meaning that educated people in towns are less likely than uneducated people to adopt small ruminants. NATION, the nationality of the respondent (as a proxy of the ethnic background of the head of the household) has a negative sign, meaning that foreigners, who have more skills than nationals in raising animals, are more likely to be small ruminant adopters. WPROCC, the wife's primary occupation (1 = does not work mainly

Table 3.1 *Check for heteroscedasticity*

Variable	Coefficient	SE	t ratio	P[|Z|>z]	Mean of X
Constant	−35.0987	22.9265	−1.53092	0.125789	
AGE	0.954395	0.435731	2.19033	0.0285005	47.719101
GEND	−29.5015	16.8357	−1.75231	0.0797198	0.83146067
EDUC	−4.49632	9.10299	−0.493939	0.621349	1.7977528
NATION	−27.4239	15.7802	−1.73787	0.0822346	0.86516854
FSIZE	−1.43061	1.9632	−0.728715	0.466176	8.0449438
NWIF	−1.23293	6.94045	−0.177645	0.859002	1.2359551
WPROCC	29.5823	13.6946	2.16014	0.0307615	0.59550562
INC	0.0125806	0.0134482	0.935487	0.349537	427.07865
PROCC	16.3502	14.6049	1.1195	0.262927	0.32584270
NYXP	1.00019	0.905652	1.10439	0.269425	8.4157303
Heteroscedasticity term					
NYXP	0.0341354	0.0223082	1.530	0.1260	8.4157303
NWIF	0.2188801	0.2725706	803	0.4220	1.2359551
INC	−0.0025193	0.0013723	−1.836	0.0664	427.07865
Disturbance SD					
Sigma	31.340421	11.394099	2.751	0.0059	

Note: See 'Definition of variables', under 'The Empirical Tobit Model' in text.

outside home) is positively correlated with the probability of adoption, as expected, because of the role of small ruminants for women. The negative sign associated with INC suggests that those who adopt small ruminants as a food security strategy are not among the wealthiest people.

NYXP, years of experience in farming, happened not to be significant. In fact, the so-called 'modern farmers' who are emerging in the country are coming from diverse horizons, not necessarily with enough experience in farming. Other variables were not statistically significant. Table 3.2 shows Tobit coefficient estimates. The relative importance of the factors considered appears in Table 3.3, columns 5 and 6, which present the partial derivatives.

From Table 3.3, we get $z = 0.411$, so the predicted probability of urban livestock adoption for a household with characteristics X (the vector of explanatory variables) is estimated as

$$F(X'B/\sigma) = 0.6591$$

where F is the cumulative standard normal distribution function. This result indicates that there is a 66 per cent chance that an average urban household would adopt small ruminants.

The expected value of small ruminant adoption is defined in the model as

$$E(Y) = X\beta F(z) + \sigma f(z)$$

Table 3.2 *Tobit estimates*

Variable	Coefficient	SE	t ratio	P value
Constant	−35.0987	22.9265	−1.53092	0.125789
AGE	0.954395	0.435731	2.19033	0.0285005
GEND*	−29.5015	16.8357	−1.75231	0.0797198
EDUC	−4.49632	9.10299	−0.493939	0.621349
NATION*	−27.4239	15.7802	−1.73787	0.0822346
FSIZE	−1.43061	1.9632	−0.728715	0.466176
NWIF	−1.23293	6.94045	−0.177645	0.859002
WPROCC*	29.5823	13.6946	2.16014	0.0307615
INC	0.0125806	0.0134482	0.935487	0.349537
PROCC	16.3502	14.6049	1.1195	0.262927
NYXP	1.00019	0.905652	1.10439	0.269425

Note: See 'Definition of variables', under 'The Empirical Tobit Model' in the text.
* Significant at 10 per cent level.

where $z = \beta X/\sigma$; and $f(z)$ is the unit normal density. Replacing this with the values obtained in Table 3.3, we get

$$E(Y) = 12.894 \times 0.6591 + 31.3404 \times 0.3668 = 19.994$$

Table 3.3 *Tobit partial-derivatives decomposition*

Variable	Mean	B	XB	dE(Y*)/dXi	dF(z)/dXi
Constant	1	−0.35098			
AGE	47.7191	0.954	45.538	0.44	0.011
GEND	0.8314	−29.501	−24.527	−13.617	−0.345
EDUC	1.7977	−4.501	−8.092	−2.078	−0.053
NATION	0.8651	−27.424	−23.724	−12.658	−0.321
FSIZE	8.0449	−1.431	−11.509	−0.66	−0.017
NWIF	1.2359	1.233	−1.524	−0.569	−0.014
WPROCC	0.5955	29.582	17.616	13.654	0.346
INC	427.0786	0.013	5.373	0.006	0
PROCC	0.3258	16.35	5.327	7.547	0.191
NYXP	8.4157	1	8.417	0.462	0.012

Note: See 'Definition of variables', under 'The Empirical Tobit Model' in the text.
XB = 12.894
$f(z) = 0.3876$
$\sigma = 31.3404$
$E(Y^*) = XB + \sigma f(z) = 30.335$
$E(Y) = F(z)EY^* = 19.994$
$\{-zf(z)/F(z) - f(z)^2/F(z)^2\} = 0.462$

This result indicates that new adopters can be expected to raise, on average, 20 small ruminants.

Similarly, the expected number of small ruminants to be raised by those who already have goats and sheep is estimated as

$$E(Y^*) = \beta X + \sigma f(z)/F(z) = 12.894 + 31.3404 \times 0.3668/0.6591 = 30.35$$

The result indicates that small ruminant owners are expected to raise an average of 30 animals, which is close to the means found in the study.

Table 3.4 presents the elasticity decomposition for changes in the explanatory variables, along with the marginal effects. Total elasticity of change has two components: the first (E_1) is the elasticity of the number of small ruminants to be raised; the second (E_2) is the elasticity of the probability to adopt. Because probabilities are being sought on only one side of the cumulative distribution function, these probabilities look high.

AGE exhibits the highest elasticity (0.69) of intensity of adoption, meaning that a unit change in age will cause the intensity of adoption to increase by 0.69, or more significantly, with a 10-year increase in age, there will be seven more animals. Similarly, the probability of adopting will increase by 8 per cent for a 10-year increase in the age of non-adopters. The elasticities of categorical variables show the effects of switching from one category to another. For instance, GEND exhibits an elasticity of adoption of –0.43, meaning that the probability of livestock adoption by women is 43 per cent higher than that by men. And among those who already have animals, it is expected that women's herds will have, on average, four more animals than men's herds.

Table 3.4 *Tobit marginals and elasticities decomposition*

Variable	Marginals		Elasticities	
	M_1	M_2	E_1	E_2
AGE	0.3388	0.2903	0.8086	0.6929
GEND	–10.4740	–8.9748	–0.4355	–0.3732
EDUC	–1.5982	–1.3694	–0.1437	–0.1231
NATION	–9.7365	–8.3428	–0.4213	–0.361
FSIZE	–0.5079	–0.4352	–0.2044	–0.1751
NWIF	–0.4377	–0.3751	–0.0271	–0.0232
WPROCC	10.5027	0.9993	0.3128	0.0817
INC	0.0045	0.0038	0.0954	0.081
PROCC	5.8048	4.9739	0.0946	0.1281
NYXP	0.3551	0.3042	0.1495	

Note: See 'Definition of variables', under 'The Empirical Tobit Model' in the text.
M_1 (marginal effect on adoption) = $EY^*(df(z)/dXi)$
M_2 (marginal effect on intensity of adoption) = $F(z)^*(dEY^*/dXi)$
E_1 (elasticity of intensity) = $dEY^*/dXi^*Xi/EY^*$
E_2 (elasticity of adoption) = $dF(z)/dXi^*Xi/F(z)$

CONCLUSION AND POLICY IMPLICATIONS

In their attempts to help households intensify livestock production systems, either to achieve food security goals for the poorest people or to reduce the meat deficit at the national level, decision-makers will find that the results of the analysis can provide useful insights. The analysis has shown the characteristics of the typical household adopter. Drawing lessons from past (unsuccessful) attempts to give a boost to the livestock sector, if new and sound policies are to be launched to improve the country's self-reliance in meat supply and food security, planners and decision-makers should take into account the following characteristics:

- Urban livestock should be regarded as an economic activity that generates income and contributes to food security. As a result, it should be monitored, and its various impacts should be measured.
- To improve the quality of the products, feedstuffs should be made available, and this could be achieved by promoting private entrepreneurs in animal feed production.
- Urban livestock should be considered an important component of the struggle to alleviate poverty.
- Particular attention should be devoted to women, as they play an important role in small ruminant keeping. A credit policy could be launched to help women gain access to inputs such as feed, to veterinary medicine and to markets.

Impacts of the field research grant

Human resources development

The AGROPOLIS grant provided a great opportunity to implement an ad hoc sampling method. During the field research, the thesis adviser visited the researcher and demonstrated the transect method as a means of taking a livestock inventory in an area where animals are always scavenging. An additional 10 surveyors were trained by the researcher and six assisted with the research.

Gender-sensitivity analysis

Gender is often considered an important variable in livestock ownership in Africa. Animals play a major role in matrimonial compensations. Women usually receive livestock as presents at the time of marriage. However, in the findings, ownership was not clearly defined in the household, even though women allocated more time to small ruminants.

Institutional capacity strengthening

At the researcher's home university, graduate research on UA was not a high priority among students, partly because the AGROPOLIS programme was not well-known.

The extension agency with which the researcher is affiliated, the National Agency for Rural Development, showed great interest in the research. The study showed that urban livestock contributes significantly to meat supply and poverty alleviation in the region. Consequently, the agency is planning to create a network on urban livestock, to help implement appropriate economic policies for the development of safe and sustainable systems for urban livestock production. Moreover, the field research made an additional contribution to the International Livestock Research Institute programmes, especially the approach taken to determine urban livestock inventory and adoption conditions in West Africa.

Outside of any formal affiliations, the researcher had extended discussions with the mayor of the city, to whom the concept of UA and its potential contribution to food security and the urban environment were explained.

One of the most important aspects of the application has been its impact on capacity-building. Among the 12 PhD candidates from developing countries, only two of us returned to our home country. Those who did not get the opportunity to work on a subject related to their country remained in the United States. To me this was a big loss for their institutions.

The findings showed that urban livestock is an important asset of households in the area. The approach used for livestock inventory (following the transect alleys) has proven to be very effective and innovative. Moreover, the field research was a great opportunity to develop discussions on the environmental concerns and sustainability of raising urban livestock. Now, people are aware of the interest in keeping urban livestock and of the need to encourage this and to provide a legal framework for it, instead of just condemning the activity.

ACKNOWLEDGEMENTS

Apart from the Fulbright Scholarship for my four years of academic training, I received an AGROPOLIS grant for the field research. During my field research, I received academic advice from the International Livestock Research Institute (Addis-Ababa, Ethiopia). Additional data were also obtained from local extension agencies. CIRES provided the administrative support.

REFERENCES

Adesina, A. and Baidu-Forson, A. (1995) 'Farmers' perception and adoption of new agricultural technology: Evidence from analysis in Burkina Faso and Guinea, West Africa', *Agricultural Economics*, vol 13, pp1–19

Barry, M. B. (1978) 'Les Peuls en Côte d'Ivoire', *Cahiers du CIRES*, vol 5, pp75–81

Barry, M. B. (1990) 'L'insécurité alimentaire en Afrique. A qui la faute?' *Cahiers du CRES*, Special Issue, pp77–84

Barry, M. B. (1992) *Impact des Mesures de Libéralisation des Importations de Viande sur les Systèmes de Production Animales dans la Zone de Contact Côte d'Ivoire–Mali–Burkina Faso*, Association canadienne des études africaines, Montréal

Dennery, P. (1995) 'Inside urban agriculture: An exploration of food producer decision making in a Nairobi slum', MSc dissertation, Wageningen Agricultural University, Wageningen, Netherlands

Due, J. M. (1986) 'Agricultural policy in tropical Africa: Is a turnaround possible?' *Agricultural Economics*, vol 1, pp19–34

Due, J. M. and Magayanne, F. (1989) 'Changes needed in agriculture policy for female headed farm families in tropical Africa', *Agricultural Economics*, vol 4, pp239–253

Ehui, S. (1997) 'Contribution of livestock to food security in sub-Saharan Africa: A review of technology and policy issues', Paper presented at the 23rd Conference of the International Association of Agricultural Economists, 1–16 August 1997, Sacramento, CA

Gladwin, C. and McMillan, D. (1989) 'Is a turnaround in Africa possible without helping women to farm?' Proceedings of Kansas State University's 1983 Farming Systems Research Symposium. Kansas State University, Manhattan, KS, Paper No. 6

Greene, W. (1997) *Econometric Analysis* (3rd edition), Prentice-Hall, Upper Saddle River, NJ

Greene, W. (1999) 'Marginal effects in the censored regression model', *Economic Letters*, vol 64, pp43–49

Henn, J. K. (1983) 'Feeding the cities and feeding the peasants: What role for Africa's women farmers?' *World Development*, vol 11, pp1043–1055

Hosmer, D.W. and Lemeshow, S. (1989) *Applied Logistic Regression*, John Wiley & Sons, New York, Wiley Series in Probabilities and Mathematical Statistics

Lele, U. (1986) 'Women and structural transformation', *Economic Development and Cultural Change*, vol 34, pp195–221

McFadden, D. (1984) 'Econometric analysis of qualitative response models', in Griliches, Z. and Intriligator, M. (eds), *Handbook of Econometrics. Vol. 2*, North Holland, Amsterdam

Maxwell, G. D. (1994) 'Internal struggles over resources, external struggles for survival: Urban women and subsistence household production', Paper presented to the African Studies Association, November 1994, Toronto

Pindyck, S. D. and Rubinfield, D. L. (1990) *Economic Models and Economic Forecasts*, McGraw-Hill, Hightstown, NY

Poats, S. (1991) *The Role of Gender in Agricultural Development*, Consultative Group on International Agricultural Research, Washington, DC. Issues in Agriculture, No. 3

Rakodi, C. (1991) 'Urban agriculture: Research questions and Zambian evidence', *Journal of Modern African Studies*, vol 26, pp495–515

Sadoulet, E. and de Janvry, A. (1995) *Qualitative Development Policy Analysis*, John Hopkins University Press, Baltimore, MD

Shapiro, B. I. and Brorsen, W. (1988) 'Factors affecting hedging decisions', *North Central Journal of Agricultural Economics*, vol 10, no 2, July

Sodepra (1985) *Rapports Annuels d'Activités Sodepra-Nord*, Ministry of Agriculture and Livestock, Abidjan, Côte d'Ivoire

Sodepra (1987) *Rapports Annuels d'Activités Sodepra-Nord*, Ministry of Agriculture and Livestock, Abidjan, Côte d'Ivoire

Sodepra (1989) *Rapports Annuels d'Activités Sodepra-Nord*, Ministry of Agriculture and Livestock, Abidjan, Côte d'Ivoire

Yapi-Gnaoré, V. C., Ehui, S. and Shapiro, B. (1995) 'Peri-urban livestock production and development in sub-Saharan Africa: A review of opportunities and constraints', *Proceedings of the International Conference of the Association of Institutions of Tropical Veterinary Medicine*, AITVM, vol 1, pp151–163

ANNEX 1. COMMENTS ON MODELS USED IN THE LITERATURE

The linear probabilistic model has been criticized for its numerous shortcomings (heteroscedasticity of the error term, unrealistic probability values of the dependent variable). As a result, the model has become obsolete. To overcome the difficulties encountered in this model, the probit model transforms the linear model in such a way that the values of the dependent variable will lie in the (0,1) interval for all values of the explanatory variables. The requirement of this process is that it translates the values of the characteristics X, which range in value over the entire real line, to a probability that ranges in value fromto (Pindyck and Rubinfield, 1990).

Estimation procedure

The model of small ruminant adoption is specified as a censored regression model, expressed as

$Y_i = Y_i^*$ $Y^* = \beta X_i + \mu_i > 0$ for those who have small ruminants
$Y_i = 0$ $Y^* \leq 0$ for those who do not have ruminants

where Y is the dependent variable; Y^* is an underlying latent variable that indexes adoption; X is socio-economic characteristics of the respondents, which, it is hypothesized, affect the adoption decision; and μ is the error term, which is assumed to have a truncated normal distribution, yielding a Tobit model. The model presents two advantages: it permits the investigation of the decision of whether to adopt and the level of adoption (Adesina and Baidu-Forson, 1995); and its coefficients can be desegregated to determine the effects of a change in one variable on changes in the probability of adoption and in the expected intensity of the adoption.

The total change in Y associated with a change in X_i can be decomposed into the change in the probability of Y's being above the limit and the change in Y when it is already above the limit (Shapiro and Brorsen, 1988).

The regression coefficients are computed using the mean values of the explanatory variables, as presented in Table 3.1. Elasticities are computed following the McDonald and Moffit decomposition (McFadden, 1984):

$$EY = F(z)EY^* \tag{A1}$$

where $z = X\beta/\delta X_i$. Taking the derivatives of EY with respect to X_i we get

$$\delta EY/\delta X_i = F(z)(\delta EY^*/\delta X_i) + EY^*(\delta F(z)/\delta X_i) \tag{A2}$$

and multiplying both sides of equation [A2] by X_i/EY we get

$$\delta EY/\delta X_i(X_i/EY) = F(z)(\delta EY^*/\delta X_i) + EY^*(\delta F(z)/\delta X_i)(X_i/EY) \qquad [A3]$$

Replacing EY with its value from equation [A1] and rearranging terms, we get the decomposition of the total elasticities into the two effects. The first effect is equivalent to the expression

$$Zf(z)/F(z) - f(z)^2/F(z)^2 \qquad [A4]$$

This is the fraction by which the β coefficients must be adjusted to obtain the correct effects for observations above the limit. The second fraction is obtained by subtracting the results obtained in equation [A4] from 1 (Shapiro and Brorsen, 1988).

ANNEX 2. LIVESTOCK INVENTORY IN KHOROGO

| | | Livestock inventory (n) | | | |
| | | Adult sheep | | Adult goats | |
Neighbourhood	Streets surveyed	Female	Male	Female	Male
Air France	1	44	5	41	7
	2	55	10	36	8
	3	35	13	46	12
	4	69	8	54	21
	5	69	20	64	9
Nouveau Quartier	1	65	7	42	15
	2	56	12	42	8
	3	48	8	40	9
	4	49	16	31	5
Dem	1	109	15	81	15
	2	62	13	44	7
	3	31	4	23	9
Koko	1	66	11	50	9
	2	62	12	77	19
	3	65	11	64	11
	4	64	10	54	17
	5	71	10	42	9
	6	54	15	45	18
	7	66	10	42	4
	8	55	12	47	12
	9	74	13	45	18
Delafosse	1	65	4	61	5
	2	43	5	57	2
	3	63	3	62	6
	4	42	7	56	4
	5	88	7	64	10
	6	72	4	64	13
	7	82	4	61	12
Tuéguéré	1	55	8	34	8
	2	38	9	51	10
	3	39	8	46	18
Petit Paris	1	11	3	23	6
	2	39	9	16	3
	3	20	6	11	4
	4	35	10	12	9
	5	20	4	14	5
	6	73	5	32	0
	7	59	0	10	0
Haoussabougou	1	93	5	91	2
	2	155	1	100	10
	3	160	1	58	12
	4	172	1	96	20
	5	75	1	59	13

	6	81	5	56	9
Banaforo	1	90	1	69	24
	2	60	1	43	6
	3	60	1	77	20
	4	71	1	61	13
	5	86	4	53	14
	6	112	1	116	4
Soba	1	50	8	30	7
	2	39	5	33	3
	3	40	5	30	4
	4	40	5	35	4
	5	47	7	36	8
	6	47	5	30	8
Sinistré	1	72	5	49	7
	2	55	7	45	12
	3	55	1	60	6
	4	60	3	42	6

4

Exploring the Gender Dimensions of Urban Open-space Cultivation in Harare, Zimbabwe

Stephanie Gabel

INTRODUCTION

Urban planning as a discipline and profession in its own right is still young. Provision of and access to affordable housing, public transportation, employment and health are issues that require urban planners and decision-makers to intervene where physical planning and market forces are deemed inadequate to ensure the well-being of the people they are planning for. Food security is one area in which few planners have yet to deliberately apply a similar rationale for intervention in urban planning. Urban food cultivation in cities around the world captured this researcher's interest, as it poignantly demonstrates a way in which people are finding food security in an urban context. In addition, it signals an area in which planners are perhaps not addressing the realities on the ground: few authorities recognize urban farming as a land-use, despite its prevalence. Such has been the case of Zimbabwe. Cultivating urban open space involves not only land-use issues that have not been addressed, but also gender issues – a second area historically neglected by planners and decision-makers the world over.

This research sought to take a closer look at open-space cultivation by women urban farmers and to gain insights into gender issues emerging from their experiences, to help inform policy. To get a more in-depth view of the experiences of urban women farmers, this label or identity of 'urban farmer' was perhaps not the most useful, as the roles of these women were diverse, overlapping and sometimes conflicting. The need to provide household food was difficult to disentangle from many other needs – most significantly, women's need for social relations that are not oppressive (for example, social relations that are not sexist, racist, ageist or classist).

Description of study area

Harare is the capital city of Zimbabwe and is home to about 2 million people. Zimbabwe has a predominantly rural population, but rural-to-urban migration has become a serious issue for Harare as it grapples with a growth rate of between 5 and 7 per cent (ZWRCN–SARDC, 1998). However, this rate increased rapidly in 2002 as a result of internal displacement due to drought and political and economic instability.

Harare is situated at an altitude of 1550m. The topography of the city is hilly in rocky areas, flatter in the south, and undulating in the north (Rakodi, 1995). The city lies on a watershed plateau between two major rivers, the Limpopo and the Zambezi. Some of the country's best agricultural soils are in this area.

Influenced by British colonial administration and planning, Harare has a formal gridiron layout, wide streets, a town square and public gardens, and has generally maintained its infrastructure. According to the acting Deputy Town Planner for Harare, Mrs Charambira,[1] open spaces account for about 10 per cent of urban land (Figure 4.1), although the percentage has been cited as higher in other reports (Zinyama, 1993). The seven women who worked with the author moved to Highfield, Harare, from rural locations in the 1950s and 1960s. At that time, abundant land was available for those who wished to cultivate, and so early residents who farmed became 'owners' of much of the undeveloped land around these areas. Only one of the seven cultivators included in this study was among these original owners.

The present situation in Zimbabwe could be described as tense and fragile – socially, politically and economically. In the past few years, food prices have soared; the price of some staple commodities, like tomatoes and rape, rose more than 100 per cent in the course of just one week (Financial Gazette, 2001a, 2001b). Other commodities such as sugar, oil, washing soap and bread are now unaffordable for many low-income families. Speculations in 2000 that the country may face grain shortages have become a reality, as Zimbabwe is now suffering from drought. The potential for immense human loss is imminent, and the international community has yet to commit the resources needed to halt the impending tragedy.

Research questions

For this research, five broad questions were proposed:

1 What are the practical and strategic needs of women with the opportunity to cultivate urban open space in Harare?
2 What are the practical and strategic needs of women without an opportunity to cultivate urban open space in Harare?
3 What are the current policies and stances of local departments and decision-makers on citywide planning and its accommodation of urban agriculture (UA)?

Legend:
- ■ CBD
- ▨ Industrial areas
- ▨ High density residential
- ▨ Low density residential
- □ Open spaces

City of Harare

Airport

0   10km

Note: The map is based on one drawn in 1989; it is still being used in most recent documents. Therefore, the amount of open space lost to development has not been adjusted for. However, the map does give a sense of how much open space the city has available, as well as showing its spatial layout.
Source: Adapted from Zinyama (1993, p10)

Figure 4.1 *Map of Harare, with particular reference to urban open spaces*

4   What are the relationships, interactions, differences or similarities between each of the three groups identified above?
5   Can any action strategies be identified within and between any of these groups to promote more accommodative planning initiatives or practices related to UA and women cultivators or noncultivators in Harare?

Research with noncultivating, poorer households (question 2) was not carried out because the women farmers expressed concern about opening up the research to others in their neighbourhood. It is difficult to say how much of this was a form of gate-keeping and how much was due to a genuine concern about their own safety and the researcher's. (Other researchers have also cited fear as a real concern during politically tense times. In fact, before the author left Zimbabwe, residents were having to inform local police before holding meetings of more than three people.) However, some insights into this group have been gained, both from this fieldwork and from that of others.

OBJECTIVES

This chapter emphasizes preliminary findings and analysis of question 1 and considers how such identified needs of the urban women farmers relates to questions 4 and 5. Some of the findings of the study continue to be analysed. The objectives of this chapter are, therefore, to share key findings as they relate to the research undertaken with the women farmers, insofar as the work has progressed to date.

METHODOLOGY

The research methodology is feminist because the author advocates feminism[2] in her own life and work. As many feminist academics have proposed (Harding, 1987; Kirby and McKenna, 1989; Stanley, 1990; Reinharz, 1992) there is no single feminist methodology – no methods are exclusively feminist. Although acknowledging many viewpoints, perspectives, standpoints, opinions and theories, some feminist scholars do share similar ideas on what forms a feminist methodology. First, feminist methodology stands at a disjuncture with positivism and has made valuable contributions to illuminating positivism's limitations, weaknesses and fallacies (Bowles and Klein, 1983; Stanley and Wise, 1983, 1990; Keller, 1985; Harding, 1987; Smith, 1987; Reinharz, 1992; Mvududu and McFadden, 2001). Second, feminism produces unique critiques of dominant ideologies that have not only left gender unexamined, but also ignored issues of race, class, age, imperialism and religion (Mohanty, 1991; Reinharz, 1992; Frankenberg, 1993; Imam, 1997; Collins, 1998; Hooks, 2000). Third, feminism advocates research for social justice and encourages engaging with others in action for positive change (Kirby and McKenna, 1989; Stanley and Wise, 1990; Slocum et al, 1995; Guijt and Kaul Shah, 1998). Fourth, feminism creates a space for the role and positionality of researchers, their personal experiences, their emotions and their feelings to be included in research and interrogated through reflexivity (Reinharz, 1983; Harding, 1987; Smith, 1987; Frankenberg, 1993; Collins, 1998). Approaches to research that have accommodated these aspects of feminism are ethnomethodology and participatory research.

Ethnomethodology[3] is an area within the social sciences that embraces the everyday and the personal. Ethnomethodology

> argues that 'data' should be used as a 'topic', and not a resource.
> The idea of using data as a topic is one which suggests that we
> shouldn't use people's accounts as unexplicated data. We should
> instead explicate them... In other words it is on understanding
> how we 'do' everyday life. (Stanley and Wise, 1983, p139)

The understanding of data within ethnomethodology embraces the ways of understanding, knowing and doing that all members of society share; this approach is referred to as the documentary method of interpretation. Stanley and Wise (1983) use the analogy of the researcher and a detective looking for evidence – evidence in the form of events, speech, ways of looking and so forth. Like detectives, researchers find themselves in new or problematic situations, in which they

> use events, speech, ways of looking and a whole variety of other evidence, as precisely evidence, and this is interpreted as 'evidence which stands on behalf of' a whole body of knowledge which we deduce from it. We use it as something which points to an underlying pattern, of which the evidence is but a small part. (Stanley and Wise, 1983, p140)

An interesting aspect of ethnomethodology is its way of confronting notions of reality and fact:

> What goes on in social life appears to us as factual; and we experience these social facts as constraining – as constraining as any other material facts. In other words, it is the consequential nature of social facts which constitute their 'factness'. We believe they have consequences; we act on the basis of this; and so they do have consequences. (Stanley and Wise, 1983, p141)

We could not name oppression or social injustice, let alone act to address or end it, if indeed we did not share some commonly held ideas of the social facts determining what oppression is, who experiences it, and how.

Participatory research

The author's own views on international development have been shaped in many ways, both by previous volunteer experiences and by the literature on participation, especially that focusing on research and action for mobilization and change (Freire, 1970; Freire and Faundez, 1989; Freire and Horton, 1990; Horton, 1990); on participatory action research (Fals-Borda and Rahman, 1991; Brinton Lykes, 1997; Chambers, 1997; Chataway, 1997; Nieuwenhuys, 1997); and on participatory development generally (Nelson and Wright, 1995; Guijt and Kaul Shah, 1998). In trying to get people involved in this research (from institutional support, to research assistants, to women urban farmers), in facilitating the research, and in acquiring information from and with the farmers, the author attempted to embrace a spirit of putting the theory and tenets of participation into practice. What was most important in terms of creating space for participation in the research, is often cited in research on participatory development.

Overall aims were to:

- develop shared ownership of the research;
- enable other participants to direct the research process, have a say on what to do, and how;
- create opportunities for collective data-gathering and analysis;
- create space for participants to reflect on the research and provide critical feedback;
- build trust;
- allow research to progress toward action and doing if desired by other participants.

Such attempts as these are made in participatory research so that the hierarchical relationships associated with research – between the researcher and those being researched can be broken down.

Key concepts

Open-space cultivation

The term 'urban agriculture' as applied in Zimbabwe has generally been defined according to location (Mbiba, 1995). The categories are on-plot, off-plot and peri-urban agriculture. For the purpose of this paper, urban will refer to open-space cultivation, a form of off-plot agriculture that entails the cultivation of food crops, primarily maize, on undeveloped public or private land that is not legally owned by the farmer.

Gender

According to the southern African feminist scholar Ruth Meena:

> Gender has been defined as socially constructed and culturally variable roles that women and men play in their daily lives. It refers to a structural relationship of inequality between men and women as manifested in labour markets and in political structures, as well as in the household. It is reinforced by custom, law and specific development policies. Whereas sex is biological, gender is acquired and constructed by society. (Meena, 1992, p1)

Although this project focused on the lived experiences of only seven urban women farmers, gender dynamics were revealed throughout the research process by examining gender relations. I should also make it clear that while this fieldwork was with women farmers only, this does not preclude the work from contributing to gender analysis (Mies, 1983; Keller, 1985; Smith, 1987; Frankenberg, 1993; Imam, 1997; Nussbaum, 2000), especially given that the researcher was actively having dialogue with representatives of government and of non-governmental organizations (NGOs) and, in fact, working with an NGO engaged in formulating a programme on UA. Furthermore, as Meena (1992, p22) explains: 'Engenderisation of the research process, however, has to go hand in hand with the bridging of the knowledge gap which exists in the region'. Meena asserts that to bridge this knowledge gap in southern Africa, research needs to be carried out on women on specific issues, as a means to challenging male control over knowledge and the primacy of male power. Imam (1997) clearly states that an examination of gender relations includes relationships of women with women and of men with men (the emphasis in this research has been on women with women); and 'relations of categories of women to social phenomena (whether the state, the division of labour, education systems, economic relations, political systems or other), and the different relations of groups of men to those same phenomena' (Imam, 1997, p5). The research effort reported in this chpater has contributed to contextualizing UA from a feminist perspective, by working with a small group of urban farmers (as well as using other research methods, such as policy reviews and interviews with government and NGO stakeholders), which helped reveal gender relations interwoven into the practice of UA in Zimbabwe.

Practical and strategic needs

Caroline Moser's work on clarifying a gender planning methodology provides definitions that distinguish between practical and strategic gender needs. Strategic needs, according to Moser:

> *are the needs women identify because of their subordinate position to men in their society... They relate to gender divisions of labour, power and control and may include such issues as legal rights, domestic violence, equal wages and women's control over their bodies. Meeting strategic gender needs helps women to achieve greater equality.* (Moser, 1993, p39)

Practical needs are those that:

> *women identify in their socially accepted roles in society. Practical gender needs do not challenge the gender divisions of labour or women's subordinate position in society, although rising out of them. Practical gender needs are a response to immediate perceived necessity, identified within a specific context.* (Moser, 1993, p40)

Although the distinction between these two types of needs can provide a useful tool to aid us in analysing how gender is being addressed in proposed policy or project interventions, it should be noted that Moser's framework has been critiqued by other feminist scholars, including scholars in Africa (Imam, 1997; Wieringa, 1998). However, the author has found applying this framework difficult and problematic and is exploring alternative methods for analysis.

Field methods

A variety of research methods were trialled through the fieldwork in Harare. With the women farmers, the methods were adapted to the needs the women were expressing, in an attempt to produce a 'thoughtful method', described by

Rutenberg (1983, p75) as one that 'is the combination of intellect and emotion and is concerned with practical and personal as well as academic application'.

Participatory tools

The participatory tools used in the research were drawn from *Power, Process and Participation: Tools for Change* (Slocum et al, 1995). They appear to be somewhat similar to participatory rural appraisal (PRA) techniques; however, the tools shared in this resource book have been specifically developed to address gender and social stratification.

The first participatory tool that was used with the small group of women is a popular tool often used at the beginning of a process. It is known as landscape mapping, and is similar to transect walks (Slocum et al, 1995). This exercise consisted in having a small group of the women take us on a walk through an area where each of the women had one field. In this exercise, the women were asked to tell the researchers about the land they were farming, what they cultivated, what some of the challenges were and so forth. This was followed, a week later, with an exercise to map out this area with the same group of women.

The second tool used in this study was a modified version of a life-history interview, conducted with each of the seven women separately, at their homes. These interviews revealed a great deal about the backgrounds of the women, which enabled the researchers to get to know each of them on a more individual level. It revealed information about their migration from rural areas to the city, their educational backgrounds, when they started cultivating in the city, their employment experiences and much more. Flip-chart paper was used so the women could see what was being written in tables such as this:

Date	Location	Household composition	Activities	Major events
Birth				
↓				
2000				

The last participatory tool used during the same interviews was a technique referred to as household-activity ranking. This was a short exercise in which each of the women named the contributions each person living in her household made and ranked these contributions in importance, according to her own criteria. The women were asked to explain their criteria. A second table was used to fill in this information:

Who	Activity	Contribution	Ranking

Focus groups

Four focus-group discussions were held with the women, all participants gathering in the living room of one of the homes (the women took turns hosting group gatherings). Generally, all seven women (20 at the beginning) would attend, although on occasion some came late or were away. Topics explored at the focus groups were as follows:

- *Meeting 1* – The women's perceptions of local decision-makers' and planners' attitudes toward UA; and the women's views on the difficulties lodgers and noncultivators had in accessing land for UA;
- *Meeting 2* – The women's perceptions of access to land by women and men, in both rural and urban settings;
- *Meeting 3* – The women's UA information, training and communication needs, which were then summarized for presentation at an upcoming workshop on the same topic;
- *Meeting 4* – Action strategies to meet the needs and concerns raised in the research.

Each meeting lasted 1.5–2 hours.

Quite often, the women did not seem to be as comfortable holding discussions in a larger group as when speaking in their own homes, where they seemed to volunteer more personal information and express their opinions more freely. Nevertheless, the focus groups presented an opportunity to observe group dynamics and hear the kinds of stories and information the women wished to exchange with one another, and these exchanges played an important role in forming and maintaining a group identity.

Postharvest interviews

From October 2000 to April 2001, detailed in-depth interviews were held with each woman individually. The interview concerned her most recent farming activities and included information-gathering on:

- the time and resources used for each major activity (planting, weeding, harvesting, etc.);
- the estimated amounts harvested, stolen and shared;
- the ways the women obtained their fields;
- other interesting details that emerged in the process of the interviews.

Once again, each interview lasted 1.5–2 hours.

Visioning interviews

To facilitate the process of determining which projects the women wanted to undertake and how, individual semi-structured interviews were held with each of the women in her own home (discussing project ideas as a group seemed to create some tension). Topics discussed at these individual interviews included what the women envisioned for themselves and their families in the years to come, how they imagined working with the other women in the group, what their own project ideas were, and what resources they required or possessed to undertake these activities.

Informal meetings with key informants and NGOs

Significant effort was put into finding out the interests, opinions and involvement in UA of local government, academics and NGOs. The author carried out informal discussions and meetings with at least 30 or more such stakeholders who, in some way or another, had an interest in UA in Zimbabwe.

Review of the literature and secondary sources

A proportion of time was dedicated to tracking down documents, research papers, reports and other such publications related to UA.

Internship

An internship placement with the Municipal Development Program for Eastern and Southern Africa (MDP–ESA) was developed by MDP and the researcher within its Urban Agriculture Program for the period May–August 2001. This allowed active engagement in the day-to-day implementation of the UA programme by writing reports, editing materials for dissemination, strengthening the participation of stakeholders in meetings and discussions on UA, developing proposals and becoming involved in other related activities. The internship created an opportunity to gain an insider's perspective on the policy side of UA, by bringing the researcher into closer contact with information that may otherwise have been difficult to obtain and with individuals who either were policy makers or had connections with policy makers.

Action strategies

Action strategies took on numerous forms and increasing importance as a result of the elevating stresses affecting the women. Action was undertaken in collaboration with the women, sometimes at their request and sometimes because a possible contact or opportunity for them had been discovered. The burden of the increasing costs of food and household expenditures (such as water and electricity bills) was greater on some women's households than others, but all were eager to participate and talk about what actions they could take as a group. Significant time and energy went into identifying ways to address the issues the women were raising. The objectives of the action strategies were to:

- work directly with local organizations;
- provide education and training;
- allow participation in meetings where NGOs and decision-makers were present;

- network and share information with others (including other urban farmers); and
- establish the women's own projects.

STRENGTHS AND WEAKNESSES OF THE RESEARCH

The inclusion of action strategies as a participatory research technique proved to be both a strength and a weakness. It revealed complexities: over time discrepancies, contradictions and group dynamics came to the surface. Unlike survey methods or other quantitative methods, this research explored the qualitative nature of the everyday lives of women urban farmers, revealing the real difficulties they faced when trying to organize themselves. Considerable discussion time and emphasis are placed on the need for farmers to be organized and in particular to organize themselves, given the limited resources of governments and NGOs. The realities of organizing for UA, especially for older women, are indeed complex, as some of the findings in this research suggest. The challenge of such research methods is that a great deal of time and personal commitment are needed so that participants develop trust and share experiences – prerequisites for action strategies.

It was anticipated that this research would be inclusive and that 'participatory' meant that the women would 'lead' the process. However, in a short-term research project with limited resources, the support was not there to allow this level of involvement. It became apparent that the women involved were not accustomed to such relationships with foreigners, development workers, politicians or indeed any other figures with perceived authority or control. Had this knowledge been available at the outset, other strategies to lead the research would have been employed. A greater personal understanding was gained of why education and awareness-raising are such important elements of participatory and action-oriented research (for example, Paulo Freire's approach, see Freire, 1970).

Overall, the participatory elements of this research allowed the author to build enduring relationships. It helped to lay a foundation for future work in Zimbabwe. This could be an important outcome, as trust and shared experience are building blocks for any successful development work. By the time it ended, the research project had built an excellent springboard for initiating a collaborative participatory-action research project.

Perhaps the greatest weakness of the research was a lack of resources to directly translate and transcribe from Shona to English. Therefore, when participants at meetings and interviews spoken primarily in Shona, the author received only a paraphrased translation. As English was spoken fluently by professionals and government employees, language was not a challenge in meetings with such individuals. However, five of the seven women farmers did not speak English fluently.

PRELIMINARY RESEARCH FINDINGS AND ANALYSIS

If we think we know who the 'women' are and set about to bring 'progress' to them, but the 'women' think of themselves in more complex ways, meanings will pass in the night and development projects that look good on paper will not necessarily work on the ground... 'Women' is not a fixed reference point, a natalist or 'shy' subject status. It is variable in the eyes of its holder and it needs, therefore, to be variable in the eyes of its assignors and helpers. It is a term that should invite some healthy confusion about the changing gender meanings in development rather than the place of women in/and 'it'. (Sylvester, 2000, p209)

The key findings and brief analysis provided in this section represent snapshots of work to be expanded (Gabel, 2003). The works of Mbiba (1995, 2000) and Mudimu (1996) sought in part to raise awareness of women's participation in UA in Harare. This research builds on their work and helps to establish a greater awareness of urban open-space farming through gender analysis. The conclusion drawn from the present research is that women's adoption of urban open-space cultivation in the 1950s and 1960s was a persistent means of resisting, deflating or blunting patriarchal control within and outside the household.[4] As in other areas where urban women have chosen to pursue independent enterprises, they have had to cope with the negative perceptions that neighbours, planners and decision-makers have of urban farming. Portrayals of women in Zimbabwe and elsewhere in southern Africa have been discussed by Gaidzanwa (1985), McFadden (1992), Meena (1992), Ncube (1995), Zhou (1995), ZWRCN (1995), Abraham (1999), Barnes (1999), Hodgson and McCurdy (2001) and Mvududu and McFadden (2001). Studies have shown that many farmers are aware of the illegality of farming without permission, yet they continue to do so (Mudimu, 1996; Martin et al, 2000). This is done, not out of ignorance or a wish to conduct illegal activities, but out of necessity, as many have claimed (Schmidt, 1990, 1991, 1992; Gaidzanwa, 1992; Zhou, 1995; Barnes, 1999; Sylvester, 2000), and – as I assert – as a form of continued resistance to the barriers these early women residents and later entrants have had to face. They have demonstrated their ability to acquire access to large tracts of undeveloped urban land and maintain control of that land through the development of a complex informal land-tenure system, established over time through a web of women's support networks. In a country where women are still fighting for legal control and ownership of land, women's predominance in urban open-space cultivation attests to the very real presence of urban women in the city, expresses their entitlement to urban land, and demonstrates how significantly women have shaped the form and function of their urban environment. In addition, other forms of power and control are operative within the UA milieu in Harare, making the analysis more complex and uncertain and expanding it beyond the issue of gender.

The research was conducted with a group of seven urban women farmers, most of whom were in their middle to late 50s. On the surface, the group could appear homogeneous, as the women were similar in age, resided in their own homes, lived within several blocks of one another, cultivated in the city, were most of them (four of the seven) the heads of their households and were all women. However, although the women were unified in the ways they defined their urban-farming needs, interviews with individual women often revealed diverse interests, ideas and experiences. For the purpose of this paper, the focus will be on their stated shared needs for urban farming.[5]

In the analysis, two major difficulties were encountered when trying to fit the findings from the research into Moser's (1993) framework on practical and strategic needs. First, the assignment of needs to the two categories seemed to force complex findings into a dualistic conceptual framework. Some needs seemed to fit both the concept of practical needs and that of strategic need, rendering the assignment somewhat purposeless and making the framework perhaps less useful for meaningful application. Second, the a priori decision to analyse and fit my findings into Moser's framework seems to be a renunciation of the feminist approach and methods, particularly that of embracing the complexity of everyday experience, rather than reinforcing reductionism and dualistic thinking. Such shortcomings of Moser's framework have indeed been documented elsewhere. Wieringa has given a detailed critique of Moser's distinction between practical and strategic needs. She states that 'Moser's conflation of needs and interests means that the more flexible, intentional and therefore political category of interests is replaced by the more static category of needs, which coheres in planning discourse' (Wieringa, 1998, p362). Furthermore, Imam (1997, p4) has questions similar to those in Wieringa's paper: 'Who has the abstract authority to define what are practical and what are strategic needs?' This critique of Moser's framework, as well as the difficulty experienced in applying the framework to this research, suggests that an alternative form of analysis is required.[6] The complexity and challenges of addressing the everyday experiences this group of women encounter, as I discovered through interviews, personal observation, action strategies and literature reviews, are illustrated in the following subsections.

Land

The farmers have acquired land in the city, but this in itself has not necessarily helped to significantly improve their food security, owing to the interdependence of land-use and other needs, as well as other dimensions of local power and control discussed in this section.

The women frequently stated that the control, use and ownership of land (without fear) would be significant to them. The complex informal land-tenure system is one manifestation of how urban women have gained control and ownership of land. In this section, an initial summary of the informal land system is presented; this summary is based on discussions with the farmers on how they have accessed land for urban cultivation.

Original ownership, a category of informal ownership (references to original ownership occur in the work of Mudimu (1996) and Martin et al (2000)), applies in the case of farmers, mostly women, who started the practice in the 1950s and 1960s. Greater amounts of undeveloped land were available at that time, as family housing was just starting to be built for African urban residents. These women were therefore able to farm large areas of land. Most people had minimal interest in urban farming at that time. One of the farmers who participated in this research had more than seven fields (some of which have now been taken over for development of housing and industry). Many of the fields of latecomers to urban farming have come from these original owners, as the women would subdivide their fields to assist friends and family in need or want. Therefore, these farmers (one woman called this group the 'Kings', which alludes to the kind of power and prestige such women hold) do possess control over these cultivated spaces, but the accommodation of so many newcomers points to the generosity of many of the original owners, as well as perhaps to the reciprocity of their social networks. Four ways were identified in which original owners have passed on land, and in many cases ownership, to other women (this is also verified by Mudimu (1996) and Martin et al (2000)): gift-giving, inheritance, selling and lending. In the first three cases, the recipients of the land become the new owners. Those who lend their fields do so with the clear understanding that they retain ownership and are free to claim their field at the onset of the next growing season. This causes some difficulties for the recipients if the owners are uncertain about using that field themselves that year. Women will often wait for permission to use the land if the owner remains uncertain and may end up planting well after the first rains have fallen, thus constraining yields, as well as inducing stress on the dependent farmer. In addition, many women are constantly on the lookout for land because of their temporary user status and the uncertainty and vulnerability that brings.

Other forms of land entitlement also exist. One type of particular interest is entitlement through provision of paid field labour (not known by this researcher to have been previously mentioned in the literature). One man who was employed by many women in one particular area made repeated use of this form of entitlement. He had built a makeshift structure on the land to keep a watchful eye on the comings and goings of farmers. When farmers came to look for fields, he would provide information, but at a cost (he might insist that they employ him to clear the field, as a finder's fee). Such stories reveal the kinds of manipulation and control that other actors have in the informal tenure system and how the kinds of networks that women have adopted may differ from those involving men.

Other informal channels that have developed for accessing land may include more overt conflict and power dynamics. One self-proclaimed community-based organization is headed by an outspoken and energetic man, who founded the organization and stated that his membership base is 99 per cent women. They came to claim the fields surrounding their suburb in what he says was a 2- to 3-month confrontation, in which his group apparently picked up their hoes to fight for the land.[7]

Questions should be raised about the stakes for women already engaged in farming when new forms of organization and participation spring up spontaneously, as in this case. The informal land-tenure system established by earlier residents, many of whom are urban women, is being challenged by new entrants, urban development and land grabbing. Many urban women do not necessarily have claim to land in rural areas (Gaidzanwa, 1992; Moyo, 1995), including six of the seven women in this research. The threat of losing the control and access they have managed to procure over the years may be very real, especially given the rapid economic decline experienced currently in Zimbabwe. Giving the women the ability to own or work land without fear is one of the crucial challenges within the field of UA.

Organizational support

Organizational support is another complex factor to consider and one that takes several forms. First, the women could use assistance in organizing their UA activities to maximize the benefits to themselves. In group discussions in preparation for a presentation they were to give at a UA workshop, the women identified a list of needs in their urban farming practices. These are presented in Table 4.1.

Table 4.1 *UA needs identified by urban women farmers*

Exact words, as agreed by the women	English translation
Kuwana munda nedurim usingatye	We want to get the land and cultivate without fear
Mitengo yakaderera pane zvinhu zvekurimisa sembeu nefetiraiza	We need affordable prices for farming inputs
Kudzidziswa nzira dzekurima dziri nyore uye dzinoda mari shoma • Kukudza goho/kukohwa zvakawanda patuminda tudiki • Kushandisa fetiraiza: Uwandu, Inoiswa sei, Nenguva ipi • Mbeu dzinoenderana nevhu uye mvura inonaya muHarare • Kuchinja kwezvinhu mukurima	We want to be trained in easier and cheaper farming methods: • How to increase yields • Fertilizer usage – what kind, how much, and how to apply • Matching seed types to soil and climate in Harare • Innovations and new technologies
Kuchengetedza minda kuti tisabirwe	We want security from theft for our little plots
Tingawana sei uye kupi mari ingatibatsira kurima nyangwe zvikwereti zvinowirirana nesu	How can we get some money to assist us in our farming – even credit or loans that are suitable for us?
Dzimwewo mbeswa/mbeu dzisiri chibage? • Dzingatiwanisa mari • Tingadzirima sei uye tinowana kupi zvingadiwa pakudzirima	What other crops can we grow besides maize? • Cash crops? • How can we cultivate these, and where can we get inputs?
Tinotenda neuyu musangano asi taifara kana muchiti yeukawo kuti muite nechishona zvizhinji	We thank you for this workshop, but we would be happier if you would consider doing most of your things in Shona
Zvingatibatsirawo pakuchengeta/kuriritira mhuri dzedu sezvo takura kudai	We want to know if there are any other alternatives that will help us take care of our families, since we are advanced in age

Table 4.2 *Estimates from seven farmers for the 2000/01 growing season*

	Estimated total quantity produced in kg (value in ZWD)	Estimated total quantity of loss from theft, spoilage, and sharing in kg (value in ZWD)	Estimated total cost of farming in ZWD
Farmer 1 (7 fields)	1800 (33,300)	450 (sharing, theft, and spoilage) (8325)	13,900 (food given to hired labour and cost of preservative not included)
Farmer 2 (2 fields)	165 (3076)	50 (just shared; unable to estimate amount stolen) (694)	714
Farmer 3 (2 fields)	80 (1387)	25 (shared and stolen) (208)	890 (plus blanket and clothes in return for labour)
Farmer 4 (3 fields)	120 (2035)	80 (just stolen; unable to estimate amount shared) (1110)	1737
Farmer 5 (3 fields)	112 (1908)	No estimate (uncertain about how much shared; little theft)	4475
Farmer 6 (2 fields)	Uncertain (just harvested green mealies that lasted only 1 week)	Uncertain	434 (cost of grinding not included)
Farmer 7 (2 fields)	195 (3029)	20 (stolen only; unable to estimate amount shared) (462)	780 (cost of grinding not included)

Note: ZWD, Zimbabwe dollars (in 2003, 816.86 ZWD = 1 USD).

The women were quite aware of their needs and constraints. Data from postharvest interviews with the farmers also suggest that the output of food from farming is sometimes marginal, especially when the significant costs of theft and inputs – particularly fertilizers and seeds that are often purchased in small quantities at inflated prices – are factored in. Table 4.2 provides a summary of the estimates given by the farmers for their 2000/01 growing season (estimates for quantities produced refer to maize only). These numbers, it should be noted, are based on the best estimates each women could give, as they do not record the costs of their expenditures. In addition, the dollar values attributed to the amounts of maize are based on several assumptions. First, the women often referred to buckets harvested, not actual kilograms; therefore, given information from the women, one bucket was estimated as equal to

Table 4.3 *Specific costs and details of the women's farming*

Farmers	Cost of inputs as a percentage of output[a]	Percentage of costs dedicated to purchasing fertilizers	Percentage of costs dedicated to hiring labour	Help provided by children or husband in farming	Help (hired or otherwise) with land preparation and planting
Farmer 1 (harvest lasted the whole year)	66	29	31	Yes	Yes
Farmer 2 (harvest lasted 8 weeks)	46	48	28 (+direct exchange)	No	Yes
Farmer 3 (harvest lasted 8 weeks)	79	49	Direct exchange only	No	Yes
Farmer 4 (harvest lasted 3 months)	140 (with high high level of 85 (with theft excluded)	30	37	No	Yes
Farmer 5 (harvest lasted 8 weeks)	235	67	0	No	No
Farmer 6 (harvest lasted 1 week)	Uncertain	38	0	No	No
Farmer 7 (harvest lasted 2 months)	41	59	32	Yes	No

Note: a) Output = quantity harvested for household consumption.

20kg. Second, the value of mealie meal (the ground maize used to make their staple food, *sadza*) was calculated using the current retail price (as of June 2001) of a 10kg bag of mealie meal if purchased at a grocery store. Third, an important part of the harvest is the green mealies (corn cobs that are roasted and enjoyed on the cob). The value of green mealies was estimated from information that one bucket of these mealie cobs would produce one bucket of mealie meal. A more conservative figure was based on the assumption that one bucket of green mealies would give a three-quarter bucket of mealie meal. Lastly, and very importantly, a dollar value was not given for the labour each of the women and their family members invested, so their labour has not been factored into the costs of their farming.

Some interesting information can be further derived from Table 4.2, especially about the cost ratio of inputs to outputs and the costs of fertilizer use and hired labour. Table 4.3 summarizes this information.

Practices

As shown in Table 4.3, in two cases, the actual cost of inputs exceeded the value of the maize consumed within the household. Generally, fertilizers accounted for the greatest proportion of the costs of farming. What is particularly distressing is that except in farmer 4's case, the benefits derived by the poorest farmers of the group (from two households that were experiencing hunger) were the most marginal. The poorest farmers were also dedicating a larger portion than the others of their actual financial resources to purchasing fertilizers (when their ability to pay with cash was most constrained). In only two cases were children or husbands going to help in the fields (which demonstrates that – in all but one case – urban farming, if classified as a household activity without clarifying who in the household engages in it, would misrepresent the realities of whose labour is provided and who bears the challenges, stress and costs of providing it). Given the age of the women (most were in their middle to late 50s), the majority of them needed and wanted assistance with land preparation and planting, the most arduous tasks of their farming. The seven in-depth postharvest interviews revealed many useful insights. Collectively purchasing inputs (as most purchases are made in small quantities, requiring additional trips, time and expense) and switching to alternative farming methods (which would decrease the reliance on fertilizer inputs) are just two simple ways the farmers could make their actual farming practices less dependent on cash (none of the women are formally employed). But both of these initiatives would require organizational support.

These tables cannot, however, show the nonquantifiable benefits UA provides to the women farmers. The women expressed pleasure at being able to share their green mealie cobs (which is a favourite treat at harvest time) with family, neighbours, friends and lodgers. The harvest time is talked about with excitement and pride (perhaps even elevating their status within the household and their neighbourhood during this period), indicating that the value they place on their maize outputs is more than dollar figures alone can account for. The marginal benefits might seem worth their labour and time if the women can bring home fresh produce and mealie cobs during the harvest.

A concern is the on-again-off-again organizational support for UA from urban authorities and decision-makers since the mid-1980s. No matter what directive is dictated from above, women in Zimbabwe have continued to cultivate with or without permission, and they have, importantly, chosen to cultivate individually, as opposed to collectively (Mbiba, 1995), as have the women farmers in this research. In 1985 (five years after Zimbabwe's independence), the then Ministry of Local Government and Town Planning sent out a circular encouraging urban authorities to promote income-generating projects through co-operatives, and it spoke directly to the need to organize UA. The prime minister was quoted as saying:

> I have discussed with the Ministries of Local Government ...
> about the need for agricultural co-operatives near all our urban
> areas. This, we feel, will harness the unguided energies of our

> *women, who till every available piece of land which is idle,*
> *including that which is near streams. These women should be*
> *properly organised by you into co-operatives so that every*
> *morning they leave the urban centres to go to their vegetable or*
> *maize fields.* (GRZ, 1985)

Male urban authorities, both pre- and post-independence, have preoccupied themselves with the control of urban women, and this circular demonstrates that fact poignantly with regard to UA.[8] Participation in the co-operative movement in urban areas became the only mechanism through which women could legally acquire land and resources for their farming activities.

The comprehensive research of Christine Sylvester speaks to the marginalization of women's productive labour by government efforts to promote co-operatives. In her analysis, Sylvester (2000) documents the shifting placement of the responsibility for the promotion of co-operatives and the promotion of women, reinforcing strong associations between women, informal employment and co-operatives. After independence, in 1980, the government pursued a Marxist–Leninist path (Sylvester documents the simultaneous influence of authoritarianism and liberalism in various policies pursued between 1980 and the early 1990s) and therefore promoted co-operative production. Women's participation in the struggle for independence had earned them dubious inclusion in the government's employment strategies, namely, designs to organize women into co-operatives for the benefit of society and the well-being of the family. However, government enthusiasm and commitment to the co-operative movement declined quickly. Initially, co-operatives were promoted within the president's office, but were subsequently delegated to the Ministry of Agriculture, Lands and Resettlement:

> *In 1986, a formal Ministry of Co-operatives was created. A year*
> *and half after that, however, the ministry was merged with the*
> *Ministry of Community Development and Women's Affairs, at*
> *which point a narrative link was established between 'women'*
> *and 'co-operatives'. Co-operatives as an authority area, was then*
> *hived off in 1989 from the Women's ministry to form half of the*
> *new Ministry of Community and Co-operative Development.*
> (Sylvester, 2000, p78)

The responsibility for co-operatives was later moved again, this time to the new Ministry of National Affairs, Employment Creation and Co-operatives, which had a mission to:

> *facilitate the creation of an enabling environment for the*
> *promotion of employment generation focusing on women, the*
> *youths and the unemployed through the provision of training and*
> *the development of small and medium scale enterprises ... and*
> *co-operatives as well as the informal sector.* (GRZ, 1996 [1995],
> p99)

Two departments were established under this ministry: one was responsible for employment creation; the other, for co-operatives, women and youth development. However, in July 2000, another shift occurred, and co-operatives are now under the jurisdiction of the newly created Ministry of Youth, Development, Gender and Employment Creation. This department is located within party headquarters and is said to be still promoting co-operatives (despite the acknowledged and evident neglect and failure of the same (Nyathi and Hoffman, 1990; Sylvester, 2000)), as well as promoting micro and informal-sector projects. Meanwhile, the Ministry of Industry and Commerce remains unfettered by gender-mainstreaming policies.

It became evident that the women in this research and many others in their neighbourhood had created a variety of support networks to assist themselves, as suggestions from local politicians to form co-operatives had never materialized and had remained a form of unconvincing propaganda. Food is often shared with those who are without; money is lent, land is given, and goods and required information are exchanged between women in their neighbourhoods. As Mvududu and McFadden (2001, p234) note: 'the reaction to economic decline may be to diversify and build social networks as a form of safety net and flexible access to new resources'. Given the networks they have, these women need a type of organizational support fundamentally different from what has thus far been thrust down from above. A precondition of many current assistance projects and programmes is that women be organized (many NGOs, and even women's organizations, expect this), and it was found during the research that even when women do get organized, the assistance will still not come easy or at all. Many examples of this are found in Sylvester's (2000) research on women and co-operatives in Zimbabwe.

In this research, one of the group action strategies the women wanted to explore was to generate ideas for projects and ways they could engage in these projects. Their preference was to do individual projects, but as a group they wished to open a group savings account and have each member make an agreed monthly contribution. This is what they did, and each started to raise chickens in their yards. However, the only women's organization that took any interest in providing them with advice told the women, without even coming to visit them or finding out what each of their plans and activities were, that they should all be engaged in the same projects. So, they are each doing the same project, despite their diverse interests. Perhaps other options could be explored, ones not negating the possibility of individual determination and needs but allowing for the expression of difference, as this seemed particularly important to each of the women. Wanzala (1998, p18) argued that individual representation and difference, although presenting 'a challenge to epistemology, methodology and policy as prerequisites to social action, ... also has the potential to act as a facilitator of epistemological transformations and ultimately of social transformation'. Finding what these new forms of organizational support are requires time, sensitivity, commitment and resources. Without organizational support for women to organize around UA, decisions will be made without their direct input or will be made by self-appointed leaders or spokespersons.

Access to decision-makers, planners and NGOs

Access alone does not seem to be sufficient for women's voices to be heard and incorporated into dialogue or decision-making processes. Despite action strategies that provided access to planners and NGOs within the research, the women derived no direct benefit, and these ties were not sustained afterward. Mention has already been made of a community-based UA organization. The leader of this group harnessed many resources for his organization, from both the private and the public sectors. Companies, such as Monsanto,[9] are giving them training, seeds and other inputs for free, and their patron is the minister of Mines and Energy. This group leader, who is without a phone or his own transportation, is very mobile and seems to know his way around. The women in this research project did not have the time or the resources to run around, nor did they desire to use his approach. The women were invited to join his group but declined. One woman said they would get lost, because the leader moved too fast. Free seeds and training were not enough to sway them. So how do these women get their voices heard and responded to? Such questions still remain and may in part be symptomatic of impacts of patriarchal relations within society, as well as within the NGO–donor community.

REFLECTIONS FOR FURTHER RESEARCH

A great deal of research could be proposed. However, from the data and analysis shared in this paper, a few ideas only will be mentioned:

- Research on women's everyday support networks would be useful, as a means of obtaining a better understanding of the ways women organize and of the barriers to developing other organizational strategies. This could be undertaken as an ethnographic study or as a study using other sociological or anthropological methods. In addition, complementary research could be undertaken to determine how women and men *want* to organize for UA, in particular examining mechanisms allowing them to effectively participate in decision-making.
- More research on urban land conflicts would also be helpful, as many types of conflicts are taking place, often beyond the awareness and knowledge of unaffected people, especially decision-makers, planners and policy makers. Using a feminist methodology helps to ensure that issues of gender, class, imperialism and race are addressed. This would be a very sensitive area of research.
- Farmers could benefit from research documenting in detail the inputs and the outputs, from planting to postharvest. An historical study could be undertaken to specifically investigate the emergence of urban open-space cultivation over time, revealing the main actors and so forth.
- It would be wonderful to document the stories of the original cultivators, most of whom were women. Such a research endeavour would further

explore UA from a gender perspective, perhaps revealing some of the push factors that led women to begin cultivation in the city.

- Finally, action research could be used to involve feminist researchers and local gender expertise in the debate on UA and, in particular, to help to identify the possible resource requirements and constraints, risks and benefits (for various stakeholders) of intervening in UA with the intent of developing strategies, plans, and policies supportive of the everyday lives and needs of women in urban areas.

IMPACTS OF THE FIELD RESEARCH GRANT

Human resources development

Although no formal training was provided, the research project gave the researcher and the research assistants new experiences in:

- doing research in an urban context;
- using qualitative methods;
- facilitating action-oriented research.

All four research assistants indicated that their participation was useful to them in some form or other. One of the women found a job in the development field during the research and claimed it was her participation in this research that helped her to clinch the job, as she drew on her experiences from the work she had done.

Another important impact of the research was that the women farmers formed their own group and even gave themselves a name. A small amount of money was fundraised by the researcher that enabled them to undertake projects of their own choice, as they indicated was their preference. They also decided to open a group savings account, to which all of them would contribute monthly. Correspondence they continue to send indicates the success of their initiatives.

Gender-sensitive analysis

The diverse nature of UA opens many opportunities for an interdisciplinary examination of the context in which the practice is embedded. The research reported here, and to be complemented elsewhere (Gabel, 2003), represents a modest (and external) attempt to integrate the gender dimensions into research on urban open-space farming in Harare. It expands the gender discourse on UA by locating the practice of urban farming by women in a wider sociopolitical context, including research on women and gender from other disciplines. This has revealed that many of the specific gender interests identified by women farmers emerge in similar forms in gender research from other disciplines or areas of study.

The research reveals the need to explore alternative, Zimbabwean strategies for analysing the concerns, experiences and needs of women so that these can be more easily taken up by policy makers. There is some indication that gender as a construct for analysis and as a platform for intervention may not be well understood as a social science methodology (Kaneez Hasna, 1998). This modest beginning, it is hoped, will provide an opening for further dialogue on what may be entailed in putting gender on the agenda of UA in Zimbabwe.

Lastly, other than this research, feminist methodology seems to be absent from studies of UA. In addition, few researchers have used qualitative methods[10] or methods other than standard survey questionnaires, on-site interviews with farmers, and quantitative techniques for analysis. It is unfortunate that the research on UA in Zimbabwe has not involved more discussion of methods and methodologies; perhaps this is the area in which this study's contribution to the research on UA in Zimbabwe is both useful and unique.

Institutional strengthening and effectiveness of local partnerships

As part of the approach taken in this research, an internship placement was organized for the author with MDP–ESA, an NGO designated as the regional focal point by the Resource Centre on Urban Agriculture and Forestry (RUAF) for eastern and southern Africa. The involvement with MDP–ESA provided institutional strengthening, as well as creating an effective local partnership during the second stage of the research. The first meeting at MDP–ESA was held near the end of the first visit to Zimbabwe. With Shingi Mushamba, the co-ordinator of the UA programme, discussion took place on the need to improve networking and information-sharing, and contacts were shared in organizing the first UA stakeholder forum, in mid-December of 2000. The forum has continued to operate, and its membership has increased. The author's role during the internship with MDP–ESA was to provide support to Mr Mushamba in the management and delivery of the UA programme. This entailed writing reports to RUAF; editing the proceedings from a workshop on the political economy of UA in eastern and southern Africa, jointly sponsored by the International Development Research Centre (IDRC) and MDP–ESA; organizing stakeholder forums; increasing the visibility of the UA programme at MDP–ESA through new contacts and public appearances; assisting with proposal development; and numerous other responsibilities. This partnership with MDP–ESA complemented the research reported here, as MDP–ESA staff allowed a flexible work schedule, encouraged the women farmers to participate in workshops and stakeholder forums, shared their own knowledge and information and because they were good listeners.

Professor Mudimu, from the Department of Agricultural Economics and Extension at the University of Zimbabwe, was also a key affiliation for the author, as he provided the necessary support during the first stage of research.

Dialogue was initiated with the Canadian Institute of Planners (CIP) to discuss opportunities for a partnership between MDP–ESA and CIP's WorldLinks Program to sponsor an intern placement at MDP–ESA to work with the UA programme. Because of a change in focus, CIP may not continue its internship programme, so other opportunities for sponsoring interns are being examined.

Also, the author's academic adviser, Nora Angeles, has gained more interest in UA. Her expertise is in rural agriculture in Southeast Asia. A paper she wrote on gender and UA in the Philippines, her native country and where she conducts much of her research, appeared in Urban Agriculture Magazine (Angeles, 2002).

Finally, information on the networking and informal meetings with stakeholders or those with interests in UA in Zimbabwe is being compiled in a resource guide on UA in Zimbabwe, which will be published through MDP–ESA.

Use of research results

Several contacts have proved to be useful in sharing information on UA in Zimbabwe. Nicoliene Oudwater at the Natural Resources Institute (NRI) undertook research in 2000 on UA in Zimbabwe, and information exchanges with her took place at the beginning of the research project. A paper by the author submitted to the NRI on methodologies used to study UA was used by NRI researchers in their analysis of methods and subsequently cited in their own paper: 'Methodologies for situation analysis in urban agriculture' (Martin et al, 2002). This was a paper prepared for the ETC-Netherlands e-Conference on Appropriate Methodologies for Urban Agriculture (the paper can be accessed through the RUAF web site). Contacts with other researchers have generally been for networking and information-sharing, but requests for publications stemming from the author's research have also been received from NGOs and academics, such as the World Watch Institute and Beacon Mbiba. Plans for further dissemination of this research are being developed, including a chapter in a book on social capital, as well as briefs focusing on planning, gender, women and UA.

CONCLUSION AND RECOMMENDATIONS

This research, conducted in Highfield, Harare with seven women farmers, provided useful insights into their needs as food providers and cultivators. It also revealed gender interests related to UA in Harare and to broader sociopolitical constraints that urban Zimbabwean women (a significantly underresearched group) confront. This, in turn, creates barriers that make it difficult to fully integrate a gender analysis in UA work in Zimbabwe. The identified need for organizational support for women cultivators must be addressed, as there is some evidence that the push to formally support and organize UA has marginalized and added to the stress on some groups of women farmers.

The incorporation of participation and action into the research took many forms and proved to be a useful way of gaining insight into the challenges that women face to be heard, to locate support and to derive benefit, as well as of gaining appreciation for the timeliness and institutional support it requires.

The field of UA research creates a space for many disciplines to embark on gender research in Zimbabwe. Disciplines such as history, sociology or anthropology could enrich our understanding of women's early involvement in UA by more profoundly documenting and contextualizing its historical beginnings. Gender-sensitive research to help farmers maximize the benefits of their urban farming would be another critical area to explore. Action research that examines how UA research and development can foster the participation of Zimbabwean (or Southern African) gender specialists and feminist scholars could broaden and enrich the work currently under way.

It is hoped that the data, analysis and insights shared in this paper, but ultimately in the thesis and future dissemination initiatives, will be of use to those involved, even if in a small way. Many wonderful things grow from small and humble beginnings.

ACKNOWLEDGEMENTS

This research project benefited from the generous support and time of many individuals and organizations, without whom this personally valuable learning experience would not have been possible. Financial and material support was generously provided by IDRC's AGROPOLIS programme, the CIP and the MDP–ESA. The CIP, through its Student Scholarship Program, awarded me $1000, which paid for my tuition fees while I was in Zimbabwe and helped me to purchase useful resource materials for my research.

I would also like to acknowledge the support of Professor Godfrey Mudimu, from the University of Zimbabwe; Mary Kabelele, from the Participatory Ecological Land Use Management Association; and Tendayi Mutimukuru, Shepherd Siziba, Regina Nyagwande, Tafadzwa Mapfawo, Nora Angeles, my family and friends, and notably the women from Highfield.

In addition to the funding mentioned above, I am grateful for various other contributions: Shingi Mushamba generously donated his combi (a minivan that provides public transportation) to allow the women farmers and myself to conduct our field trip. When all the local support avenues we explored did not materialize, my family and friends, donated US$400. This provided the start-up capital the women farmers needed to initiate their individual projects. Each woman was given the equivalent of US$50 in Zimbabwe dollars, and the remaining money was used to open a group savings account. RUAF generously gave me an honorarium for the use of the paper on methods submitted to the NRI. Approximately US$150 of that money was shared between the women farmers and used for their individual projects. MDP–ESA provided material support in various ways. During my second trip, they furnished me with a workspace, rented office furniture for me, and gave me access to their computers and email. Other contributions they made were not directly related to my research per se.

NOTES

1   Mrs. Charambira, acting Deputy Town Planner, Harare, Zimbabwe, personal communication, 2000.
2   See Bell Hooks (2000, p31) for her explanation of why it might be more beneficial to feminism for a person to state, 'I am an advocate for feminism', rather than state, 'I am a feminist'.
3   I would like to thank Diana Lee-Smith for her helpful recommendation that I read up on ethnomethodology (after I did so, I seemed to stumble across references to it frequently).
4   The appropriate wording is difficult to find here, as the emergence of urban food cultivation in open spaces can be viewed through so many lenses. A fuller treatise (Gabel, 2003) endeavours to expound on this proposition more adequately.
5   Although the women will be referred to as the women or the farmers, these are perhaps not the most desirable labels.
6   Alternatives are currently being explored and will be shared in future publications.
7   This was not the only case where the increased male interest in involvement in and control of urban open-space cultivation was witnessed. This may not necessarily be negative, but it becomes important to acknowledge the implications and impacts it produces.
8   During this same period, the early 1980s, the government instituted Operation Cleanup, an effort to clean up prostitution in cities. As Rudo Gaidzwana, a leading academic writer on gender and feminism in Zimbabwe, explained, this culminated in the round-up and arrests of women who were walking at night but were unable to produce marriage certificates. She explained further that 'the arrests ... were an attempt to reassert the social dominance of men, as well as the elders who were smarting from the perceived threats to their dominance over women within and outside households' (Gaidzwana, 1992, p115). As can be imagined, this initiative raised a lot of controversy. Although less confrontational, the organization of women into co-operatives can be categorized as one of many forms of patriarchal control. Efforts to control women and their sexuality have also been researched (McFadden, 1992; Amanor-Wilks, 1996; Zinanga, 1996).
9   Monsanto has been offering free inputs and training to urban farmers as part of their efforts to expand the marketing of their products to rural households and farmers.
10   Beacon Mbiba, although he does not discuss his methodology or methods specifically, has used qualitative methods, such as participant observation, photography, and ethnography, to some degree (Mbiba, 1995).

REFERENCES

Abraham, K. N. (1999) 'Resistance innovations in African feminist literary discourse: African women negotiating cultures of resistance', in McFadden, P. (ed), *Reflections on Gender Issues in Africa*, Sapes Books, Harare, Zimbabwe, pp1–18

Amanor-Wilks, D. (1996) 'Invisible hands: Women in Zimbabwe's commercial farm sector', *Southern African Feminist Review*, vol 2, no 1, pp58–80

Angeles, N. (2002) 'The struggle for sustainable livelihood: Gender and organic agriculture in Valencia City, Philippines', *Urban Agriculture Magazine*, vol 6, pp32–33

Barnes, T. (1999) *We Women Worked So Hard: Gender, Urbanization and Social Reproduction in Colonial Harare, Zimbabwe, 1930–1956*, Heineman, Portsmouth, NH

Bowles, G. and Klein, R. D. (eds) (1983) *Theories of Women's Studies*, Routledge, London

Brinton Lykes, M. (1997) 'Activist participatory research among the Maya of Guatemala: Constructing meaning from situated knowledge', *Journal of Social Issues*, vol 53, no 4, pp725–746

Chambers, R. (1997) *Whose Reality Counts? Putting the First Last*, Intermediate Technology Publication Ltd, London

Chataway, C. J. (1997) 'An examination of the constraints on mutual inquiry in a participatory action research project', *Journal of Social Issues*, vol 53, no 4, pp747–765

Collins, P. H. (1998) *Fighting Words: Black Women and the Search for Justice*. University of Minnesota Press, Minneapolis, MN

Fals-Borda, O. and Rahman, M. A. (eds) (1991) *Action and Knowledge: Breaking the Monopoly with Participatory Action Research*. Apex Press, New York, NY

Financial Gazette (2001a) 'Fingaz food price monitor', *Financial Gazette*, 14–20 June

Financial Gazette (2001b) 'Fingaz food price monitor', *Financial Gazette*, 23–29 August

Frankenberg, R. (1993) *The Social Construction of Whiteness: White Women, Race Matters*, University of Minnesota Press, Minneapolis, MN

Freire, P. (1970) *Pedagogy of the Oppressed*, Continuum Publishing Company, New York, NY

Freire, P. and Faundez, A. (1989) *Learning to Question: A Pedagogy of Liberation*, Continuum Publishing Company, New York, NY

Freire, P. and Horton, M. (1990) *We Make the Road by Walking: Conversations on Education and Social Change*, Temple University Press, Philadelphia, PA

Gabel, S. (2003) 'Urban agriculture, policy, planning and feminism: Revealing complexity through hands, hearts and actions', The University of British Columbia, Vancouver, BC, Canada. MA thesis.

Gaidzanwa, R. (1985) *Images of Women in Zimbabwean Literature*, College Press Publishers, Harare, Zimbabwe

Gaidzanwa, R. (1992) 'Bourgeois theories of gender and feminism and their shortcomings with reference to southern African countries', in Meena (1992), pp92–125

GRZ (Government of the Republic of Zimbabwe) (1985) Local Government Circular, No. 81, 10 Jan. Ministry of Local Government and Town Planning, GRZ, Harare, Zimbabwe

GRZ (1996 [1995]) Constitution of Zimbabwe (revised edition). GRZ, Harare, Zimbabwe

Guijt, I. and Kaul Shah, M. (eds) (1998) *The Myth of Community: Gender Issues in Participatory Development*, Intermediate Technology Publication Ltd, London

Harding, S. (1987) *Feminism and Methodology*, Indiana University Press; Open University Press, Stratford, UK

Hodgson, D. and McCurdy, S. (eds) (2001) *'Wicked' Women and the Reconfiguration of Gender in Africa*, Heinemann, Portsmouth, NH

Hooks, B. (2000) *Feminist Theory: From Margin to Center*, South End Press, Cambridge, MA

Horton, M. (1990) *The Long Haul: An Autobiography*, Doubleday, New York

Imam, A.M. (1997) 'Engendering African social sciences: An introductory essay', in Imam, A., Mama, A. and Sow, F. (eds), *Engendering African Social Sciences*, Council for the Development of Social Science Research in Africa, Dakar, Senegal, pp 1–30

Kaneez Hasna, M. (1998) 'NGO gender capacity in urban agriculture: Case studies from Harare (Zimbabwe), Kampala (Uganda) and Accra (Ghana)', International Development Research Centre, Ottawa, ON, Canada. Cities Feeding People Series, Report 21. Available at http://www.idrc.ca/cfp/rep21_e.html

Keller, E. F. (1985) *Reflections on Gender and Science*, Yale University Press, New Haven, CT

Kirby, S. and McKenna, K. (1989) *Experience, Research, Social Change: Methods from the Margins*, Garamond Press, Toronto, ON

Martin, A., Oudwater, N. and Meadows, K. (2000) 'Urban agriculture and the livelihood of the poor in southern Africa', Paper presented at the International Symposium on Urban Agriculture and Horticulture: The Linkage with Urban Planning, 7–9 July, Berlin, Germany. Sponsored by TRIALOG, Vienna, Austria; Humboldt-University, Berlin, Germany; HABITAT, Havana, Cuba

Martin, A., Oudwater, N. and Gundel, S. (2002) 'Methodologies for situation analysis in urban agriculture', Paper presented at the e-Conference on Appropriate Methodologies for Urban Agriculture: Research, Policy Development, Planning, Implementation and Evaluation, 4–16 February, ETC-Netherlands, Netherlands

Mbiba, B. (1995) *Urban Agriculture in Zimbabwe*, Ashgate Publishing Ltd, Aldershot

Mbiba, B. (2000) 'Urban agriculture in Harare: Between suspicion and repression', in Bakker, N., Dubelling, M., Gründel, S., Sabel-Koschella, U. and de Zeeuw, H. (eds), *Growing Cities, Growing Food*, Deutsche Stiftung für Internationale Entwicklung, Feldafing, Germany

McFadden, P. (1992) 'Sex, sexuality and the problems of AIDS in Africa', in Meena, R. (ed), *Gender in Southern Africa: Conceptual and Theoretical Issues*, SAPES Books, Harare, Zimbabwe, pp157–195

Meena, R. (ed). (1992) *Gender in Southern Africa: Conceptual and Theoretical Issues*, SAPES Books, Harare

Mies, M. (1983) 'Toward a methodology for feminist research', in Bowles and Klein (1983), pp117–139

Mohanty, C. (1991) 'Under Western eyes: Feminist scholarship and colonial discourses', in Mohanty, C., Russo, A. and Torres, L. (eds), *Third World Women and the Politics of Feminism*, Indiana University Press, Bloomington, pp51–80

Moser, C. (1993) *Gender Planning and Development: Theory, Practice and Training*, Routledge, New York, NY

Moyo, S. (1995) 'A gendered perspective on the land question', *Southern African Feminist Review*, vol 1, no 1, pp13–31

Mudimu, G. (1996) 'Urban agricultural activities and women's strategies in sustaining family livelihoods in Harare, Zimbabwe', *Singapore Journal of Tropical Geography*, vol 17, no 2, pp179–194

Mvududu, S. and McFadden, P. (eds) (2001) *Reconceptualizing the Family in a Changing Southern African Environment*, Women in Law Southern Africa Research Trust, Harare

Ncube, S. (1995) 'Ideologies on everyday life among finalists at the University of Zimbabwe' in Sithole-Fundire, S., Zhou, A., Larsson, A. and Schlyter, A. (eds), *Gender Research on Urbanization, Planning, Housing and Everyday Life*, Zimbabwe Women's Resource Centre and Network, Harare, pp145–162

Nelson, N. and Wright, S. (eds) (1995) *Power and Participatory Development: Theory and Practice*, Intermediate Technology Publication Ltd, London

Nieuwenhuys, O. (1997) 'Spaces for the children of the urban poor: Experiences with participatory action research', *Environment and Urbanization*, vol 9, no 1, pp233–249

Nussbaum, M. (2000) *Women and Human Development*, Cambridge University Press, Cambridge

Nyathi, A. and Hoffman, J. (1990) *Tomorrow is Built Today*, Anvil Press, Harare

Rakodi, C. (1995) *Harare: Inheriting a Settler-Colonial City – Change or Continuity*, John Wiley & Sons, Inc., New York

Reinharz, S. (1983) 'Experiential analysis: A contribution to feminist research', in Bowles Klein (1983), pp162–191

Reinharz, S. (1992) *Feminist Methods in Social Research*, Oxford University Press, New York, NY

Rutenberg, T. (1983) 'Learning women's studies', in Bowles and Klein (1983), pp72–78

Schmidt, E. (1990) 'Negotiated spaces and contested terrain: Men, women, and the law in colonial Zimbabwe, 1890–1939', *Journal of Southern African Studies*, vol 16, no 4, pp622–648

Schmidt, E. (1991) 'Patriarchy, capitalism, and the colonial state in Zimbabwe', *Signs: Journal of Women in Culture and Society*, vol 16, no 4, pp732–755

Schmidt, E. (1992) *Peasants, Traders, and Wives: Shona women in the History of Zimbabwe, 1870–1939*, Baobob Books, Harare

Slocum, R., Wichhart, L., Rocheleau, D. and Thomas-Slayter, B. (eds) (1995) *Power, Process and Participation: Tools for Change*, Intermediate Technology Publication Ltd, London

Smith, D. (1987) *Everyday World as Problematic: A Feminist Methodology*, Northeastern University Press, Boston, MA

Stanley, L. (ed.) (1990) *Feminist Praxis: Research, Theory and Epistemology in Feminist Sociology*, Routledge, London

Stanley, L. and Wise, S. (1983) *Breaking Out: Feminist Consciousness and Feminist Research*, Routledge, London

Stanley, L. and Wise, S. (1990) 'Feminist praxis and the academic mode of production: An editorial introduction', in Stanley (1990), pp3–19

Sylvester, C. (2000) *Producing Women and Progress in Zimbabwe: Narratives of Identity and Work from the 1980s*, Heinemann, Portsmouth, NH

Wanzala, W. (1998) 'Towards an epistemological and methodological framework of development', *in* McFadden, P. et al (eds), *Southern Africa in Transition: A Gendered Perspective*, SAPES Books, Harare, pp1–26

Wieringa, S. (1998) 'Rethinking gender planning: A critical discussion of the use of the concept gender', *Gender Technology and Development*, vol 2, no 3, pp349–371

Zhou, A. (1995) 'Women's access to trading space at growth points in Zimbabwe: A case study of Mataga', in Sithole-Fundire, S., Zhou, A., Larsson, A. and Schlyter, A. (eds), *Gender Research on Urbanization, Planning, Housing and Everyday Life*, Zimbabwe Women's Resource Centre and Network, Harare, pp163–184

Zinanga, E. (1996) 'Sexuality and the heterosexual form: The case of Zimbabwe', *Southern African Feminist Review*, vol 2, no 1, pp3–6

Zinyama, L. (1993) 'The evolution of the spatial structure of Greater Harare: 1890–1990', in Zinyama et al (1993), pp7–32

Zinyama, L., Tevere, D. and Cumming, S. (eds) (1993) *Harare: The Growth and Problems of the City*, University of Zimbabwe Publications, Harare

ZWRCN (Zimbabwe Women's Resource Centre and Network) (1995) *Zimbabwe Women's Voices*, ZWRCN, Harare

ZWRCN–SARDC (Zimbabwe Women's Resource Centre and Network; Southern Africa Research and Documentation Centre) (1998) *Beyond Inequalities, Women in Zimbabwe*, ZWRCN–SARDC, Harare

5

Gender, Commercial Urban Agriculture and Urban Food Supply in Greater Gaborone, Botswana

Alice J. Hovorka

INTRODUCTION

Urban agriculture(UA)[1] is changing the way people feed themselves in cities, and academics and practitioners alike are increasingly turning their attention to the current form and future potential of this activity. This research builds on existing literature by addressing three interrelated gaps in our understanding of UA in Africa. First, the activity has been viewed primarily as an informal household-level survival strategy in many African cities; we are well informed about its contribution to household food security in terms of providing fresh and nutritious produce and saving or generating family income. This conceptualization has overshadowed investigations of how formalized commercial agriculture in and around cities may be encouraged and sustained in order to increase urban food supply and enhance food security. Second, our understanding of the productivity or net outcomes of these commercial (as well as subsistence) systems is hindered by studies that tend to aggregated data, thus masking the differential opportunities and constraints of different groups of urban dwellers in creating, shaping and sustaining agricultural systems. This aggregation has been particularly detrimental to a full understanding of how net outcomes, specifically quantity and types of foodstuffs produced, vary along gender lines. It has also masked our understanding of how a gendered UA sector influences urban food supply beyond the household scale. Third, studies do not adequately consider the key factors that influence agricultural productivity, namely socio-economic status, location and human–environment relations. Who you are, where your plot is located and how you interact with the environment in that location matter. These elements are treated separately or are neglected altogether in the existing literature.

This research addresses the above issues by focusing on formal commercial UA systems, highlighting gender as a means by which to disaggregate data, and exploring the socio-economic, locational and human–environment factors influencing the quantity and type of crop and livestock species produced. Gaborone, Botswana, was chosen as a case study given that agriculture in and around the city is primarily commercial as opposed to subsistence-oriented, and that an equal number of men and women participate in this activity, a scenario not often found in commercial agriculture sectors in sub-Saharan Africa.[2] Botswana also presented a favourable policy environment, whereby the Government expressed an interest in baseline information exploring the present form and future potential of UA in national development plans. Finally, with little research conducted on UA in Botswana to date, this research adds to the growing literature on agriculture in and around cities of Southern Africa.

OBJECTIVES, HYPOTHESES AND CONCEPTS

The objective of the research is to understand the relationship between a gendered commercial UA sector and the nature of urban food supply in Greater Gaborone, Botswana. This requires an exploration of the productivity of male- and female-owned agricultural enterprises in and around the city. Specifically, the research investigates how and why gender influences the net outcomes of commercial UA systems. It is expected that gender differentials in socio-economic status, location and human–environment interactions in the city will affect the type and quantity of crop and livestock species produced by men and women. Such differences may generate a segmented labour market within the commercial agriculture sector or encourage varying levels of productivity amongst the urban entrepreneurs. In turn, a gendered UA sector will have implications for the ability of local production to contribute foodstuffs to the urban food supply, ultimately shaping the accessibility and appropriateness of crop and livestock products available for city dwellers.

Gender as an analytical category is meant to capture a complex set of social processes that are inextricably linked with power relations. Gender analysis involves the examination of men's and women's roles, responsibilities, and social status in relation to cultural perceptions of masculinity and femininity (Feldstein and Poats, 1989; CCIC, 1991; Overholt et al, 1991; FAO, 1995; Thomas-Slayter et al, 1995; Woroniuk et al, 1997). To this end, gender analysis allows us to disaggregate data on UA and to explore why certain processes and structures generate different opportunities and constraints for different people (Hovorka, 1998). We need to interpret gender difference as a complex phenomenon (Bondi and Domosh, 1992, p201) that occurs at multiple and interconnected scales. In reformulating gender as a theoretical category and an analytical tool, we can better explore the division of social experiences that tend to give men and women different conceptions of themselves, their activities and beliefs, and the world around them (Harding, 1986, p31). Those researchers who explore gender dynamics to this depth provide some of the most comprehensive, interesting, and thought-provoking pieces in the field of UA (Rakodi, 1988, 1991; Memon and Lee-Smith, 1993; Maxwell, 1994; Mbiba, 1995; Mianda, 1996; Mudimu, 1996).

This research begins with the premise that location and human–environment relations within the city will affect the form and extent of men's and women's participation in commercial UA, as well as the nature of the production systems that result. On the one hand, gender is an important organizing principle of social life and spatial patterns. Just as there exists a sexual division of social and economic roles, so there exists a sexual division of space whereby relationships of ownership and of possession, as well as positions in social structure are stretched-out over space. Moreover, because it is constituted out of social relations, spatiality is always and everywhere an expression and medium of power that serves to simultaneously reflect and reinforce particular social relations (Massey, 1996, p104). In many contexts, the socio-spatial dynamic reveals variations in the construction of gender relations, and more often than not spatial arrangements tend to work for men and against women (Hanson and Pratt, 1995, p17). On the other hand, gender is also an important delineation of human interactions with the environment. Men and women interact with the environment in different ways for different purposes, with differential rights of access to, control over and use of productive resources, such as land and labour, because of their relative position and power within socio-structural hierarchies and the wider political economy. Gendered resource tenure and responsibilities are concrete expressions of gendered power relations that delineate differential interactions with the environment for men and women (Rocheleau et al, 1996). In sum, the ability to make an agricultural system productive depends upon who you are, where your plot is located, and how you interact with the environment in this location.

METHODOLOGY

The research methodology was designed to collect information regarding the general form and function of commercial UA,[3] the larger structural context in which it has emerged,[4] and the specific gender differences within this economic sector. It was not designed to explore in-depth gender relations within the household or to illuminate how such micro-scale dynamics are constituted of and by relations at the meso- and macro-scales. The research methodology should not be interpreted as a dismissal of the household as an integral and important part of understanding the (re)production of gender inequality. Rather it is an attempt to shed light on men's and women's positionality within the urban economic sector, demonstrate how gendered positionality is (re)produced through productivity dynamics, and highlight the implications of this on urban food supply. Using the enterprise owner and/or enterprise as the unit of analysis, it illuminates the linkages between local level commercial production and political economic forces at larger scales. The methodology brings together socio-economic, locational and human–environment factors to provide a holistic view of this urban economic sector. Data analysis involved quantitative methods to determine the statistical associations between gender and commercial UA systems, and qualitative methods to support these linkages. Fieldwork took place in Greater Gaborone, Botswana from October 2000 to September 2001.

Primary data collection involved interviews with the owners of UA enterprises in Greater Gaborone. The study site of Greater Gaborone, as delineated in Figure 5.1, includes Gaborone City and its surrounding peri-urban areas (approximately 15–25km radius from the city proper). The Greater Gaborone Planning Area (GGPA) has been designated by the Government of Botswana as the unit area that will be most affected by the growth of the city proper. The primary objective of GGPA is to provide a framework for integrating economic, social, institutional and physical development within this urban area in order to serve the expansionary needs of Gaborone City, Tlokweng, Mogoditshane, Mmopane, Gabane and Metsemotlhabe (MLGLH, 1998, p19). This study site was large enough to generate an adequate sample size, and it proved relevant for local planning authorities in their considerations of policy initiatives and action related to UA in and around Gaborone.

Commercial UA is defined here as a system of farming aimed primarily or exclusively at commerce and income-generating. The objective of a commercial system is to produce a maximum yield for regular sale on the market at an adequate rate of return such that the profit is reinvested in the system of farming to produce further yield and expand outputs, employment opportunities, fixed assets and so on. Urban agriculture activities in Greater Gaborone are primarily formal commercial agricultural enterprises, as well as some informal enterprises operating without official recognition. 'Formal' enterprises include those operations registered as companies or business trading names, receiving grants through the government-funded Financial Assistance Program (FAP), or occupying land specified for 'agricultural purposes'. To establish a complete listing of formal UA enterprises (given that no complete listing existed at the time of the fieldwork) it was necessary to consult and continually verify a number of sources and organizations. These included Ministry of Agriculture extension officers, Registrar of Companies, Tribal Land Board and Department of Lands allocation records, key informants, agriculture suppliers/distributors, veterinarians, farmers' organizations, and general word-of-mouth. In each instance, the selection criteria of 'formal' and 'commercial' production were made clear. This definition became cloudy on occasion when persons claimed to be 'commercial' yet were selling only one or two cattle or goats a year for special events or when extra finances were required. In these few instances, no interviews were conducted. As data collection progressed, it became clear that a number of entrepreneurs operate informally; in many cases these individuals are women involved with poultry and horticulture on 'residential' plots. These individuals were included in the sample.

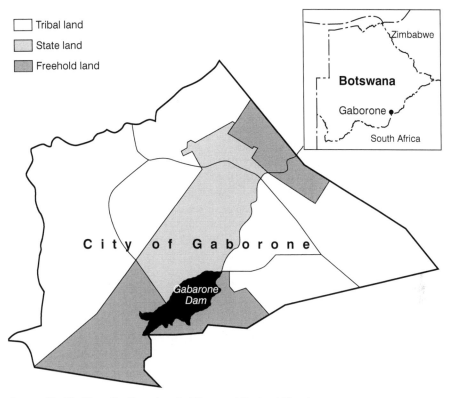

Tribal land
State land
Freehold land

Botswana

Zimbabwe

Gaborone ●

South Africa

City of Gaborone

Gabarone Dam

Source: Modified from the Department of Town and Regional Planning, Government of Botswana, 2001

Figure 5.1 *Greater Gaborone Planning Area*

The study sample consists of a total of 109 commercial agriculture enterprises (including 44 per cent male-owned and 47 per cent female-owned enterprises), 80 of which are 'formal' while 29 are 'informal'. By the end of the 12-month fieldwork season there were no more commercial farmers to be interviewed; all sources of information and identification methods were exhausted, and the researcher had driven around Gaborone and peri-urban areas searching for any enterprises that may have been overlooked. The author can conclude with a high degree of certainty that interviews have been conducted with the entire 'formal' population (save for five interviews on account of scheduling difficulties), as well as the 'informal' population, which was more difficult to verify given the relative invisibility and lack of records on such enterprises. The statistical sample represents some 95 per cent of the commercial UA population in Greater Gaborone.

The empirical investigation of male- and female-owned commercial UA enterprises involved an interview survey that took on average 45 minutes to complete. Interviewees were asked a combination of short-answer and open-ended questions relating to:

(a) net outcomes (eg type of agriculture production, gross earnings and amount of foodstuffs produced in 2000);
(b) socio-economic variables (eg gender, age, ethnicity, citizenship, income, access to capital, labour, natural resources, inputs, information, services, social networks, etc.);
(c) locational variables (eg plot location, tenure system, cost of land, size, on/off plot production, process of acquisition, etc.);
(d) environmental variables (eg water sources, soil type/quality, pests/disease, climate, etc.).

Following the formal interview session, participants were asked for a 'tour' of their agricultural enterprise. This allowed participants to relax somewhat, providing the researcher with further insights into their operations and experiences. Photographs were taken with the permission of participants for reference and presentation, as well as a gesture of appreciation for individuals' time (the photos were sent to participants upon processing).

These structured interviews and farm-tours generated a relatively rich data set adequate for both quantitative and qualitative analysis. Two issues, however, require further discussion. First, few participants were able to provide official records documenting their productivity levels, investment into fixed assets, or running cost expenditure for their enterprise. Their ability to estimate such figures had to be relied upon. In many cases, gross earnings were calculated from participants' figures on, for example, the number of chickens produced per cycle multiplied by the number of cycles per year multiplied by the selling price during 2000. Calculating running costs for 2000 required using standard figures for inputs such as day-old chicks, feed, water costs, etc. in the poultry broiler sector. I do not feel that this issue jeopardizes the statistical analysis. Moreover, this situation is telling of the financial and management problems facing commercial UA enterprises in Greater Gaborone.

Second, the ecological sampling did not progress as initially proposed. Information was assembled on soil type and quality, water sources, pests/hazards, slope/drainage and climate, but in-depth ecological conditions regarding crop species (eg density, cropping patterns, etc.) did not become a major focal point of the research. The dominance of the poultry, and indeed livestock, industry in and around Gaborone resulted in only a few horticultural producers being included in the sample. Furthermore, it became clear early on that standardized ecological sampling across various agricultural activities would be difficult. It is intended that future research endeavours will pursue this element, following in particular the implementation of the Glen Valley Horticultural Site in Gaborone, which will provide a case study of commercial horticultural production by urban dwellers initiated by the Government of Botswana.

Secondary data collection involved key informant interviews with government officials (Ministry of Agriculture, Department of Town and Regional Planning, Department of Lands, Department of Water Affairs, Ministry of Finance, Women's Affairs Department), Tribal Land Board authorities, municipal authorities (Gaborone City Council), agricultural extension officers, academics and researchers (University of Botswana, Botswana College of Agriculture, Botswana National Productivity Centre), non-governmental organizations (Women and Law in Southern Africa Trust, FONSAG: Forum on Sustainable Agriculture), farmers' organizations (Botswana Agricultural Union, Botswana Poultry Association), veterinarians, agricultural suppliers/distributors, and local business organizations (Women's Finance House, Botswana Confederation of Commerce, Industry and Manpower). A total of 42 key informant interviews were conducted. Secondary data collection also consisted of the review and documentation of some 350 references, including government documents, academic papers, statistical summaries and maps gathered from libraries and resource centres in Gaborone. Using this information, several 'thematic papers' and bibliographies were compiled on issues relating to agriculture, food systems, urbanization, gender and political economy in Botswana.

Data analysis combined quantitative with qualitative techniques in order to give the research statistical and conceptual significance. Using a statistical software program for social science research, SPSS, the researcher used a number of quantitative techniques to identify trends and characteristics of the data set. Specifically, I used multiple regression analysis to test which variables, be they socio-economic, locational, environmental, or a combination thereof, best explain levels of gross income generated by urban agricultural enterprises in 2000. Discriminant analysis allowed an exploration of whether or not there are significant differences between male- and female-owned enterprises, and what variables best account for such variation. Finally, factor analysis was used to illuminate complex groupings in the data set, and this provided insight into the potential underlying structure and character of the information collected. The qualitative component of the research focused on (semi-) structured personal interviews, key informants and secondary data. Qualitative information was used to generate a meaningful understanding of the statistical relationships between gender and commercial UA systems in Greater Gaborone.

RESEARCH FINDINGS

Although an equal number of men and women participate in commercial UA in Greater Gaborone, gender segregation and inequality plague this urban economic sector. Ideas and social norms regarding the roles and responsibilities of men and women at the macro-scale influence opportunities and constraints for individual men and women, particularly in terms of access to productive resources, which in turn influences the quantity and type of foodstuffs produced for the urban market. The fact that men and women are positioned on unequal terms in political, economic and social realms in Botswana (Mogwe, 1992; Kidd et al, 1997) means that there are significant differences between male- and female-owned commercial UA enterprises. In short, women are in a disadvantaged position relative to men within this urban economic sector both in terms of quantity and type of production.

Gender differences in productivity levels stem from differential socio-economic status given income disparities between male and female entrepreneurs. Men feature prominently in middle- and high-income categories, while women are concentrated in lower-income brackets.

Specifically, income levels clearly favour men in Greater Gaborone with men earning on average BWP12,818 and women generating on average BWP7985 gross earnings per month (BWP is Botwana's currency, the pula; BWP1 = USD0.21 (May 2005)). Such income disparities are linked to the fact that men often have higher levels of education, hold well-paid and/or alternative employment, and live in a two-income household. Figures on education show that 42 per cent of men in the sample hold a diploma or Bachelors degree while 66 per cent of women have less than a secondary education. Men are also more likely to have a steady income through their participation in non-agricultural activities that are well paid, including, for example, construction or the civil services. One-third of men in the sample are involved in production full-time compared to only half of the women. In terms of marital status, there are only 12 single men while there are 27 single women in the sample, which impacts on the total 'household' income available for enterprise investment.

Socio-economic gender differences have a major impact on women's access to productive resources, including capital, labour and land. For example, investment in fixed assets for commercial UA is much higher for the 41 men than for the 47 women interviewed, with total investments of BWP4,063,690 and BWP2,836,400 respectively. Men invest on average BWP99,114 in their agricultural enterprise whereas women invest on average BWP60,349. There is also a definitive gender trend as to the labour pool for agricultural production, whereby the male-owned enterprises employed a total of 287 full-time[5] and 51 part-time labourers, whereas female-owned enterprises employed 123 full-time and 12 part-time labourers in 2000. On average, men employ 7.07 labourers and women employ 2.65 labourers. The strong relationship between socio-economic status and access to land influences the spatial distribution of male- and female-owned enterprises across the urban landscape. Men are located on plots of agricultural land that are larger in size, more expensive, and located throughout tribal, leasehold and freehold tenure categories. Men occupy a total of 465ha of land with an average plot size of 9.7ha. Their female counterparts have 125ha of land with an average of 2.4ha per plot. Even more discrepancy exists with the actual area under agricultural production: men cultivate a total of 262ha with an average 5.1ha versus women who cultivate 45ha total agricultural land with a 0.9ha average. Also, men generally spend more money on acquiring land in Greater Gaborone than women; 43 men have spent BWP816,556 whereas 47 women have spent BWP391,338 on purchase or lease price(s) for urban land. Women more often occupy tribal land that is allocated free of charge, and in some instances is associated with the residential homestead. Specifically, there is a high concentration of women in the peri-urban villages of Mogoditshane, Gabane and Metsemotlhabe.

There is a strong statistical relationship between the quantity of foodstuffs produced and those variables representing socio-economic status and location on the urban landscape. Put differently, men and women generate differential gross earnings on account of their differential socio-economic status and access to land. Figures for 2000 indicate that male-owned enterprises grossed BWP12,173,615[6] while female-owned enterprises grossed BWP7,801,037. Specifically, men earn on average BWP23,522 per month, whereas women earn on average BWP13,368 per month. Statistical analysis reveals that there are a number of significant socio-economic and locational variables affecting the gross earnings[7] of commercial UA enterprises in Greater Gaborone. Specifically, higher education (Pearson Correlation Coefficient of 0.360 at the 0.01 level), high number of employees (0.513), large fixed asset investment (0.506), high cost of land (0.268), formal status (0.399), and off-plot production (−0.472) statistically lead to higher gross earnings. Looking at the gendered nature of these categories, it is clear that women have a disadvantaged position relative to their male counterparts. As detailed above, men are more educated, hire more labourers, invest in fixed assets and pay more for access to prime agricultural land. Additionally, women are more likely than men are to operate enterprises informally. Many more men formally registered their enterprises as companies or business trading names in Greater Gaborone. Women tend to be formally registered by receiving FAP grants or occupying land specified for 'agricultural purposes'; they also dominate the informal commercial UA sector (the sample has 20 women and 7 men in this category). Also, 28 men are involved in off-plot (non-residential) production while only 17 women occupy land that is not combined with the primary residence. In sum, gender differences within this urban economic sector are linked to differential socio-economic status, which ultimately translates into access to land and ability to put this land into agricultural production.

There is a clear spatial distribution of male- and female-owned enterprises across the urban landscape, reflecting a strong correlation between levels of capital and ability to purchase land for agricultural production. Men are located on plots of agricultural land that are more expensive, larger in size, and located throughout tribal, leasehold and freehold tenure categories. Women more often occupy tribal land that is allocated free of charge, and in some instances is associated with the residential homestead. In turn, this gendered socio-economic and locational positioning of men and women in the commercial UA sector has major implications on their human–environment interactions in terms of the scale, intensification and type of agricultural production systems in particular urban locales. Analysis reveals that women operate at smaller scales, to greater intensity and within limited agricultural subsectors (namely broiler production) on tribal land (both residential and agricultural zoning), while men participate more broadly in terms of scale and type of agricultural production on land across tenure categories.

When considering type of agricultural subsector, there are 38 female-owned enterprises involved in intensive broiler production compared to 22 male-owned enterprises. More men than women are involved in other activities found in Greater Gaborone, including dairy, fisheries, horticulture, livestock (beef cattle), piggery, poultry (eggs) and and smallstock production. The tendency for female commercial producers to gravitate to broiler production in general is attributed to numerous factors relating to its local popularity as an accessible, adaptable, visible subsector that is well supported and offers lucrative results. Broiler production yields a relatively quick cash turnover with little investment and capital requirements relative to other agricultural sectors. It also allows producers to overcome the harsh and unreliable climate by creating an artificial environment (the poultry house) to avoid any dependence on Botswana's climate, water access and soil conditions. Broiler systems are highly adaptable to small plots of land that can only sustain a small number of chickens, yet remain lucrative endeavours. The broiler subsector was initially vertically integrated, whereby a large-scale producer employed contract growers within Greater Gaborone in order to expand productivity. Social networks and word-of-mouth, particularly amongst low-income women in peri-urban areas, have created a snowball effect with increased visibility and discussion around this activity leading to greater interest in the establishment of similar enterprises. Furthermore, the Botswana Poultry Association disseminates information on technical and management issues to producers in the area, providing guidance and support to entrepreneurs. Many female enterprise owners noted that they had become involved in such production because of the influence of friends, neighbours or family members, and because of the relatively fast income generation this activity provides without a significant amount of investment or a source of support for such endeavours.

When considering scale and the intensity of agricultural production, gender analysis along class lines reveals that low-income women operate highly efficient and effective broiler production systems (generating high yields compared to their middle-income counterparts), drawing on their own resources (eg social networks, homemade equipment) to sustain production at the small scale. Yet their efforts are constrained by urban zoning, given that their plots of land are relatively small and located in residential areas, and their ability to accumulate enough capital to acquire larger plots of land is limited. Middle-income women have access to larger plots of tribal land zoned for agricultural purposes, yet continue to choose intensive and smaller-scale broiler production. This is largely on account of the fact that their participation in this sector has been facilitated by government assistance, thus artificially inflating their socio-economic standing. Many of these women noted their inability to sustain, let alone expand, production given a lack of capital for everyday running costs. Unlike low-income women, middle-income women operate more independently and are reliant on state-supported extension services, information dissemination and training rather than on personal support networks. The majority of male entrepreneurs operate at the middle-income level and have larger systems that are often mechanized (reflecting a substantial investment of capital into fixed assets and labour) in a broad range of subsectors that may be intensive (eg broilers) or extensive (eg horticulture, smallstock). The small number of men and women operating in the high-income bracket are reliant on their own resources and have significant options for larger-scale and diversified production systems.

The above analysis reveals that socio-economic status, location and human–environment relations shape the gendered nature of agricultural production systems. Patterns of land-use in and around the city delineate the locations in which agricultural production can occur. Access to these plots of land is gained through access to capital, whereby economic rent for more favourable land requires more capital. As demonstrated, women are socio-economically disadvantaged compared to men; hence they tend to occupy the least expensive land (and most marginal in terms of size, zoning and quality), and on occasion use land that is not officially designated for agricultural purposes. The resulting class-based gender hierarchy, with women found in lower-income brackets and men in middle- and high-income brackets, takes on a spatial expression and in turn facilitates the type, scale and intensity of human–environment interactions (i.e. agricultural production systems) in different locales. Ultimately those entrepreneurs who find themselves with limited socio-economic status and location, primarily women, face more limited opportunities for their agricultural systems.

In turn, the gendered nature of commercial UA Greater Gaborone has implications for the urban food supply and food security in Botswana. Certainly with differential experiences existing along gender lines, this agricultural production sector is not reaching its potential in contributing to the supply of foodstuffs to the urban market. Although men's and women's equal participation in commercial UA shows relatively equal access to the sector as a whole, smaller gross earnings and the concentration of female-owned enterprises into the broiler subsector reflect the segregation and marginalization of women. In terms of the urban food supply this means that it is neither reaching its maximum potential in the quantity of foodstuffs available to urban dwellers nor is there a adequate range of foodstuffs availed through local commercial production in Greater Gaborone.

REFLECTIONS FOR FURTHER RESEARCH

The research provides detailed information on the gendered positionality of men and women in the commercial UA sector in Greater Gaborone, and the implications of such gender segregation and inequality on the urban food supply. Further research will explore the intricacy of gender relations at the household scale that may further contribute to the production and reproduction of gender inequality at meso- and macro-scales. Specifically, to what extent do the delineation of power around productive resources within the household and the negotiation of access to and use of such resources influence men's and women's ability to participate effectively in commercial

UA? Beyond household dynamics, it will consider in-depth the role of complex social networks and marketing channels in the UA sector. Illuminating the complexity and subtlety of such household power relations and personal networks will enrich a gender analysis of UA in Botswana, adding conceptual and empirical depth to the present study. Additionally, future investigations of UA in Greater Gaborone will provide historical depth to gender dynamics within this economic sector. Few studies to date have documented the evolution of this activity over the long term, particularly with respect to gender. Forthcoming fieldwork in Greater Gaborone (2004 or 2005) will consider men's and women's experiences with agricultural enterprises over a number of years (with new data complementing the 2000 data set presented here) as well as their ability to sustain production levels or expand operations.

FIELD RESEARCH GRANT IMPACTS

Human resource development

the author received language training in Setswana during the course of the fieldwork and completed courses at the beginner and intermediate level. No other specific training activities were received and/or conducted.

Institutional capacity strengthening and effectiveness of local partnerships

The local partnerships developed through an affiliation with the Ministry of Agriculture (MoA), Department of Town and Regional Planning (DTRP), and the Department of Environmental Science, University of Botswana were exceptional. These institutions provided much support and encouragement and were a pivotal factor in the author's ability to contribute to planning and policy initiatives. My relationship with the MoA was particularly strong, and initial support from Mr Masego Mphathi, Deputy Permanent Secretary, quickly expanded to numerous departments, including Crop Production, Animal Health and Production, Soils, Extension, and Agricultural Planning and Statistics. Officials in the last department were instrumental in the organization and support of the First National Workshop on (Peri-)Urban Agriculture. The Department of Town and Regional Planning provided access to key informants, documents and digital data. Finally, the researcher's relationship with faculty and students at the Department of Environmental Science, University of Botswana provided access to equipment and facilities, as well as support and encouragement. The above partnerships facilitated a mutual contribution to knowledge of UA in Botswana. This research was the catalyst for institutional capacity building in this area, while insights, information and support from persons in these institutions allowed me to successfully complete the study.

Methodological and scientific advances

The contributions of this research to innovative methods and advancement of knowledge are threefold. Conceptually, the research furthers understanding of how people interact with the environment in urban areas and draws out the linkages between socio-economic status, location and human–environment interactions. Methodologically, the research redresses the paucity of empirical evidence documenting women's disadvantaged position in UA realms relative to men. The research provides gendered insights through in-depth quantitative analysis, as supported by qualitative insights, to illuminate the linkages between gender and agricultural production in and around cities. Substantively, the research involves gender analysis at multiple scales, rather than solely focusing on the household level. By doing so, it reveals the impact of local gender differences on urban food supply. It furthers an understanding of how gender manifests itself at multiple levels, is continually (re)produced, and may have significant consequences in a particular context.

Utilization of research results

The research has had a significant and immediate impact on the planning and policy initiatives of the Government of Botswana, both as a means of information dissemination and as a catalyst for UA focused activities. Throughout the fieldwork, the author provided information to key stakeholders on UA issues through interviews with government officials, private sector companies, non-governmental organization (NGO) workers, and individual entrepreneurs. As interest grew, I co-organized the National Workshop on (Peri-)Urban Agriculture with Ms Daphne Keboneilwe, Senior Rural Sociologist at MoA. The event was hosted by the MoA in May 2001, and was officially opened by the Assistant Minister of Agriculture. It brought together representatives from Government Ministries and Departments of Agriculture, Lands, Water, Health and Sanitation, and Town Planning, as well as municipal authorities, Tribal Land Board officials, academics, the NGO community, private sector companies and urban farmers themselves. Ms Keboneilwe and the present author compiled the workshop proceedings (Keboneilwe and Hovorka, 2001).

Increased awareness of and interest in UA on account of the workshop provided the impetus for further activities aimed at exploring the current role and future potential of the activity in Botswana. A Task Force was established in September 2001 in order to formulate a draft policy paper for UA. The second National Workshop on (Peri-)Urban Agriculture was held in July 2003 to discuss the policy document in preparation for its eventual presentation to the Government of Botswana. The Task Force is currently reviewing the specific gender issues raised by this research and will evaluate potential avenues for addressing the gender segregation and inequality present in the UA sector. While the author continues to assist Ms Keboneilwe periodically with relevant issues, including the Task Force and draft policy paper, UA has become a genuine focal point for government officials in Botswana and is receiving much enthusiastic interest and support from key stakeholders.

The urban entrepreneurs who participated in the research are also a focal point for information dissemination. In the latter part of the fieldwork, packages were mailed out to interviewees providing details about immediate impacts of the research in order to keep participants abreast of new developments. Specifically, a summary of the national workshop was included, highlighting future initiatives and steps in the process of planning and policy formulation. Participants have been encouraged to contact Ms Keboneilwe, or the present author directly if possible, to voice comments regarding UA activities in Botswana.

Preliminary research results were presented twice during the 12 months of fieldwork; first at the said workshop in May 2001, and second, to faculty and students at the Department of Environmental Science, University of Botswana, in September 2001. Both venues provided an excellent opportunity to review tentative findings of the investigation, and to disseminate baseline information on commercial UA in Gaborone. Subsequently, conclusive results were presented at the Association of American Geographers Annual Meeting in Los Angeles and the AGROPOLIS Review Workshop in Ottawa, both in March 2002, and the Canadian Association of Geographers Annual Meeting in Victoria in May 2003. The research forms the basis of four manuscripts, three of which are currently under review with peer-refereed journals and one that has been accepted for publication.

ACKNOWLEDGEMENTS

The author acknowledges financial support from the following institutions: AGROPOLIS Award for Urban Agriculture Research, International Development Research Centre (IDRC); National Science Foundation, USA; and Social Sciences and Humanities Research Council of Canada. This research was conducted as partial fulfillment of a PhD degree at the School of Geography, Clark University, Worcester, MA, USA (Hovorka, 2003). The Department of Environmental Science, University of Botswana, provided access to equipment and facilities in-kind, including a personal office with a computer, library privileges, mailbox, and scanning/photocopying access that was beyond expectation. I am grateful for their support, both professional and material, during my time in Greater Gaborone.

NOTES

1   The term 'urban agriculture' in this chapter refers to both peri-urban and urban locales given the scope of research within the Greater Gaborone Planning Area, as detailed in the methodology section.

2   For an in-depth analysis of the gender-balanced entry into and participation within this sector see Hovorka (2003) 'Gendered experiences, changing gender relations?

A feminist political ecology of commercial urban agriculture in Botswana'. Unpublished manuscript under review.

3   For an overview see Hovorka, (2004) 'Commercial urban agriculture in Greater Gaborone: Form & function, challenges & prospects', Pula: *Botswana Journal of African Studies* (in press).

4   For an in-depth analysis of this issue see Hovorka (2003) 'Urban opportunities: Entrepreneurial urban agriculture in Botswana'. Unpublished manuscript under review.

5   This figure does not include two enterprises that together employ some 618 full-time labourers.

6   This figure does not include two of the largest grossing producers in Greater Gaborone whose turnover well exceeds the norm.

7   Gross turnover here is used as the most reliable estimate of quantity or productivity. There are no significant statistical correlations to suggest that the type of agricultural activity influences this figure. Moreover, given the difficulties in standardizing quantities of foodstuffs across dairy, horticulture, livestock, poultry broiler, poultry layer, piggery, and smallstock production, gross turnover remains the best estimate of quantity at this point in the analysis.

REFERENCES

Bondi, L. and Domosh, M. (1992) 'Other figures in other places: On feminism, postmodernism and geography', *Society and Space*, vol 10, pp199-213

CCIC (Canadian Council for International Cooperation) (1991) *Two Halves Make a Whole: Balancing Gender Relations in Development*, CCIC, Ottawa

FAO (1995) *Gender Analysis and Forestry*, FAO Forests, Trees and People Programme, Rome, Italy

Feldstein, H. S. and Poats, S. V. (1989) *Working Together: Gender Analysis in Agriculture*, Kumarian Press, West Hartford, CT

Hanson, S. and Pratt, G. (1995) *Gender, Work and Space*, Routledge, London

Harding, S. (1986) *The Science Question in Feminism*, Cornell University Press, Ithaca, NY

Hovorka, A. J. (1998) 'Gender resources for UA research: Methodology, directory and annotated bibliography', *Cities Feeding People Report 26*, IDRC, Ottawa

Hovorka, A. J. (2003) 'Exploring the effects of gender on (peri-)urban agriculture systems in Gaborone, Botswana'. PhD Dissertation, School of Geography, Clark University, Worcester, MA

Keboneilwe, D. and Hovorka, A, J. (eds) (2001) *Proceedings of the National Workshop on (Peri-)Urban Agriculture*, 28–29 May 2001, the National Veterinary Laboratory, Ministry of Agriculture, Government of Botswana, Sebele, Botswana

Kidd, P. E., Makgekgenene, K., Molokomme, A., Molamu, L. L., Malila, I. S., Lesetedi, G. N., Dingake, K. and Mokongwa, K. (1997) *Botswana Families and Women's Rights in a Changing Environment*, The Women and Law in Southern Africa Research Trust, Gaborone, Botswana

Massey, D. (1996) 'A global sense of place', in Barnes, T. and Gregory, D. (eds), *Reading Human Geography: The Poetics and Politics of Inquiry*, Arnold, London

Maxwell, D. G. (1994) 'The household logic of urban farming in Kampala', in Egziabher, A., Lee-Smith, D., Maxwell, D. G., Memon, P. A., Mougeot, L. and

Sawio, C. (eds), *Cities Feeding People*, International Development Research Centre, pp47–65, Ottawa

Mbiba, B. (1995) *Urban Agriculture in Zimbabwe: Implications for Urban Management and Poverty*, Avebury Ashgate, Aldershot, UK

Memon, P. A., and Lee-Smith, D. (1993) 'Urban agriculture in Kenya', *Canadian Journal of African Studies*, vol 27, no 1, pp25–42

Mianda, G. (1996) 'Women and garden produce of Kinshasa: The difficult quest for autonomy', in Ghorayshi, P. and Belanger, C. (eds), *Women, Work, and Gender Relations in Developing Countries*, Greenwood Press, Westport, CT, pp91–101

MLGLH, Republic of Botswana (1998) *Gaborone City Development Plan (1997–2021): Final Draft Plan*, Ministry of Local Government, Lands and Housing, Gaborone City Council, and Department of Town and Regional Planning, Gaborone, Botswana

Mogwe, A. (1992) *Country Gender Analysis: Botswana*, Swedish International Development Authority (SIDA), Sweden

Mudimu, G. D. (1996) 'Urban agricultural activities and women's strategies in sustaining family livelihoods in Harare, Zimbabwe', *Singapore Journal of Tropical Geography*, vol 17, no 2, pp179–194

Overholt, C. A., et al (1991) 'Gender analysis framework', in Rao, A., Anderson, M. B. and Overholt, C. A. (eds), *Gender Analysis in Development Planning*, Kumarian Press, West Hartford, CT

Rakodi, C. (1988) 'Urban Agriculture: Research questions and Zambian evidence', *The Journal of Modern African Studies*, vol 26, no 3, pp495–515

Rakodi, C. (1991) 'Women's work or household strategies?' *Environment and Development*, vol 3, no 2, pp39–45

Rocheleau, D., Thomas-Slayter, B. and Wangari, E. (1996) *Feminist Political Ecology*, Routledge, London

Thomas-Slayter, B., et al (1995) *A Manual for Socio-economic and Gender Analysis: Responding to the Development Challenge*, Clark University, Worcester, MA

Woroniuk, B., Thomas, H. and Schalkwyk, J. (1997) *Gender: The Concept, Its Meaning and Uses*, SIDA, Department for Policy and Legal Services, Stockholm, Sweden

6

Moving between the Plan and the Ground: Shifting Perspectives on Urban Agriculture in Havana, Cuba

Adriana Premat

INTRODUCTION

The current global trend toward ever-increasing urbanization, ongoing food insecurity, and environmental degradation – particularly in countries of the so-called South – makes it imperative to study and understand urban agriculture (UA) as a food provisioning alternative that addresses the nutritional needs of city dwellers while potentially contributing to the environmental health of cities and their surrounding territories. Although numerous valuable studies have been conducted on various dimensions of UA, the vital question of its sustainability from a sociocultural perspective has received little attention. This research project attempts to redress this lacuna through a case study of how sociocultural differences that shape people's UA discourses and practices in Havana, Cuba, may significantly affect the long-term fate of UA.

Recognized as a world leader in alternative organic agriculture (Rosset and Benjamin, 1994) and UA (Murphy, 1999), Cuba presents an ideal site for the exploration of these research interests. UA became particularly important in Cuba during the post-Soviet economic crisis, which began in 1989 and resulted in, among other things, great food insecurity. Although primary food-production practices were not unknown in Cuban cities before this time,[1] the intensity that these practices then acquired was unprecedented.

Cuban cityscapes were redrawn as plantains and chicken coops took the place of rose bushes in home gardens and as previously abandoned city lots were sown with food crops of all kinds. Today, almost a decade later, nationwide UA efforts account for almost 60 per cent of all Cuban vegetable production (Bourque and Cañizares, 2001), and the average production outputs in some municipalities already reach the level required to meet the daily dietary vegetable intake of 300 grams per person recommended by the Food and Agriculture Organization of the United Nations (Cruz Hernández and Medina, 2001, p7). In the area of food-animal production, results have been equally impressive; in 2000, small spaces, such as *patios*, were alone said to have produced 326.9 million eggs and 7 tonnes of poultry meat.[2] In a short time, UA efforts in Cuba appear to have successfully reduced food insecurity for a considerable portion of the population, as well as contributing to the amelioration of environmental problems through, for example, the elimination of abandoned lots, which were often used as garbage-disposal sites (Cruz Hernández and Medina, 2001).

Although Havana is not the only Cuban city where UA flourishes, a number of factors made it an especially promising site for this study. First, the city is central to the country's UA movement: Havana has not only been repeatedly praised vis-à-vis other Cuban cities for its UA performance, but it also is the place where most UA-related research, decision-making and support networks are based. Havana's UA sites are said to involve more than 22,000 producers (Cruz Hernández and Medina, 2001) and are reported to have met up to 30 per cent of the subsistence needs of entire neighbourhoods (Murphy, 1999). Second, in Havana's UA landscapes the whole gamut of types of production space is represented, from the high-yield, high-investment *organopónicos* (organoponic gardens), which commercialize their outputs,[3] to the low-yield household gardens geared toward self-provisioning (Table 6.1). Third, as the capital and the most urbanized area of the country, with a population of 2,185,076 (20 per cent of the total population of the country; Cruz Hernández and Medina, 2001), Havana also affords an optimal opportunity to explore the intersection of urbanity and agriculture. Fourth, as the densest urban area of the country, this city is the best site in which to explore the limitations of UA, as well as its potential to contribute to food security and the ecological sustainability of the urban environment. Fifth, previous research had provided the researcher with helpful contacts in this city.

Without doubt, the success of UA in Cuba, and in Havana in particular, has been greatly facilitated by extensive government support. This support has taken various forms, including the allotment of state lands to be used as garden lots in usufruct; the promotion of research on sustainable technologies; the dissemination of related knowledge by agricultural delegates appointed to every level of government; and the provision of affordable agricultural inputs to urban farmers through the Tiendas Consultorias Agropecuarias (TCA, agricultural goods and services centres).[4] Yet, despite this support, the future of the food-production dimensions of UA in Havana is uncertain, particularly those of small-scale, self-provisioning activities.

Statistics show that although some types of UA spaces (such as the high-yield organoponic gardens) have almost doubled in number over the last five years (Cruz Hernández and Medina, 2001), small-scale, self-provision-oriented food-production sites, such as *parcelas*, have decreased considerably. By 1997, Havana had 26,600 officially registered urban agriculture plots geared toward

Table 6.1 *Main food-oriented urban agricultural sites in Havana*

Production sites	Land tenure	Area occupied	Commercialization as main objective	Year of creation
Farms	Private–state	NA	Yes	NA
Popular organoponics (m²)	State	2000–5000	Yes	1993
Intensive gardens (m²)	State	1000–3000	Yes	1991
High-yield organoponic plots (ha)	State	>1	Yes	1994
Factory/enterprise self-provisioning gardens (ha)	State	>1	No	1989
Usufruct plots (m²)	State (some private)	<1000	No	1991
Patios (m²)	Private	<1000	No	NA

Note: NA, not available.

family self-provisioning (Murphy, 1999), but by 2000 this number had dropped to 7944 (Cruz Hernández and Medina, 2001).[5] Cruz Hernández and Medina considered this decrease primarily a reflection of the country's economic recovery and the shift by some successful farmers to large-scale, commercially oriented forms of agricultural production. The authors added, however, that the disappearance of some of these sites could also be linked to the transfer of these lots to 'investments *more appropriate for a city*' (Cruz Hernández and Medina, 2001, p41, emphasis in the original).

The expressed perception that non-agricultural (as in food-producing) functions are 'more appropriate for a city' recalls an anti-agricultural bias in Cuba's urban population at large and within decision-making circles in particular, previously identified in the literature (for example, Murphy, 1999). This bias found past expression in Havana's by-laws prohibiting the cultivation of 'agricultural' crops in front yards, permitting only ornamental plants (Benjamin et al, 1984, cited in Murphy, 1999). As will be argued, this attitude, rather than being based on the real limitations to urban land-use for UA, appears to derive from a preconceived notion of what is 'proper' to the city. This sense of propriety, in turn, largely determines the activities decreed legitimate and hence institutionally serviced and enabled.[6]

Why should one care about small-scale, household-oriented UA sites in the first place? Despite the ongoing economic recovery of Cuba, the small-scale site for self-provisioning is still a feasible food-security option for that sector of the population lacking easy access (financially and spatially) to food products sold at agricultural markets or UA-specific commercial outlets. Although organoponic production is significant, these sites and the produce they generate are not accessible to everyone. And prices at *organopónicos* are lower than those at *agromercados* (agricultural markets), but they are still high for many Cubans. These sites are also unevenly distributed and not always easy for city residents without a personal vehicle, be it a car or a bicycle, to reach.[7] The variety of produce available at *agromercados* or at UA-specific agricultural stalls (*puntos de venta*) varies throughout the city and does not always approximate the variety found in family plots, with the notable exception of those well-provisioned *agromercados* in more affluent city neighbourhoods (such as that located at 19 and B in the comparatively well-to-do municipality of Vedado). As Murphy (1999, p14) put it, residents of core municipalities such as Old Havana, Central Havana and El Cerro 'have to leave their neighbourhoods to find simple food items', unless they can produce these themselves. The same applies to animal protein. Rabbits, for example, are not sold to Cubans, except in a few expensive restaurants in well-to-do neighbourhoods. Above the ration quotas,[8] more common items, such as chicken and eggs, have to be purchased in dollar stores at prices that are still high for most citizens. An increase in larger scale, high-output UA spaces that commercialize their products, therefore, should not be considered synonymous with universal access or be taken to imply enhanced food security for all.

Although recognizing the accomplishments of the UA movement in Cuba, we should also be concerned about how it is changing and the prospects for its long-term survival, particularly with regard to expanding, improving on, or even sustaining achievements to date in food security. As argued above, the fate of the small-scale, self-provisioning plot, so rapidly decreasing in number, presents itself as a phenomenon requiring further exploration. To the extent that this form of UA is a feasible path to food security for those unable to benefit from recent market-oriented economic reforms and related food sales outside the ration, it is of more than academic importance to identify and redress the causes of diminishing UA in Cuba.

This chapter offers insights into this problem through an exploration of the various ways UA professionals[9] and small-scale agricultural producers discursively and in practice define UA, its proper domain and its benefits. The paper begins by reviewing the concepts, questions and methodology guiding the research, noting necessary revisions made as the project progressed. It continues with a discussion of preliminary findings, focusing primarily on only two of the variables included in the study: occupation and institutional affiliation. The impacts and benefits of the research are then discussed in relation to these findings. The chapter concludes with some final remarks on the significance of the research to UA practitioners and researchers.

CONCEPTS, QUESTIONS AND METHODOLOGY

Concepts

The key concepts that frame this research – namely, UA, sociocultural factors, discourse and practice – merit detailed definition.

UA has been broadly defined as including:

> *all agricultural activities located within (intra-urban) or on the*
> *periphery (peri-urban) of a settlement, city or metropolis,*
> *independently or collectively developed by people for self-*
> *consumption or commercialization purposes; involving the*
> *cultivation or raising, processing, and distribution of a diversity*
> *of products – be these edible or not – largely via the (re)utilization*
> *of human and material resources, products and services located*
> *in and around the urban area in question, in turn contributing*
> *considerable material and human resources to that area.*
> (Santandreu and Dubbeling, 2001, p2, my translation)

Although a similarly comprehensive definition is also used at present in the Cuban context, a distinction is made, as part of this analysis, between the production of edible products (such as food animals, fruit trees, vegetables, and medicinal and culinary herbs) and non-edible products (such as ornamental plants). This disaggregation of the broad definition is particularly important because of the research objective of identifying perspectives that may work against the promotion of the food-security dimensions of UA. To treat both activities as indistinguishable would render the data and the conclusions useless. The decision to focus on the food-security aspects of UA is also grounded in the usage of the term in the Cuban context: the term first gained currency during the economic crisis of the early 1990s, when it was used to refer solely to food-production activities in the city (Cruz Hernández and Medina, 2001).

Sociocultural factors here refers to socially or culturally constructed and maintained axes of identity, such as those associated with gender, generation, education, profession, occupation and family background (for example, being of peasant or urban stock). All of these variables were prioritized for exploration in the initial proposal, but as the research progressed the list was modified somewhat. Interviews and participation at various institutional meetings and workshops helped the researcher to realize that multi-disciplinarity is very common in Cuba, with urban planners, agropecuarian engineers and architects working side by side everywhere, from the Ministry of Agriculture (MINAGRI) to the Department of Urban Planning. Because, in this context, institutional boundaries and visions appeared to be more closely guarded and more influential than disciplinary ones, institutional affiliation was added to the list of prioritized variables.

Discourse in this paper refers to the narratives, concepts and ideologies that individuals express in writing or in speaking about a particular realm of social practice. *Practice*, on the other hand, refers to the actions of individuals as they go about their routine activities, be these institutionally based or independent. Discourse and practice need not parallel each other, and discourse, in the sense used here, need not necessarily reflect actual knowledge or experience.

Questions

On the basis of the hypothesis that the above-mentioned sociocultural factors shape people's perspectives on UA and therefore play a significant role in determining the long-term success or failure of UA in Havana (as elsewhere), the research explored the following questions:

1   How is urban farming described or practised by various differently positioned actors within Havana?
2   What might these differing perspectives imply for the future of UA in this city?

Although these questions remained unchanged throughout the research, their specific focus – target population and UA sites – was narrowed as the research progressed. The data-gathering techniques originally proposed also shifted as new insights were gained into the research context.

Methodology

Overall, the research followed the data-gathering techniques outlined in the original proposal. Archival and library research was conducted at public libraries, city archives and institutional documentation centres to identify official, expert or other publicly influential Cuban perspectives on UA and the ideal of the city produced since the beginning of the economic crisis in 1989. Sites regularly visited to carry out this phase of the research included the Cuban National Library and City Archives, the Centre for the Americas Library, the Ministry of Agriculture Library, the Information Centre of the Group for Holistic Development of the Capital, and the Special Collections Library at the Foundation of Nature and Humanity. The resources consulted included books or scholarly articles describing past or current practices of primary food production in the city of Havana; city maps, urban plans, government legislation and state newspaper articles pertinent to UA; and publications, in-house reports and records produced by Havana-based non-governmental organizations (NGOs) working in the area of urban food production.

The following brief summary of the treatment given to 147 newspaper articles on UA will illustrate how data were analysed and used in the research. The material covers the period 1989–1998 and represents various newspapers with a city- or nationwide distribution, collected at the information centre of the Grupo para el Desarrollo Integral de La Capital (GDIC, Group for the Holistic Development of the Capital). A content analysis was performed on the articles, attention being paid to the kind of UA production emphasized and the type of actors, sites and functions they highlighted. Accompanying images were also analysed in terms of the actors (by gender, age and race), sites and activities (group or individual) depicted. This analysis provided a sense of the official story of the evolution of UA in Havana; insights thus gained were integrated into interview questions and helped put into a broader institutional context the discourses of the specific UA professionals included in the study (particularly those coming from MINAGRI, who constituted the primary sources for the newspaper articles).

Heeding the advice of both Harley (1988) on maps, and of Comaroff and Jean (1992) on archival material in general, the analysis was taken beyond the examination of 'textual traces', 'audible ideologies', and 'visible institutions' to uncover the ideas hidden behind silences and omissions. Although detailed analysis is still under way, it was noted, for example, that beginning in the mid-1990s, the images accompanying newspaper articles on the subject of UA were predominantly of high-output *organoponic*-type gardens, rather than family plots, which were more frequently depicted in previous years. Such a shift in representation could be seen as reflecting not so much actual changes in the practice of UA as a shift in official priorities (after all, at that time family garden plots appeared to be thriving, with official statistics counting 26,600 in Havana).

Because of time restrictions, city residents with no connection to UA were excluded from the study, although they were initially considered part of the target population. Following the initial plan, however, open, semi-structured interviews organized by theme (Montañes Serrano, 2001a) were carried out with urban farmers, as well as with professionals from governmental organizations and NGOs whose work and opinions influenced the practice of UA. The interviews were designed to gather information about the interviewees' pertinent life experiences, their conceptions of the city in general, their knowledge and opinions about the current urban agricultural system (that is, of the set of official governmental bodies and NGOs with a mandate to regulate or support the practice of UA), and their views on the appropriateness of various spaces (such as neighbourhoods, parks and households) for growing edible crops or raising food animals. With urban farmers in particular, information was also sought on their places of residence, as well as the physical characteristics of their agricultural spaces (for example, open to the street or closed to public view, proximity to residence) and their land-tenure status (for example, private, state owned usufruct). The latter factor, in particular, emerged as a significant variable in shaping some of the actions of producers, with UA professionals exercising a higher degree of influence over the practices of those holding usufruct rights.

As originally proposed, the field investigations emphasized multi-sited ethnographic research (Marcus, 1995, 1998), prioritizing first-hand experience, observation and detailed description (what anthropologists call participant observation) in various settings, from primary food-production sites to institutional meetings. The researcher observed and participated in the everyday farming practices and other relevant activities of interviewees. With respect to farmers, their ways of dwelling in the city, the neighbourhood and the household, as well as their relationships to services available through the UA system were noted. To gain insight into the culture promoted by various institutions or groups involved in UA, the author sought to participate in their planning meetings and workshops. These included a permaculture course and numerous working meetings organized by the Antonio Nuñez Jiménez Foundation (Fundación Antonio Nuñez Jiménez, FANJ), as well as meetings and social gatherings organized by the Botanical Association, the Environmentalist Group of San Isidro, MINAGRI, and mass organizations, such as the Committees for the Defence of the Revolution (CDR).

The analysis of the research data involved the systematic coding of interview transcripts, meeting notes and field notes (recording observations), as well as news clippings and other supplementary documentation. Computer software designed for qualitative analysis was used in this coding process to disaggregate the data by topic, theme, question and participant attributes, such as gender, age, education, occupation, institutional affiliation, family background and place of residence. Because the data often contained the discourses of the same individuals in various settings or situations (such as private informal conversation, formal interview, informal gathering or public meetings) at various times over the period of research, the analysis was designed to remain sensitive to temporal, as well as contextual, shifts. These temporally and contextually variegated discourses were, in turn, compared with the observed practices of the same individuals, as noted in the field notes, allowing for a nuanced and complex understanding of the processes under study. In this manner, participant observation allows one to note the differences (and the convergences) between what people say in various settings and what they do, better contextualizing people's discourses or conscious representations of a given subject. This offers great advantage over other data-gathering and analytical techniques and analyses that assume a perfect fit between discourse and practice.

The only adjustment made to the initially proposed data-gathering techniques was a decision not to ask the producers to draw 'counter-maps'. Although counter-maps have been successfully used by researchers in other settings (Gould and White, 1980; Peluso, 1995; Rocheleau et al, 1995) to gather information on producers' perception and knowledge of local land-use, the construction of counter-maps would have been inappropriate in the Cuban context. Interviewees felt uncomfortable about drawing maps that noted private neighbourhood land-use, as this could be considered tantamount to 'informing' on others. Instead, farmers were asked to subjectively describe their garden or animal-raising spaces and the larger territories surrounding them (neighbourhood, municipality and city). They were specifically asked to comment on their assessment of UA practices within their territory but were not required to specify individuals or locations.[10]

Site selection

The research focused on small-scale production sites – including *patios*, rooftops, house alleys and abandoned city lots – that did not exceed 1000 m^2, were exploited by a family or individual with the goal of self-provision, and may have been privately owned or held in usufruct,[11] referred to as *patios* or *parcelas*, respectively (Cruz Hernández and Medina, 2001). The sites were selected for attention for a number of reasons, including those outlined in the introduction. First, even though their numbers have decreased considerably over the last few years, they are still the most extensive and popular expression of UA in Havana, which currently has 7944 officially registered *patios* and *parcelas* occupying 1030ha and engaging 16,869 producers (Cruz Hernández and Medina, 2001). Second, the small-scale production sites, particularly those involving privately owned spaces, are also the most spontaneous, independent and voluntary (as opposed to governmentally guided and regulated) individual expressions of UA in the city – an expansion of expressions long present in Havana. Third, with an average annual production rate of 4989kg of vegetables per producer (Cruz Hernández and Medina, 2001), these sites are the UA spaces most closely linked to household food security. Fourth, they are the most centrally located instances of UA – the most organically integrated into the urban physical and social environment. Other types of production spaces, such as *fincas* (farms) and even *organopónicos* (see Table 6.1), tend to be located on the outskirts or in the least densely populated areas of the city. Indeed, in two of the most central municipalities included in the study (Old Havana and Central Habana), *patios* and *parcelas* are the only UA activity present in the area. Fifth, despite their significance, these spaces have been the least studied.[12] Therefore, any concern for the sustainability of UA, and specifically its contribution to food security, arguably needs to place special value on these expressions – all the more so, considering that these expressions of the practice, although most closely linked to household food security, are the least well served by the formal UA system.

Definition of the study area

The sample of farmers was drawn from three neighbourhoods located in various municipalities: Old Havana, Central Havana and El Cerro. These territories were chosen because, despite some commonalities (such as a deteriorating, old housing stock), they offered interesting contrasts in patterns of land-use (such as availability of open spaces and *patios*), agricultural history (such as past and present recognition by authorities of their agricultural function), and resources available (for example, alternative sources of livelihood, such as tourism). The two most densely populated of these municipalities, Old Havana and Central Havana, had few open spaces and no large-scale UA production sites. According to a still ongoing census by the Agricultural Inputs Enterprise for the City of Havana (Empresa de Suministros Agropecuarios Ciudad Habana, ESACH), in 2001 the former had 37 and the latter had 49 officially registered, small, productive *patios* and *parcelas* (ESACH, 2001).[13] The main difference between the two territories is that Old Havana is a well-developed tourist site, where few vacant lots escape assignment for related uses. However, it is also a territory where at least a portion of tourism revenue has been earmarked for community development projects that sometimes involve small *parcelas*, particularly on the municipality's periphery. The municipality of El Cerro contrasts with the two others in that it not only enjoys a long history of agricultural production but also contains a number of high-output agricultural sites, such as *organopónicos*. The level of small-scale agricultural activity in this municipality is also impressive by comparison with the other two: the ESACH census (2001) reports a total of 1329 registered productive *patios* and *parcelas* in its territory.

Sample definition

As explained, *parcelas* and *patios* have not received much attention in the literature. Moreover, the above-mentioned census is still incomplete and does not provide enough detail to systematically characterize the universe under study, making it impossible to speak of a truly representative sample of producers. For these reasons, and given the restrictions faced by foreign researchers when carrying out comprehensive surveys, a snowball survey technique was considered most appropriate. Three urban farmers from the three municipalities were initially contacted through activities organized by the FANJ. These farmers then assisted the researcher in compiling a list of other local producers, and so on. Everyone suggested for inclusion was incorporated into the study, and no one declined the invitation to participate. The resulting sample encompassed 30 urban farmers associated with 19 UA sites. A wide range of UA activities were represented, from the raising of animals (such as rabbits, chickens, ducks, guinea pigs and pigs) to the cultivation of fruit trees, medicinal and culinary herbs, root crops, coffee, leafy greens and other edible vegetables. Three of those interviewed were exclusively engaged in raising animals, 14 of them engaged only in gardening, and 13 did both. The sample allowed for gender-sensitive analysis, as it included 19 men and 11 women, with three married couples and one father–daughter partnership. Eighty per cent (24) of the sample comprised people over 50 years of age – reflecting a generational pattern representative of this type of activity across the city (Premat, 1998; Murphy, 1999; Cruz Hernández and Molina, 2001). Of the 30 producers included in the sample, 19 were associated with usufruct land and 11 worked in privately owned spaces. The size of the sample was considered optimal to allow for an in-depth investigation of the selected sites and producers through participant observation.

The professionals included in the study were selected, as planned, to reflect various positions in the decision-making hierarchy, as well as the diversity of institutions involved in regulating or promoting UA in Havana. The initial selections were made with the assistance of the FANJ, but the list was expanded as the research progressed and actors were identified by interviewees or the researcher as being important within a given locality. In total, 41 interviews (with 21 women and 20 men) were conducted with representatives of 27 official bodies, including agencies of the state and NGOs. Included were MINAGRI, the Institute for Fundamental Research on Tropical Agriculture, the agricultural supplies industry, the agricultural goods and services stores, the Ministry of Housing, the Ministry of Public Health, the Ministry of the Environment, CDR (neighbourhood-based organization), the Municipal Assembly of Popular Power (government body), the Cuban Association for

Animal Production, the city's peasant sector, the Revolutionary Armed Forces, the Provincial Urban Planning Office, GDIC, Habitat Cuba, FANJ, the Cuban Council of Churches, the Ministry of Alimentary Industry, the Office of the City Historian, the Cuban Botanical Association, the Wine-makers Club, the Community Food Conservation Project, the Environmentalist Group of San Isidro, and the Community Patio Project of El Cerro.

PRELIMINARY FINDINGS

Preliminary analysis of the gathered data indicates that a significant disjuncture exists between the discourses and practices of, on the one hand, those who officially plan, support, and regulate UA in Havana and, on the other, those who practise it as small-scale, self-provisioning producers. Although a number of variables have been included in the study, the discussion here will be centred on occupation within the UA system ('professional' or 'producer')[14] and institutional affiliation. As will be shown, these variables help to account for significantly different perspectives on UA, which should be taken into account in understanding the full potential and limitations of the practice in all its diversity in Havana.

Discourses and practices of UA professionals

In general, the discourses of UA professionals included in the study reflect a strong technocratic bias, not necessarily unique to the Cuban context. These professionals expressed a common concern with defining, counting, formalizing and ordering UA spaces. Their discourse had its practical counterpart in practices such as mapping, granting of usufruct rights and census-taking. Although these practices appeared to stem from a genuine desire to better know and organize the constituency so as to serve it better, they are also associated with a formalization and institutionalization of UA activities that, in turn, can be linked to a desire for professional self-preservation, at least in some instances. These practices should also be understood as 'disciplinary technologies' (Foucault, 1979) that have the effect of moulding and influencing the target population's behaviour. In Cuba, this moulding should not be equated with oppression; instead, it appears to be motivated, at least in part, by the desire to highlight and encourage already existing practices contributing to the common good. However, in some important respects the current practices of defining, counting, formalizing and ordering UA spaces involves the inadvertent disenfranchisement of some UA producers.[15]

Important silences were noted in the discourses of UA professionals during interviews or at meetings as they defined UA, identified its principal actors, and described its evolution. These discourses corresponded to practices that, from the point of view of some small-scale urban farmers, were seen to have exclusionary effects.

When pressed, many UA professionals included the raising of food animals in their definition of UA. However, their discourses tended to submerge this aspect of the activity, equating UA primarily with the 'proper' exploitation of the soil in the less controversial activity of gardening. When mentioning animal-raising, most interviewees carefully characterized the practice as an exception that had taken place at the height of the 'special period' and suggested that its most aberrant manifestations (such as pig-raising in the core of Havana) no longer occurred. In fact, their discourses mirrored what was proper according to the law, not necessarily what was actually done (or was known to be done). This same perspective was also reflected in their reporting practices. Thus, the statistics reported by MINAGRI representatives at the local level were found to reproduce the official zoning of food-animal-raising. For example, a report from the municipality of El Cerro (CDR Municipio Cerro, 2001) tallied production involving chickens and rabbits – activities sanctioned within this territory by the UA guidelines put out by the Urban Planning Sector – whereas an equivalent report from the more central municipality of Central Havana (MINAGRI, 2002), again reproducing the guidelines, did not mention such animal-raising activities, although they are known to occur there. The reporting practices of Cuban UA professionals, then, tend to produce a normative picture of UA practices in the city and reflect an identifed pattern of behaviour in the production of official records by professionals in other settings (Whyte, 1985; Hammersley and Atkinson, 1990), where the main objective of reporting is to prove the competence of incumbent authorities.[16] What is important to underscore here is that this reporting (or, rather, underreporting) has the effect of making certain practices invisible, hence excluding them from consideration by UA professionals as they devise UA policy.[17] That such exclusion may be conscious and geared toward moulding the direction of UA activities within certain territories, thus encouraging some expressions while disabling others, was suggested by an agricultural representative in one of the areas where such activities were glaringly absent from official reports, although very noticeable on the ground. The representative stated that 'the current level of animal raising within the territory should be tolerated, but it should not be institutionally encouraged'.

The discourses of UA professionals also consistently depicted the typical actor involved in food production – from organoponic gardens to *patios* – as male. When asked to comment on the role of women, even those professionals in technical positions closer to the ground downplayed women's direct involvement in food production.[18] In fact, professionals consulted in a recent study estimate that women make up only 10–15 per cent of Havana's UA producers (Cruz Hernández and Medina, 2001). Such statements, however, are not based on actual statistics, because these are either non-existent or unreliable (Cruz Hernández and Medina, 2001). Rather, they are grounded on professionals' impressions and anecdotal evidence. These findings suggest that such impressions may be mistaken in relation to small-scale, self-provisioning spaces, where women do participate in food-producing activities by themselves, or jointly with men, often playing an important – although less public – role.

Although the perceptions of professionals in this respect deserve a fuller investigation, they appear to be partly founded on established gender roles that consider agriculture a male domain, as well as on established professional practices that give less import to independent producers and small-scale food production aimed at household self-provisioning, where women's involvement may be higher than expected.[19] It is not surprising to find that in this context, gender-sensitive analysis is largely absent from the reporting practices of UA professionals, as well as from their research agendas.[20]

When asked to comment on the development of food production in the city, most UA professionals emphasized its novelty, particularly in the city core, tracing its origins to the economic crisis of 1989. In this manner, they 'silenced' its previous, albeit more modest, existence while defining it as an exception needing redress. In fact, UA professionals coincided in the opinion that, now that the food-security crisis had been attenuated, there was an urgent need for reordering UA spaces. Expert knowledge was needed to correct both individual and institutional initiatives conceived and implemented at the height of the crisis, when there was little time for reflection and careful planning (Cruz Hernández and Medina, 2001). In the majority of the discourses of the UA professionals analysed, this 'ordering' was connected with the gradual relocation of food-production activities from the core of the city to its outskirts, a policy that, once again, disregarded the desires, established practices, and food-security concerns of many small-scale producers.

Despite these shared characteristics within the professional group, the research revealed that expressed perspectives within this broadly defined sector were far from homogeneous. Data gathered through interviews and various meetings with architects, urban planners, geographers and agricultural professionals suggest that differing perspectives within this group regarding the 'proper' place and function of UA did not correlate to differences in age, race, gender, education, profession, personal background (urban or rural) or role within the UA system (decision-maker or service provider).[21] Rather, these differences correlated with institutional affiliation. The mandate and resource investment of the professionals' institutional base emerged as important factors in shaping their discourses on UA.

To illustrate, consider the professionals in the Urban Planning Sector and MINAGRI, both with official authority to act on and influence the practice of UA in Havana. Employees of the Urban Planning Office have the authority to approve or reject the location of UA-related sites on urban public land[22] – whether commercial stalls, organoponic gardens or *parcelas*. Having committed themselves, as of 2000, to the incorporation of UA as a permanent element of Havana's master plan (Cruz Hernández and Medina, 2001), professionals in this sector now face the challenge of deciding how this incorporation can be best achieved. It is here that the distinction between UA geared toward food production and that oriented toward ornamental crops becomes important.

Urban planning professionals interviewed about UA divided the city into broad, internally homogeneous areas considered to have a differential 'vocation' for agricultural food production.[23] While conceding that agriculture as a food-producing activity has a place in the city, people interviewed in this sector felt that its optimal location is not in the core municipalities, which are densely built and lacking in appropriate water resources and soil availability. This position is consistent with the sector's mandate to promote economic growth in the city while maximizing the efficient use of state investment and resources. It further underscores this sector's understandable concern with how UA might best be inserted into the urban context while taking into account the inputs the activity requires (for example, soil, water), as well as how it may compete with other urban functions, such as housing and industry. But what this position does not take account of is the possibility of food-production alternatives that need not take up much space or soil or require a total reliance on conventional water sources (using instead, for example, recovered rain or recycled water). This exclusion seems to be partly founded on a traditional vision of food production as large scale and extensive and on an institutional 'blind spot' that automatically excludes private domestic spaces from serious consideration. Moreover, the data gathered suggest that this exclusion may be linked to an anti-agricultural (as in anti-food-production) bias within this sector that resists, primarily on subjective grounds, the possibility of the positive integration of food production into the urban environment.

This anti-agricultural bias becomes particularly evident in the discourses of urban planners speaking of UA during interviews and at meetings. During the six private interviews and the seven public meetings the researcher attended with people in this sector, they made only two references to food security and food production, while these same professionals employed terms such as *verde* (green) and *medioambiente* (environment) in their every mention of UA. Careful analysis indicates that such wording does not merely reflect a broader understanding of the multiple functions of UA, without necessarily excluding food security per se; rather, *greening* in these discourses was used systematically as an antonym of *food production*.[24] In several cases, speakers clarified that when they spoke of greening they referred explicitly to ornamental trees and plants. For example, an agronomist at the Provincial Urban Planning Office who supported greening of the city core elaborated her position by stating that the most urban of spaces (she was referring to municipalities like Old Havana and Central Havana) are fit at best for only an ornamental type of noncomestible agriculture that would beautify the environment. The correlation of *ornamental* and *noncomestible* with *greening* is significant, as is the consistency in this usage within the sector.[25] As Montañés Serrano (2001b) pointed out, different words are not different forms naming the same thing; rather, different words construct different realities. In this case, the reality constructed excludes certain practices from acceptability in the city, particularly its core.

This vision is further reproduced in the official *lineamientos* (guidelines) on UA put out by the Provincial Urban Planning Office. These guidelines unequivocally state that the central zone, which encompasses two of the municipalities included in this study (Old Havana and Central Havana), 'can only support silviculture in front yards and urban parks'. (DPPFA Ciudad de La Habana, 2001) These guidelines locate the most suitable zone for agricultural activity in the city's periphery – where, incidentally, such activities had been included in previous master plans – and consider the intermediate zone, which includes the outer districts of the municipality of El Cerro, suitable for activities ranging from *organopónicos* and *parcelas* to poultry- and rabbit-raising. This discursive construction of the possible (and by extension the permissible) has clear implications for the actual practices of UA professionals. As illustrated by the selective counting practices of MINAGRI representatives, such discourses influence the behaviour of professionals, even outside the Urban Planning Sector.

The mapping practices of professionals in the Urban Planning Sector also parallel their discourses in important ways. Although the Urban Planning Office's official map of the current agricultural landscape of Havana notes the presence of UA in the core, in the form of a few large-scale, high-investment endeavours such as *casas de posturas* (seedling houses) and high-yield *organopónicos*, small-scale efforts in this area go unrecorded, even on maps depicting activities at the level of the municipality. This situation is no doubt a reflection of an institutional emphasis on the management of large public spaces, particularly those dedicated to UA projects requiring considerable investment on the part of the state (Cruz Hernández and Medina, 2001). However, it is clear from other maps that even the inclusion of these larger spaces is seen as a temporary concession. Thus, the planners' vision of the future of UA in Havana does not accommodate even these higher output expressions of UA, not even in the intermediate zone, where a number are currently located. Future agricultural activity has been localized on this map on the outskirts of the city – an indication of the entrenched anti-agricultural (that is, anti-food-producing agricultural) bias alluded to in the literature (Murphy, 1999) and partly confirmed by the data presented here.

The map in question can be said to reflect what some theorists of space (such as Certeau (1988) and Lefebvre (1998 [1974])) have identified as a typical planner's or decision-maker's gaze, guided by the metaphor of the map that re-creates a univocal and abstract space governed by the laws of the 'proper', a space where differences and specificities that are known to exist are often erased to give way to a unified vision. Although the planners' vision may seek to ensure a permanent space for UA in Havana, such an image of the future may translate into a shortfall in services for small-scale UA practices located well within the urban fabric, thus muffling other UA with the potential for growth that, as explained, contributes differently to the food security of the most vulnerable of city residents.

MINAGRI, which has been officially in charge of promoting and overseeing UA for at least a decade, presents a different perspective. For ministry people,[26] particularly those involved with UA since the early 1990s and who identify themselves as members of a kind of UA vanguard, the story of UA in Havana has been one of a struggle against entrenched attitudes that oppose food production in the city, attitudes that they feel they have partly succeeded in changing through perseverance and hard work. As one high-level official put it, this involved convincing others in the decision-making sector that lettuce plants could in fact be as decorative as flowers.

In fact, the discourses of MINAGRI officials, contrary to those of the Urban Planning Sector, suggest that when they speak of UA, they are usually referring to food crops, rather than to ornamentals. With the exception of extension workers in Central Havana, they also consistently emphasize the food-security dimension of the practice, rather than its greening effects. Although most acknowledge that UA can contribute positively to the environment (*medioambiente*), they generally add this as an afterthought. This is a position also reflected in the ministry's literature, such as a recent brochure entitled 'Basis of the System', which lists the environment last in the list of the 28 sub-programmes to be promoted by this sector.

MINAGRI's concern with UA sites and their productivity, independent of the urban environment in which they are embedded, can be observed in the practices of its staff as they go about collecting statistics and selecting model UA sites (chosen every year for every form of production at the various territorial levels). In both cases, what is prioritized is the quality and quantity of outputs and the technical aspects of the practice (for example, the effectiveness of an irrigation system or the presence of intercropping), rather than the degree of integration between the production site and the surrounding urban environment. This narrow focus on the productive dimension in measuring the success of UA has been criticized by those in the Urban Planning Sector (Cruz Hernández and Medina, 2001), yet there is evidence of change. A member of MINAGRI's UA group who participated in a series of workshops on this subject organized by the FANJ commented, 'Today, things have changed, and one has had a chance to reflect more about the city and how it is not just unidimensional; it is made up of many parts, and we have to reconcile these different parts.' Indeed, such reconciliation seems imperative to ensure that all the positive dimensions of UA are fully developed in Havana. This task could very well begin with a true reconciliation of the perspective of the MINAGRI with that of the Urban Planning Sector, a reconciliation that, as the valuable work of Cruz Hernández and Medina (2001) attests, has already begun.

Less questioned by studies such as that by Cruz Hernández and Medina (2001) has been the manner in which UA professionals express a desire to segregate food-production practices in the city: they have a tendency to prioritize only some areas (or sites) for development. Although less so than in the case of the Urban Planning Sector, this tendency was also pronounced within MoA.

For the same reasons given by urban planners (lack of space and inputs like water), ministry staff consistently acknowledged the difficulty of developing UA in the core municipalities of Old Havana and Central Havana. Still, with the exception of two staff, none ruled out these municipalities as sites for food production, albeit on a minor scale. More importantly, all but one of the MINAGRI staff coincided in identifying other municipalities in the urban planners' central zone as feasible for food production. Staff often illustrated this point by referring to the municipality of Plaza de la Revolución, which, although the civic centre of the country, possesses a number of successful *organopónicos*. Moreover, the same ministry staff consistently highlighted the importance of small-scale producers working in these areas, particularly those associated with *patios* and *parcelas*.[27]

Superficially, the practices of the UA sector of the MINAGRI appear to correspond to its discourses. The recent appointment of a delegate of agriculture to the two core municipalities of Old Havana and Central Havana, which – unlike other city municipalities – had been without such a delegate for years, underscore that this sector is reconsidering the potential of UA in the city's inner core. The location of, and the plan to multiply, TCAs in these and other centrally located municipalities also suggest that more than purely ornamental cultivation is being promoted. The TCAs' primary objective is to promote UA activities in all its forms through the provision of agricultural inputs and services, as well as through the dissemination of relevant educational material. Although permitted to sell ornamental plants, the TCAs are obliged to carry a stock of vegetable seeds and hence could be seen as promoting food production. The launching by MINAGRI in 2000 of the *patio* and *parcela* movement further indicates that for the ministry, small-scale UA spaces centred on the household constitute an important component of the practice. The official *patios* and *parcelas* movement began with the stated aim of promoting agricultural production in every potentially suitable urban space. It was also designed with the explicit goal of assisting in the organization of already existing small-scale UA producers, to serve them better.

Still, data collected during this research shows that MINAGRI resources are not evenly allocated across the city and not all UA activities are equally supported. Thus, although key extension workers in the municipality of El Cerro have recently been given their own means of transportation, those of Central Havana and Old Havana must cover the territory on foot. TCAs are required to have vegetable seeds in stock, but the prices are fixed and the stores must derive their revenues from other 'non-essential' items, such as ornamental plants and agricultural accessories (for example, garden implements and straw hats). In this context, even though low-priced vegetable seeds should encourage food production, TCA staff have little incentive to promote cultivation of food crops in neighbourhoods where such practices are not already common.[28] The majority of those interviewed did not acknowledge any shortcomings in the support system for food-animal-raising. The fact that TCAs carry vegetable seeds and gardening implements but do not offer comparable inputs for food-animal-raising was not identified as a problem.[29]

Although acknowledging the importance of *parcelas* and *patios* in some contexts, ministry staff nonetheless consistently highlighted, instead, high-output UA spaces, such as the high-yield *organopónicos*, often equating these gardens with UA as a whole.[30] This is not surprising, considering that these spaces are associated with projects managed by the ministry and represent considerable state investment. This also sheds light on media accounts that, at a time when *parcelas* appeared to be thriving, focused instead on organoponic gardens, turning them into the icon of UA in Havana.[31] Notwithstanding the importance of the volume of the organoponic gardens' outputs, this emphasis hints at a hierarchy of institution-based priorities biased against the small, independent food producer.

Yet, it would be unfair to ignore how some MINAGRI actions in fact legitimate and encourage small-scale producers and their activities. A case in point is the recent census[32] of small-scale agricultural sites, associated with the *patio* and *parcela* movement.

More than noting the location and type of production taking place in small-scale UA sites, this census has entailed the literal labelling of these sites with stickers, usually applied to the door of the producer's private residence. The stickers read, 'This house participates in the Popular Movement for Agricultural Production of the Neighbourhood, by the Neighbourhood and for the Neighbourhood. United we will win this battle as part of the war of the people.' In a sense, these stickers reassert the need to harmonize the activities of private or semi-private sites with the revolutionary goals that emphasize the community over the individual. They publicly label the sites (and by extension the private households and citizens associated with them) as fulfilling a social rather than a private function. Particularly in the case of *parcelas*, over which producers are granted usufruct rights, the stickers mark the power and jurisdiction of the state over the spaces in question and denote their proper function with respect to the surrounding community. This public demarcation also seems to invite surveillance, not just by state functionaries, but by local residents, who thereby gain official sanction to assert their expectations over the use of this 'public' land. In this manner, the census acts as an example of what Foucault (1979) would call a disciplinary technology, which, through the counting, labelling and ordering of spaces, indirectly moulds the individuals who occupy them, in this case, after the image of the Guevarist ideal of the *hombre nuevo* (new man), who puts collective goals ahead of individual ones. Importantly, the census also acts to legitimate the role of the producer whose activities – even when private – thus appear to be sanctioned and encouraged by the state.

Finally, if the project of reconciling institutional perspectives to strengthen Havana's UA system is to be taken seriously, the above-mentioned convergences and divergences in the visions and practices of UA professionals need to be clearly acknowledged and reflected on. But the job cannot end with an interinstitutional dialogue. The perspectives of urban farmers, including the small-scale urban farmers in the city core, also need to be brought into the debate. It is to their opinions and practices that we now turn.

Urban farmers' discourses and practices

The data analysed to date indicate that the producer directly engaged in small-scale primary food production perceives and experiences UA very differently from the professionals.

Note: The proximity of this garden to the city core is underscored by the figure of the centrally located *Capitolio* (Capital).

Figure 6.1 *View from urban garden in Old Havana*

Interviews with producers indicate that most are less concerned with definitions and claims about the novelty of UA than with more practical problems. Most do not define themselves as urban farmers unless they see an advantage to doing so (for example, to gain access to services or resources). Also, most commented on the continuity of the practice, tracing it to familial or neighbourhood precedents from before the 1989 crisis.

The practices of small-scale farmers show the creative use of space for food production, even in settings that present considerable constraints. The now well-established gardens in previously abandoned lots of the core municipalities of Old Havana and Central Havana (Figures 6.1 and 6.2), as well as gardens created where no soil used to exist (Figure 6.3), illustrate the extent to which producers' sense of what constitutes an appropriate space for UA differs from that of people in the Urban Planning Sector. Acknowledgement of their creative accomplishments by UA professionals would necessitate a reconsideration of what those professionals understand as the standard requirements for food production, and this in turn might lead to an institutional incorporation of new spaces into the officially sanctioned and supported UA system.

The obscured practices of these producers demonstrate how despite official regulations on, and restrictive definitions of, UA, some practitioners continue to engage in their own creation of UA space, within limits dictated by their own economic and human resources. Certeau's writings on this general phenomenon seem applicable here; he considered the typical space of those

Note: This is in the centrally located and densely built municipality of Central Havana.

Figure 6.2 *Two views of an urban garden created out of a previously abandoned city lot*

Note: This illustrates the use of recycled truck tires to create a cultivable area on top of a cement patio.

Figure 6.3 *Urban garden in the municipality of El Cerro*

without formal power who, while lacking the authority to tabulate and impose their own vision of space, 'insinuate their countless differences into the dominant text' and reveal through their everyday practices the ambiguity of the space conceived as abstract and univocal by the planner's map (Certeau, 1988, pxxii). To ignore such diversity in the actual use of space is to be trapped in a particularly restrictive and impoverished notion of UA that does not take account of reality on the ground, and therefore, does little to address the needs of all practitioners.

Producers interviewed in this study described themselves as relating differently to the community, depending on the land-tenure status of spaces they cultivated. Those producers working on private spaces saw themselves primarily as sacrificing for their immediate family, not for their neighbours, whereas those working in usufruct plots, although acknowledging the self-provisioning goals of their *parcelas*, were also quick to point out how they contributed to the immediate community by sharing produce with neighbours, free of charge; donating of a portion of their outputs to community institutions; or donating their time toward onsite community activities (such as educational programmes involving children). Their claims were corroborated by observations of the producers' practices.

Further analysis suggests that such practices derive in part from producers' personal beliefs in the correctness of sharing, as well as from their perception of a need to legitimate their right to continued use of the usufruct space. The labelling component of the MINAGRI census could be seen to contribute to these motivations, as could other factors, such as the material and moral incentives to participate in the community, as promoted by neighbourhood institutions such as the CDR.

Data collected through participant observation of urban farmers further suggests that, in general, sharing of UA products and knowledge does take place within the community but that such intraterritorial practices do not necessarily characterize UA. Instead, UA practices often involve the crossing of neighbourhoods, as well as municipal boundaries, in a manner that contradicts the MINAGRI slogan that UA is of the neighbourhood, by the neighbourhood, for the neighbourhood. Far from claiming a pronounced sense of belonging to the local community, most producers felt the opposite; many described their gardens or animal-raising spaces as a refuge from the social tension or physical decay of the surrounding neighbourhood. This finding contrasts sharply with those of Cuban scholars studying the role of UA in the development of territorial attachment and neighbourhood-based community movements in the district of Santa Fé in the Havana of the early 1990s (Fernández Soriano and Otazo Conde, 1996, 1999; Fernández Soriano, 1997) and may be explained by a change in historical circumstances, as well as by the uniqueness of the community and effectiveness of the leaders in question.

During interviews, most producers identified the greatest value of their UA efforts to be the important contribution UA provides to the family diet; some even calculated the concrete savings facilitated by the practice. Thus, a small *patio* owner told me that the plantain bushes in his garden gave him 2400 plantains in a good year. With plantains selling for about 1 peso each in the agricultural market, this amounts to a savings of 2400 pesos a year (the equivalent of about nine average monthly salaries) (in 2003, 2.348 Cuban pesos (CUP) = 1 United States dollar (USD)). Another producer, who raises rabbits for family consumption and who at the time of the interview had 50 rabbits in a small rooftop area, commented that his family of five eats at least one rabbit a week. Considering that a small rabbit of about 3kg, unavailable in the formal market except in restaurants, sells for about 140 pesos (more than half an average monthly salary), this represents quite a saving, even when one factors in the high cost of feed. The contribution to household food security is even more impressive when one considers that most producers diversify their efforts. Thus, the rabbit raiser also had 60 chickens on his rooftop, and the gardener's cultivation also included root crops like yucca; vegetables, such as tomatoes, lettuce, and a Cuban variety of spinach; and a slew of medicinal and culinary herbs (for example, parsley, basil, ginger, oregano, rosemary, turmeric, mint and aloe). Notwithstanding impressive official statistics on the subject, then, it is evident from these few examples that UA practices make an important contribution to the food security of city households, particularly when one considers that state ration stores meet only minimal dietary needs, and prices at agricultural markets – and even at *organopónicos* – are still high for a large portion of the population. In this sense, the known potential of such spaces for contributing to food security could be realized through official support and encouragement in the form of UA education and services.

The raising of food animals, largely unmentioned by professionals, seems particularly important to most producers, who identify this practice as a source of much needed protein – considered a necessity in the ideal diet of most Cubans (Figure 6.4).[33] Some complain that despite the importance of the practice, the support of governmental institutions is uneven. Lack of needed resources – from fodder to cages – was a particular focus of comment. For example, although MINAGRI makes chicks available to the population at accessible prices, official venues for acquiring feed are virtually nonexistent, and hence most producers end up paying exorbitant prices for feed in the black market.[34]

The resilience and resourcefulness of some producers in this context should not be mistaken for the long-term survival chances of the practice. One rabbit raiser humorously commented, 'The day they prohibit me from raising rabbits, I will raise something else. I will raise a smaller animal. There will come a point when I might even raise ants or mosquitoes. Always trying to breed the biggest specimen, of course!' He added, more seriously, that his situation was exceptional because he had built equipment that allowed him to produce his own animal feed; other producers in his neighbourhood were not as resourceful, and their practice was seriously undermined by the difficulty in acquiring feed.

Producers further mentioned that while requiring work, food production brings pleasure, satisfaction, and even health – not just from its material output

Figure 6.4 *Family of proud rooftop animal raisers in the municipality of El Cerro*

but from its creative and recreational dimensions – an issue only partly acknowledged by urban planners who primarily consider the greening elements of UA (although not its food-production dimension) as raising the quality of life of city residents.[35]

The importance of production sites for those involved also has a symbolic dimension that has to do with the meanings producers attach to these spaces. With gardens close to the producer's residence, production space becomes an extension of the home, a site for cultural accumulation and display of individual or family identities, intertwined with acts of home-making as well as identity-making – a characteristic noted of gardening practices more generally in various parts of the world (Mukerji, 1990; Chevalier, 1998). This symbolic dimension was vividly illustrated by the garden of an artist who, following his creative urge, had hung among the vegetables pieces of coloured glass, discarded toys and even a tea cup given to him by his last lover (Figure 6.5). Although the garden design emphasizes the producer's individuality, it can also underscore a personal connection to society. Gardens that have been purposely opened for public viewing appear to lose their personalized quality, becoming virtually absorbed by dominant space through, for example, the display of official iconography (such as pictures of revolutionary heroes).

Although UA professionals generally played down the participation of women as producers, the data collected show that women do participate in food production, by themselves or with others. Six of the 11 female producers included in the study considered themselves independent producers working by themselves or with other women. (Three of these engaged in all facets of

Note: Some decorative touches are illustrated here, such as a hanging bicycle bell and tin plate.

Figure 6.5 *Gardener posing in his garden in the municipality of El Cerro*

the raising of chickens and rabbits.) The other five considered themselves producers jointly with their husbands or male relatives. A number of the male producers interviewed noted the assistance they received from their wives or mothers. In all cases where work was shared, a gender division of labour seemed to apply, with women primarily engaging in tasks such as cleaning animal cages or pens and watering the gardens. The males, in these instances, were publicly identified as the producers, even if the women's contributions were key to the success of the activity. Thus, for example, a garden publicly associated with the male head of the household was on further investigation found to be quite dependent on the labour, knowledge and willpower of the wife. She not only prepared the seedlings on the terrace of the house, but also usually decided where each crop should be planted in the garden lot. She was the authority on how the produce was to be used and held the knowledge of the culinary and medicinal properties of the plants in the garden. It was she who, for example, informally prescribed medicinal herbs to neighbours to deal with their various ailments. As the cook in charge of managing the household's food resources, she decided what needed to be harvested or slaughtered on a particular day. Although this subject deserves further exploration, enough data have been gathered to question the representation of urban farmers as primarily males and to point to a possible inadvertent exclusion of women practitioners by UA professionals trying to promote the practice.

These preliminary findings illustrate how sociocultural factors largely affect the manner in which UA, its proper spaces, and its actors are defined in Havana. The biases based on professional status and institutional affiliation, identified here, influence decisions regarding which UA spaces and practices are considered possible, legitimated and addressed by service providers. Although caution is required when interpreting the silences of official maps and discourses, these omissions often translate into real forms of exclusion. What is mapped is what is noticed and acknowledged. This applies even to research agendas that, echoing official maps, have tended to exclude the less formal practices of UA in private home spaces. These spaces are predominantly administered by women and generally constitute the primary sphere of action for the elderly, so this omission may lead to gender- and age-based exclusion. In the long run, non-acknowledgement translates into deficient identification of needs and hence a corresponding lack in the development of necessary services. Moreover, rigidity in the way UA spaces are conceived can preclude the long-term persistence of certain practices (such as animal raising in the city core) by relegating them to the realm of the illicit and therefore of the temporary.

To promote only one or another institutional vision of what UA spaces, activities and functions ought to be often alienates those producers whose practices do not fit the vision. The permanence of UA – with its environmental and food-security benefits and the livelihoods that have been created through its development – depends vitally on those who do the actual work: the urban farmers. If UA in Havana is to remain sustainable and the functioning of state supports are to be effective, the views of producers – particularly those associated with the small-scale sites discussed in this paper – have to be considered, and their specific multidimensional needs must be taken into account.

CONTRIBUTIONS TO THE FIELD OF URBAN AGRICULTURE AND IMPACTS OF FIELD RESEARCH

This study has made a number of contributions to the advancement of knowledge in the field of UA. Through the close investigation of a particular case (Cuba), the research has initiated a grounded exploration into important issues, such as the existence of an anti-agricultural (as in anti-urban-food production) bias within decision-making groups – issues about which only broad generalizations have been made in the existing literature (UNDP, 1996). The research has further illustrated how serious consideration of this bias must distinguish between various kinds of UA practices (for example, food-producing or non-food-producing) and various kinds of UA spaces present in the research context.

On a conceptual and methodological level, this work can also be seen as expanding the established frontiers of UA research. First, the focus on the impact of sociocultural factors addresses the existing imbalance in UA scholarship, which tends to have a 'hard-science' bias and to overemphasize the technical dimensions of the phenomenon, disregarding its social dimensions.[36] Considering that sociocultural obstacles to UA have been identified in other contexts (UNDP, 1996), such a broadening of research agendas is important beyond the Cuban case. Second, the use of a multi-sited ethnographic approach to the study of UA constitutes a methodological innovation in a field that has usually focused on isolated sites and actors, rather than on the interrelationship between these as part of a cultural system. The use of participant observation in various settings not only allows for the proper contextualization of interview data but also leads to a better understanding of what are no doubt complex and fluid practices.

To date, the research process and its outcomes have had a number of impacts that merit mention. In terms of the researcher's own professional development during the research, she participated in a permaculture course offered by the hosting NGO, the FANJ. This course not only provided important research contacts but also imparted valuable knowledge on technical aspects of sustainable agriculture that, given a training in social anthropology, she was lacking.

The research process allowed the establishment and strengthening of ties with local Cuban institutions, such as the FANJ and the Casa de Altos Estudios Don Fernando Ortiz (CAEFO, Don Fernando Ortiz institute of advanced studies, an academic institute associated with the University of Havana). Through CAEFO, a history course allowed the researcher to better contextualize current UA practices. Although this organization is not directly involved with UA, the author's contact in CAEFO, the late historian José Tabares del Real – an original member of the revolutionary 26th of July Movement – was instrumental in helping the researcher schedule interviews with high-level officials whose work has been central to the UA movement. The FANJ – with which there had been collaboration before this research – supported the author in a number of ways, including writing formal letters of introduction that facilitated access to various data sources (for example the Cuban television network, the National Library, the Casa de las Américas (Institute of the Americas) library), and made it possible for some high-level decision-makers to be interviewed. Staff at the FANJ furthered the research by including the author in relevant activities (UA-related field trips and workshops) and by openly sharing relevant literature, their field contacts and their accumulated knowledge and experience.

The impact of the research process on institutional capacity-strengthening was most clearly reflected in the author's direct involvement with Cuban NGOs generally and in particular with the host organization, the FANJ. At an informal level, almost daily conversations about findings with FANJ employees positively influenced their work 'on the ground' by making them aware of practitioners' needs for services and support. More formally, there were opportunities to share findings from the author's current and past research at a number of venues, including a workshop organized by the FANJ to introduce its staff to a database program designed to monitor the development of UA sites and at a series of five more formal workshops, attended by 12–20 UA professionals each, in which the writing of a book on UA in Havana was debated. The researcher also copy-edited and gave written feedback – which highlighted methodological gaps and challenged preconceived ideas (particularly regarding the issue of gender and participation in UA) – on that book, which was recently published by the FANJ, with the support of the International Development Research Centre (IDRC).

As well as contributing to the work of the host NGO, the author also advanced and promoted the work of other Cuban institutions and groups involved in UA. Having the luxury of access to meetings and events organized by various groups and institutions throughout the city, she willingly acted as bridge between them – bringing to their attention each other's ongoing projects or available resources. She assisted groups with the translation of funding proposals and the promotion of their work in international circles, sharing with them information on funding possibilities overseas, including those offered by AGROPOLIS and IDRC. In the case of the Community Patio Project of El Cerro, the researcher's assistance led to its securing financial support from a Dutch NGO for a small video project.

These research findings are expected to assist Cuban UA professionals in addressing problems of a practical nature in their everyday work. More specifically, the findings will likely influence FANJ's future plan of action and research agenda by helping that organization evaluate the effectiveness of its existing UA programmes and projects. Aside from FANJ, people from the Provincial Urban Planning Office in Havana, as well as MINAGRI have expressed an interest in the findings of this research. Once these are compiled, it is intended that they will be made available to these organizations.

CONCLUSIONS

The research data discussed above present insights of relevance to those interested in UA in Cuba and beyond. At the most general level, the findings to date underline the importance of sociocultural factors in shaping people's perspectives on UA and, in turn, affecting the long-term survival of certain UA practices. More concretely, the findings presented here point to a perspectival gap – possibly not limited to Cuba – related to occupation within the UA system (professional versus producer status), as well as to institutional affiliation. As shown in the Cuban case, this gap can result in the inadvertent exclusion of certain small-scale, household-oriented food production activities from the agendas of professionals who currently plan the future of UA in Havana – a situation that entails further inadvertent exclusions along gender and generational lines.

Insofar as UA everywhere is embedded in a sociocultural matrix, the study suggests possible research agendas applicable to other settings where sociocultural variables, such as those discussed above, may also play an important role in shaping divergent perspectives on UA. Although the social variables identified as important will no doubt vary from context to context and could be further refined, the research approach outlined here could be reproduced elsewhere.

In terms of findings more specifically relevant to the immediate case study, the insight that occupational status within the UA system and institutional affiliation account for significantly different perceptions of the phenomenon in the Cuban context will hopefully allow for constructive interventions, as these differences constitute a potential obstacle to the long-term consolidation of certain UA practices. For example, with respect to the conflicting mandates and needs of various institutions and practitioners, one action that could be taken is the conscious encouragement of initiatives that bring together – and encourage the exchange of ideas among – the diverse actors involved with or concerned about the practice of UA. This process has in fact already been initiated in Havana through the workshops organized by the FANJ and facilitated in part by IDRC funding, but it needs to be sustained and expanded, particularly to ensure the inclusion of small-scale, household-oriented urban farmers working in areas often ignored by the professional sector.

Finally, not all differences in perspective among the actors involved represent immovable positions. Even long-entrenched sociocultural values are susceptible to reconsideration and change; this is perhaps especially true in a country such as Cuba, where radical change seems intrinsic to people's lives.

ACKNOWLEDGEMENTS

This research was undertaken with generous financial assistance from IDRC (AGROPOLIS Program) and York University. I would especially like to thank my thesis adviser, Professor Margaret Rodman, of the Department of Social Anthropology, York University, and my field adviser, Armando Fernández Soriano, a researcher at the Fundación Antonio Nuñez Jiménez de la Naturaleza y el Hombre.

NOTES

1   My current research data indicate that urban farming, particularly so-called Chinese family-run vegetable gardens, was common in some areas of pre-revolutionary Havana. As for post-1959 Havana, notwithstanding the ambitious 1967 Havana Greenbelt project, which was intended to make the city self-sufficient in some comestible products, the extant literature suggests that there have always been individuals within the city who have engaged in farming practices to maintain family traditions or supplement government rations (see Butterworth, 1980).

2   These statistics were cited by Adolfo Rodriguez, the national delegate of UA at the first national meeting of the *patio* and *parcela* movement, which took place on 13 September 2001. The citation is derived from a transcript of this meeting, which was taped on site.

3   *Organopónicos* in Cuba are located on non-agricultural state land and use a modality of row-vegetable farming that officially relies on organic inputs.

4   The TCAs are now known as Consultorios Tiendas Agropecuarios (CTA), with the word *consultorio* (literally translated as 'consulting centre'), now placed before the word *tienda* (literally meaning 'store') to emphasize the social, as opposed to the commercial, function of these places.

5   This broad trend is corroborated by Cruz Hernández and Medina's (2001) case study on an area known as Camilo Cienfuegos, in the municipality of East Havana, where out of 152 small-scale producers organized in clubs in 1995, only 53 remain.

6   Data gathered during my fieldwork on former producers associated with small-scale spaces suggest that lack of appropriate services targeting the specific needs of this type of producer (such as affordable and accessible feed and medicine for food-animal raising) has discouraged some from continued participation.

7   Although public transportation has improved considerably since the earlier years of the economic crisis, long waits and crowded conditions are still the norm on many of the city bus lines. Statements such as those made by Murphy (1999), that a 5- to 10-km trip is a short commute by public-transportation standards in Havana, reflect a singular lack of awareness of the way most Cubans experience mobility within the city.

8   Today, provisions through the state-subsidized ration in Cuba fill 55 per cent of the nutritional requirements of an individual, according to recent studies (Díaz Vázquez, 2000). This is assuming that what is given through the ration is consumed in its entirety, something which, as Benjamin et al (1984) suggest, is not always the case, given personal tastes and the desire for variety.

9   The term *professional* in this context is used to refer to salaried workers whose jobs involve the encouragement, support or regulation of UA activities.

10   Participatory techniques requiring the involvement of the community as an active participant in the research process (such as the rapid visual diagnosis described by Santandreu (2001)) were equally not an option in the Cuban context for a foreign researcher, although they could very well be implemented by institutions having official jurisdiction over the counting and mapping of UA practices.

11   In the case of usufruct lots, the right granted is temporary. Few explicit restrictions apply to the use of these spaces; the only obligation of the *parcelero* is to keep the lot under agricultural production.

12   More studied have been the larger scale, more productive, higher input *huertos intensivos* (intensive gardening plots) and organoponic gardens geared toward commercial production. Incidentally, these spaces were not readily accessible to an outside researcher.

13   These numbers are growing as the census continues. Thus, in the case of Central Havana, according to a report by the municipal delegate for UA (MINAGRI, 2002), by 2002 the number of registered *patios* had gone up to 232 (almost five times the number counted in 2001). What should be emphasized here is that these numbers do not represent actual available spaces for UA. According to estimates made by the Central Havana Municipal Housing Office, 8000 spaces (ranging from *patios* to balconies) could be used for UA. If accurate, this figure would mean that 16 per cent of the 49,253 households in this municipality could engage in some kind of UA. The number of UA sites counted to date, however, only accounts for 3 per cent of these spaces.

14   Although other differentiations can be made in terms of occupation within the UA (such as decision-maker, TCA manager, extension worker), the broad distinction between producer and professional was found to be most important in relation to the findings discussed here.

15   The word *inadvertent* is used here to underscore that the data do not allow us to assume that this disenfranchisement is the result of a conscious plan on the part of UA professionals.

16 The practice of inflating statistics for UA spaces 'permissible' within certain territories can be linked to the same motive.

17 It should be acknowledged that with activities such as pig-raising that are legally authorized only in certain parts of the city, underreporting may also reflect a policy of leniency or silent toleration.

18 The only instance in which the typical producer was described as female was an interview with a professional working in the municipality of Central Havana, where the bulk of UA activities was said to concentrate on the cultivation of ornamentals.

19 An exception worthy of notice is the work of NGOs, such as FANJ, which in its day-to-day work has prioritized such small spaces.

20 I have only encountered one article in the Cuban literature that dealt with women in UA (that is, Cruz and Murciano, 1996). This article described the experiences of three female producers but made no generalizations about the role of women in UA. It is interesting to note that in the more recent study conducted by Cruz Hernández and Medina (2001), women's role in production remains underinvestigated.

21 This is not to deny that decision-makers and service providers have significant differences of opinion on other related issues outside this analysis (such as the merit of organic agriculture and diversified production). Nor is it my intention to suggest that gender does not constitute an important axis of difference when it comes to allocating tasks within the UA system. Indeed, the division of labour within MINAGRI, for example, appears highly gendered, with women minimally represented in the higher echelons of the decision-making hierarchy yet abounding in its technical sector (Cruz Hernández and Medina, 2001). Although positions in this latter sector may be more lucrative (as in the management of agricultural input and service stores), they also involve greater health risks (such as in the application of toxic substances by extension workers).

22 Although a subdivision of the Urban Planning Sector concerns itself with the application of by-laws pertaining to private domestic spaces, these by-laws refer primarily to building regulations and do not mention UA practices.

23 The analysis that follows is based on the opinions of six individuals working in relevant areas of the urban planning sector, including the Office of National Planning and the Provincial Headquarters of Planning and Architecture. Also included, because of close links to the sector, were three employees from GDIC.

24 This analysis suggests that the proposed inclusion of UA as part of Havana's Green Areas System (Cruz Hernández and Medina, 2001) may not necessarily lead to the full development of its food security dimensions.

25 It is also significant that these professionals did not identify water supply as a problem when it came to the cultivation of ornamentals in these territories. This concern simply did not arise, although it was always mentioned when people discussed the cultivation of food crops.

26 The analysis that follows is based on data gathered from 11 individuals positioned differently in the institutional hierarchy of MINAGRI. Included were provincial and municipal delegates (for each of the municipalities in the study), representatives working at the neighbourhood level, and employees of the agricultural input enterprise and the TCA.

27 Indeed, it was this ministry that had, from the beginning of the post-Soviet economic crisis, the authority and resources to encourage this type of food production, which led to, among other things, the creation of the TCAs.

28 It is not my intention to question the fairness of a policy that fixes prices for essential agricultural products, but rather to point out that such policies may not always have the desired effects.

29 These stores do, however, carry goods related to the keeping of domestic animals, such as dog leashes.

30 When one considers the absence of *organopónicos* from certain core municipalities and the fact that a quarter of them are dedicated to production for the tourist industry (Cruz Hernández and Medina, 2001), the ubiquitous ministry slogan that UA is production of the neighbourhood, by the neighbourhood and for the neighbourhood (initially used to underscore the bringing together of producer and consumer in the space) loses some of its original import.

31 As of the mid-1990s, photos of *organopónicos* regularly accompanied articles on UA. Previously, the image of the *parcelero* (plot holder) was the preferred representation of UA in the print media.

32 The census is actually carried out by agricultural representatives, who are paid by ESACH (a dependency of MINAGRI) but are based at municipal headquarters of the CDR.

33 Some authors have suggested that the purportedly rural background of many urban farmers might lead to practices that clash with urban aesthetic sensibilities, reinforcing non-practitioners' attitudes about the appropriateness of this activity in an urban environment. Contrary to the literature, my research data so far indicate that although gardeners may often be of peasant background, animal raisers, the most controversial of urban food producers, are primarily of the city; neither they nor their families originated in the countryside.

34 This shortcoming of the system is acknowledged by some in MINAGRI and the Cuban Association for Animal Production, a Cuban NGO closely associated with MINAGRI that is seeking to address the needs of at least some animal raisers in the city.

35 Among the food producers interviewed, those who spoke of a commitment to organic agriculture were few, as were those who spoke of the positive impact of UA on the environment. This position, which contrasts with that of most UA professionals who seem committed to sustainable practices, may correlate with generational and educational differences between professionals and producers: the former are predominantly young (mostly in their 40s) and university educated, whereas the latter have at most a secondary-level education and are older (in their 50s and 60s). Of course, other more practical considerations – such as the fear of losing an entire season's work and its associated benefits – may be at play in producers' willingness to look for 'modern' solutions (for example, the application of chemical pesticides) to production problems. Clearly, this is an area that requires further attention by UA professionals.

36 This research also contributes to expanding the scope of social sciences, such as anthropology, that – although incorporating work on urban environments for decades – have largely ignored the subject of UA.

REFERENCES

Benjamin, M., Collins, J. and Scott, M. (1984) *No Free Lunch: Food and Revolution in Cuba Today*, Grove Press, New York, NY

Bourque, M. and Cañizares, K. (2001) 'Agricultura Urbana en La Habana (Cuba)', *Revista Agricultura Urbana*, vol 1, no 1, pp27–29

Butterworth, D. (1980) *The People of Buena Ventura: Relocation of Slum Dwellers in Postrevolutionary Cuba*, University of Illinois Press, Urbana, IL

CDR (Comité de Defensa de la Revolución) Municipio Cerro (2001) Agricultura urbana informe (September), Havana

Certeau, M. de (1988) *The Practice of Everyday Life*, University of California Press, Berkeley, CA

Chevalier, S. (1998) 'From woolen carpet to grass carpet: Bridging house and garden in an English suburb', in Miller, D. (ed), *Material Cultures: Why Some Things Matter*, University of Chicago Press, Chicago, IL, pp47–71

Comaroff, J. and Jean, C. (1992) *Ethnography and the Historical Imagination*, Westview Press, Boulder, CO

Cruz Hernández, M. C. and Medina, R. S. (2001) *Agricultura y Ciudad: Una Clave para la Sustentabilidad*, Fundación de la Naturaleza y el Hombre, Havana

Díaz Vázquez, J. (2000) 'Consumo y distribución normada de alimentos y otros bienes en Cuba', in Burchardt, H. J. (ed), *Nueva Sociedad*, La ultima reforma del siglo, Caracas pp33–56

DPPFA (Dirección Provincial de Planificación Física y Arquitectura) Ciudad de La Habana (2001) *Lineamientos para la Agricultura Urbana*, Havana

ESACH (Empresa de Suministros Agropecuarios Ciudad de La Habana) (2001) Informe sobre los resultados del movimiento popular en torno a la estimulación de la poducción en patios y parcelas con cierre 15 de Junio del 2001, Havana

Fernández Soriano, A. (1997) 'Movimientos comunitarios, participación y medioambiente', *Temas*, vol 9, pp26–32

Fernández Soriano, A. and Otazo Conde, R. (1996) 'Comunidad, autogestión, participación y medioambiente', in Dilla, H. (ed), *La Participación en Cuba y los Retos del Futuro*, Centro de Estudios Sobre América, Havana, pp225–237

Fernández Soriano, A. and Otazo Conde, R. (1999) 'Realidades, retos y posibilidades de los municipios Cubanos en el fin de siglo', in Zemelman H. et al (eds), *Gobiernos de Izquierda en América Latina: El Desafío del Cambio*, Plaza y Valdes, Mexico City, pp166–170

Foucault, M. (1979) *Discipline and Punish: The Birth of the Prison*, Vintage Books, New York

Gould, P. and White, R. (1980) 'Mental maps', in Press, I. and Smith M. E. (eds), *Urban Place and Process: Readings in the Anthropology of Cities*, Macmillan, New York, pp96–104

Hammersley, H. and Atkinson, P. (1990) 'Documents', in *Ethnography: Principles in Practice*, Routledge, New York, pp127–143

Harley, J. B. (1988) 'Maps, knowledge, and power', in Cosgrove, D. and Daniels, S. (eds), *The Iconography of Landscape*, Cambridge University Press, New York, pp277–312

Lefebvre, H. (1998 [1974]) *The Production of Space*, Blackwell, Oxford

Marcus, G. (1995) 'Ethnography in/of the world system: The emergence of multi-sited ethnography', *Annual Review of Anthropology*, vol 24, pp95–117

Marcus, G. (1998) *Ethnography through Thick and Thin*, Princeton University Press, Princeton, NJ

MINAGRI (Ministerio de la Agricultura) (2002) Informe de balance de la agricultura urbana. en Centro Habana (April), Havana

Montañés Serrano, M. (2001a) 'Dinámica, funcionamiento, y contenido de las entrevistas individuales y grupales', in Villasante, T., Montañés, M. and Martín, P. (eds), *Construyendo Ciudadanía. Vol. 1: Prácticas Locales de Creatividad Social*, Ediciones El Viejo Topo, Barcelona

Montañés Serrano, M. (2001b) 'Introducción al análisis e interpretación de textos y discursos', in Villasante, T., Montañés, M. and Martín, P. (ed), *Construyendo Ciudadanía. Vol. 1: Prácticas Locales de Creatividad Social*, Ediciones El Viejo Topo, Barcelona

Mukerji, C. (1990) 'Reading and writing with nature: Social claims and the French formal garden', *Theory and Society*, vol 19, pp651–679

Murphy, C. (1999) 'Cultivating Havana: Urban agriculture and food security in the years of crisis', Food First, Institute of Food and Development Policy, Oakland, CA. Development Report 12

Peluso, N. (1995) 'Whose woods are these? Counter mapping forest territories in Kalimantan, Indonesia', *Antipode*, vol 27, no 4, pp199–217

Premat, A. (1998) 'Feeding the self and cultivating identities in Havana, Cuba', York University, Toronto, ON, Ottawa. MA thesis.

Rocheleau, D., Thomas-Slayer, B. and Edmunds, D. (1995) 'Gendered resource mapping: Focusing on women's spaces in the landscape', *Cultural Survival Quarterly*, Winter, pp62–68

Rosset, P. and Benjamin, M. (1994) *The Greening of the Revolution: Cuba's Experiment with Organic Agriculture*, Ocean Press, Sydney

Santandreu, A. (2001) 'Rapid visual diagnosis: A rapid, low cost, participatory methodology applied in Montevideo', *Urban Agriculture Magazine*, vol 1, no 5, pp13–14

Santandreu, A. and Dubbeling, M. (2001) 'Los qué, como, y por qué en el proceso participativo y constructivo de diagnostico para la agricultura urbana', in *Diagnósticos Participativos de Agricultura Urbana. Lineamientos Metodológicos y Conceptuales*, Workbook No 86, Urban Management Program, Regional Coordinating Office for Latin America and the Caribbean, PGU-ALC/UNHABITAT, Quito-Ecuador, pp1–13

UNDP (United Nations Development Programme) (1996) *Urban Agriculture: Food, Jobs, Sustainable Cities*, UNDP, New York

Whyte, W. F. (1985) 'Interviewing strategy and tactics', in Whyte, W. F. and Whyte, K. K., *Learning from the Field: A Guide from Experience*, Sage Publications, New York, NY, pp97–112

7

Urban Agriculture and Local Sustainable Development in Rosario, Argentina: Integration of Economic, Social, Technical and Environmental Variables

Eduardo Spiaggi

INTRODUCTION

This research was carried out in the Empalme Graneros neighbourhood of Rosario, Argentina. Rosario is a city with a population of 1.1 million and is located in the central part of the country, in what is known as Pampa Humeda, where the main agricultural production is concentrated.

The combination of neoliberal policies and structural adjustment, together with the high levels of corruption among the leading class (politicians, business people, union leaders, etc.), has caused a serious deterioration of the productive and social sectors of the country and has, since 1998, led to four years of continuous economic recession (depression): 50 per cent of the population is now below the poverty line, almost 20 per cent is unemployed, and regional economies are devastated (*Clarín Newspaper*, 1998–2001). As a consequence, the population is constantly migrating from impoverished rural areas to the cities, where immigrants occupy scattered settlements known as *villas miseria* (slums). The project activities were directed toward these new city dwellers.

The government made its first attempts in urban agriculture (UA) in 1989 – one of the most serious periods from a socio-economic point of view – to lessen to some degree the food problems that large sectors of the population were facing. The Pro-Huerta Programme (promoting gardens programme) of the National Institute of Agricultural Technology was created under this umbrella and is still in operation.

Since the beginning of our research activities the main objective was to demonstrate the feasibility of UA and its impact on sustainable local development (Biasatti et al, 1999; Spiaggi et al, 2000a). Several variables were evaluated to quantify feasibility and impact under four headings:

- social (degree and type of participation, gender aspects, institutional development, respect for cultural diversity, increase in the beneficiaries' empowerment);
- economic (genuine income generation, commercialization, costs of production, human resources, inputs);
- technical (introduction of vermiculture as a waste processor, intensification and diversification of production); and
- environmental (water quality, presence of pollutants in soil, vermicompost and vegetables, treatment and exploitation of house wastes, biodiversity status).

CONCEPTUAL FRAMEWORK AND HYPOTHESES

Our approach is based on a wide concept of UA coinciding with that of other authors (Mougeot, 2000), in which UA not only provides food production and self-employment but also helps to 'create an improved microclimate and conserve soils, to minimise waste in cities and to improve nutrient recycle, and to improve water management, biodiversity, the O_2–CO_2 balance, and the environmental awareness of city inhabitants' (Deelstra and Girardet, 2000, p47).

It has been widely reported in the literature that food production in cities runs some risks, mainly owing to pollutants produced by exhaust fumes from vehicles and factories. Another important aspect is animal breeding in urban areas, with its zoonotic risk and manure generation (*Urban Agriculture Magazine*, 2000–2001). Other reservations about UA are related to land access and competition with other land-uses (real estate, sports, etc.).

The need to incorporate UA into urban planning has become apparent (de Zeeuw et al, 2000), and this requires appropriate, broad, flexible and participatory policies at the municipal level.

This research is based on experience that began in the Empalme Graneros neighbourhood and is supplemented by experiences at the regional level, by visits to other active projects in Chile (Tomé) and Cuba (after an invitation from the Ministry of Higher Education of Cuba and with the objective of co-operating in the development of a network of universities for UA research), and by information on the marked development of UA at the international level. The initial questions posed in the project were as follows:

1   Can urban production systems for processing organic waste include large-scale vermiculture technology to derive fertilizer (vermicompost)?
2   Can UA projects be put into practice in low-resource urban sectors to start a process leading to sustainable local development?

Although the two central questions are different, in that the first is of a technological nature and the second is of a general nature, they are closely related. Thus, when considering vermiculture as the technology for processing organic waste, it leads to thoughts of the city's social problems and the people who suffer such extreme poverty that they live on garbage.

The second question was directed at evaluating the role of UA as a local development tool for social sectors suffering extreme poverty. The approach, in this case, was based on the integration of all the productive and training activities in a community development context and on the search for improvement of the beneficiaries' self-esteem and quality of life (Spiaggi et al, 2000b).

A new hypothesis grew as the project evolved. One of the variables studied in this project, as an indicator of sustainability, was the role of UA systems in increasing the biodiversity of the urban ecosystem. By gaining an understanding of the close relationship between the inhabitants and the biota – that is, between the cultural background and the use of natural resources – it becomes appropriate to use the concept of sociobiodiversity, or biocultural diversity, which refers to the relationships between sociocultural diversity and biological diversity (*Developing Ideas*, 1997).

It is possible to preserve biological diversity as far as sociocultural diversity is preserved (Toledo, 2000). And it is evident that we are currently facing a worldwide process of cultural homogenization, an imposition of a monoculture (*Developing Ideas*, 1997), which to a lesser or greater degree is imposing rules and styles of consumption, production, information and so forth and incorporating various societies and ethnic groups.

Therefore, the objectives of this paper are to report on the following:

- the introduction of large-scale vermiculture as an appropriate technology for processing organic waste and producing fertilizer in productive UA systems;
- the quantification of environmental and social indicators of system sustainability; and
- the strengthening of community participation and organizational capabilities.

METHODOLOGY

From a theoretical point of view, the systemic approach used was based on that suggested by García (1994), as the problem under study can be considered that of functioning as an organized whole, involving the biophysical environment, production, technology, social organization and the economy. Because such a situation is characterized by a coming together of multiple processes in which interrelations constitute the structure of a system working as an organized whole, we can call it a complex system. And, like any system made up of living organisms, it is also an open system, exchanging substance, energy and information with the environment. This approach is also based on what Morin (1994) defined as complex thought:

> *What is complexity? At first sight complexity is a net (complexus: a whole made up of interwoven parts) of heterogeneous inseparably associated constituents presenting the paradox between the one and the multiple. On close attention, complexity is, in effect, the net of events, actions, interactions, determinations, chances that make up our phenomenic world...*
>
> *Reality is both in the link as in the distinction between an open system and its environment. This link is absolutely crucial from the epistemological, methodological, theoretical, empiricist point of view. Logically, the system cannot be understood but as including the environment in itself, an environment that is both intimate and foreign and part of itself being, at the same time, external.*[1] (Morin, 1994, pp32, 44, 45)

From the ethical point of view, I must make it clear that I do not consider myself an external observer who attends a site daily to take down notes, leaves the place and objectively analyses data afterwards, but as a researcher as subject – not object – who tries to sustain a commitment of solidarity with people who suffer an unfair situation. Therefore, I cannot set the researcher aside from my persona, as can be observed in this chapter from the results and the data reached together with the neighbourhood inhabitants and other colleagues.

The philosophical and technical principles of agroecology (Altieri, 1999) structure this researcher's methodological approach. This approach is based on the use of a technical and productive strategy grounded in the above-mentioned principles as sustained in temporal and spatial diversification. This strategy is linked to the maintenance of high rates of recycling of animal and vegetable wastes and urban residues, to the optimization of the use of space, and to the implementation of low-cost technologies in a participative research–action framework (Spiaggi et al, 1996; Montero, 1997).

From a technical point of view, vermiculture was introduced as an appropriate technology for processing organic waste and transforming it into biofertilizers (Spiaggi et al, 2000a; Spiaggi et al, 2001). For this, intensive training was carried out in April and May 2000: a theoretical and practical course, designed for 25 inhabitants, was given at the 17 de Agosto Community Centre. This eventually led to the design of trials with the beneficiaries on the use of vermicompost with various vegetable species (tomato and chicory) from June 2000 to March 2001.

In parallel, work was carried out from June 2000 to December 2001 on the intensification and diversification of production, preparation of aromatic and medicinal plants, and the organization of efforts to commercialize these. A field assessment of the community gardens in Rosario to determine the dissemination of the vermiculture technology is yet to be performed

The fieldwork was carried out in the Empalme Graneros neighbourhood, in its most impoverished area. The working sites were two community farms of about 1ha each, 15 blocks from each another. This experience did not start from a zero point: from 1991 to 1996, the municipality's Community Gardens Department gave intense training, but the programme suffered problems and was finally interrupted in 1997.

The methodology also included the analysis of some indicators to allow evaluation of project sustainability; thus, the analysis of the following indicators was proposed (Nickerson, 1993; CET, 1998): environmental, social, economic, technical and productive factors.

Environmental factors

Biodiversity

Periodic samples were taken to quantify the number and abundance of plant and animal species in the production systems and surrounding environment. Studies were made of the inter- and intraspecific relationships, as well as diversity and density of various populations.

This activity, as already pointed out, is of vital importance and highly complex. The area studied represents extremely intense anthropization of the soil, and consequently only a few species of the original biota still grow there. Therefore, it should be considered an 'artificial' (eco)system. From the agroecological-productive point of view, it is clear that an increase in biodiversity favours system stability (Altieri, 1999), but this concept is more readily applicable to agroecosystems. The methodology applied in agroecosystems is not wholly transferable to urban systems. The studies on the role of diversity in areas destined for UA must be deepened and contextualized to the environmental issues of cities – for example, can areas destined for UA be integrated into the net of green spaces in cities? To what extent can they contribute to regulation of temperature and to regulation of water drainage and absorption? More complex still is the relation between biota and inhabitants. As I have already said, the majority of the inhabitants are immigrants from rural areas, who bring not only their cultural baggage but also various species – mostly plants, such as manioc, tobacco, cotton, and medicinal and aromatic species. This results in an increase in cultural diversity in cities and has a subsequent effect on biodiversity.

Soil and vermicompost

Soil and vermicompost analyses were carried out in the productive system and surrounding environment. Percentages of organic matter, bio-availability of minerals (P, N, K, Ca), concentration of heavy metals, and quantity and diversity of microbial colonies were determined.[2]

The most critical aspect of this section was the sampling and subsequent determination of the presence of heavy metals in soil and harvested vegetables, in terms of both the sampling design and the quantity and type of analyses performed. More analyses should probably have been performed, and the behaviour of these elements in the environment should be permanently monitored.

Water

Water analyses (chemical and microbiological) were carried out on samples taken from the running water and from existing wells (groundwater).

Social factors

Social diversity

The number of individuals surveyed (sex and age) and the nature of their roles (active or passive, direct or indirect) were determined. The integration of various groups (men, women, youths and children) from the community was also noted.

Participation

The level of participation was measured by recording attendance at the training meetings and in the production activities. Besides absence or presence, the level of participation (active, moderate or passive) was also registered.

Economic factors

By the end of 2000, a methodology was designed to evaluate some economic aspects of the project to allow an analysis of the costs and benefits of activities. This methodology included keeping monthly records of input costs (seeds, tools, greenhouses, fences, water consumption, etc.); human resources (time devoted by the beneficiaries); technical advice; social plans (temporary income paid to some of the beneficiaries); and income (from vegetables, vermicompost, earthworms and commercialization of plants and medicinal products). Some costs, such as that of some of the necessary inputs (seeds and tools, for example) were easier to estimate than others, such as that of land restoration (from informal dumps to fertile and productive land for UA). A methodology designed to deliver realistic results should take into account economic costs and values that are sometimes difficult to quantify.

This methodological approach offers the advantage of analysing the system in its complexity and requires the use of qualitative as well as quantitative data. Such data include, for example, information on the quantity of waste processed, the quantity of vermicompost produced, the income obtained from commercialization, the degree of participation of the beneficiaries, the women's situation, and the level of organization of the community. In addition, difficulties arise in the delimitation of the system studied and an adequate deconfounding of the influence of external variables (macroeconomy, recession, unemployment, reduction of social plans) and their permanent interaction with the local variables (pressure on the use of the land, problems of wastes, current water access, interpersonal relations, among others).

Technical and productive factors

Production factors were also considered, and these were quantified through the use of two small experiments: trials to determine the effect of vermicompost as a biofertilizer, both in its traditional form (that is, as obtained from the bed) and diluted in water (1kg per 3L of water, settled for 14 days and filtered). All studies were based on the following pattern: plots with established doses of fertilizer were compared with control plots without them. It would be interesting to compare the use of various doses as well as vermicompost mixed with manure from various animal species in future trials.

Trial 1 (vermicompost as fluid biofertilizer) – in this trial, 22 tomato plants (*Lycopersicum esculentum* variety *platense*) were studied (this variety of tomato was obtained in the region of La Plata, Argentina, and is widely used by horticulturists). Plants 1-11 were allotted a treatment with liquid fertilizer, prepared using 1kg vermicompost per 3L water (settled for 14 days and filtered). Plants 12-22 constituted the control plot, and they were given no fertilizer. Treated plants received a 200-mL dose per plant at the moment of transplanting and a second 200-mL dose 49 days after transplanting.

Trial 2 (vermicompost as standard biofertilizer) – of 36 tomato plants (*L. esculentum* var. *platense*), 18 were considered the control plot: that is, they received no treatment; and 18 were fertilized with vermicompost as obtained from the beds: that is, they were treated. Treated plants received a 200-g dose per plant at the moment of transplanting and a second 200-g dose 49 days after transplanting.

The total number and weight of fruits produced by the plants of each treatment (a number had been assigned to each plant) were determined. The number of fruits produced and the total fruit weight per plant were then calculated. Fruits were collected every three days. Four people took part in conducting these trials.

RESEARCH FINDINGS

Vermiculture training

The use of vermiculture for both the processing of organic waste and the production of biofertilizers and animal protein was widely successful. Of the 25 beneficiaries offered a course on vermiculture, 18 attended the whole course (eight classes), and four of these are currently active as monitors and disseminators of this technology.

Annually, a total of about 6t of organic waste, processed in 20 production modules on the two community farms, in the beneficiaries' houses and in the 17 de Agosto Community Centre, renders about 2.6t of vermicompost.

This result is particularly important because approximately 40 per cent of the people in this neighbourhood live on informal waste collection, separating glass, metal, plastic and cardboard and selling these to storers and discarding the organic waste as being traditionally of no use. Also, the municipal waste-collection system does not function in most sectors of this neighbourhood; thus, waste constitutes a great environmental problem.

Vermicompost as biofertilizer

A summary of the results of the trials is given in Tables 7.1 and 7.2. An increase in the number and weight of fruit was observed with the use of vermicompost, both standard and diluted, although for the latter the average weight per fruit was lower for the treated group than for the control. It is important to highlight that diluted vermicompost is easier to use and more efficient, as 3L of diluted vermicompost can be obtained from 1kg of standard vermicompost. This kind of trial, based on the idea of trying organic fertilizers obtained from the production system itself, needs further implementation and research, as more consistent support to strongly advise its massive use can be achieved through more trials with more plants and various species. No conventional fertilizers were used in these trials, as these low-income urban farmers, whose only capital to invest is their time and labour, could not have afforded them.

Table 7.1 *Effects of fluid vermicompost on tomato yields and components of yield*

	Control	Treatment
Total fruit (n)	67	116
Average fruit–plant ratio	6.09	10.54
Total weight obtained (g)	9850	13,358
Average weight per plant (g)	895	1214
Average weight per fruit (g)	147	115

Table 7.2 *Effects of standard vermicompost on tomato yields and components of yield*

	Control	Treatment
Total fruit (n)	262	299
Average fruit–plant ratio	14.55	16.61
Total weight obtained (g)	32,613	42,651
Average weight per plant (g)	1811	2396
Average weight per fruit (g)	124	143

Note: Statistical analyses were not significant at 0.05 per cent.

The results show that vermiculture is an appropriate technology (biotechnology) for processing organic waste (agricultural and urban) at a small to medium scale. It allows the reuse of the derived high-quality biofertilizers in productive systems, transforming waste into an input. Its low cost and simple handling make it available to small producers and urban inhabitants with few financial resources (Spiaggi et al, 2001). It is worth mentioning that because of high unemployment rates, the people in this study were eager to invest their time and skills in productive activities, such as those offered by UA. Earthworms were supplied at no cost by the Faculty of

Veterinary Sciences of the National University of Rosario, and the community made a commitment to sharing the worms with any new beneficiaries that became involved in UA in the neighbourhood.

Medicinal plants and natural products

Another aspect to be highlighted is the work done with medicinal and aromatic plants, which started many years ago with the classification and rescue of existing species in the neighbourhood. This project proceeded mainly after meetings with the inhabitants – both *criollos* (creoles) and indigenous – who, coming from rural areas, had a wide knowledge of and tradition in the use of the various plants. In 1993–1996, the first attempts to capitalize on this knowledge were made in the community centre when professionals (biochemists and doctors) from the municipal health centre and the Community Gardens Department participated (Lattuca, 1999). There, the first medicinal products (creams, lotions and ointments) were processed, as well as the external antiparasite and anti-inflammatory medicines that were then used and prescribed by the health centre.[3] The initial results led the doctors at the health centre to recommend that the local authorities spread the experience to other neighbourhoods in the city. In three neighbourhoods, various species will be grown, and the simplest products will be produced in the community centre; more complex products will be prepared at the municipality's medicinal laboratories.

This is a clear example of how technical, sociocultural, economic and environmental factors can interact. On the one hand, the traditional knowledge of the community is respected and valued; on the other hand, the sociobiodiversity is preserved and economic resources are generated and returned to the community in the forms of income for the neighbourhood producers and cheaper medicines.

Environmental education and generation of genuine income and employment

Training in vermiculture had a strong component of environmental education that allowed participants to become aware of the issue of waste and to begin concrete activities in this field. Another achievement was their joining a working group consisting of 21 people. They also developed a proposal to allow them to offer an urban-hygiene service to the municipality, on the one hand, and to adapt a place to process the organic fraction (through composting and vermiculture), classify inorganic materials and set up a plastic-recycling plant, on the other.

At present, agreements are being discussed with the municipal authorities, who are backing up the establishment of a co-operative (the Cooperativism Department is training the members of the group), and arrangements are being made with a private landowner to enable the group to carry out the proposal's activities.

Another source of income is the produce of the gardens (vegetables, seedlings, vermicompost, flowers and worms), which each beneficiary takes home for self-consumption, thus saving money. Barter sites, known as *clubes del trueque*, enable the beneficiaries to exchange their products for other goods, such as clothes, sugar, and flour – a practice that expanded in the face of the economic crisis the country is still experiencing. In addition, the beneficiaries make direct sales in the gardens and have a home delivery service. In mid-2002 the municipality's UA programme created a fair for vegetables and other community products in the centre of the city; people from various community projects can sell their products at this fair once a week.

The strategies for income generation are varied, and they do not exclude, but rather combine with, one another. Once again, it becomes difficult to quantify these activities. We have estimated a value of 1 United States dollar (USD) a day for the quantity of products that each beneficiary takes home, exchanges at the barter sites and sells directly.

It becomes necessary to state that almost none of the beneficiaries works full-time at these activities, that most of them are women in charge of several children, and that both men and women alternate their UA activities with occasional jobs (many alternate them with informal waste collection, performed at night).

Sustainability indicators

Given that sustainability can be considered to be the dynamic equilibrium of a triad of social, economic and environmental variables and given the extreme poverty of the urban inhabitants in this project, the results have a real application at the local (neighbourhood) scale. The extreme poverty, which affects more than 30 per cent of the inhabitants, leads to a strong social imbalance that threatens the sustainable development of the city. The complexity of microsustainability (at a local scale) adds to the complexity of the sustainability at the city.

The results should be considered within the framework of the tension between the socio-economic context of the neighbourhood and the greater forces at the city level.

Urban agriculture in community development

Another feature to highlight is the project working system: fortnightly discussions were held at the community centre with representatives of the community, the National University of Rosario, the nongovernmental organization (NGO) Ecosur, the health centre, the 'Crecer' centres (places where children under five years of age are assisted together with their mothers), the health secretary, the Environmental Policy Department and the social promotion secretary. At these meetings, in addition to the members (five to eight representatives) of the community regularly attending, professionals in various disciplines took part, thus allowing an interdisciplinary approach to the various neighbourhood problems, to the generation of local intervention policies and to the interaction with local authorities.

REFLECTIONS FOR FURTHER RESEARCH

Although successful in its own right, the project has also highlighted topics for future research. From a technical point of view, vitally important issues for sustained success are: the generation of production technologies to increase products and make a more efficient use of resources (energy, fresh water and sewage, manure, etc.); the practical relationship between urban waste and manure production; the productive and environmental implications of vermicompost; and the monitoring and control of pollutants.

From the sociopolitical point of view, some other issues to be studied are: the systematic introduction of UA in official urban planning; the development of new regulations on the use of land; and the establishment of commercialization channels. Another aspect to explore is the relationship between biodiversity, sociocultural diversity and UA (Smit, 2000). Also needed is continuing and deepening research to systematize a methodology for assessing the impacts (today and in the future) of UA on the sustainable development of cities.

OTHER IMPACTS OF FIELD RESEARCH

Development of human resources

So far, 60 people (41 women and 19 men) from the community have been trained in vermiculture, in organic production techniques for vegetables and aromatic and medicinal plants, and lately, in environmental and urban waste problems. Twelve assistants from Niagara College (Ontario, Canada) and the NGO LifeCycles (British Columbia, Canada) have been trained and have participated in the field activities.

Gender-sensitive analysis

As experiences around the world have shown, UA involves mostly women (Jaramillo, 1997; Moya, 1998). In this project, 65–70 per cent of participants were women (figures vary because of the dynamics of the relationship with beneficiaries – for instance, some of them left the project because they gained temporary employment, and others joined the group because of the constant rise in the unemployment rate). Women mainly joined to initiate an individual development process, which was important. It allowed them, without education or training, to get out of the family context, traditionally associated with child raising – the majority have many children – under stressful conditions, such as men's alcoholism and violence.

When making the decision to attend the training meetings, the participating women started a process that not only allowed them to train in some technique – and this is sometimes just an excuse – but also to meet peers in the same situation and those who had a higher degree of personal development and could share their problems and experiences. This coincides with what the researcher personally observed in the community of Tomé, Chile, where most of the participants in the project were women who clearly found this opportunity important for their personal growth and for the possibility of getting in touch with their peers.

Women played a central role in the development of the Rosario project, both in designing activities and in discussing, proposing and following up on new initiatives. Two women presided over the two most representative institutions in the community: the community centre and the farmers' co-operative. These two women also had the opportunity to go to Chile for a fortnight and share training activities and exchange experiences with their Chilean peers.

Institutional capacity strengthening

Students in the ecology course taught at the Centre for Environment Studies of the Faculty of Veterinary Sciences at the National University of Rosario expressed interest in UA and have requested literature and visited the project.

For the two NGOs involved (Ecosur and Asamblea por los Derechos Sociales (assembly for social rights)) the UA programme had already been institutionalized. For them, it meant becoming involved in a new area of activity when the project started, but today it is part of their annual plans.

Effectiveness of local partnerships

Good participatory integration of the various institutions involved – the National University of Rosario, NGOs, community centre and municipal departments – was achieved. The main difficulty has been the permanent reduction of official funds allotted to social development activities.

Methodological and scientific advances

From the technical point of view, what has been achieved is the introduction of vermiculture as an appropriate technology for the processing of organic waste, the production of biofertilizers, and the acquisition of animal protein (used as animal feed in farms or for commercialization). Worms contain high-quality proteins (57–60 per cent of their dry matter), and in cases of overproduction, these proteins can be used to feed other animals, such as poultry and swine.

From the methodological point of view, the systematic approach taken in this study, which included the examination of technological, environmental, social and economic variables, may contribute to the recognition of UA as a tool for localized sustainable development in cities.

CONCLUSIONS AND RECOMMENDATIONS

The socio-economic situation of the country has worsened since this project began in the Empalme Graneros neighbourhood. More than 50 per cent of the country's population lives below the poverty line, unemployment is officially about 20 per cent, and the economy is undergoing a four-year recession. A decrease is also occurring in the gross national product, and future international payments are likely to be suspended.

In this scenario, it is evident that the weakest social groups are likely to be disadvantaged the most, and these were the people with whom this project was carried out. Bearing this in mind, the author has reached the following conclusions:

- The UA activities have had a remarkably favourable impact in four areas: (i) on productive aspects of the neighbourhood (production of more and better products for self-consumption and commercialization); (ii) on social aspects (strengthening of community participation and organizational capabilities); (iii) on economic aspects (generation of genuine income and employment); and (iv) on environmental aspects (use of agroecological techniques, restoration of informal dumps, provision of environmental training). The beneficiaries have more food for self-consumption, and they are gaining income from the commercialization of various products. Estimates allow us to conclude that each family gets about 1kg of vegetables a day, and whenever they have surplus – something that depends on seasonal patterns – the average income (including self-consumption and barter) is equivalent to about US$1 a day. The commercialization aspect should be strengthened, but it becomes difficult if the inhabitants live in extreme poverty and have no access to credit.
- Vermiculture training and environmental education have resulted in a local ability to convert organic waste into biofertilizer, as well as an appreciation of the environmental problems of the neighbourhood and the establishment of a project to create an urban-hygiene co-operative.
- An interesting articulation of work in the neighbourhood, with the local authority's participation, has been achieved during the last year. The results of this work may have contributed to some extent to the launching of the Urban Agriculture Programme within the Social Promotion Division of the Municipality of Rosario at the end of 2001.
- The most important result is the increase in the self-esteem of the participants (mostly women). They can now argue for their rights and for a better quality of life.

To conclude, I consider UA a powerful tool for engaging urban inhabitants with limited resources and for initiating local development processes. In Argentina, the National University of Rosario should be aware of the importance of UA in helping to ease the economic crisis this social sector has been undergoing so dramatically and should strengthen its research and practical actions in this field, as well as in all fields related to sustainable human development.

ACKNOWLEDGEMENTS

My sincere thanks go to the Organization of American States, the International Development Research Centre (through the AGROPOLIS Program), and the Canadian International Development Agency (through LifeCycles, for the material support given to carry out this project).

Special mention should be made of my colleagues at the National University of Rosario, Liliana Marc and Ricardo Biasatti; Antonio Lattuca (research supervisor of the AGROPOLIS project); Mariana Guillén, member of Ecosur, who has shared the project activities with me for more than a year; translator Virginia Serenelli; Professor John Middleton (supervisor of my master's thesis); and especially the neighbours of Empalme Graneros, with whom we have been sharing the project during these four years of work.

NOTES

1   The translation is our own. The source text says: 'Que es la complejidad? A primera vista la complejidad es un tejido (complexus: lo que esta tejido en conjunto) de constituyentes heterogéneos inseparablemente asociados: presenta la paradoja de lo uno y lo múltiple. Al mirar con mas atención, la complejidad es, efectivamente, el tejido de eventos acciones, interacciones, retroacciones, determinaciones, azares, que constituyen nuestro mundo fenoménico.

   'La realidad esta, tanto en el vinculo como en la distinción entre el sistema abierto y su ambiente. Este vinculo es absolutamente crucial desde el punto de vista epistemológico, metodológico, teórico, empírico. Lógicamente, el sistema no puede ser comprendido mas que incluyendo en si al ambiente, que le es a la vez íntimo y extraño y es parte de sí mismo siendo, al mismo tiempo, exterior.'

2   These results have been presented and analysed in detail in the final report for the AGROPOLIS Award Project (IDRC 1999–2000).

3   A web page for this project has been developed by John Middleton, Director of the Centre for the Environment, Brock University, Canada: www.brocku.ca/envi/au/lacapital20020516/

REFERENCES

Altieri, M. (1999) *Agroecología: Bases Científicas para una Agricultura Sustentable*, Editorial Nordan-Comunidad, Montevideo

Biasatti, R., Krug, K. R., Lattuca, A., Lemos, C., Middleton, J., Montero, A. and Spiaggi, E. (1999) 'Desarrollo local sustentable: Desarrollo de una estrategia de agricultura urbana, en Rosario, Argentina', *Revista UNR Ambiental*, no 3, pp79–93

CET (Centro de Educación y Tecnología) (1998) *Software: Sustainability Assessment*, CET, Asambleas de Dios, Chile

Clarín Newspaper (1998-2001) *Clarín Newspaper* [Buenos Aires], various editions

Deelstra, T. and Girardet, H. (2000) 'Urban agriculture and sustainable cities', in Bakker, N., Dubelling, M., Gründel, S., Sabel-Koschella, U. and de Zeeuw, H. (eds), *Growing Cities, Growing Food*, Deutsche Stiftung für Entwicklung, Feldafing, pp43–65

Developing Ideas (1997) Edited by International Institute for Sustainable Development (IISD), Winnipeg, Canada. Issue 7 (Jan–Feb)

de Zeeuw, H., Gündel, S. and Waibel, H. (2000) 'The integration of agriculture in urban policies', in Bakker, N., Dubelling, M., Gründel, S., Sabel-Koschella, U. and de Zeeuw, H. (eds), *Growing Cities, Growing Food*, Deutsche Stiftung für Entwicklung, Feldafing, pp161–180

García, R. (1994) 'Interdisciplinariedad y sistemas complejos', in Leff, E. (ed), *Ciencias Sociales y Formación Ambiental*. Editorial Gedisa, Barcelona

IDRC (International Development Research Centre) (1999–2000) 'The utilization of agroecological techniques in urban agriculture: The implementation of a new productive system (vermiculture) for local sustainable development', final report of the AGROPOLIS Award Project, IDRC, Ottawa

Jaramillo, S. (1997) 'Development from the base: Necessary condition to achieve an urban sustainable development process', *Revista Agroecología y Desarrollo*, no 11/12, pp82–88

Lattuca, A. (1999) 'Huertas familiares, escolares y comunitarias en la ciudad de Rosario, Pcia. de Santa Fe', in *Participación de las Organizaciones de la Sociedad Civil (OSC's), a Nivel Municipal*, Inter-American Development Bank, Buenos Aires

Montero, A. (1997) 'Desarrollo local sustentable: Agricultura urbana, microemprendimientos y manejo de residuso solidos', *Revista Agroecología y Desarrollo*, no 11/12, pp89–98

Morin, E. (1994) *Introducción al Pensamiento Complejo*, Editorial Gedisa, Barcelona

Mougeot, L. (2000) 'Urban agriculture: Definition, presence, potentials and risks', in Bakker, N., Dubelling, M., Gründel, S., Sabel-Koschella, U. and de Zeeuw, H. (eds), *Growing Cities, Growing Food*, Deutsche Stiftung für Entwicklung, Feldafing, pp1–42

Moya, R. (1998) 'Mujeres y desarrollo desde la base', *Revista Agroecología y Desarrollo*, no 11/12, pp104–108

Nickerson, M. (1993) *Planning for Seven Generations: Guideposts for a Sustainable Future*, Voyageur Publications, Quebec

Smit, J. U. (2000) 'Agriculture and biodiversity', *Urban Agriculture Magazine*, vol 1, no 1, pp11–12

Spiaggi, E., Biasatti, N., Marc, L., Mansilla, M. and Di Masso, R. (1996) 'Implementacion de un sistema productivo integrado nutrias – lombrices en el marco de un desarrollo agropecuario sustentable', *Revista UNR Ambiental*, no 2, pp103–112

Spiaggi, E., Biasatti, R. and Marc, L. (2000a) 'Minilivestock in Rosario, Argentina: Vermiculture for organic waste processing', *Urban Agriculture Magazine*, vol 1, no 2, p36

Spiaggi, E., Guillén, M. and Latucca, A. (2000b) 'Urban agriculture and local sustainable development in Rosario, Argentina', Presented at the International Symposium on Urban Agriculture and Horticulture, 7–9 July, Berlin, Germany.

Organized by TRIALOG, Humboldt University of Berlin, Faculty of Agriculture and Horticulture and HABITAT Havana Cuba. Published on CD Rom.

Spiaggi, E., Bisatti, R., Marc, L. and Benaglia, A. (2001) 'Aplicación de lombricompuesto para incrementar la producción de tomates', *Revista UNR Ambiental*, vol 4, pp15–23

Toledo, V. (2000) *Economía de la biodiversidad*, Environmental Training Network for Latin American and the Caribbean, United Nations Environment Programme, Regional Office for Latin America and the Caribbean, Mexico City

Urban Agriculture Magazine (2000–2001) *Urban Agriculture Magazine*, various issues

8

Agri-urban Development from a Land-use Planning Perspective: The Saclay Plateau (France) and the Sijoumi Plain (Tunisia)

Moez Bouraoui

INTRODUCTION

Peri-urban agriculture, in a strict etymological sense, is agriculture that is practised on the periphery of cities, regardless of the type of production system concerned.[1] Depending on the particular case, the relationship of this agriculture to the city can take the form of either shared ownership or a reciprocal exchange of functions. In the latter case, agriculture becomes part of the urban equation, with the result that farmland and built-up land then jointly take part in the urbanization process as parts of the urban space. Urban agriculture (UA) thus becomes the agricultural activity whose resources, products and services have, or can have, a direct urban use. This is the definition that is currently provided by the UA team at the research laboratory of the École nationale supérieure du paysage de Versailles and that the author adopted in this research when speaking more specifically about UA's transforming processes.

It was during a geography course on the peri-urban and intra-urban agricultural environments that this researcher became interested in studying the agricultural–rural environment in an urban context. The central question in this agricultural degree course was to know whether the effective management, planning and organization of a city could be designed with farmland so as to maintain the rural areas as part of the process of ensuring the sustainable organization of large cities. After this course, the decision was taken to investigate the circumstances of agri-urban development in France and Tunisia.

Since the end of the 19th century, urban growth has transformed nearby rural agricultural areas. From the middle of the 20th century on, this process has both accelerated and diversified, with the result that it has modified the morphology and spatial organization not only of the urban space but also of the surrounding countryside. This phenomenon is called peri-urbanization.

Peri-urbanization involves a long, complex, evolving process that takes place within several interacting systems – social, spatial, economic and political. In most of the world's large cities, expanding peri-urbanization has generally had a transforming effect on the farmland within the urban area. The organization, operation and evolution of farmland have given rise to much research in various disciplines. In France, the main studies dealing with questions of peri-urbanization and peri-urban agriculture include those by: David (1980); Kayser (1981, 1996); Jaillet and Jalabert (1982); Kayser and Schektman-Labry (1982); Berger (1984, 1986a, 1986b, 1989); Luginbühl (1995); Taffin (1985); Terrier (1986); SEGESA (1994); Hervieu and Viard (1996); Donadieu and Fleury (1997a, 1997b); Donadieu (1998a, 1998b); and Fleury and Moustier (1999). In Tunisia, the best-known studies on the same topic have mainly been carried out by geographers at the Faculty of Literature and Human Sciences, Université de Tunis in Tunis, especially Attia (1972); Kassab (1976); Belhedi (1979, 1989, 1992); Signoles (1985); Sethom (1992); Sethom et al (1992); and Sebag (1998).

These studies operate at two levels; the research reported in this chapter operates at the intersection of both. One level focuses on the formation of peri-urban 'crowns' and the absorption of farmland by urbanization. Studies at this level have explained the mode of operation of the socio-spatial and economic mechanisms characterizing the peri-urban zone and differentiating it from both the central urban zone and the rural countryside. The other level focuses on measuring and understanding the changing social relations in the urban and peri-urban farming and rural zones, as well as the future and specific nature of peri-urban agriculture. Studies at this level are now beginning to make a profound contribution to our understanding of the genuine emergence of new forms of urban–rural relations.

On the basis of these two primary orientations, the thesis can be summarized in the following three objectives:

1 Provide urban planners with new data likely to be relevant to their efforts to regulate or control the conflicts inherent in peri-urbanization.
2 Show how the environment produced by peri-urban and intra-urban farming can play roles as a negotiating tool and as a goal in developing new land-use plans.
3 Help generate, especially in Tunisia, fresh discussion on the spatial and social relations that the city and its inhabitants could maintain with the rural–agricultural environment surrounding them.

SELECTION AND PRESENTATION OF THE SITES – THE SACLAY PLATEAU AND THE SIJOUMI PLAIN: TWO PERI-URBAN SITES

To improve our understanding of the dynamics of the peri-urban-rural agricultural environment, the research attempted to examine how farming and farmland evolved and was organized in two peri-urban zones in two different countries: the Saclay Plateau, near Paris, France, and the Sijoumi Plain, near Tunis, Tunisia.

These sites were selected because they present virtually identical morphological and geographical characteristics, while differing considerably in urban planning and the physical environment. On the Saclay Plateau, urban planning primarily consists of restricting new building and landscaping to preserve and develop farmland as an essential component of a new way of organizing peri-urban zones. However, urban planners for the Sijoumi Plain seem to favour another approach: the installation of a major industrial zone, construction of housing on 1000ha of land, and the creation of a typical urban park to compensate for the loss of open land currently used for farming. These sites were also chosen because they appear to be ideally suited for understanding the specific modalities of the urban–rural relationship in two countries with different cultures and mechanisms for the transformation of farmland near major urban centres.

Only 20km from Paris, the Saclay Plateau covers almost 5000ha, of which 2600ha is primarily used for grain-farming (Figure 8.1). This region constitutes

Figure 8.1 *A vast sea of cereal plants, Saclay Plateau, southwest of Paris*

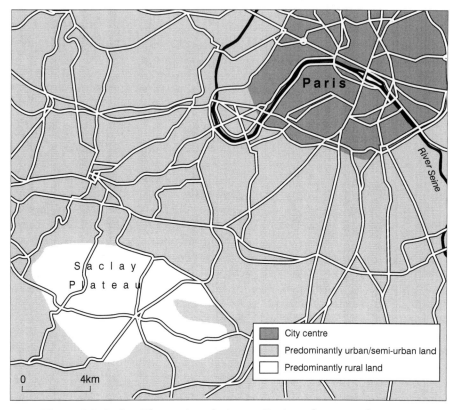

Figure 8.2 *Saclay Plateau in relation to Paris and surrounding area*

the main open space in the southwest zone of the Paris region (Figure 8.2). For at least the last 300 years, this land has been acknowledged to be the most productive in Île-de-France. However, because of its proximity to Paris, it is constantly threatened by urban sprawl.

There were two objectives involved in choosing the Saclay site. The first was to understand the sociopolitical process of the transformation of agriculture's role in the formulation of local and regional land-use policy. And the second was to describe the various strategies developed by farmers to adapt to changes in their social and spatial environments. Indeed, the reason for selecting Saclay as the French site was because it constitutes a particular example of the integration of peri-urban farmland into a new system of land-use planning (the countryside action plan (CAP)). The coherence of this system is based on the recognition of agriculture's contribution both to the economy and to the provision of green space to enhance the urban environment.

Like the Saclay Plateau, in Paris, the Sijoumi Plain is the most important open-space area in the southwest zone of the Tunis region (Figure 8.3). Located 15km from the city, the plain covers an area of nearly 7000ha, more than 3000ha of which is used for crops such as cereals, market garden vegetables, tree fruits and olives (Figure 8.4).

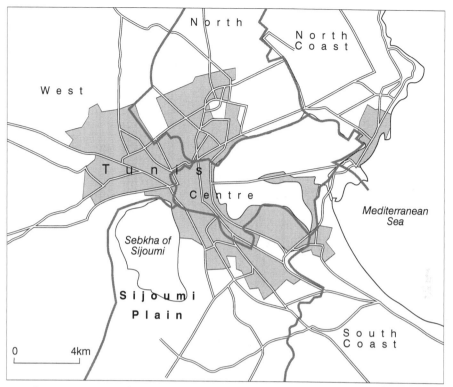

Figure 8.3 *Map of Tunis and surrounding area, including Sijoumi Plain*

Figure 8.4 *A vast rural agricultural space, Sijoumi Plain, southwest of Tunis*

Since the 1960s, this plain has been subject to increasingly forceful urban pressure and has become the first area in Tunisia affected by the phenomenon of peri-urbanization, which has created what may be called hybrid zones.[2] The destructuring effect of the urban sprawl around Tunis is reflected in varying degrees throughout the region's countryside, but especially at the urban–rural interface. The Sijoumi Plain offers many advantages for a study of how farmland in the hybrid zones has progressively been affected, because this area has been subject to many, primarily economic, changes through the installation of new industrial facilities, including some spatial changes, as a result of the expansion of the Tunis urban area into Sijoumi farmland.

RESEARCH FOCUS, HYPOTHESES AND OBJECTIVES – THE SUPRA-AGRICULTURAL FUNCTIONS OF URBAN FARMING AND HOW THESE ARE TAKEN INTO ACCOUNT AT THE LEVEL OF PUBLIC POLICY

Any attempt to characterize the various stages in the transformation of the urban countryside and assess the capacity of this zone to produce agricultural areas that are socially recognized as countryside ultimately leads to one central question and four subsidiary questions. The overall thrust of this research revolves around these five questions:

1   How and under what circumstances, especially in France, are agri-urban land-use policies developed?
2   What are the underlying causes of the urban development process that has transformed peri-urban farmland and what has been the impact of urban growth on the operation and organization of farms?
3   What are the advantages and limitations of public policy on these issues?
4   What social and physical form does the urban–rural relationship take?
5   To what extent does analysis of the social relationship with farmland help in understanding the process of change that is affecting forms of agriculture in urban areas?

From question 1 (the central question) arose the four other questions, constituting the scientific focus of this study. These questions are the research avenues for verifying two main hypotheses:

1   Urban farming has not only the economic function of producing foodstuffs, but also a spatial component that enhances the urban environment and the living conditions of urban residents.
2   Maintaining agriculture inside urban areas requires, first, social recognition and, second, integration of agriculture into a specifically urban system of land-use.

The first and most important hypothesis is the main axis of the whole project. The overriding goal reflected in this hypothesis was to check whether UA, in addition to its economic contribution, has the role of an open green space that fulfils other land-use and social functions that are just as important as agriculture itself. For example, farmland offers attractive landscapes to urban residents. It helps to enhance city outskirts, provides breathing space in the urban environment, and balances out the spatial occupancy of urban land. Moreover, farmland often constitutes the only element of cultural identity for a city, region or country. We speak, for example, of the vineyards of France (of Bordeaux, Champagne, and so on) and of the olive or orange groves of Tunisia (more specifically, the citrus groves of Cap Bon, the orange groves of Soukra, the olive groves of Sfax, etc.). In addition to sustaining a gene bank, or 'ecomuseum', of immediate value, UA can play a basic ecological role by recycling certain forms of urban waste.

The goal of the second hypothesis was to verify whether the type of farming practices used in UA and the countryside environment that UA provides city dwellers were sufficiently appreciated to enable UA, without losing its social identity and functional role, to occupy a major place in social and political projects designed to promote alternative ways of organizing urban space.

RESEARCH METHODOLOGY –
A SOCIOSPATIAL AND POLITICAL ANALYSIS
OF THE URBAN–RURAL RELATIONSHIP

With a view to developing perspectives likely to help take more advantage of the connections between the urban community and the farmland surrounding it, the project used a methodology approaching the topic along three axes: spatial, social and political. With its emphasis on these dimensions of the transformation of the role of the peri-urban-rural agricultural environment in the Saclay and Sijoumi regions, the study required an analysis of urban-planning documents, aerial photographs and classic cartography. With this latter tool providing physical indications of the countryside and its dynamics, as well as of how the territories are organized, it was possible to show changes in space and time and the effects of the various forms of urban growth on agricultural land.

A series of interviews were conducted with the main actors in the Saclay and Sijoumi regions (see the interview questionnaire in Annex 1). This group of respondents included Saclay and Sijoumi farmers, the inhabitants of the two regions, and institutional actors and urban planners in Paris and Tunis. An additional survey was conducted of the residents of Greater Tunis.

Farmer survey

The main objective of the farmer survey was to collect basic information on both the current situation of farming operations and their future prospects. It was a question of understanding the dynamics of the changes affecting farms on the Saclay Plateau and the Sijoumi Plain. This approach involved studying the various types of farms and their situation in the urban context. It was also a question of determining the constraints imposed by the city's proximity and how these affected not only the farming operations but also the farms' output and future. Depending on the nature of these constraints, an attempt was made to identify the various adaptive mechanisms the farmers used and to evaluate the additional expenses they incurred in coping with these problems.

Resident survey

We asked residents of both regions three questions:

1   How do you experience and describe your region?
2   What do you think of farming?
3   Is farmland a recognized part of the landscape in Saclay or Sijoumi?

The main objective of this line of questioning was to discover what people thought of UA and how they described it.

Institutional and urban-planner survey

Various officials and urban planners were asked their views on the role of farmland in the organization of urban space and in the issue of preserving agricultural space, not as a land reserve or food-producing economic area, but as a place for nature, leisure and recreation and as an urban-planning tool with considerable potential for reorganizing urban space.[3] In other words, the research aimed to draw their attention to an overlooked part of urban space, but one that could prove to be very useful for urban planners.

Additional survey of the residents of Greater Tunis

Considerable research work has been carried out in France to identify and assess the relationship the French people have with the surrounding space, nature, the city and the countryside. (On the basis of this research, some researchers and land-use specialists – geographers, agronomists, sociologists, landscape professionals and urban planners, for example – are adopting a new approach to the issues of peri-urbanization.)

Because the scientific community in Tunisia has not yet looked into this aspect, the methodological approach was reinforced with an additional survey of the inhabitants of Greater Tunis to collect some data on the nature of their relationship with the surrounding space.

RESEARCH FINDINGS – SACLAY AND SIJOUMI: TWO EXAMPLES OF PERI-URBAN AGRICULTURE FROM A LAND-USE-PLANNING PERSPECTIVE

The case studies of the Saclay Plateau and the Sijoumi Plain are intended to show how urbanization affects the changing character of rural agricultural space, by examining farming operations in these areas. In the process of this research, the author was led to broaden the research to characterize the urban, agricultural, social and spatial dynamics differentiating the two sites. This approach pursued three lines of investigation, focusing on spatial, sociological and public-policy dimensions.

The study of the spatial dimension (analysing the land itself, as well as urban-planning documents, aerial photos, and so on) revealed the changes in space and time affecting both regions – from the time their farming identity emerged to the beginning of the peri-urbanization process affecting them. Driven by economic and social forces, this process was reflected in:

- *A major increase in the level of urbanization* – in the Saclay Plateau, this is a result of the policy of decentralizing the scientific and industrial activity of Paris; in the case of the Sijoumi Plain, this is a result of significant population growth in Tunis, combined with increased intra-urban movement within Greater Tunis.
- *Major absorption of farmland* – more than 1200ha of agricultural land has been lost on the Saclay Plateau; more than 600ha, on the Sijoumi Plain. This phenomenon is the direct result of the convergence of four separate intentions: (i) that of public servants in Tunis, who want to meet a high demand for housing, and elected officials in Saclay, who want to benefit from the direct revenues contributed by private housing and zones of economic activity (residential taxes, business taxes, etc.); (ii) that of local people, who aspire to own property; (iii) that of landowners and real-estate developers, who hope to benefit from capital gains in real estate; and (iv) that of industrialists, who want to profit from being close to large urban centres.
- *Land-use disparity and dysfunctionality* – this is the result of the insertion of heterogeneous urban forms and the hemming in or parcelling up of farmland.

The spatial approach revealed the problems created by the process of settling urban overflow on the surrounding rural areas, in terms of both the land-use arrangements in these areas and the resulting urban–rural relations. Indeed, such urban–rural relationships have rarely been based on complementarity, but they have often led to conflict. In response to this situation, the French authorities (since the late 1960s) and the Tunisian authorities (since the late 1970s) have been establishing land-use and urban-development master plans or urban-development plans in areas where they did not previously exist. In addition, each of these countries took legislative measures (the *Land Use Act* of 1967 in France and the *Farmland Protection Act* of 1983 in Tunisia) to protect agricultural land close to cities.

The sociological approach was based on analysing the results of the interviews with farmers, institutional actors and local residents.

Farming and the situation of Saclay and Sijoumi farmers today

The interviews were conducted with 13 of Saclay's 18 farmers and 30 of Sijoumi's 300 fellahs.[4] The main objectives of the interviews were to understand the dynamics of the changes to farming operations in each area, to quantify the constraints stemming from the proximity of the urbanized area, and to determine the various ways agriculture has adapted to urban life.

Located around the central farming area, the silty land of the Saclay Plateau is shared by 18 farms, with an average size of 200ha. The main crops grown here are wheat, canola, corn and peas. Average yields are very high: 7000kg per ha for wheat, 3700kg per ha for canola, 7500kg per ha for corn, and 4700kg per ha for peas. In addition to the good soil and the favourable climate, the farmers' technical expertise contributes to these high yields. Most of the farmers are fairly old (around 63 years of age) and have their successors waiting in the wings.

On the Sijoumi Plain, the 3000ha of farmland is shared among 300 operations practising extensive agriculture on an average 10ha each. Although most of the useful agricultural area (UAA) is devoted to grains, other crops compete for the land. These other crops include market garden vegetables (tomatoes, hot peppers, lettuce, etc.), fruit or nuts (almonds, pears, peaches, plums, apricots, grapes), forage crops (sorghum, hay and clover), and olives. However, this study conducted on the dynamics of the changes affecting the 30 farms on the Sijoumi Plain revealed that agriculture there is in a critical state because of the small size of the farms: a maximum of 22ha for wheat, 1–4ha for market garden vegetables and forage crops, 2–5ha for fruit, and 2–20ha for olives. The small size of the agricultural parcels is also the main reason for the low level of productivity on Sijoumi farms: wheat, 700–1300kg per ha; grapes, 6–10t per ha; peaches, 4–7t per ha; and apricots, 7–10t per ha. These low yields are also the result of a combination of several other factors: irregular water supply in the irrigated zone, the high cost of farming inputs, an increase in urban interference, a shortage of agricultural equipment, and a lack of expertise in farming techniques. At an average age of 54 years, the Sijoumi farmers are younger than their Saclay counterparts, but they are also less well off: most of them have no successors, and they moonlight as taxi or bus drivers, truckers, artisans, shopkeepers and so on.

In both Saclay and Sijoumi, the increasing influence of urbanization creates a growing number of constraints for the farmers. In Saclay, the farmers report that their main constraints are:

- *Difficulty in moving around* – reflected in significantly higher production expenses for the purchase of stowable equipment.
- *Vagrants* – surreptitious encampment by vagrants is the most difficult constraint, because of the lengthy, cumbersome procedure for evicting them.
- *Relations with neighbours* – confrontations between farmers and local residents are particularly acute over the noise and odours produced by farm operations. To mitigate these conflicts, the grain farmers are trying to change the way they operate (direct burial of manure, manure spreading based on wind direction, etc.).

Although such constraints are virtually nonexistent in Sijoumi, certain constraints common to both regions seem to impede agricultural development more in Sijoumi than in Saclay:

- *Pilfering* – in Saclay, crop theft does not result in direct losses, whereas in Sijoumi, it is the most annoying constraint, especially for the fellahs who operate small farms near the urban areas. Despite the severe nature of these losses, more than 50 per cent of Sijoumi's farmers have not developed any strategy to counter this problem.
- *Trampling* – crop trampling is becoming an increasing problem in Saclay, as a result of clandestine racing by owners of vehicles or all-terrain motorbikes; in Sijoumi, as a result of schoolchildren and secretive young lovers. Although these practices are more a moral than a financial nuisance in Saclay, in Sijoumi they result in serious monetary loss. Unfortunately, the fellahs say that they are too poor to fight these activities.
- *Dumping* – many of the farmers and the fellahs say that the dumping of garbage on fields beside roads is an ever-growing problem. However, the losses are generally low.
- *Animal depredation* – the greatest menaces are pigeons in Saclay and the neighbours' cows and wandering sheep and goats in Sijoumi. Apparently, in Sijoumi the fellahs deal with this problem fairly well by regularly keeping watch over the most exposed plots. But in Saclay, the struggle against pigeons is becoming increasingly difficult because of the new pigeon-removal policy in Paris, which involves capturing pigeons in nets and freeing them in the surrounding countryside.

Generally, the increases in production costs caused by urban nuisances and the strategies developed to deal with them have been estimated at nearly 500 euros (EUR) per ha per year for the Saclay farmers and at more than 350 EUR per ha per year for the Sijoumi fellahs (in 2003, 0.92022 EUR = 1 United States dollar (USD)).[5]

To mitigate these costs, the Saclay farmers constantly adapt their procedures to the changing environment in which they operate and introduce subsidiary revenue-generating activities. Their Sijoumi counterparts, on the other hand, cannot afford to develop parallel projects to take advantage of the nearby urban market.

Figure 8.5 *Picking apples (top) and strawberries (bottom) at Viltain farm, Saclay Plateau*

Ancillary activities developed by the Saclay farmers include making more use of the farm's facilities (for offices, commercial space, accommodation or boarding horses). Direct selling of produce or 'U-pick' operations are other sidelines continually developing on the plateau (Figure 8.5). Three farms were already diversified in this way, and a number of other farmers were planning to do this in the near future. Another strategy Saclay grain farmers had developed to adapt to the urban environment was to create composting systems.

The behaviour of locals toward UA

The objective of the interviews with the main actors in the two territories[6] was to know whether urban space could be built to include farmland.

Between 1960 and 1980, the dominant perception in France, Tunisia and elsewhere of farmland peripheral to urban centres was urban centred: that is, this land is reserved for urban development.

In Saclay, this perception seems completely obsolete. For more than 10 years, most of the institutional actors prescribing land-use in Saclay have seemed, in response to strong pressure from local residents, to be in favour of rational, controlled expansion of the built-up area. Additional pressure has come from almost 20 local nature and environmental conservation associations that are members of the Union des associations de sauvegarde du plateau de Saclay (UASPS, union of associations for the preservation of the Saclay Plateau). For the UASPS president, agriculture represents the sole means of preserving a healthy environment and an enjoyable landscape. Agriculture also slows down urbanization and provides a natural transition area between the city and the rural heartland. As he says:

> *Picking strawberries on the Viltain farm or walking on edges of fields are ways of having concrete, meaningful contact with nature [see Figure 8.5]. Also, farming on the plateau provides verdant breathing room around Paris and an important recreational area for its inhabitants' well-being.* (Mr. Lionel Champtier, UASPS president)

Healthy environment, green space, pleasant landscape, inhabitants' well-being, 'green lung' and *natural transition zone* – these are just some of the terms used to describe the apparent development of a predominantly aesthetic approach to transforming Saclay farmland. This approach is so evident that political actors and urban planners find themselves forced to take new steps to organize and develop the Saclay region so as to limit urbanization and avoid degradation of the rural agricultural environment. According to most of the actors interviewed, features inherent in agriculture allow it to play an active role in improving urban landscapes and the living conditions of city residents. These features include green fields that enhance and beautify the roads and railways leading into the city, vast expanses of green or open cropland that extend the green belt around Paris, and an opportunity for young city dwellers who know little about the rural environment to learn about it first hand.

In contrast, the findings from our interviews on the Sijoumi Plain show that hybrid-zone farmland has primarily been seen by almost all planners and institutional actors as a land reserve to be used for urbanization. According to some of these people, agriculture cannot be considered an urban planning tool for organizing multi-use urban space. The reasons given to justify these views are 'functional', in the sense that, it is argued, a field within a city entails spatial dysfunction. Moreover, one of the two urban planners responsible for preparing the land-use master plan for Greater Tunis believes that 'the presence of farmland in an urban environment represents a physical handicap to the proper functioning of the area it is located in'. In general, according to many of the actors interviewed, urban and hybrid-zone agriculture, as practised in the heart of the Tunisian countryside, is a purely economic activity that cannot fulfil any other role than the production of foodstuffs.

Forms and social practices of peri-urban farming

This research, which was aimed at studying the forms and social practices of peri-urban farming, was conducted with a 40-person sample in Saclay and a 171-person sample in the Greater Tunis area, 110 of whom were city residents and 61 of whom were from Sijoumi.[7]

More than 50 years ago, both the plateau and the plain comprised immense expanses of farmland occupied by a few rural and agricultural families, but they now contain several thousand inhabitants, who belong to two distinct social classes: lower classes (workers, employees, etc.) in Sijoumi; and a more well-off class of middle-level and senior managers in Saclay.

To learn the main reasons for people's settling on the plateau and the plain in the first place, the interviews included a question about what motivated the first occupants to settle there. Apparently, it was for purely economic reasons (attractive land prices, easy access to the labour market, etc.) that 55 per cent of the first Saclay residents and 90 per cent of the first Sijoumi residents arrived in their respective regions almost 40 years ago.

However, the situation seems quite different today. According to the respondents, the main reasons for new arrivals now include the search for an attractive setting and pleasant living conditions. In Saclay, more than 70 per cent of the recent arrivals (in the last 2–10 years) say that they came to benefit from the rural environment of the Saclay countryside. In Sijoumi, 46 per cent of the inhabitants gave the same reason. Overall, what the inhabitants in both regions wanted was to be able to pursue a typically urban lifestyle (recreational centres, shopping centres, sports facilities, etc.) in a rural setting. This setting needed to be exclusively composed of natural elements (farming, woods, bodies of water, etc.) in a clean, healthy, pure, calm, free (unoccupied) and peaceful environment. The questionnaires revealed that the search for such a setting was based on an essentially aesthetic approach to agricultural land. For 75 per cent of the people in Saclay and 55 per cent of the people in Greater Tunis, farming was seen as supportive of the countryside image of both the

Saclay and Sijoumi regions – an open space that protects its residents 'from the harmful effects of urbanization' and a green space that is needed to improve their living conditions and to provide breathing room for the city dwellers of southwest Paris and Greater Tunis, respectively.

On the Saclay Plateau, this aesthetic relationship with the farmland was foreseeable, given the socio-professional profile of the local population (primarily upper management and well-off families accustomed to appreciating the countryside). However, in the Greater Tunis area, especially on the Sijoumi Plain – where the vast majority of the inhabitants are fairly poor, with limited education – these findings were totally unexpected. Barely 15 years ago, research by geographer P. Signoles showed that Tunisians' aspirations were solely focused on urban life, which was synonymous to them with modernity, freedom, beauty and well-being, and they totally disparaged the rural agricultural environment (Signoles, 1985). However, the findings of this study call for a rethinking of this apparent fascination with the city and the accompanying ignorance of the world of farming, at least in Greater Tunis and on the Sijoumi Plain. For 23 per cent of Tunis's inhabitants and 10 per cent of the people in Sijoumi, the *rif* (countryside) is an environment they want to live in. Whether on the city outskirts or in the rural heartland, this countryside embodies certain values that are absent in the city. For more than 40 per cent of the inhabitants of Greater Tunis and more than 30 per cent of the people on the Sijoumi Plain, the countryside is a calm, peaceful, simple, beautiful, natural, free (unoccupied), healthy, and pure place that represents traditional values. Almost 50 per cent of the residents of the Sijoumi plain, who regularly visit the farming area for recreation and relaxation, say that farming for them represents *mandhar jamil* (landscape) and *tabïa* (nature). However, the most striking finding was the wish of most residents of Tunis (52 per cent) and Sijoumi (48 per cent) to live in the countryside close to a large city but surrounded by fields of various crops – in other words, a hybrid-zone countryside. This surprising finding brought the realization that a quite recent social phenomenon had been generated by the spread of new lifestyles, as well as by new possibilities of access to urban countryside. One of the motivations for moving to this type of countryside is not difficult to discern. It is simply a matter of wanting to live in a nicer and more attractive setting than the city. Although limited, these data seem to indicate that a new social image of UA is, in fact, currently developing.

A study of public policy relating to the countryside of the Saclay Plateau reveals design rules for a new land-use plan. This is reflected in the construction of a land-use system whereby the urban environment and the rural agricultural environment cohabit in an active way that still meets the residents' need for nature and the farmers' need for land tenure and ongoing agricultural activity. After an intercommunal structure was created to ensure the harmonious development of the Saclay region, the local actors – with the help of the region's land-use professionals – focused their initial efforts on the regulated management of the region's land base. As pointed out by the president of the Intercommunal District of the Saclay Plateau (IDSP) and the operators affected by the land-use development of the plateau, this is the first step toward establishing a genuine land-use policy specific to peri-urban environments. In this way, farmers will have security concerning the availability of their tools of the trade and will thus be able to develop projects that make the best use of their operations in relation to the depreciation rates of their capital investments (buying heavy equipment, building silos, installing drainage, etc.). This land-use policy, as formulated by the Saclay authorities, is reflected in the preparation of a master farmland-management agreement between the Société d'aménagement foncier et d'établissement rural (SAFER, land-use and rural-settlement corporation), the Agence des espaces verts (AEV, agency for green spaces) of Île-de-France, and IDSP. The policy is also reflected in the freezing of a critical mass of 2000ha of UAA.

However, in addition to the critical-mass concept (which seems to meet the farmers' needs well), the success of a peri-urban development seems to entail complementary land-use measures. In Saclay, these measures make up the second part of the new land-use policy for the plateau and were formulated as the CAP (at the joint request of the IDSP and the AEV) by urban planners and rural specialists working for the Institut d'aménagement et d'urbanisme de la région Île-de-France (institute for urban planning and development of the Île-de-France region). This plan is a technical reference document that describes a series of indicators representing improved guidelines for planning land-use development in the Saclay region. Seven basic measures were formulated:

1   preserve a modern, dynamic image of farming;
2   protect and enhance the region's heritage;
3   organize road landscaping;
4   integrate new construction into the landscape;
5   develop the presence of water in the landscape;
6   create a network of pathways and green spaces;
7   mould the landscape at each stage of development.

These seven principles of countryside action have been incorporated into the local master development plan and are now being applied. To ensure the sustainability of some of these lines of action, the French government is currently using the CAP as the basis for preparing land-use contracts with local farmers. As a result, the CAP has essentially become a land-use development project that reconciles agricultural production, land-use management and preservation or enhancement of the rural agricultural environment. It has thus become a project generated by local urban policy, one that does not seek to remove farmland for parks and public gardens, but rather encourages city dwellers and farmers to work to their mutual benefit, giving farmland a new role in the land-use organization of the peri-urban environment. Indeed, the system of spatial organization that the IDSP now proposes offers both farming and farmers definite economic and social advantages – namely, improved access to the land, a refurbished drainage system, secure land tenure, and the enhancement of the farmland itself.

Two cases of agri-urban development from a land-use-planning perspective

Depending on whether it benefits from being close to the city (direct sales, U-pick operations, urban markets) or suffers from the same proximity (pilfering, crop damage), peri-urban farming often develops in contrasting ways. This contrast arises because this kind of farming does not really belong to the rural production system: it is too dependent on the urban system (Prost, 1994). The goal of our research was to determine the nature of the niche achieved by agriculture in the new social, spatial, and political processes of production in the urban areas of emerging cities.

Through the two case studies in Saclay and Sijoumi, we have been able to define two examples of agri-urban development from a land-use-planning perspective. These two examples are similar in terms of:

- *Geographical morphology* – two extensive, open, flat, isolated areas;
- *Land use* – primarily farmland, expansion of human settlement, spread of industrial or technological installations, and significant water resources, such as the ponds in Saclay and the saltwater lake in Sijoumi;
- *Type of activity* – predominantly grain-farming;
- *Nature of the urban constraints* – pilfering, crop trampling, indiscriminate dumping, etc.;
- *Social relations with farmland* (to a lesser extent) – on the Saclay Plateau these are mainly based on an aesthetic approach to farmland; on the Sijoumi Plain, they are just developing an aesthetic aspect.

The differences are more complex:

- *Farmers and their operations* – the Saclay farmers head up large, modern, high-yield operations, whereas most of the fellahs in Sijoumi operate small, traditional farms, with fairly low production, and unlike their counterparts in France, moonlight to augment their incomes.
- *Adaptive strategies* – adaptions to the urban environment (direct sales, U-pick, etc.), like pressure from local community organizations, are well developed in Saclay but almost totally absent in Sijoumi.
- *Local inhabitants* – inhabitants are primarily at the managerial level on the Saclay Plateau, whereas they are predominantly working class on the Sijoumi Plain.
- *Land-use management, planning, development and countryside preservation* – the most marked differences are found in the overall set of public policies relating to the peri-urban zone. These differences exist largely because administrative management of the land is decentralized in Saclay but centralized in Tunis.

Table 8.1 shows the similarities (in bold) and differences (in regular type) in more detail.

Table 8.1 *Saclay and Sijoumi: two examples of agri-urban development in a land-use-planning context*

	Saclay	Sijoumi
Geographic context	**Large flat area (5000ha) constituting the main open space in the southwest zone of the Paris region**	**Large flat area (7000ha) constituting the main open space in the southwest zone of the Tunis region**
Land use	**Farming, scientific research, environment (planned), channels, and ponds**	**Farming, private environment (regulated and free), diversified industry, and *sebkha* (saltwater lake)**
Agricultural land use	**Intensive grain farming (2600ha divided among 18 operations)**	**Grain farming and horticulture (3000ha divided among 300 operations)**
Type of operation	Modern, well-equipped operations with high yields and an average size of 200ha, the main function being farming	Traditional, poorly equipped operations with low yields and an average size of 8 ha, the main function being *enzel*
Farmers	Fairly old grain farmers operating large-scale enterprises, with successors and no other source of income	Fairly young fellahs operating small-scale enterprises, with no successors, moonlighting to survive economically
Main urban constraints	**Pilfering, animal depredation, trampling, indiscriminate dumping, sensitive relations with neighbours, difficulty moving around, and vagrants**	**Pilfering, indiscriminate dumping, animal depredation, and trampling**
Adaptive strategies	Modification of work itinerary, silos, stowable equipment, direct sales, U-pick, scarecrows, etc.	Lack of effective strategies
Local population	Primarily managerial class	Primarily working class
Social relations with the farmland	**Recognition of the farmland as a green space that enhances the plateau environment and the local residents' living conditions**	**Emergence of a new appreciation of farmland as a setting that residents look for**
Social actors	UASPS (strong pressure from community organizations)	Absence of local NGOs
Public actors	Government, IDSP, communes	Government, no intercommunal structure
Viewpoint of public actors	Saclay farmland is no longer a land reserve	Sijoumi farmland is a land reserve
Urban-planning	Regional master plan for Île-de-France (1994), land-use plan, and local master plan. Objectives: Preserve 2000ha of farmland and develop the rural countryside	Regional development plan, Greater Tunis master land-use plan, development plan. Objective: Make the plain the major axis of Greater Tunis expansion

	Saclay	Sijoumi
Land management	SAFER–AEV–IDSP agreement. Objectives: Counteract land speculation and provide secure land tenure to farmers	1983 *Farmland Protection Act*. Objectives: Counteract land speculation and provide secure land tenure to farmers
Green policy	Natural-balance zones, green belt, and CAP. Objectives: Include farmland in the urban region's production system and develop the landscape of urban agriculture	Government countryside policy. Objectives: Create parks and public gardens and protect wooded areas and distinctive natural sites
Nature of each situation	Public interest > private interests	Private interests > public interest

Note: Similarities are shown in boldface type, whereas differences are shown in regular type. AEV, Agence des espaces verts (agency for green spaces); CAP, countryside action plan; IDSP, Intercommunal District of Saclay Plateau; SAFER, Société d'aménagement et d'établissement rural (land-use and rural-development corporation); UASPS, Union des associations de sauvegarde du plateau de Saclay (union of associations for the preservation of Saclay Plateau).

In practice, the question of government centralization or decentralization plays an important role in the operation, evolution and management of the peri-urbanization process.

Since its *Decentralization Act* was passed, in 1983, France has witnessed the emergence of a wide range of peri-urban actors: from ordinary citizens, to local and regional authorities, to national government representatives. Power-sharing among these various actors is often crucial to improving control over the peri-urban phenomenon. On the Saclay Plateau, intercommunal collaboration has played a particularly important role in improving the management of this phenomenon. After the intercommunal structure was created, the IDSP actors have, in response to strong pressure from local community organizations, consistently attempted to preserve and develop the farming area. Their first step to this end was to take action on the main peri-urban problem – land ownership. This was achieved by the signing of an agreement with two land-related agencies (SAFER and AEV) to combat land speculation and give farmers the secure land tenure they need. This agreement was also incorporated into urban-planning documents so as to preserve 2000ha of farmland.

But in Tunisia, under the current national constitution, land-use management decisions – whether urban, hybrid zone or rural – fall under the jurisdiction of the national government. However, our study of the Sijoumi situation also showed that the decisions made by the various administrative services concerned with land use on the plain have no joint management programme for the urban perimeter, that is, specific to the hybrid zone. This state of affairs basically explains the failure of urban planners' attempts to protect farmland on the plain. For example, the regional development plan of 1977 quickly proved unsuitable for the effective socio-economic and spatial development of the hybrid zones, because it focused its lines of action on the

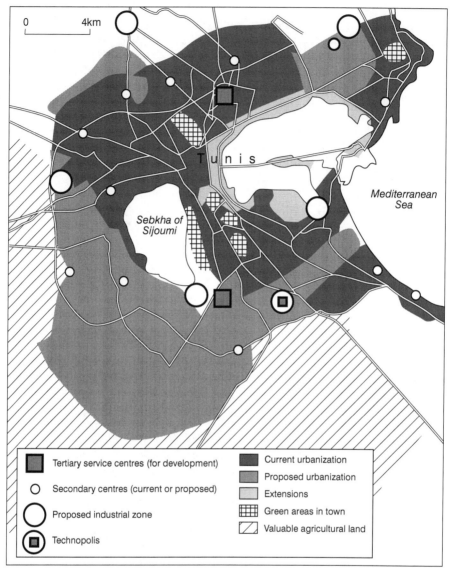

Figure 8.6 *Map of land-use master plan for Greater Tunis*

urban cores of Tunisia's cities. The same goes for the *Farmland Protection Act* of 1983, which is still the predominant instrument for land-use management for the whole country. By focusing mainly on the technical aspects of farmland preservation (soil type, crop type, etc.), the 1983 Act, as Sethom (1992, p162) pointed out, 'ignored the key problem of land speculation and the ways in which the countryside is being degraded', which makes the Act difficult to apply. Thus, in practice, in Tunisia, the government has no countryside policy specifically for the rural or green areas of the hybrid zone, such as the policies in France relating to the natural balance zones of the green belt, the regional natural park or even the CAP. One of the main objectives of the CAP is to encourage landscaping of farmland by including it in the alternative land-use projects of peri-urban zones. Indeed, quite the opposite is the case in Tunisia. The latest urban planning documents being prepared for the Greater Tunis region – the development plan for the *sebkha* (saltwater lake) zone of Sijoumi and the master land-use plan for Greater Tunis – both envisage urbanization of almost all the farmland on the plain (Figure 8.6), which will be only partially offset by new urban green spaces, such as parks and public gardens.

The Saclay situation generally corresponds to a style of management in which local public authorities supervise private interests and regulate activities governed by other public policies. However, the Sijoumi situation reflects a process of regulating use of urban and agricultural land in the hybrid zone that is dominated by private interests that, ironically, attempt to regulate the public operators. For urban authorities developing future policy in Tunisia, the Saclay example may be an inspiration – for instance, the urbanization process in Tunisia as a whole and specifically in Greater Tunis could adopt a fair policy of providing a public framework for the private practices that determine the city's layout.

CONCLUSION AND RECOMMENDATIONS

The analysis of the Saclay situation helps to identify the main rules applied in pursuing joint agri-urban development in a land-use-planning context. But farmland on the Sijoumi Plain is a marginal consideration in the current plans to develop the land in the southwest zone of Greater Tunis. This is because no collective land-use management plans apply specifically to the rural agricultural parts of the hybrid (peri-urban) area and no local community organizations are likely to promote the appreciation of the merits of UA among certain social groups.

A challenge for both managers and planners in Tunis is how to rethink the role of agriculture in the new urban-planning strategies, and the example of the Saclay situation could be used as a reference. For instance, a number of key ideas could be drawn from the Saclay situation and applied to the Sijoumi Plain, even though some of them would require a certain measure of institutional adaptation. For our purposes, we will identify only three major ideas that might provide avenues for future investigation and input into new studies on sustainable development of urban farming in Tunisia:

- *Recognizing the multifunctional character of urban or peri-urban farming and its advantages for the community* – the expansion of urbanization into the Sijoumi Plain has had a destabilizing effect on agriculture. This process has not only caused a direct loss of UAA, but also undermined farming activity and compromised its development by making the future of agriculture uncertain and by destabilizing the land market. However, as the

Saclay example clearly shows, it is not necessarily the destiny of farmland to be totally built on. The Saclay example is proof that urban development and the preservation of agriculture are compatible. The idea is thus to consider farming activity as both nurturing and economically feasible, as well as a landscape-friendly tool for managing the urban–rural interface.

- *Going beyond a simply passive cohabitation of the rural and urban environments* – on the Sijoumi Plain, passive cohabitation has created land-use conflicts and extremely strong social tensions between farmers and non-farmers, owing to the constraints the small-scale fellah operations are unable to overcome. On the Saclay Plateau, in contrast, land-use conflicts are resolved through implementation of a specifically designed land policy. Although some social tension still exists, it is not very serious, because the region's farmers are constantly finding new ways to adapt – through direct sales of fresh produce, U-pick operations, teaching farms, etc. In addition, through the new policy for managing the Saclay region (the CAP), the IDSP now offers both city dwellers and local residents an opportunity to discover the importance of the rural agricultural world to their well-being on the plateau. It is therefore recommended that similar policies be developed on the Sijoumi Plain to improve its 'livability' and that the cohabitation there be made more active by encouraging limited and controlled visits from city dwellers to the farming areas.

- *Fostering an intercommunal approach to the formulation and application of appropriate soil-management rules* – this intention is reflected in the Saclay Plateau urban-planning documents, which do not cover just one commune, but several communes constituting a large area. These documents prescribe land use for long periods (20–30 years). This approach has given the region's farmers sufficient confidence in the future to make capital investments to develop their operations. This kind of intercommunal collaboration does not seem easily transferable to Sijoumi, because the Tunisian constitution does not provide for this type of action. This is considered as falling more within the jurisdiction of legislators than as being a matter decided at the local or regional level by planners, public land-use developers or private actors (especially farmers and the other residents).

These three closely interrelated principles could, by themselves, constitute a coherent basis for a genuine agri-urban policy in Tunisia. This theme could also be the basis for a programme of scientific and technical cooperation between the two countries, France and Tunisia.

ACKNOWLEDGEMENTS

Although this research may appear to be the work of one person, it could not have been completed without the help, advice and support of too many organizations and people for me to name. I would like to express my whole-hearted gratitude to all of them. At the same time, I must specifically thank

Pierre Donadieu for agreeing to supervise this project and André Fleury for agreeing to cosupervise it. I am also grateful for the valuable collaboration provided by managers in administrative departments such as the IDSP, the Regional Directorate of the Environment and the Regional Directorate of Agriculture and Forests, in France; and the Directorate General for Town and Country Planning, the National Agency for Environmental Protection, the District of Tunis, and the Soils Branch of the Ministry of Agriculture, in Tunisia. I would also like to thank the farmers of the Saclay Plateau and the fellahs of the Sijoumi Plain for their warm welcome and invaluable input, as well as all the residents of Saclay, Tunis and Sijoumi, who gladly responded to my inquiries. Finally, I owe an immense debt to the International Development Research Centre, whose field-research grants enabled me to complete the research and organize two seminars on UA in Tunisia.

NOTES

1   The aim of this paper is to provide a concise report on the research I conducted for my thesis: *L'agriculture: nouvel instrument de la construction urbaine* (*Agriculture: A New Tool for Planning Urban Space*). The thesis was submitted on 13 December 2000 in partial fulfilment of the requirements for a doctorate in environmental sciences at the École nationale du génie rural des eaux et des forets (French Institute of Forestry, Agricultural and Environmental Engineering), in Paris.

2   Since 1998, in France, *peri-urban space* has been defined by the Institut national de la statistique et des études économiques (national institute for statistics and economic studies) and the Société d'études géographiques, économiques et sociologiques appliquées (society for applied geographic, economic and sociological studies) as a territorial entity in its own right (in terms of geographic boundary, number of inhabitants, land settlement, etc.). But in Tunisia, as in most developing countries, the search for criteria to define peri-urban space has apparently not resulted in any consensus. Whether at the level of urban-land-use planning or territory or at the level of social and economic research, few researchers use the same criteria to define *peri-urban space*. Furthermore, the neologism *peri-urban*, which has emerged from the practice of contemporary geographical science in Western countries, does not really have an equivalent in Arabic or its Tunisian dialect. This was why I decided to use the term *hybrid zones* to evoke the concepts of peri-urban space and peri-urbanization as they related to Tunisian cities.

3   On the Saclay Plateau, we interviewed the president and the former and current vice-presidents responsible for the environment; the urban planner of the Saclay Plateau district; a landscape specialist from the Institut d'aménagement et d'urbanisme de la région Île-de-France (institute for urban planning and development of the Île-de-France region); a programme officer at the Agence des espaces verts au département de l'Essonne (green-spaces agency of the department (administrative district) of Essonne); an engineer from the Regional Directorate of Agriculture and Forests; a site inspector from the Regional Directorate of the Environment; and the presidents of two local associations for the protection of nature and the environment, the Union des associations de sauvegarde du plateau de Saclay (union of associations for the preservation of Saclay Plateau) and the AVBs (Amis de la Vallée de la Bièvre). On the Sijoumi Plain, we interviewed the

director-general of land-use planning; the town planner; the head of the industrial land-use section at the Tunisian Ministry of the Environment and Land Use; the general urban planner and the head urban planner of the District of Tunis; the head architect of the Commune of Tunis; the head engineer of the Soils Branch of the Tunisian Ministry of Agriculture; two private urban planners responsible for preparing both the master land-use plan for Greater Tunis and the Sijoumi zone development plan; an agronomist from a private research company mandated to prepare a study of the traditional farming systems in the peri-urban area of Tunis; and the presidents of three nongovernmental organizations, Union Régionale de l'agriculture et de la pêche de Tunis (URAPT), Association de protection de l'environnement (APE), and Association alliance, femmes et environnement (AAFE).

4   The farmers and fellahs were met on their farms, and the interviews, which were recorded in their entirety, lasted 45–60 minutes.

5   Despite this attempt to make an economic assessment, it should be noted that the figures cited are not necessarily accurate and are only meant to provide an indication of the problems faced by farmers in peri-urban environments.

6   The interviews, at the interviewee's place of work, lasted an average of 35 minutes each and had a semi-structured format.

7   The interviews, in the interviewee's home, lasted an average of 30 minutes each and had a semi-structured format.

REFERENCES

Attia, H. (1972) 'L'urbanisation de la Tunisie', *Revue Tunisienne des Sciences Socials*, vol 28–29, pp91–117

Belhedi, A. (1979) 'L'espace tunisois: Organisation. Fonctionnement et structure typique', *Revue Tunisienne de Géographie*, vol 4, pp9–39

Belhedi, A. (1989) 'Espace et société en Tunisie', University of Tunis, Tunis, Tunisia. Doctoral dissertation

Belhedi, A. (1992) 'Le système urbain tunisien: Croissance urbaine et structuration hiérarchique', *Revue Tunisienne de Géographie*, vol 21–22, pp177–185

Berger, M. (1984) 'Proposition pour un bilan des recherches sur les espaces ruraux périurbains', *Cahiers de Fontenay*, vol 35, pp53–64

Berger, M. (1986a) 'La division sociale des espaces périurbains: État de la question', *Strates*, vol 1, pp25–33

Berger, M. (1986b) 'L'interface villes/campagnes en France: Bilan des recherches sur la production d'espaces périurbains', *Cahiers de Fontenay*, vol 41–43, pp193–212

Berger, M. (1989) 'Vers de nouveaux types de rapports villes–campagnes: La production des espaces périurbains en France et dans les pays développés d'économie libérale', *Strates*, vol 4, pp89–106

David, J. (1980) *Du Rural au Rurbain: l'Avant-pays Savoyard (Analyse Régionale et Géodémographie)*, Institut de géographie alpine, Grenoble, France

Donadieu, P. (1998a) 'L'agriculture peut-elle devenir paysagiste?' *Les Carnets du Paysage*, vol 1, pp100–117

Donadieu, P. (1998b) *Campagnes Urbaines*, Actes Sud; École nationale supérieure du paysage de Versailles, Paris

Donadieu, P. and Fleury, A. (1997a) 'De l'agriculture péri-urbaine à l'agriculture urbaine', *Le Courrier de l'Environnement de l'INRA*, vol 31, pp67–78

Donadieu, P. and Fleury, A. (1997b) *Programme de Recherches Agriculture Urbaine*, L'École nationale supérieure du paysage de Versailles, Versailles

Fleury, A. and Moustier, P. (1999) 'L'agriculture périurbaine: Infrastructure de la ville durable', *Cahiers Agriculture*, vol 8, pp81–89

Hervieu, B. and Viard, J. (1996) *Au Bonheur des Campagnes (et des provinces)*, Éditions de l'Aube, Marseille

Jaillet, M. C. and Jalabert, J. (1982) 'La production de l'espace urbain périphérique', *Revue de Géographie des Pyrénées et du Sud-Ouest*, vol 1, pp7–26

Kassab, A. (1976) *Histoire de la Tunisie: l'Époque Contemporaine*, Société tunisienne de diffusion, Tunis, Tunisia

Kayser, B. (1981) 'Vendeurs des terres à la périphérie des villes', *Annales de la Recherche Urbaine*, vol 10, pp129–136

Kayser, B. (1996) *Ils ont choisi la campagne*, Éditions de l'Aube, Saint-Étienne, France

Kayser, B. and Schektman-Labry, G. (1982) 'La troisième couronne périurbaine: une tentative identification', *Revue de Géographie des Pyrénées et du Sud-Ouest*, vol 1, pp27–36

Luginbühl, Y. (1995) 'La demande sociale de nature et les espaces périurbains', in Luginbühl, Y. (ed), *L'Agriculture dans l'Espace Périurbain: Des Anciennes aux Nouvelles Fonctions*, Bergerie nationale de Rambouillet, Rambouillet, France

Prost, B. (1994) 'L'agriculture périurbaine: Analyse d'une marginalité', *Bulletin de l'Association des Géographes Français*, vol 1994, no 2, pp144–151

Sebag, P. (1998) *Tunis: Histoire d'une Ville*, L'Harmattan, Paris

SEGESA (Société d'études géographiques, économiques et sociologiques appliquées) (1994) *Entre Ville et Campagne: Les Espaces de Périurbanisation (identification et problèmes; propositions pour l'action publique)*, Ministry of Agriculture and Forestry, Paris

Sethom, H. (1992) *Pouvoir Urbain et Paysannerie en Tunisie*, Cérès Productions; Fondation nationale de la recherche scientifique, Tunis, Tunisia

Sethom, H., Cherif, A. and Khaled, M. (1992) 'Les rapports villes–campagnes dans le domaine foncier: Le cas de la plaine de Medjez-El-Bab', in Sethom, H. (ed), *Le Déficit Alimentaire dans la «Verte» Tunisie. Qui est Responsble?* Institut supérieur de l'éducation et de la formation continue, University of Tunis, Tunis, Tunisia, pp3–67

Signoles, P. (1985) *L'Espace Tunisien: Capitale et État-région*, Centre d'étude et de recherches sur l'urbanisation du monde arab, Université de Tours, Tours

Taffin, C. (1985) 'Accession à la Propriété et Rurbanisation', *Économie et Statistique*, vol 175, pp55–67

Terrier, C. (1986) 'Les déplacements domicile–travail en France: Évolution de 1975 à 1982', *Espace, Populations, Sociétés*, vol 2, pp333–342

ANNEX 1: INTERVIEW QUESTIONNAIRE

Main questions asked during the interviews with various stakeholders:

Land-use planners and institutional decision-makers in Saclay
1/ RESPONDENT INFORMATION
- Name
- Occupation
- Nature of the mission in relation to the land-use program for the Saclay plateau

2/ PERCEPTION AND FUTURE OF AGRICULTURE ON THE PLATEAU
- If you had to describe the plateau to a person not familiar with it, what would you say?
- What, in your opinion, are the advantages and drawbacks of agriculture on the plateau?

  Drawbacks: ☐ Obstructions   ☐ Noise

  ☐ Odours   ☐ Pollution

  Advantages: ☐ Nature   ☐ Setting

  ☐ Living conditions   ☐ Farm products

- Do you think that agriculture contributes to the setting and living conditions of the plateau residents?
- How do you foresee the future of agriculture on the plateau (disappearing, no change, etc.)?

3/ IMPLEMENTATION OF THE COUNTRYSIDE PROJECT (CAP, OR THE COUNTRYSIDE ACTION PLAN) AND LAND-USE DEVELOPMENT ON THE PLATEAU
- How, in your opinion, did the idea of the countryside action plan (CAP) emerge?
- In your opinion, does the CAP meet the expectations of the farmers, residents, and conservation associations on the plateau? How?
- CAP's first line of action emphasizes preserving a modern, dynamic image of agriculture. What do you think 'a modern image of agriculture' means?
- In its sixth line of action, CAP announced the creation of a green-spaces network. Are farmlands part of this network? If so, how?
- CAP is not an urban-planning document. What, in your opinion, are the policies (laws, ordinances, etc.) that can be used (or implemented) to ensure sustainable preservation of the plateau's farmland?

Institutional planners and decision-makers in Tunis and Sijoumi
1/ RESPONDENT INFORMATION
- Name:
- Occupation:
- Nature of the mission in relation to the land-use program for Greater Tunis and the Sijoumi Zone:

2/ CITY, 'RIF' (COUNTRYSIDE), AND LANDSCAPE
- What does the term *landscape* mean to you?
- What do you think a city is?
- What do you think the 'rif' (countryside) is?
- What do you think *tabïa* (nature) is?
- Can we speak of a relationship between a city and the rif that surrounds it? If so, how?
- Can the peri-urban rif be a spatial and landscape component of the city? If so, how?
- Can agriculture and farmland become, just like a city park, an urban-planning tool for organizing urban space?
- Do you think that agriculture contributes to the plateau landscape and to the residents' living conditions?

3/ PERCEPTION AND FUTURE OF AGRICULTURE ON THE SIJOUMI PLAIN
- If you had to describe the plain to a person not familiar with it, what would you say?
- Do you think that the agriculture on the plain is

  ☐ Dynamic ☐ Not dynamic ☐ Other

- What, in your opinion, are the advantages and drawbacks of agriculture on the Sijoumi Plain?

  Drawbacks: ☐ Obstructions ☐ Noise

  ☐ Odours ☐ Pollution

  Advantages: ☐ Nature ☐ Setting

  ☐ Living conditions ☐ Farm products
- How do you foresee the future of agriculture on the plain (disappearing, no change, etc.)?
- Do you think that the farmland on the Sijoumi plain can play a role in the development and land-use planning of Greater Tunis? If so, how?

Saclay and Sijoumi farmers

1/ RESPONDENT INFORMATION

- Name:
- Age of the farmer and level of training:
- Number of children and other people subsisting from the farm (including young children):
- How long have you lived on the plateau or plain:
- Outside income:
  Other activities of farmer:
  Outside work of spouse:

2/ STATUS OF THE FARM AND ITS LAND

- Legal status (owner, tenant with government contract, etc.):

- Total area (useful agricultural area [UAA], in hectares):

- Types of crops grown in the corresponding land areas:

- Problems related to land tenure (precarious, renewable lease, etc.):

- Does the farm consist of land in different locations (in several parcels):

- Have there been any offers to purchase (property pressure):

3/ PRODUCTION EQUIPMENT

A — CROPS

- Changes in production:

CHANGES IN GROWING AREA	Decrease	Stable	Increase
Over the last 5 (or 10) years			
Outlook for the next 5 (or 10) years			

- Were the changes in response to:

  The situation of the particular crop:

  The peri-urban environment (interference, markets, etc.):

B — LIVESTOCK

- Type (cattle, sheep, etc.):

- Changes in production:

	CHANGES IN HERD NUMBERS AND WHY			
	Increase or start	Stable	Decrease or stop	Changes in animal type and why
Over the last 5 (or 10) years				
Outlook for the next 5 (or 10) years				

- Have the changes been in response to–
  The particular situation of the livestock concerned:

  The peri-urban environment (interference, markets, etc.):

C — WORK FORCE

- Total number, including–
  Family members:
  Permanent employees:
  Casual employees:

D — EQUIPMENT

- What degree of autonomy does the farm have (owner, co-owner, etc.)?

- Recourse to outside help to do certain jobs? Which jobs and why?

4/ FARM INCOME

- Is the income from the farm satisfactory?
- Has it been necessary to earn income outside the farm?

5/ STATEMENT CONCERNING CITY-RELATED CONSTRAINTS AND ADDITIONAL COSTS

A — CROPS AND GEOGRAPHICAL LOCATION

Note: 0: not annoying; 1: slightly annoying; 2: quite annoying; 3: very annoying.

Constraint	Note (0 to 3)	Response	Crops or fields concerned	Quantification and estimation
Pilfering (theft)				
Animal depredations				
Trampling (strollers, children, etc.)				
Unauthorized dumping				
Theft of equipment				

Difficulty of access
or moving around
Vagrants or nomads
Crop harvesting or
delivery
Relations with neighbours
Other constraints

B — ABANDONMENT

- If, over the last few years, certain constraints have become so serious that you have had to give up growing a crop or operating a given piece of land, indicate the specific cause and its impact on your farming system (decrease in UAA, etc.). Indicate how you offset this loss.

I gave up...	*Because...*

- After mentioning these constraints, indicate which ones would force you to leave or stop farming if they became too serious?
- Assuming your system is more or less transferable to a location where the constraints are not so serious, what makes you stay?

6/ RELATIONSHIP BETWEEN THE FARMER AND THE LOCAL COMMUNITY

- Do you consider yourself a city dweller or a farmer?

- Have you noticed any changes in recent years? If so, what is your view of these changes?

- Do you consider yourself as living in the city or the country?

- How do you foresee the future of agriculture in this region?

- What relations do you maintain with the local residents and the other activities in the region?

- If you were to describe the plateau or plain to a person who does not know it, how would you describe it?

(Questions addressed specifically to the Saclay plateau farmers)
- Do you know what the CAP is and its mission?

- Does this interest you? Would you like to make an active contribution to it?

- It is planned to keep at least 2000ha for farming on the plateau. What do you think of this?

(Questions addressed specifically to the Sijoumi plain farmers)
- It is planned to urbanize the plain — what do you think of this?

Residents of the Saclay plateau

1/RESPONDENT INFORMATION

- Age:
- Occupation:
- Where do you live? Place:
- Number of children:

2/ RESIDENT'S RELATIONSHIP TO THE PLATEAU
A — PLATEAU ACTIVITIES

- How long have you lived on the plateau?

- Why did you settle here?

- Could you describe the places where you like to stroll from time to time?
  Where:
  Why:
  With whom:
  How often:

B — THE PLATEAU AS SEEN AND EXPERIENCED BY THE RESIDENTS

- Do you consider yourself living in the city or in the country?

- Do you consider yourself as a city or country dweller?

- In one sentence, explain what the term *landscape* means to you?

- On the plateau, do you feel that you are in the countryside?

- The following photographs were taken on the plateau, do you recognize these locations?

  ☐ No   ☐ Yes

  If yes,
  Where is it?
  How did you recognize it?

If you go there, when? With whom? How often? To do what (stroll, jog, bike, etc.)?
- In which order of preference would you put them? Why? What do you see on the first photo?

C — SOCIAL RELATIONSHIP WITH FARMING ON THE PLATEAU

- If you had to describe the plateau to someone who did not know it, how would you describe it?

- What, in your opinion, are the advantages and drawbacks of agriculture on the plateau?

  Drawbacks: ☐ Obstructions   ☐ Noise

  ☐ Odours   ☐ Pollution

  Advantages: ☐ Nature   ☐ Setting

  ☐ Living conditions   ☐ Farm products

- Do you think that agriculture contributes to the plateau landscape and to your living conditions? If so, how?

3/ THE IDSP8 POLICY AS SEEN BY THE RESIDENTS
- Since you've known the plateau, what, in your view, has changed the most?
- Are you aware of the district's CAP? What do you think of it?

4/ THE PLATEAU'S FUTURE AND ITS RESIDENTS' EXPECTATIONS
- How do you foresee the future of agriculture on the plateau (disappear, no change, etc.)?

- Do you agree with the introduction of other scientific facilities on the plateau? Why?

- What kind of improvements would you like to see to the plateau landscape (in terms of hedges, groves, vegetable fields, alignment, recreational amenities, etc.)?

Residents of Greater Tunis
1/RESPONDENT INFORMATION
- Age:
- Occupation:
- Where do you live? Place:
- Number of children:

2/ WHAT DO THESE WORDS MEAN TO YOU?
- *Mandhar jamil* (landscape)?
- *Medina* (city)?
- *Rif* (countryside)?
- *Tabïa* (nature)?

3/ RECREATIONAL ACTIVITIES
- What recreational activities do you practice?

  ☐ Walking   ☐ Jogging

  ☐ Soccer   ☐ Cycling   ☐ Other (specify)

- Where and why?
- How often?
- Alone or with others?:

4/ IS THERE AN AGRICULTURAL COUNTRYSIDE AROUND TUNIS?
- Do you prefer living in the city or in the 'rif' (countryside)? Why?
- What, in your opinion, is the extent of farming around the capital? A lot, a little, or just traces?
- In your opinion, what is the most commonly grown crop around the capital?

☐ Vegetables ☐ Tree fruit

☐ Grains ☐ Other

5/ In your opinion what are the advantages and drawbacks of agriculture on the city outskirts?

Drawbacks ☐ Obstructions ☐ Noise

☐ Odours ☐ Pollution

Advantages: ☐ Nature ☐ Setting

☐ Living conditions ☐ Farm products
- Do you think that agriculture contributes to the mandhar jamil (landscape) of Greater Tunis? If so, how?
- How do you foresee the future of agriculture around Tunis (disappearing, no change, increasing, etc.)?

Residents of the Sijoumi plain
1/RESPONDENT INFORMATION
- Age:
- Occupation:
- Where do you live? Place:
- Number of children:

2/ RESIDENT'S RELATIONSHIP WITH THE PLAIN: COUNTRYSIDE SEEN/EXPERIENCED
A — ACTIVITIES ON THE PLAIN
- How long have you lived on the plain?
- Why did you settle here?
- Are there places on the plain where you like to stroll from time to time?
Where:
Why:
When:
With whom:

B — PERCEPTION OF AGRICULTURE ON THE PLAIN

- Do you consider yourself a city or country dweller?
- Do you prefer living in the city or in the 'rif' (countryside)? Why?
- Do you consider that you are living in the city or in the country?
- In your opinion, what are the advantages and drawbacks of agriculture on the Sijoumi Plain?

Drawbacks   ☐ Obstructions   ☐ Noise

                       ☐ Odours   ☐ Pollution

Advantages: ☐ Nature   ☐ Setting

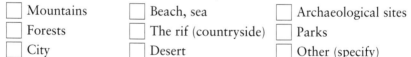

                       ☐ Living conditions   ☐ Farm products

- If you had to describe the *mandhar jamil* (landscape) of the plain to a person that does not know it, what would you say?
- Do you think that agriculture contributes to the *mandhar jamil* (landscape) in this region and to your living conditions? If so, how?

3/ THE FUTURE OF THE PLAIN

- Since you've known the plain, what, in your opinion, has changed the most?
- How do you foresee the future of agriculture on the plain (disappearing, no change, etc.)?
- It is planned to urbanize the plain. What do you think of that?

4/ GENERAL QUESTIONS

- Which place do you like the most for your recreation?

☐ Mountains   ☐ Beach, sea   ☐ Archaeological sites
☐ Forests   ☐ The rif (countryside)   ☐ Parks
☐ City   ☐ Desert   ☐ Other (specify)

- In one sentence, explain what the term mandhar jamil (landscape) means to you?
- What does the term *medina* (city) mean to you?
- What does the term *rif* (countryside) mean to you?
- What does the term *tabïa* (nature) mean to you?

ANNEX 2. PHOTOGRAPHIC SUPPORT USED TO DETERMINE THE LANDSCAPE PREFERENCES OF THE INHABITANTS OF THE SACLAY PLATEAU

Figure 8A1:
*Line of wells
(between
Trou Salé
and Orsigny)*

Figure 8A2:
Trou Salé farm

Figure 8A3:
*Trou Salé farm in
the mist*

Figure 8A4:
*Trou Salé
southern fringe
of Buc, seen
from the
Orsigny plain*

Figure 8A5:
INRA experimental plots

Figure 8A6:
Limon Abbey

Figure 8A7:
Saclay Pond

Figure 8A8:
Fields and woods of Saint Marc

9

Assessing Benefits from Allotments as a Component of Urban Agriculture in England

Arturo Perez-Vazquez, Simon Anderson and Alan W. Rogers

INTRODUCTION

Allotments are conspicuous elements of urban agriculture (UA) in England. They provide fresh and healthy food and many non-market benefits, such as relaxation, enjoyment and recreation. Allotments promote and support a variety of natural functions, such as green open spaces and habitats for wildlife (Garnett, 1996). However, allotments are under threat: many sites have disappeared in the past few decades (HoC, 1998a) as a result of the pressures of urbanization and development.

The current allotment scenario is a function of many complex, interrelated factors, including social, ecological, economic and political issues. Urban development pressures and urbanization have caused a decline in allotment provision in many English cities. The performance of local authorities in promoting and supporting allotments varies across the country (Crouch et al, 2001). Also threatening allotments are ecological factors, such as pollution and soil contamination; and social aspects, such as theft, vandalism and a lack of interest in allotments (Garnett, 1996; HoC 1998a, 1998b).

The value of allotments has been often underestimated. In fact, the non-tangible benefits from allotments may be undervalued, and their environmental importance is not often considered. The environmental and socio-economic benefits of English allotments have not been investigated and valued in economic terms. It has been suggested that future development of allotments should be sought through political processes (Crouch et al, 2001). However, one might try to incorporate the value of non-market benefits as an additional dimension of allotment importance. Other studies have recognized the cultural, social and recreational values associated with allotments and community gardens (Gröning, 1996; Drescher, 2001) – values that show gardening is an enjoyable outdoor social activity. If the whole value of allotments is estimated, it may provide significant justification for preserving and developing them, wherever there is a demand.

This paper comprises two pieces of research: a participatory appraisal of allotment gardening and a contingency valuation study. After this a brief introduction, the objective and hypothesis are presented; then a theoretical framework for participatory rapid appraisal (PRA) and the contingent valuation method (CVM) is explained. The participatory and contingent valuation methodologies used to assess the role of allotments and to monetize the benefits derived from allotments are presented, together with the findings, their impacts and general conclusions.

GENERAL OBJECTIVE AND HYPOTHESIS

Little research has been done in England to analyse allotment agriculture as a component of UA with consideration of its ecological and socio-economic aspects. This research intends to clarify some of these factors and to explore the implications for the short and long terms. The general objective and hypothesis were as follows:

- *Objective* – the main objective of this research was to identify the main determinants (environmental and socio-economic) that have influenced allotment development in England, as well as the constraints on, and opportunities for, action to improve urban food production and urban well-being.
- *Hypothesis* – differences in keeping allotments between settings must be explored if we are to avoid misleading generalizations and to understand the local factors and causal influences that have contributed to a variety of strategies, management and use in local food production.

Concepts definition

Allotments

In Britain and particularly in England, the normal forms of UA are allotments, city farms, and home and community gardens. The term *allotment* is defined in the *Allotments Act* of 1925 as 'an allotment garden or any parcel of land not more than five acres [about 2ha] in extent cultivated or intended to be cultivated as a garden farm, or partly as a garden farm and partly as a farm'. The birth of the allotment movement in Britain has a political origin and occurred in response to food shortages (Crouch and Ward, 1988; Burchardt, 1997). Allotments have had an important role at various times in English history – during wartime, for instance. Interest in allotments declined in England at the end of World War II but returned during critical moments, that is, during the 1960s, when there was a concern for self-sufficiency, coupled

---

Box 9.1 WTP and WTA

Willingness to pay (WTP) is the total amount of money a consumer would be willing to pay, at a given level of income, *to gain* the benefits associated with an environmental resource.

Willingness to accept (WTA) is the total amount of money an individual would be willing to accept *to forgo* all the benefits associated with an environmental resource.

Source: OECD (1994)

---

with a new interest in recreation (HoC, 1998a). Now, at the start of the 21st century, allotments are again on the agenda, with updated concerns for local food supply, healthy living, ecological diversity and sustainable cities.

Participatory rural appraisal

Participatory research methods have been used in studying a wide range of topics. Participatory rural appraisal (PRA) comprises a growing family of approaches and methods to enable local people to share, enhance and analyse their knowledge of life and conditions so that they can plan and take action (Chambers, 1992). It involves significant innovations in being less extractive and providing more empowering ways of collecting and using information in development. It is seen as combining techniques or approaches from several disciplines to increase relevance via triangulation (Chambers, 1994). This sort of study needs interdisciplinary interaction to address the complexity and multidimensionality of the phenomena and to improve accuracy. A participatory approach has not been used previously to assess the local knowledge of allotment gardening, although participatory methods have been used to examine the situation of UA in South Africa (May and Rogerson, 1995); to determine the significance of UA in Belem, Brazil (Madaleno, 2000); and to monitor urban and peri-urban agriculture in Dar es Salaam (Jacobi and Kinago, 2001). In other countries participatory methodologies have proved to be reliable instruments for harnessing local knowledge, assessing agricultural performance, and designing better scenarios from farmers' points of view. Edwards-Jones (2001) mentioned that no scientific or technical reason invalidates the use of participatory methods in the UK.

Contingent valuation

An increasingly popular approach to estimating the value of environmental goods is CVM. This method originated in the early 1960s but did not become widely used until the mid-1970s (Blore, 1996; Hanley et al, 2001). Contingent valuation is a method of estimating the economic value of public goods. CVM uses a variety of techniques, such as mail surveys, telephone interviews, face-to-face interviews, group discussion or a combination of these (Willis and Garrod, 1993; OECD, 1994). In contingent valuation surveys, citizens are asked to reveal how much they would be willing to pay for a particular public good or service. Total willingness to pay (WTP) for an entire population thus represents the total economic value (TEV) of the good or service (Box 9.1).

Typically CVM has five main components:

1   an introductory description of the good being valued, which helps set the general context for the decision to be made;
2   a description of the policy impacts or the logical but hypothetical scenario the respondents have to be asked to consider, to elicit their opinion;
3   questions related to WTP to preserve or willingness to accept (WTA) compensation for the environmental good;
4   questions concerning the general socio-economic profile of the respondent or interviewee;
5   questions concerning general attitudes toward the good being valued (Blore, 1996; Carson et al, 2001).

In addition, photographs, maps, diagrams and other visual aids are important to illustrate the contingent valuation scenario. Many surveys now include debriefing questions, which seek to analyse how well respondents understood the survey questions, what exactly they thought they were paying, how credible they found the survey, and whether the survey had changed their opinions on the issue in question (Hanley et al, 2001). Basic principles of CVM can be found in OECD (1994) and World Bank (1998).

WTP is used as a measure of value to an individual, and this measure depends on preferences and income (Carson et al, 2001). WTP is a pretty useless concept unless backed up by ability to pay (Hanley et al, 2001). The value of a particular resource use can be measured in terms of the sacrifice people are willing to make to have it. But it is accepted that this measure is sensitive to changes in the distribution of income. If preferences differ, then people with similar incomes will have different WTPs for the same resource allocation (Carson et al, 2001).

Carson (1997) and Edwards-Jones et al (2000) provide extensive reviews of the technique addressing theoretical and methodological issues. CVM has been used to estimate the value of a wide range of public and environmental goods (Loomis et al, 2000). Today, a number of federal and international agencies recommend contingent valuation in their regulations and policies (Bateman, 1993). Since 1972 many contingent valuation studies have been undertaken in Britain (Green et al, 1990; Hoevenagel, 1994). Most of these studies have concluded that CVM is capable of measuring the benefits produced in environmentally sensitive areas in terms of use and non-use values (Willis et al, 1995). CVM has been adopted in law as a basis for establishing the value of natural-resource damages (Hoehn and Randall, 1982). The evidence suggests the acceptance of this method in the context of public policy decision-making in England.

The main characteristics that make CVM particularly useful in measuring environmental values are the following (Brookshire et al, 1982):

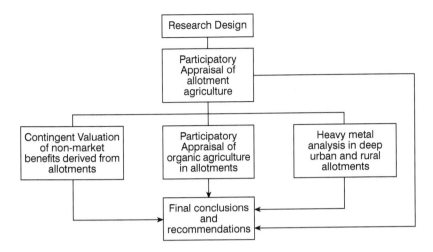

Figure 9.1 *Research design*

Source: Oultwood LG web index. http://www.oultwood.com/localgov/uk/london.htm, 2002

Figure 9.2 *Location of study areas in southeast England*

Source: www.london.gov.uk, 2002

Figure 9.3 *Boroughs covered in Greater London (inner city)*

- it is flexible enough to value a wide range of policy impacts (Freeman, 1979);
- with adequate research design, contingent value data are entirely comparable to those obtained using other valuation techniques (Schulze et al, 1981);
- when rigorous hypothesis tests are possible, outcomes are consistent with the validity of contingent value data.

Two studies on UA have used CVM. A study was carried out in Havana, Cuba, to elicit urban growers' WTP for the land they use (*jardines populares*, 'popular gardens') to guarantee access to water and better security from theft. The average WTP estimated from 121 respondents was 23.5 Cuban pesos (CUP) per 1000m² per month under current conditions (status quo) and 34.4 pesos per 1000m² per month with improvements in water and security from theft (in 2003, 2.348 CUP = 1 United States dollar (USD)). Aggregate WTP for popular gardens was estimated as being 6.88 million pesos per year (344,000 USD at the time of the study) and 10.07 million CUP per year (503,500 USD) with the proposed improvements (Henn, 2000). A CVM study for cocomposted urban organic waste (solid waste and human faeces) among urban farmers and other potential consumers was carried out in Ghana (Danso et al, 2001). The authors found that 70 per cent of the farmers had positive perceptions and were willing to pay for compost, and the rest were unwilling to pay. Ten per cent of those who were willing to pay could not express any bid (amount). The authors concluded that farmers without experience in compost expressed a higher mean WTP than those with this type of experience.

RESEARCH DESIGN AND METHODOLOGIES

Figure 9.1 shows the research design and aspects covered using various research methods to assess the social, ecological and economic issues of allotment gardening. First, we used the participatory method to assess allotment agriculture's main characteristics, constraints and potentials. As a result of this exploratory work, we found some issues that we then considered in further studies. For example, one issue was the 'total economic value' of allotments in relation to the diverse benefits derived from them. Second, it was considered important to determine the heavy-metal concentration in soil and vegetables from urban and rural allotments. Third, considering that organic agriculture is gaining an important role in allotments, a participatory appraisal was carried out to characterize and financially analyse food produced conventionally and food produced organically. Finally, general conclusions and policy recommendations were drawn from the results obtained. This paper focuses only on the participatory appraisal of allotments and the contingent valuation study.

Participatory research methodology

The main purpose of this study was to analyse and compare the function, use and management of allotments across various settings in the southeast of England. These settings were Greater London, and Ashford and Wye in Kent. These sites are representative of the 'deep urban' (inner city), 'urban' (market town) and 'rural' (village) allotment situation, respectively (Figure 9.2). These areas were chosen because they are representative of allotment gardening in England and because they have a historical record of growing food in allotments.

The allotment sites covered in Wye village were Bean Field and Church Field. In Ashford, the sites were Burton Farm, Cryol Road Cemetery, Gas House Fields, Henwood, Musgrove Farm, Musgrove New, Westrees and William and Jemmett (see Figure 9A1 in Annex 1). In Greater London (inner city), allotment holders from 17 allotment sites were interviewed; of particular interest were allotment holders in Islington, Southwark, Camden, Lewisham and Greenwich boroughs (Figure 9.3).

An extensive literature review about UA and allotments was carried out. The researchers then contacted key informants (see Table 9A1 in Annex 1) and organizations (Ashford Borough Council and the National Society of Allotment and Leisure Gardens Ltd (NSALG)) to obtain advice or information. These individuals and organizations work with, or are related to, UA, particularly allotment gardening, in England.

A list of the allotment sites and allotment holder representatives from each location was then obtained from the local authority. For each allotment site, a

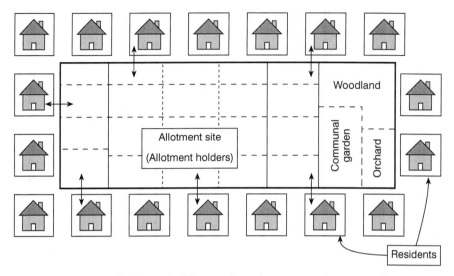

Figure 9.4 *Allotment holders and residents were the respondents*

list of respondents was elaborated, and finally a randomized list of allotment holders was prepared and appointments were made either face-to-face or by telephone. Opportunistic allotment holders were also interviewed. In general, allotment holders were interviewed because they were available and willing to participate at a given time.

To analyse allotment management and use and to highlight themes, opportunities, problems and strengths of the allotment agriculture, participatory methods were used, including semi-structured interviews. Allotment holders were asked to map their allotment plots, time lines (a description of major events in the period of ownership of the allotment) and seasonal calendars (with main activities). Ranking exercises were carried out to reveal and enable understanding of preferences and priorities about the purpose of holding the allotment. Finally, a 'force-field' analysis (a technique to visually identify and analyse forces affecting a particular situation and to design a strategy for planning a positive change or development) and analyses of strengths, weaknesses, opportunities and threats were performed.

After the information was gathered, the process of systematization followed. Information matrixes were formed, and a number of question guides were analysed. For each theme, similarities and contrasts were identified among the respondents, and existing trends were spotted. Finally, tentative conclusions were drawn and presented in a feedback meeting with allotment holders and local authorities. Qualitative and quantitative observations were registered, and conventional statistical analyses were performed. Microsoft Excel was used to process the data. Statistical analyses were performed by SPSS.1 Cross-tabulation analysis was performed to give an understanding of patterns and differences among the variables.

Contingent valuation methodology

The purposes of the contingent valuation study were, first, to identify and assess the benefits and services that allotment holders and residents derive from either allotment plots or sites; and, second, to estimate the value of allotment benefits through allotment holders' and residents' willingness (or intention) to pay or accept compensation for the allotment plots or site.

This study was carried out in the same study areas (Wye, Ashford and London). Two categories of respondent were sampled: allotment holders and residents (meaning people who live at the allotment sites), as shown in Figure 9.4.

The contingent valuation survey was conducted during 2000 and 2001. A questionnaire with closed and open-ended questions was used. The CVM survey involved the creation of a hypothetical and credible (to respondents) scenario for the allotment site. Respondents were asked to state the *maximum* they would be willing to pay to keep the allotment plot and to preserve it in its present situation and the *minimum* they would be willing to accept in compensation to give up the contract with the landlord or local authority and lose the benefits derived from allotments. Allotment holders were asked to rank each benefit identified for them on a scale of 1 (not important) to 5 (very important). A total of 180 and 230 questionnaires were distributed among allotment holders and residents, respectively. Forty-five questionnaires were delivered in Wye, 135 in Ashford and 230 in London. A total of 198 completed questionnaires were returned (Table 9.1).

Table 9.1 *Total number of questionnaires delivered to, and returned by, plot holders and residents*

Location	Questionnaires delivered (n)		Questionnaires returned (n, %)	
	Plot holders	Residents	Plot holders	Residents
Wye	20	25	16 (80)	9 (36)
Ashford	50	85	35 (70)	28 (33)
London	110	120	73 (66)	37 (31)

Statistical analyses, such as descriptive statistics and cross-tabulation, correlation and regression analyses, were performed. The analysis of the information focused on comparing responses across settings (Wye, Ashford and London) and contrasting WTP and WTA in respondents' categories (allotment holders and residents).

RESULTS AND DISCUSSION

Participatory appraisal

The profile of allotment holders across settings is shown in Table 9.2. Significantly more allotment holders in Wye and Ashford were men, in comparison with London, which had a better balance of gender participation. Among allotment holders, variation in ethnic background was less in Wye and Ashford than in London. Most allotment holders in Ashford and Wye were retired, whereas in London those retired were in the minority. A contrast in ages was also evident: Wye and Ashford had more elderly allotment holders than London.

Table 9.2 *Allotment holders' profile across settings, participatory appraisal*

	Wye (n = 19)	Ashford (n = 36)	London (n = 74)
Gender			
Male (%)	84	92	54
Female (%)	16	8	46
Ethnic background			
English (%)	87	97	76
Other (%)	13	3	24
Occupation			
Retired (%)	53	76	43
Full- or part-time job (%)	27	24	57
Student (%)	20	–	–
Age group (years old)			
20–29 (%)	–	1	1
30–44 (%)	40	17	40
45–60 (%)	40	34	35
>60 (%)	20	48	19

Source: Data from interviews

In general, the main purpose for holding allotments was to grow safe, fresh food. Secondary purposes were to have a hobby, to get some exercise, to have something to do, to keep active, to enjoy a source of relaxation and to be outdoors. For most people, keeping allotments was not intended to be a way of saving money. People do allotment gardening for recreation or because they can eat better if they grow food themselves. Thus, there is not just one purpose for keeping allotments, but a combination of purposes. The NSALG (1993) pointed out that in its research 75 per cent of plot holders mentioned the desire for fresh food, and fewer than 20 per cent noted the potential of the allotment to save money.

Relationship between gender and purpose for keeping allotments

We found a clear relation between gender and the purpose for keeping allotments. Women keep allotments to be outdoors in the fresh air, to have a place for meditation, to grow their own produce and to be able to grow flowers and herbs. Elderly men (those over 55 years old or retired) were most interested in keeping allotments to grow their own food, to get some exercise, and to have something to do and somewhere to go. Men with full-time jobs keep allotments for the pleasure of being outdoors, taking exercise and relaxing.

The reasons suggested here for more women becoming involved in allotments, particularly in London, are lack of a garden beside city houses to grow food and the need to be outdoors; the trend is also associated with media promotion and the presence of women on TV gardening programmes. Crouch (1992) mentions that vegetable growing was considered women's work up to the 20th century, when the allotment became the men's domain and women became more exclusively involved with child-rearing. But it seems that this trend is again reverting, or at least a trend has emerged toward a gender balance in many places. The NSALG (1993) found that the proportion of women who are plot holders has increased at the national level, from 3 per cent (in 1969) to 16 per cent (in 1993). In our study, we found that 16, 8, and 46 per cent of plot holders in Wye, Ashford and London, respectively, were women.

Relationship between gender and crops cultivated

On average, each plot had 16 crop species. The crops most often cultivated were potatoes, spinach, onions, courgettes (zucchini), runner beans, leeks, Brussels sprouts, tomatoes and cabbage. Women grew more flowers and herbs (33 per cent) than men, but potatoes were seldom grown by women on their own, as it was said to be hard work.

Herbs, flowers and vegetables were equally important for women, whereas for most men potatoes, onions, crop salads and soft fruits were more important. Women grew flowers for relaxation, for beauty (as decorative plants), to brighten up the plot, to pick for the house or to give away. Thus, women's plots were normally delightful to look at. Men grew flowers basically to attract interesting insects, to encourage beneficial insects for biological control or just to enjoy them as well. It seems that women were more sensitive about the appearance of their allotment and not just concerned with what they could produce. To them, therefore, it was the overall vision that was important. Significantly ($p < 0.05$) more women than men in Ashford used organic approaches. Women usually wanted to break allotment gardening rules, in comparison with elderly allotment holders, who normally grew food in straight rows. Overall, elderly men spent more time than women in the allotment.

A large number of plots were run by couples, particularly in Wye: allotments run by couples in Wye, Ashford and London represented 40, 17 and 20 per cent of the plots. The roles played by women in this case were picking flowers, vegetables and fruits; watering; hand-weeding; processing food; and providing companionship. In plots managed by couples, decisions on how and which types of crops should be planted were generally made by consensus, and activities were self-assigned. Plots run by couples were also fully coloured with flowers and herbs. Women who ran their own plots had to do the same tasks as men, such as digging, weeding, watering, collecting manure and composting.

Relationship between occupation and time spent in allotments

We found a clear relation between age and occupation and between these and the amount of time spent in the allotment. Retired people usually spent more time, in comparison to the employed. On average, retired people or adults above 50 years of age spent much more than 15 hours a month more in their allotments during the busy time than people under 50 years of age. Some allotment holders were full-time (those who were always in the allotments), and others were part-time (those who worked in their allotments two or three days a week or on their days off).

The occupational difference was related to how people used and managed their allotments. Nearly 100 per cent of younger allotment holders, but only 37 per cent of the elderly ones, grew their crops organically. Retired people kept allotments more for growing food, for having something to do and somewhere to go, and for exercising. For employed people, allotment holding was more to provide a beautiful place to be, to stay in, to relax in and to enjoy. Allotments were for recreation and leisure, and not merely for the food or money that people could save by growing their own food. Because of time constraints, plots run by those in the full- and part-time groups were less neat and tidy than those of the retired group. Employees grew crops that did not need to be looked after as often or were easy to grow. Retired people were more likely to grow any kind of crop without distinction (short- and long-term crops) and to have a complete plot rather than a small or half plot. Younger allotment holders tended to be working class or professionals with a reasonable income. Thus, they were not people in need, and they did not keep allotments out of economic necessity but to satisfy other needs, such as pleasure, relaxation, and a pastime spent with others to improve quality of life.

Relationship between ethnic identity and allotment management

No statistically significant difference appeared between ethnic identity and allotment management. However, ethnic diversity was reflected in an increasing agrodiversity of crops cultivated in allotments, particularly exotic crops. A number of crops were related to ethnic identity and preferences. For example, Afro-Caribbean gardeners more frequently grew maize, squashes, callaloo (spinach-like leaves), and scallion (a type of spring onion); Pakistani gardeners, coriandrum, callaloo, squashes, and onions; Chinese gardeners, the usual Chinese vegetables; Italian gardeners, salad crops, beans and various tomatoes; Indian gardeners, a wide range of herbs (thyme, coriander, garlic, etc.); Spanish gardeners, tomatoes ('Alicante' cultivar) and occasionally potatoes, in contrast with Irish allotment holders who, perhaps not surprisingly considering the historical importance of this crop to them, grew large quantities of potatoes (100 per cent of interviewees). English gardeners grew a wide range of conventional vegetables with conspicuous flowers, salad crops, runner beans and potatoes. Afro-Caribbean gardeners used a machete to clean up and preferred an intercropping management style; and Chinese gardeners preferred to kneel while working in their plots. The wide range of crops and varieties cultivated in allotments reflected new cooking methods adopted by English society and an increase in the number of television programmes featuring various cuisines.

Relationship between occupation and allotment's profitability

Forty-two and 58 per cent of people in Wye and Ashford and only 21 per cent of people in London considered allotments profitable. Retired people (on average, 40 per cent) mentioned that allotments were profitable, but employees (on average, 67 per cent) mentioned that allotments were not cost-effective. In London, 79 per cent of allotment holders found that allotment gardening was not cost-effective because of the distance they travelled to get to their plots, sometimes up to 5km.

Retired people in Wye and Ashford found that their allotments were reasonably profitable: they were not concerned about time constraints, they were entitled to their allotments free of charge or they paid low rent, or their allotments were behind their home or less than a kilometre away. Retired people, unlike full- or part-time employees, were not obliged to pay rent for plots at many council allotment sites, and they were more likely than employed and younger allotment holders to purchase and use chemicals.

Allotment holders' perceptions of the future for allotments

A close relation existed between allotment holders' ages and their perception of the future for allotments. Eighty-three per cent of younger allotment holders (those in their 30s and 40s) were optimistic and said that the allotment movement was increasing. Seventy-three per cent of allotment holders above 50 years of age were pessimistic and thought that allotments did not have much of a future. Elderly allotment holders in Wye and Ashford thought that younger people were uninterested in allotments, as most plots were used by the elderly and almost 40 per cent of the plots were abandoned, in contrast to London, where 80 per cent of allotment holders were optimistic about the future of allotments and most sites had a long waiting list.

Today, it is an exception to find any allotment holder who makes regular and intensive use of pesticides, and even those who do are being more influenced by the organic movement. Diverse organic (ashes, manure, household wastes, and crop and garden remains) and nonorganic (concrete slabs, plastic tubs, bottles, pallets, old tires, fences and old washing machines) waste materials were recycled in allotments to increase soil fertility, keep plants in place, store water or hold compost. Considering these facts, it is expected that organic production in allotments will increase in the future due to food safety, environmental concerns and the popularity of organic food for its healthy qualities.

The common problems found to all settings were pests, weeds, poor soil fertility, birds, plots abandoned (because of weeds and pests), vandalism and theft. Additional problems reported in London were pollution, contamination, loss of allotments to development, lack of allotment facilities and more severe problems of vandalism and theft. In Wye and Ashford, people were concerned

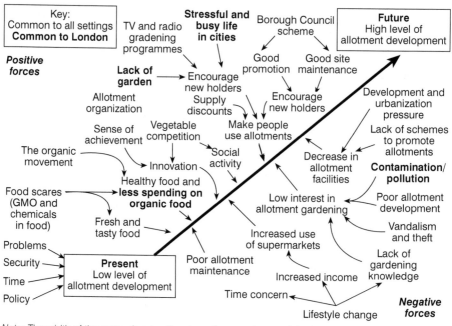

Note: The width of the arrow denotes the strength or weakness of the force depicted. GMO stands for genetically modified organisms.

Figure 9.5 *Force-field analysis (positive and negative forces) of allotments in London*

about the use of chemicals in allotments and therefore cross-contamination. They also had problems of accessibility, as people have allotments in the countryside but live in towns or cities. Therefore, factors that can increase future demand for allotments are an effective allotment promotion, the quality of the sites (services and facilities), and security as allotments with low record of vandalism are more attractive to potential tenants.

UA through allotments was seen as an integral part of the urban infrastructure and an asset to enhance a much better quality life in cities, especially for people who lived in flats and did not have access to gardens. Allotments promote open spaces in cities, encourage biodiversity, and build communities, as well as improving the urban microclimate. However, allotments have not yet received the attention they deserve from many borough councils (Martin and Marden, 1999).

A force-field analysis was performed to identify negative and positive forces affecting allotment development. The force-field analysis (Figure 9.5) revealed that people are motivated to take on allotments by several *positive forces*:

- food and environmental concerns;
- relief from the stressful and busy life in cities;
- organic-food movement and improvements in diet;

Figure 9.6 *Urban agriculture means cultivating plants, cultivating people and promoting a different landscape in cities*

- significant promotion of gardening through media (TV, radio, magazines, and newspapers);
- flats and houses with no gardens or gardens that are too small for growing food on any scale;
- an interest (especially among the retired) in keeping occupied or keeping healthy with gentle exercise;
- the satisfaction of producing one's food.

Some people are discouraged from becoming involved in allotments by several *negative forces*:

- contamination and pollution;
- development and urbanization pressure that has led local authorities to sell off allotment sites to developers;
- lack of policy schemes to promote and support allotments;
- lack of facilities (toilets, clean water, etc.) at the allotment sites;
- theft and vandalism to plots;
- abandoned or poorly-maintained plots.

A strategy to develop allotments should be designed to consider all these forces.

Planning land-use in cities

From the perspective of urban land planners, a civilized relationship is needed between open spaces, buildings, roads, streets and houses in cities. The loss of allotments and other green open spaces will undermine the sustainability of cities and their environmental capacities. Despite the long cultural and historical importance of allotments, policy makers and local authorities still have little recognition of the need to preserve these open sites. The problem now in many boroughs is lack of allotment facilities. Thus, local authorities need to be encouraged to promote the use of existing allotments and set up more in brownfields or on derelict land. In inner London, according to a survey a few years ago by Wickens et al (1995), derelict land and brownfields accounted for 622ha, which represented 39 per cent of the total derelict land (1591ha) usable for allotment gardening. In Ashford, the total land available is 19ha. Without doubt, land is available in every borough for greening the cities with allotments and parks and for other city needs.

Sustainable urban development means integrating the city with its surroundings and hinterland where food can be grown, thus promoting a better environment and human well-being. Drescher (2000) emphasized the importance of integrating urban and peri-urban agriculture into present and future urban planning as an important factor in sustainable city development.

In our study, we found that most of the allotment plots were smaller in London than in Ashford and Wye. The average area of the plots in Wye, Ashford and London was 230, 187and 110m^2. The reasons for this disparity were land scarcity in London and the reduction in plot size to accommodate more people as demand increased. Average plot size shrinks in larger urban areas (from 280m^2 down to 30m^2), and distance to plots from home tends to increase in these areas (up to almost 5km in London). Although many plots were abandoned in Ashford and Wye, London had high demand and little vacancy. Contrary to a common perception that urban gardening is primarily leisure driven, at all locations the main purpose of allotment gardening was said to be the growing of food – safe, fresh household food. By growing their own food, people obtained diverse benefits (enjoying recreation and health, socializing, learning new skills and so on) at the same time (Figure 9.6). Most allotment sites in London were beyond housing areas, in contrast to the situation in Wye and Ashford, where allotments were close to residential areas and were often an extension of the allotment holder's garden.

The relationship between allotments and society

To sum up, among allotment holders, differences appear in gender, occupation and ethnic background. Allotment holders are rejuvenating and are becoming more diverse in generation, gender and ethnic background, and this is reflected in allotment holders' ways of growing food and using the allotments. We also found differences in terms of gender and occupation and purposes for keeping allotments and the benefits expected. Allotments on marginal land involve local people in a variety of land uses, such as meeting local social needs in terms of recreation, health, exercise, food and many others. Allotment gardening is still a

Table 9.3 *Allotment holders' profile across settings, contingent valuation*

	Wye (n = 16)	Ashford (n = 35)	London (n = 73)
Gender			
Male (%)	88 (14)	83 (29)	52 (38)
Female (%)	12 (2)	17 (6)	48 (35)
Occupation			
Retired (%)	50 (8)	60 (21)	37 (27)
Full-time job (%)	31 (5)	26 (9)	48 (35)
Part-time job (%)	6 (1)	14 (5)	10 (7)
Semi-retired (%)	13 (2)	not known	5 (4)
Age group (years old)			
31–40	6 (1)	9 (3)	22 (16)
41–50	19 (3)	20 (7)	22 (16)
51–60	19 (3)	14 (5)	18 (13)
> 60	56 (9)	57 (20)	38 (28)

Source: Data from survey.

very low-cost activity that contributes towards creating a much better environment in cities, supplying food according to people's food preferences, and keeping people in contact with nature.

Two other texts are related to this study. One is by Crouch and Ward (1988), who pointed out the social and cultural importance of allotments in building communities and the way people relate to each other. The second is a report on UA in the UK by Garnett (1996), who mentioned the wide range of benefits – such as biodiversity, health (mental and physical), and leisure – to be derived from growing food in allotments.

Contingent valuation

The overall sample of respondents was 198: 124 (62.6 per cent) allotment holders and 74 (37.4 per cent) residents. The sample (allotment holders and residents) was 65 per cent men and 35 per cent women. Forty-six and 30 per cent of allotment holders and residents had a mean age of more than 60 years old. The distribution of ages was heavily skewed toward the younger generation in London, in contrast to the situation in Wye and Ashford. Occupations varied in each location. The majority of allotment holders were retired (45 per cent), but 40 per cent were employed full-time and 10 per cent part-time (Table 9.3). The majority of residents were full-time employees (44 per cent), whereas 36 per cent were retired and 13 per cent were working part time.

Allotment holders were asked to assign a level of importance to the benefits derived from allotments on a 5-point response scale: fresh food (4.5), enjoyment (4.1), fresh air (4.0) and exercise (3.9) were considered very important, and saving money (2.2) and socializing (2.4) were considered less important.

Table 9.4 *Direct and indirect benefits derived by residents from allotments*

Type of use value	Social	Economic	Ecological
Direct	• New horticultural skills • Peaceful neighbourhood, no traffic or other noise • Nice view • Organic food and good food • Socializing • Exchange of ideas and vegetables, fruits, and flowers • Contact with a green population • Friendship • Exercise • Health (knowing what you are eating, keeping your mind active, and having some occupational therapy) • Enjoyable company • Relaxing hobby	• Fresh vegetables and fruits from time to time • Money saved • Chance of buying vegetables	• Green area for living things • Space between houses (providing privacy) • Open natural space • Fresh air • Enjoyment of wildlife associated with the allotments • Habitat for wildlife
Indirect	• Quality of life • Satisfaction from watching things grow • Privacy • Sense of community • Sense of security	• Site saved from being built on • Improved value of resident's house	• Attractive open space • Peace and quiet • Green space • Nice view behind the houses • Buffer zone • Less noise from urban roads • More rural atmosphere

Residents identified direct and indirect benefits derived from allotments, and these were linked to social, economic and ecological benefits (Table 9.4). The social benefits were health, recreation, healthy food, learning horticultural skills, having nice view from people's houses, a social space to meet people and so on. The ecological benefits were habitat for wildlife, promotion of biodiversity, reduction of pollution, a different urban landscape, etc. The economic benefits all had to do with saving money. Few residents noted that allotments bring negative effects when they are abandoned or not well maintained.

The non-market benefits reported by allotment holders and residents were monetized as an individual's WTP and WTA. A few residents, particularly in

Table 9.5 *Pearson correlation coefficient between WTP, WTA, and HHI*

	Wye (n = 11)	Ashford (n = 33)	London (n = 67)
WTA–WTP	0.852*	0.544**	−0.010
WTA–HHI	−0.107	0.738*	−0.292
WTP–HHI	−0.394	0.627**	0.188

Note: HHI, household income; WTA, willingness to accept compensation for allotment; WTP, willingness to pay for allotment. **, * Correlation significant at the 0.01 and 0.05 levels (two tailed), respectively.

Ashford, noted that allotment plots bring negative effects when they are abandoned, underutilized or not looked after properly.

Correlations between WTP and WTA were highly significant; those between household income (HHI) and WTA and between HHI and WTP were not (Table 9.5). In Ashford, the correlation between WTP and WTA was significant (0.544), and the correlations between WTP and HHI (0.627) and between WTA and HHI (0.738) were highly significant. It was clear that people who had a higher income would be willing to pay and willing to accept in compensation much more money that those whose income was smaller. In London, no significant relationships between WTA, WTP and HHI were found, because many respondents failed to answer the question related to HHI. Figures from Wye should be taken with caution, as the sample size was too small.

The interlocation comparison revealed that WTP and WTA values were higher in London than in Ashford and Wye. The allotment holders' mean annual WTP amounts per plot were 78.93 ± 134.05, 35.64 ± 42.22, and 79.43 ± 83.29 GBP in Wye, Ashford and London. The WTA amounts, in the same order, were 134.09 ± 132.42, 321.15 ± 379.13, and 1148.82 ± 1449.77 GBP. The residents' mean annual WTP amounts were 41.66 ± 52.04, 46.14 ± 42.81, and 283.57 ± 338.46 GBP in Wye, Ashford and London. The residents' mean annual WTA amounts were 50 ± 50, 638 ± 1541.9, and 1554 ± 1552 GBP for the same locations (Table 9.6). Allotment holders and residents tended to be willing to pay and willing to accept more compensation as the level of urbanization increased. This is partially explained by the higher household income, lack of open spaces (land scarcity) and people's tendency to value more highly green open spaces and the opportunity to be outside. Also the value of land in London (inner city) is among the highest in the world. The WTA–WTP ratios were pretty consistent with those of other mail surveys that indicate that the disparity in WTA–WTP ratio is between 1.5 and 18.0 (Edwards-Jones et al, 2000). In this study, the WTA–WTP ratios were 1.2 (Wye), 9.0 (Ashford) and 14.5 (London). Most people were able to monetize the non-use values, as their responses were internally consistent. Very few allotment holders stated that they did not understand the WTP or WTA questions. Depending on their status (allotment holder or resident), respondents put less or more effort into arriving at a reasonable value for WTP, as most residents failed to answer this question

Table 9.6 *Summary of the results for WTP and WTA in the three study areas*

	Wye		Ashford		London	
	Allotment holder	Resident	Allotment holder	Resident	Allotment holder	Resident
WTP (GBP)						
Mean	78.93	41.66	35.64	46.14	79.43	283.57
Minimum	10.00	0.00	0.00	0.00	10.00	0.00
Maximum	500.00	100.00	200.00	150.00	500.00	1000.00
SD	134.05	52.04	42.22	42.81	83.29	338.46
Protest bids (*n*, %)	2 (12.5)	6 (66.6)	4 (11.1)	14 (50.0)	12 (16.4)	16 (43.2)
Sample size (*n*)	14	3	31	14	61	21
WTA (GBP)						
Mean	134.09	50.00	321.15	638.00	1148.82	1554.54
Minimum	25.00	0.00	0.00	0.00	0.00	0.00
Maximum	500.00	100.00	1000.00	5000.00	5000.00	5000.00
SD	132.42	50.00	379.13	1 541.93	1 449.77	1 552.22
Protest bids (*n*, %)	5 (31.2)	6 (66.6)	15 (42.8)	18 (64.2)	47 (64.3)	19 (51.3)
Sample size (*n*)	11	3	20	10	26	18
Average rent payment (GBP per plot per year)	10		27		30	
WTA–WTP ratio	1.7	1.2	9.0	13.8	14.5	5.5

Note: GBP, British pounds (in 2003, 0.618 GBP = 1 USD); WTA, willingness to accept compensation for allotment; WTP, willingness to pay for allotment.

or send the questionnaire back. The use of a mail survey worked well with allotment holders, but not with residents. In the case of residents, other techniques to collect the information, such as a telephone interview or a hybrid technique (mail and telephone; mail and face-to-face interview), should be used. For WTP and WTA, 144 and 88 usable responses were received, respectively, from an overall 198 respondents. Fifty-four and 110 protest bids (WTP and WTA values of zero) were received for WTP and WTA, respectively. Allotment holders gave several reasons for these protest bids: they felt that local authorities would not pay the right compensation, that having allotments was the allotment holders' right, that being retired they could not afford to pay any amount to keep holding the allotment, or that they would expect at least one year's notice. The estimated value of WTP and WTA may have been affected by protest bids from those who thought that access to allotments was their right. Those more concerned about allotment protection and importance may have offered a premium price. The allotment holders' WTP figures in Ashford were almost the same as the amounts paid in rent per year, and in London they were almost twice the amounts of rent. The low WTP values can be viewed as strategic behaviour. The strategic behaviour of reporting low WTP values, compared with WTA values, was perhaps due to the suspicion that the local authority or landlord would misuse the contingent valuation results to impose higher rents. Strategic behaviour is not inevitable in preference-revelation situations, but it is not nearly as severe a phenomenon in consumer decision-making about public goods as many economists fear (Mitchell and Carson, 1989). Also, respondents experience significant uncertainty in answering open-ended questions and may exhibit free-riding or strategic overbidding tendencies (Bateman et al, 1995).

Respondents could identify both use and non-use benefits (attributes) derived from allotments, and through the CVM substantial values were attached. The allotment holders and residents were willing to pay annually on average 64.83 GBP per plot and 123.79 GBP per site, respectively. The standard deviation and variance were bigger for WTA than for WTP. The maximum values were 5000 GBP for WTA and 1000 GBP for WTP. Other studies have reported that WTA is usually significantly greater than WTP for the same goods (Edwards-Jones et al, 2000). The difference between the amounts people would be willing to pay and those they would be willing to accept has several possible explanations. First, it may reflect strategic behaviour, as allotment holders would not like to see any increase in allotment rents. Allotment holders probably were acting strategically in stating their WTP, considering they were offering almost the same or twice the price they were paying for rent. Other studies have demonstrated this strategic behaviour (Whittington et al, 1990; Atlaf et al, 1993). Second, the discrepancy could be due to the fact that many allotment holders are retired and not in a position to pay more, even if they wished to do so. The discrepancy might also reflect an aspect of human protest – if the allotments were to be taken away, the allotment holders would demand that the local authority pay high compensation as retribution for taking away the benefits they derive.

Nonresponse could be the result of a number of factors. For example, respondents might have decided not to exert the mental energy required to think of a reasonable monetary value for the benefits derived from allotments. People might have found the household income question very sensitive, as they refused to answer it in most cases. According to Hoevanagel (1994), a nonresponse rate of 20–30 per cent is not uncommon for valuation questions related to WTP, and it can be even higher in WTA settings. In fact, nonresponse bias is inherent in any stated-preference approach (Lindberg et al, 1999).

In conclusion, differences occurred in WTP and WTA across settings and types of respondent. The estimated values for WTP and WTA for allotments varied between allotment holders and residents: values obtained from residents were higher. A consistent strategic behaviour was demonstrated by allotment holders in stating their WTP. Therefore, WTP figures seem less valid than WTA for estimating TEV.

Allotments provide a wide range of benefits to residents, and they were able to monetize them in terms of WTP and WTA. The most important benefits derived by allotment holders were safe and fresh food, health, fresh air, enjoyment, relaxation, recreation and pleasure. Allotments were important to residents because they brought social, economic and ecological or environmental benefits.

The high correlation of WTP and WTA with HHI was confounded by settings. The allotment holders' and residents' stated WTAs were greater than their stated WTPs. The allotment holders' stated WTPs were similar to the actual payments for keeping an allotment. The values for WTPs and WTAs tended to be higher in London than in Ashford and Wye.

This is the first study to value non-market benefits of UA. Individual preferences for keeping and preserving allotments were based on various aspects (social, economic and environmental). The value of allotments should be considered the holders' and residents' values in estimating an aggregate TEV and capturing the complete value of allotments. The contingent valuation study provided information about WTP that could be useful in policy design, such as in exploring the various ways in which people use allotments, not only for well-being, but also for making cities more environmentally friendly.

The residents' WTP to keep the allotment site in its current situation would depend on the type of development proposed (supermarket, parking lot, houses, etc.) and the availability of alternative leisure facilities.

This study calls for the continuation and expansion of future research in allotments in issues such as:

- The economic value of the various benefits, considering that no desegregation was attempted in this study. The WTP could vary if a different format were used to state it, such as bidding games, budget allocation, trade-off games, priority evaluation, or costless choice.
- Alternative methodologies for exploring the economic value of the non-market benefits and services derived from UA and for providing additional information to decision-makers and local or national authorities.

To significantly reduce the environmental impact of cities, two other aspects need also to be investigated: the impact of allotments on health (physical and mental) and the energy analysis (budget) of growing food in allotments.

Studies have estimated the value of a wide range of ecosystem services, but very few are related to UA. This is perhaps one of the first studies attempting to value the benefits derived from UA in allotments. Other studies (Henn, 2000; Danso et al, 2001) have been already mentioned. Some contingent valuation studies have looked at urban areas in terms of green open spaces, such as parks and forests (Tyrvainen and Vaananen, 1998).

SIGNIFICANCE OF THE FINDINGS

This research presents information that could help reverse the trend of abandoned or disappearing allotments and could assist in the design of a plan to improve allotment development.

Giving back to the allotment holders the report for each location helped them to know more about how other allotment holders dealt with soil fertility, pest and disease control, and other issues.

This research was the seed at the Agriculture and Horticulture Department at Imperial College at Wye that initiated action for a research programme on UA. At the time of writing, the Imperial College at Wye was planning to launch a postgraduate programme on urban and peri-urban agriculture in 2002 (Box 9.2).

BOX 9.2 NEW POSTGRADUATE PROGRAM IN URBAN AND PERIURBAN AGRICULTURE

'Within MSc SARD (Sustainable Agriculture and Rural Development), a new specialist option in **Urban and Periurban Agriculture (UPA)** is currently being prepared. This will address the major ecological, environmental and socio-economic factors affecting UPA worldwide, with an emphasis upon urban regeneration and improved quality of life. Participants will gain and develop analytical skills to understand the holistic nature of UPA agroecosystems and the options for their sustainable development. It is planned that this new option will be available from October 2002. Any academic enquiries should be addressed to Dr Joe Lopez-Real: j.lopez-real@ic.ac.uk'

Source: Howard Lee, Imperial College at Wye, University of London, UK, personal communication, 21 February 2002

Findings have been used by local growers to strengthen their organizations and to design future actions. It is hoped that this research will have an impact on decisions regarding the future development of allotments and that the extended value of the allotments will be considered in policy design.

Finally, the information gathered could be easily used for a series of alternative analyses by scholars, allotment holders and policy makers who wish to learn more about the value of allotments and the allotments' use and management strategies according to gender and ethnic identity.

The participatory approach, integrating the main aspects of allotment gardening, provided a number of insights at various levels – plot, site and location – and demonstrated a location difference in gender, ethnic background and occupation. Differences occurred in gender participation, problems, threats and many other issues. The participatory study gave us a good understanding of allotment gardening, and the contingent valuation study helped us to fine-tune and confirm results obtained through participatory methods, and through this research method the identified non-market benefits and services were monetized.

CONCLUSIONS AND RECOMMENDATIONS

From the results presented in this paper, the following conclusions can be drawn:

- This is probably the first research in England in modern times that has attempted to revitalize the local knowledge and to understand the differences between settlement size and allotment use and management. The hypothesis stated for this research is supported by the results mentioned above, in that allotment gardening is determined partially by gender, ethnic identity and occupation.

- The allotment holders' participation appeared in two main aspects: first, in their intentions and willingness to participate through points of view and comments they gave; and second, their involvement in the workshops and feedback meetings. Allotment holders' participation was not passive, and their involvement was important to fine-tuning findings and defining issues to be investigated (some of them addressed in this research).
- Allotments should be viewed as an integral part of the urban infrastructure and as an asset and enhancement, giving a better quality of life in cities and towns, especially for people who live in flats and houses with no gardens, for people with stressful and busy lives, and for people who wish to grow their own food and who enjoy gardening. UA practised in allotments is promoting open spaces in cities, encouraging biodiversity and building communities. To develop and sustain allotment gardening in England, there is a need for allotment holders, their organizations and local authorities to combine their efforts.
- The CVM used in this study was capable of capturing the value of allotments. However, some other tools for valuing benefits derived from UA should be field-tested to determine which is most suited to people's socio-economic circumstances. The figures derived from this study suggest that the value of allotments is considerable, when we put together allotment holders' and residents' values. WTA–WTP ratios were similar to those of other studies using CVM. A significant correlation was encountered between HHI and WTP. This means that there was a clear trend that people who had higher HHI would be WTP more for keeping allotments, among allotment holders and residents.

Finally, through this study, the researchers were able to identify the social, environmental and economic benefits that holders and residents derive from either allotment plots or sites. This study brings diverse elements together to help decision-makers understand allotments and their importance, not only in monetary terms, but also in terms of social and ecological values. The value of allotments depends on their location, the services and facilities provided, and the availability of alternative leisure facilities. In general, in small towns with few leisure activities, allotments were important. They allowed people to enjoy gardening, to keep active by doing exercise, and to eat fresh produce.

The findings presented in this document, fully presented in Perez-Vazquez's thesis (2002), justify further public efforts to preserve and develop allotments in England. Local authorities should be committed to providing allotments and planning potential areas for allotment development in the future.

To improve the allotment situation:

- Gardening should be taught again at primary schools or in gardening workshops or through frequent visits to allotments or communal gardens. Local authorities should implement programmes to promote the use of allotments for many purposes (food, health, leisure, relaxation and so on). A mass media campaign about allotment gardening and nutritional education should be encouraged.

- Free-of-charge rentals should be available to retired and disabled people, and the government and local authorities should update the law on allotments, to promote allotment gardens.
- Finally, further research should be undertaken on the valuation of the non-market benefits of allotments, on organic production in allotments, and on other issues relevant to the promotion of allotments and urban food production. Academic and governmental institutions should be encouraged to perform the relevant research on allotment gardening and UA as a way of helping people improve their health and nutrition while enhancing urban ecology in English cities and towns.

ACKNOWLEDGEMENTS

The first author would like to thank International Development Research Centre (IDRC) through the AGROPOLIS Award and Conacyt–Mexico for their generous financial assistance. We would like to thank all the allotment holders who agreed to take part in this study and the local authorities at Ashford and London who generously provided important information. Thanks to Richard Wiltshire and Harriet Festing for providing information and advice. The authors are highly appreciative of the role played by Uwe Latacz-Lohmann in giving advice on the contingent valuation study. Many thanks to Luc Mougeot for his comments on the final report and to Wendy Storey for her information and friendship. Finally, the authors would like to thank the reviewers for their interesting comments.

REFERENCES

Atlaf, M. A., Whittington, D., Jamal, H. and Smith, V. K. (1993) 'Rethinking rural water supply policy in the Punjado, Pakistan', *Water Resource Research*, vol 23, pp63–72

Bateman, I. (1993) 'Valuation of the environment, methods and techniques: Revealed preference methods', in Turner, R. K. (ed), *Sustainable Environmental Economics and Management*, Belhaven Press, London

Bateman, I. J., Langford, H. I., Turner, K. R., Willis, K. G. and Garrod, G. D. (1995) 'Elicitation and truncation effects in contingent valuation studies', *Ecological Economics*, vol 12, no 2, pp161–179

Blore, I. (1996) 'How useful to decision-makers is contingent valuation of the environment?' *Public Administration and Development*, vol 16, pp215–232

Brookshire, D. S., Schulze, W. D., Thayer, M. A. and d'Arge, R. C. (1982) 'Valuing public goods: A comparison of survey and hedonic approaches', *American Economic Review*, vol 93, pp369–389

Burchardt, J. (1997) 'Rural social relations, 1830–50: Opposition to allotments for labourers', *Journal of Agricultural and Rural History*, vol 45, part II, pp165–175

Carson, R. T. (1997) 'Contingent valuation surveys and tests of insensitivity to scope', in Raymond, J. K., Werner, W. P. and Norbert, S. (eds), *Determining the Value of Non-market Goods*, Kluwer Academic Publishers, Dordrecht, pp127–163

Carson, R. T., Flores, N. E. and Meade, N. F. (2001) 'Contingent valuation: Controversies and evidence', *Environmental and Resource Economics*, vol 19, pp173–210

Chambers, R. (1992) 'Rural appraisal: Rapid, relaxed and participatory', Institute of Development Studies, University of Sussex, Brighton, UK. Discussion Paper 331

Chambers, R. (1994) 'The origins and practice of participatory rural appraisal', *World Development*, vol 22, no 7, pp953–969

Crouch, D. (1992) 'Popular culture and what we make of the rural, with a case study of village allotments', *Journal of Rural Studies*, vol 8, no 3, pp229–240

Crouch, D. and Ward, C. (1988) *The Allotment: Its Landscape and Culture*, Faber & Faber, London

Crouch, D., Sempik, J. and Wiltshire, R. (2001) *Growing in the Community: A Good Practice Guide for the Management of Allotments*, Department of the Environment, Transport and Regions; Greater London Authority; Local Government Association; Shell Better Britain Campaign, London

Danso, G., Fialor, S. C. and Drechsel, P. (2001) 'Farmers' perception and willingness to pay for urban waste compost in Ghana', Paper presented at the International Conference on Waste Management and the Environment, 4–6 September 2002, Cadiz, Spain. ASCE UK International Group, University of Portsmouth, Southampton, UK

Drescher, A. W. (2000) 'Urban and peri-urban agriculture and urban planning', Discussion paper for an electronic conference on Urban and Periurban Agriculture on the Policy Agenda, 21 August–30 September 2000, Food and Agriculture Organization of the United Nations – ETC Netherlands – Resource Centre on Urban Agriculture and Forestry. Available at http://www.fao.org/urbanag/Paper3-e.doc

Drescher, A. W. (2001) 'The German allotment gardens: A model for poverty alleviation and food security in southern African cities?' in Drescher, A. W. (ed.), Proceedings of the Sub-Regional Expert Meeting on Urban Horticulture, 15–19 Jan 2001, Stellenbosch, South Africa. Food and Agriculture Organization of the United Nations – University of Stellenbosch, Stellenbosch, South Africa. Urban Agriculture Notes. Available at http://www.cityfarmer.org/germanAllot.html

Edwards-Jones, G. (2001) 'Should we engage in farmer-participatory research in the UK?' *Outlook on Agriculture*, vol 30, no 2, pp129–136

Edwards-Jones, G., Davies, B. and Hussain, S. (2000) *Ecological Economics: An Introduction*, Blackwell Sciences Ltd, Oxford

Freeman, A. M. (1979) 'Hedonic prices, property values and measuring environmental benefits: A survey of the issues', *Scandinavian Journal of Economics*, vol 10, no 10, pp154–173

Garnett, T. (1996) *Growing Food in Cities: A Report to Highlight and Promote the Benefits of Urban Agriculture in the UK*, National Food Alliance, London

Green, C. H., Tunstall, S. M., N'jai, A. and Rogers, A. (1990) 'Economic evaluation of environmental goods', *Project Appraisal*, vol 5, pp70–82

Gröning, G. (1996) 'Politics of community gardening in Germany', Paper presented at Branching Out: Linking Communities Through Gardening, annual conference of the American Community Gardening Association (ACGA), 26–29 Sep, Montréal, QC Urban Agriculture Notes. Available at http://www.cityfarmer.org/german99.html

Hanley, N., Shogren, J. F. and White, B. (2001) *Introduction to Environmental Economics*. Oxford University Press, New York

Henn, P. (2000) 'User benefits of urban agriculture in Havana, Cuba: An application of contingent valuation method', McGill University, Montréal. MSc thesis.

HoC (House of Commons) (1998a) Fifth report: The future for allotments. Report and proceeding of the Committee. Environment, Transport and Regional Affairs Committee, Environment Sub-Committee. Session 1997–98, House of Commons, London

HoC (1998b) The future for allotments: Minutes of evidence. Environment, Transport and the Regions. Session 1997–98, House of Commons, London

Hoehn, J. P. and Randall, A. (1982) 'Aggregation and disaggregation of program benefits in a complex policy environment: A theoretical framework and critique of estimation methods', Paper presented at the annual meeting of the American Agricultural Economics Association, 1–4 Aug, Logan, UT

Hoevenagel, R. (1994) 'A comparison of economic valuation methods', in Pethig, R. (ed), *Valuing the Environment: Methodological and Measurement Issues*, Kluwer Academic Publishers, Netherlands, pp251–270

Jacobi, P. and Kinago, S. (2001) 'Different ways to monitor urban and periurban agriculture in Dar es Salaam, Tanzania', *Urban Agriculture Magazine*, vol 5, pp43–44

Lindberg, K., Dellaert, B. G. C. and Rassing, C. R. (1999) 'Resident tradeoffs: A choice modelling approach', *Annals of Tourism Research*, vol 26, no 3, pp554–569

London (2002) http://www.london.gov.uk/.

Loomis, J., Kent, P., Strange, L., Fausch, K. and Covich, A. (2000) 'Measuring the total economic value of restoring ecosystem services in an impaired river basin: Results from a contingent valuation survey', *Ecological Economics*, vol 33, pp103–117

Madaleno, I. (2000) 'Urban agriculture in Belem, Brazil', *Cities*, vol 17, no 1, pp73–77

Martin, R. and Marden, T. (1999) 'Food for urban spaces: The development of urban food production in England and Wales', *International Planning Studies*, vol 4, no 3, pp389–412

May, J. and Rogerson, C. M. (1995) 'Poverty and sustainable cities in South Africa: The role of urban cultivation', *Habitat International*, vol 19, no 2, pp165–181

Mitchell, R. C. and Carson, R. T. (1989) *Using Surveys to Value Public Goods: The Contingent Valuation Method*, Resources for the Future, Washington, DC, USA; Johns Hopkins University Press, Baltimore, MD

NSALG (National Society of Allotment and Leisure Gardens) (1993) *National Survey of Allotment Gardeners' Views in England and Wales*, NSALG, Birmingham, UK

OECD (Organisation for Economic Co-operation and Development) (1994) *Project and Policy Appraisal: Integrating Economics and Environment*, OECD, Paris

Oultwood LG web index (2002) http://www.oultwood.com/localgov/uk/london.htm

Perez-Vazquez, A. (2002) 'The future role of allotments in the south east of England as a component of urban agriculture', Imperial College, Wye, UK. PhD dissertation

Schulze, W. D., d'Arge, R. C. and Brookshire, D. S. (1981) 'Valuing environmental commodities: Some recent experiments', *Land Economics*, vol 57, pp151–169

Tyrvainen, L. and Vaananen, H. (1998) 'The economic value of urban forest amenities: An application of the contingent valuation method', *Landscape and Urban Planning*, vol 43, pp105–118

Whittington, J., Briscoe, J., Mu, X. and Barron, W. (1990) 'Estimating the willingness to pay for water sources in developing countries: A case study of the use of contingent valuation survey in southern Haiti', *Economic Development and Cultural Change*, vol 38, no 2, pp32–45

Wickens, D., Rumfilt, A. and Willis, R. (1995) *Survey of Derelict Land in England 1993. Vol. II: Reference tables*, Department of the Environment; Her Majesty's Stationery Office, London

Willis, K. G. and Garrod, G. D. (1993) 'Valuing landscape: A contingent valuation approach', *Journal of Environmental Management*, vol 37, pp1–22

Willis, K. G., Garrod, G. D. and Saunders, C. M. (1995) 'Benefits of environmentally sensitive area policy in England: A contingent valuation assessment', *Journal of Environmental Management*, vol 44, pp105–125

World Bank (1998) *Economic Analysis and Environmental Assessment*, World Bank, Washington, DC, Environmental Assessment Sourcebook Update No. 23, April

ANNEX 1: KEY INFORMANTS AND ALLOTMENT SITE LOCATIONS IN ASHFORD, KENT

Table 9A1 *Key informants interviewed, 1999–2000*

Date and location	Interviewee	Position
8 Mar 1999, Ashford	Sara Andrews	Co-ordinator of the allotment desk at Ashford Borough Council
23 May 1999, Wye	Alexander Kasterine	Chair of the Wye Allotment Association
24 May 1999, Wye	George Cadish	Professor at Wye College and allotment holder
29 Jun 1999, London	Martin Smith	Allotment holder representative (One Tree Hill Allotment Association)
28 Jul 1999, London	Adrian Hill	Allotment holder representative (Dulwich Grove Common)
1 Aug 1999	Jack Rickards	Allotment holder representative (Gilliespie Allotment Association)
16 Aug 1999, Ashford	Tony Fagg	Allotment holder representative
26 Aug 1999, Ashford	Howard Green	Allotment holder representative
15 May 2000, Wye	Mr Lepper	Garden shop owner
15 Sep 2000, Nottingham	David Crouch	Professor of cultural geography at Anglia University
15 Sep 2000, Nottingham	Richard Wiltshire	Professor of Asian and African studies at Kings College
16 Sep 2000, Nottingham	Simon Badley	Lecturer at University of Birmingham

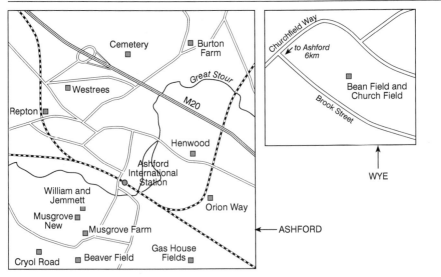

Figure 9A1 *Location of allotment sites in Ashford Borough Council*

10

Neglected Issues on Form and Substance of Research on Urban Agriculture

Luc J. A. Mougeot

This book clearly points to the need for new and deeper ways of doing research into the issues addressed by the various contributions. This conclusion reflects on these studies and highlights aspects of research on urban agriculture (UA) that, either on form or substance, should merit more attention over the coming years.

ROLE OF UA IN URBAN FOOD SUPPLY AND SECURITY: URBAN CONTEXTS AND RURAL/URBAN ENTITLEMENTS

Urban food systems are significantly re-structuring themselves. Unprecedented concentrations of people living in increasingly crowded spaces are trying to reduce their vulnerability to insecurity, and questionable safety of food supplies, by balancing better local self-reliance with external dependence. The circumstances leading to these changes and particular cities' ability to implement such changes will define the way systems will be re-structured (Koc et al, 1999). The role of UA in these transformations, namely the extent and nature of its contribution to urban food supply and food security, will also vary from city to city, both in the North and the South. The logic behind these inter-city differences needs to be understood.

There seem to be different urban contexts for UA but these still need to be identified, typified, characterized, explained and compared. There will be those where UA has become an important source of food (and particular types of food) and others where this will be less true: why the differences? Differences between the North and the South may be easier to explain than differences among particular regions and countries.

Also the evolution of UA's contribution to a given urban food supply system over time needs to be documented: why is it that this may have grown or declined? Is growth or decline associated with greater intensification, specialization or diversification, a combination with other activities or exclusive zoning? Is large-scale peri-urban agriculture encouraged only, or is UA being promoted at multiple scales throughout the urban area, on permanent land-uses or on flexi-zoning stressing combined and temporary uses? What is the place of the urban poor in these dynamics over time? Why is it that UA policy may continue to develop even in the absence of a major food supply role for UA? This book collects valuable baselines from which a new generation of researchers is well positioned to launch such studies; in fact, this is exactly what several of the authors plan to do.

This research across cities and over time can supply policy makers with the 'bigger picture'. This is needed if policy makers are to make timely decisions about whether they should implement policies to curb or promote particular types and scales of UA with particular groups. This might be to mitigate the disruptive effects of macro or contextual changes, particularly those that affect the urban poor. We can now safely say that most Latin American and African governments were largely not prepared to deal with the spectacular growth in urban food insecurity and hunger that was spurred in the 1990s by economic structural adjustment policies, and this is without taking into account any sudden onset disasters. Economic recovery in many instances has meant resolving the supply side of the equation, but much less so the demand side. Governments essentially responded to and endorsed people-driven UA. Research to identify and characterize different urban food supply systems, as these affect the urban poor, could assist governments to develop more robust local food supply systems. Well-advised city governments in contexts of high vulnerability, as in Rosario in the early 2000s, are integrating UA into municipal agricultural policies.

One important criterion in this typology of urban food systems is the effectiveness of migrancy and reciprocity systems on the ground. These systems are used by urban and rural members of extended households and kin networks, as documented by Frayne in this volume. We need to clarify the link between the importance of UA for the urban poor's food security and the extent to which these hold rural and urban entitlements. Frayne's findings suggest that a loss of rural entitlement by the urban poor increases vulnerability to hunger. UA tends to be practised by households that cannot count on food transfers from rural areas. This is mainly because they do not have or have lost rural entitlements (the reader will have noted that households' savings from self-provisioning compare favourably with the retail value of rural food transfers secured by others, in the Namibia study).

How long can 'reciprocal urbanization' sustain the kind of exchanges that are critical to the urban poor's food security? Beyond the first-generation urban poor, will more of the second- and third-generation urban poor lack such rural entitlements? It is probable that they will. Will they therefore be even more vulnerable to hunger and more compelled to resort to other options, including self-provisioning through UA? How does this reasoning apply to impoverished middle-class workers? In some countries urbanization has been closely associated with economic growth and eventually poverty reduction. In many more and over the same number of generations this has not been the case; some may even argue that this is actually proving more difficult to achieve, as developing economies now compete globally in order to attract growth.

These questions lead to another: if, as urbanization proceeds, more of the urban poor lose access to rural entitlements, do they develop a new set of urban entitlements? If so, under which conditions, and how effective are these urban entitlements in reducing their food insecurity, in enabling them to engage in UA production for self-provisioning and trade? As the Togo and Zimbabwe case studies show, access to resources for UA is far from being straightforward and seems to be conditioned to entitlements. Does UA in turn enable those engaged in it to increase their urban entitlements and if so, how? On a policy plane, is a better future for poor urban producers and UA not linked to their showing that, beyond feeding families, they can benefit the city and other urban actors in other ways? Is the construction of a new reciprocity system, this time in the urban arena, the key to entitling UA and its practitioners to be accepted as part and parcel of the urban space economy? Can we find evidence that such a process is at work, where there has been greater acceptance of some forms of UA? Given the diversity and concentration of actors and activities in cities, the resulting competition and collaboration among them, does building urban entitlements for UA require a more sophisticated discourse and strategy of alliances, a more multi-functional system of reciprocity?

Comparative analysis of different urban contexts is stressed here for urban food security studies. But it is obviously also useful on other counts. It has been used in this volume to reveal differences in local governance systems (Bouraoui) and in the social and amenity profiles of cities (Pérez-Vasquez), which affect the incorporation of UA into urban management and the very value which people assign to particular forms of UA in their city.

IMPROVING THE QUALITY OF SURVEY DATA AND OFFICIAL STATISTICS

There is a fundamental need for improved policy and technology interventions in UA, a sector of urban activity that officially remains largely unquantified, if not invisible. Data adequacy, accuracy and reliability can only be bettered if field survey data and official statistics used in scientific reports are scrutinized more often than ever, for both limitations and implications. UA continues to challenge data gatherers' skills, as evident from the case studies in this book. For instance, techniques such as snowballing or 'convenient' sampling, or the use of data from statistical directorates, must be scrutinized and new research should use these tools with full awareness and improve on them.

Several city, municipal, provincial or national governmental agencies are already collecting and publishing data on certain types of agricultural production in urban areas (eg Kampala in Uganda, Dar es Salaam in Tanzania, La Habana in Cuba, Lomé and England in this volume). This trend will only grow and academic research is already using more and more of these data. So the demand is there.

Assessments of secondary databases are few and represent a goldmine of opportunity for research by statisticians and others. In these statistical monitoring systems, how is UA defined? What does it include or exclude? What questions are used to generate the data and how adequate are they? What is the census or sampling framework used, area covered, size and distribution of the sample across the city? When and how are data actually collected from households or producers? What are the consistency checks and scales at which data can be disaggregated (urban and rural, intra- and peri-urban, city zones, districts, wards, city blocks, households)? How often and in which seasons of the year are data collected? How consistent are definitions and sampling frameworks, categories of tabulations from one census to another? How comparable are urban data with rural data? One source of data that needs to be further exploited is aerial photography, at different scales right up to high-resolution satellite imagery. There are still very few accurate maps showing the spatial distribution of different UA systems at different scales in any given city or over time. Larger-scaled maps tend to show much more UA than smaller-scaled maps and spatial distribution of particular systems may vary greatly from season to season.

With the growing institutionalization of UA in many cities of the developing world, more public policies, programmes, projects and offices will be set up and mandated to support and manage different UA activities and issues. Research assistance will be needed to monitor progress and to evaluate and adjust these mechanisms.

All these needs can generate several theses and dissertations or mobilize whole teams of researchers. Unless more attention is devoted to this information frontier, progress on data quality and informed policy-making will remain slower than possible. Comparative studies can be particularly useful to national and municipal census offices: these could identify, describe, analyse and contrast different statistical monitoring systems already in place, draw lessons and advise interested cities on how to improve existing systems or create new systems for various policy needs. In this process scientific survey methods already tested by academics and others, when objectively reviewed, can inform the collection and processing of official statistics on UA. In selecting particular city sites, care should be exerted to discourage the temptation for governments to use official statistical monitoring to harass, rather than assist, poor producers who may be engaged in irregular or illegal UA practices. Priority should be given to assisting cities that commit to keeping this risk down to an acceptable minimum.

FROM BASELINES TO ACTION RESEARCH FOR CHANGES ON THE GROUND

A growing number of UA field research sites and local informants are bound to experience survey fatigue, in the absence of follow-up actions. As Tallaki found in his study, researchers are likely to confront more of this fatigue. It is important for baselines to be designed so that they can be followed up with action-oriented research that can inform interventions responsive to the needs of those involved in the diagnoses in the first place. Researchers should be concerned with those informants who stand to lose the most if there is no follow-up. Rapid Participatory Appraisal methods and variants (Lomé, Harare, La Habana, England) do allow the researcher to survey, compare and contrast the viewpoints and practices of different groups of actors. As in the case of urban vegetable marketing in Lomé, the commodity perspective enables the researcher to cover the wide spectrum of actors involved with a particular commodity file at different stages on a particular issue (in this case, from customs officials to urban consumers in the import, distribution, sale, purchase, application and consumption of pesticides).

The baseline results in turn can be reflected in an action-oriented research agenda, which define specific roles, responsibilities and actions for different actors engaged in resolving the issue. Developing a rapport of trust with relevant institutional actors is critical for the researcher wishing to follow up on baselines with useful action-oriented research. Policy-driven research should be convened and led by public policy agencies as opposed to research institutions, the latter playing an indispensable supportive role in the process (eg Rosario study, follow-up to Botswana study).

STAKEHOLDER ASSESSMENT: AN OFTEN NEGLECTED AND IMPORTANT FIRST STEP IN POLICY ANALYSIS

An important initial step in policy research is an assessment of the playing field, including discourse and practice by the various stakeholders on the issue at stake. In the case of UA, the producers themselves and the public officials are critical stakeholders and central actors. The case studies in Lomé (agrochemicals), Harare (access to land), Paris (landscape value of agriculture) and Habana (status of self-provisioning) are particularly illustrative of this stakeholder assessment.

The Habana case study is particularly rich, methodologically. It shows that conventional research on isolated sites and actors is clearly insufficient; the relationships between actors and sites must be documented to put the data into context. This is also required for an understanding of actors' discourses, practices and overall strategies within a particular cultural system. It is difficult to see how policy-making in UA can be improved without professionals and practitioners bridging gaps among and between themselves, to develop a shared language, vision and strategy. Such assessments can lead into participatory consultations, where diverse stakeholders voluntarily come together and resolve particular issues. The case studies of Rosario, Paris and Lomé are suggestive of contexts in which the conditions for such developments are present and should be supported by research.

The Habana case study shows what stakeholder assessment can document. It revealed marked discrepancies between the discourses and practices of those who officially plan, support and regulate UA on one hand and, on the other, those who practise it on a small-scale, for self-provisioning in the central city. Different actors not only hold different concepts of UA and of its place in the city, they also hold different views of their and others' role in this sector. Nor is this situation exclusive to Cuba, and yet for such a basic piece of information it is rarely inventoried and analysed.

Stakeholder assessments should be attentive to gender dimensions of stakeholders' attitudes and actions. These affect policy design, implementation and performance. In La Habana public officials' discourse depicted the typical urban producer as being a man. Women's involvement in food production was downplayed, even though reliable statistics were not available to support this attitude. Gender analysis was found to be largely absent from research agendas and reporting practices of UA professionals (Cruz and Sanchez Medina, 2003, pp65–66, 187).

By contrasting public officials' with producers' views, stakeholder assessments can show the extent to which professionals' assumptions, visioning and planning may disregard desires, practices and food security concerns of many small-scale producers. Additionally in La Habana, perspectives on the proper place and function of UA were found to differ considerably among professionals. Differences were very much shaped by the mandate and resource investment of each professional's institutional base.

There are grounds for believing that in many cities of the developing world urban planners' challenge to mesh UA into the urban fabric seems to be fed, at least partly, by an anti-agricultural bias (Quon, 1999; *Urban Agriculture Magazine*, 2001). This could be due more to self-inflicted myopia than to the actual range of admissible systems. It is one important aspect of UA planning and management from which agronomic expertise has been missing until now. The range of admissible systems currently in the view of urban planners often excludes systems that can be accommodated in smaller spaces, that combine other uses on the same plot, and often require fewer resources than assumed. Some urban planners, in La Habana as elsewhere, tend to associate UA with a kind of ornamental beautification that excludes rather than combines food production (Quon, 1999). Others have certain types of UA in mind when viewing its place in the city. Premat found, for example, that maps at various scales tend to record only larger, high-investment, public UA projects – and even then, not all of them; also, those planned sites that were mapped were all located on the city's outskirts. Inner city and intra-urban UA had hardly any place on their paper maps, and it is difficult to comment on their mental maps. For bad or good, discourses and practices in urban planning circles often influence the behaviour of professionals in other public sectors (selective counting, technical extension in agriculture in La Habana).

In contrast, for agriculture officials UA usually refers to food production and they stress generally its food security rather than its greening effects. Agricultural agencies are usually the ones that collect data on UA, have a network of extensionists and relate more directly with UA practitioners. However, in the field, they tend to concentrate on the production aspects of UA systems, worrying less about their interaction with surrounding land-uses and activities, and in cities such interactions are critical, which is why UA cannot be left to Ministry of Agriculture professionals alone.

If it is important to assess differences of views and practices between urban and agricultural agencies, it is probably more important for policy change around the developing world to document how reconciliation is reached where and when it has taken place. National legislation that clearly assigns a role to local governments on UA and decentralized governance at the municipal level seems to be critical in many regions of the world (on Eastern and Southern Africa, see MDPESA, 2003) in order to draw up guidelines for urban planning and for agricultural agencies to work together (see Bouraoui on France, this volume). In La Habana, what explains a revival of interest in and assistance to central-city food production by agricultural bodies? This has included the appointment of delegates, the location of input and service outlets, the launch of a backyard and plot movement, a recent census of small-scale sites, and physical labelling and state legitimization of small-scale producers.

Where gaps persist between what UA professionals and producers consider to be urban space for agriculture, or the two groups are divided on other issues, research can assist with supporting stakeholder consultations. These can lead professionals to recognize such gaps, and then offer options for re-visiting current standard requirements for food production. Only then can new spaces (or solutions to other issues) be incorporated into the officially sanctioned and supported UA system. Can the kind of land-use policy developed and implemented for the peri-urban region of Paris – between urban planners, rural specialists, city dwellers and farmers – serve as a reference for developing-country adaptations? Is a version possible for intra-urban agriculture as well?

Data collected from producers may help to challenge views common among the professionals. One often-held view is that UA practitioners tend to have a rural background and that this explains why some UA practices clash with accepted urban aesthetics; but the livestock raisers in La Habana and the market growers in Lomé were found to come primarily from the city (a growing trend across UA worldwide). Moreover, the participation of women in small-scale UA, either on their own or as part of a couple, also contradicted officials' views that women's involvement in UA is limited. Even when a husband acknowledges his wife's contribution, officials may still identify him publicly as the producer, as in La Habana. Gender-sensitive training to technical extension units will only work if gender blindness is understood in the first place.

The findings in this book underline the potential benefits of perceptual analysis to public policy design and adjustment for UA. A detailed assessment of the public agencies involved seems particularly important. It can reveal differences in levels of support for UA, between politicians and technocrats (a frequent source of tension) on one hand, and then within each group on the other. This might show that all-out assumptions that urban policy-making circles are fraught with an anti-agriculture bias may be only partly true at best, and is surely useless for prescription. Any bias will rarely equate with complete and indiscriminate opposition, nor will it be impossible to remove over time. But it should be investigated in depth, if it is to be understood and acted upon. And this means that the mesh of the net should be suited to catch the right fish. Using the right net very often leads one to find that a bias may only be aimed at specific UA practices or types of UA spaces, that this bias is held by some official actors only, and that it has a solution.

THE WORLD OF LOCAL ORGANIZATIONS FOR UA

The organization of urban producers into recognizable groups is deemed critical by agencies, governments, non-governmental organizations (NGOs) and other social actors. Organization will allow practitioners to better access resources, services and markets, practise more sustainable and profitable forms of UA, negotiate the resolution of conflicts, bring their know-how, perspectives and interests to bear on policy design and take on responsibilities in their implementation. This is an important need and was identified by a conference of six Ministers of Local Government from East and Southern African countries in 2003 (MDPESA, 2003).

In cities, organization is key to being invited, heard, listened to, accounted for, supported and rewarded. Urban producers' organizations must not only defend their own interests but also speak the 'urban language' and show they can help other urban actors solve their problems. Organization is essential to urban producers becoming valued urban actors. In La Habana, a large constituency of self-provisioning home-based producers who did not have a strong enough voice, had been left out of the official UA programme. In Rosario, partnerships between organized producers and public urban actors rendered local UA multi-functional and enabled it to connect usefully with the rest of the city (employment, waste recycling, public health care, food markets). In Rosario, as on the Saclay Plateau in the Paris region, governance regimes that encourage multistakeholder forms of decentralized resource management considerably facilitated the participation of urban producers in local policy-making.

Although it is often assumed that urban farmers are individualistic, we still know little of the organizational aspects of UA; and the more researchers look into it, the more they seem to find. Is UA becoming more organized over time, consistent with trends on other fronts of urban activity? If UA is becoming more organized, it is probably doing so very unevenly across the sector. The type of urban actors in UA that seem the least organized are the poor urban producers themselves. This may be due in part to the prevailing illegal status of their location, production or practices. But how much of this is true? As in rural areas, we know of instances where urban producers have been deceived by would-be organizers or leaders and have turned to alternate forms of association and collaboration. Reconnaissance efforts should probably target this category initially.

Formal and informal organizations need to be defined and documented: those whose membership is largely composed of self-provisioning producers (household consumption) and others that are market-oriented. The case studies in Harare and Gaborone suggest that there may be significant differences in the way men and women organize themselves to carry out UA activities (women are more likely than men to operate enterprises informally). Socio-economic differences may only be part of the explanation.

It is important to understand both the internal and external aspects of the poor urban producers' organizations. Internally, how do they emerge and evolve, what is their mandate, their membership and geography, what are their constraints and successes? Externally, how do they relate to other organizations in the city and, beyond that, bear on their fate? These include organizations of actors directly involved in UA (public and private-sector suppliers of information, training, other services and inputs; customers and traders, processors and consumers, farmers' unions). They also include organizations of the larger community of actors indirectly involved in UA (community-based organizations, NGOs, city councils, public utilities, employment centres, health and education establishments, food-processing and catering, etc.). Also, international actors are coming into play, as market-oriented UA not only exports increasingly but also uses inputs provided by transnationals. The Harare case study points to one company with global reach now providing free inputs and training to urban producers, a stepping stone from which to conquer the rural market.

As the Lomé study suggests, the more accepted and important market-oriented systems are probably more organized than systems focused on self-provisioning. The Lomé case study points to the importance of external analysis. One will not necessarily perform better if one is organized; but organization may help to negotiate access to land and share input costs. However, even when producers and their partners are fairly well structured, it does not follow that they will receive the kind of extension services that will make their practices safer, healthier, more productive and sustainable. Producers' organizations probably need to thread alliances and partnerships with other organized actors in the field of UA and beyond.

An increasing trend is for higher income individuals and groups to engage in UA and employ or out-source production to a poorer, often female-dominated work force (ornamentals is a booming sector). What are the trade-offs for the urban poor when their production is actually organized from without? Is this trend growing in cities and under which conditions? Is it a promising one for more equitable, productive and sustainable involvement of the poor in UA? To what extent can the vast associative experience of rural agriculture be useful to UA producer organizations?

As regards the non-market or self-provisioning urban producers, a hypothesis still to be tested is whether their organizations are comparatively smaller, more localized, more informal and multipurpose. Is this true? If so, are these less effective in building urban entitlements? Is there a growth in scale and formalization over time? The Harare case study shows that, as in rural areas, informal support networks are often created in reaction to top-down and ineffective (public) co-operative systems. Would organizations including UA in a broader social agenda be better positioned or networked than strictly market-oriented and more formal organizations to 'Sell UA' and partner with other urban actors? What can we learn from successes and failures? Do market and self-provisioning organizations have much to learn from one another?

In any event, more research is needed to both improve the functioning of existing organizations and create new ones, or affiliate poor urban producers with existing organizations. Few will dispute that UA will help to make cities more inclusive, productive and sustainable if UA has a stronger role in urban policies – and this can only be achieved through better organization.

THE ROLE OF UA IN NURTURING SOCIO-BIODIVERSITY

UA is very much part of the forces which are transforming the socio-biodiversity of 21st century cities. An unprecedented concentration of people from widely diverse origins is creating a mosaic of food cultures never seen before, in any given city today, anywhere in the world. Food items whose consumers were largely rural and scattered in space, now find larger markets within much smaller, but often more distant areas. In the cities, traditional cuisine tends to become the luxury of a few of the better-off. There is anecdotal evidence that some of the agriculture and livestock keeping in and around the larger urban markets may be supplying increasingly those niche markets with traditional specialty food, ornamental, aromatic and medicinal products; these products could enable more people to reassert their local territorial identity and communal cultures (in the face of global trends). Very little research has concentrated on the links between UA, socio-biodiversity and the safe-food agenda. What are the niche markets for these local specialty products? What role can UA play in supplying these expanding markets? How much support is there in the general public for this type of UA? How safe are its products and how can current practices be improved? What is the potential for expanding the variety of crops or livestock for niche markets?

Medicinal plants are particularly interesting, as these can be grown in small spaces; in natural and processed form they fetch good market prices at a reasonable production cost. Spiaggi in his study describes how a partnership between researchers, Creole and indigenous residents, the local municipality's biochemists and medicinal doctors, and its community gardens department, has helped to identify and grow local medicinal plants, process these into creams, lotions and ointments, as well as antiparasite and anti-inflammatory medicines that supply local health centres. Similar systems have been observed in La Habana, Cuba and in Fortaleza, Brazil.

MEASURING THE LESS TANGIBLE BENEFITS AND COSTS OF THE UA FUNCTION

The UA advocacy literature often claims that UA benefits the city society, economy and environment in many ways. Considerable effort has been spent so far in measuring the more directly quantifiable benefits and costs of UA, although methods do vary greatly. As many such results often fail to capture the full balance sheet, more needs to be documented and measured than has been the case so far. Contingent valuation methods have been used for some time in environmental economics but their application to UA is still in its infancy. Until Perez-Vasquez's own study, not even one of the most famous UA systems worldwide, the English allotment gardens, had been submitted to such an analysis. The wide range of UA systems are particularly fertile ground for further work in this area, given the multiple functions that they are believed to fulfil in urban settings.

Perez-Vasquez's study showed that both allotment holders and residents are able to identify direct and indirect benefits that are social, economic and ecological. They were also able to monetize these as individuals' willingness to pay (WTP) and willingness to accept (WTA) compensation. As such values are individual, beyond calculating overall averages it is important to account for gender, economic or cultural differences among those individuals. Different groups of urban actors may attach different values to forms of UA and such surveys could help to identify and rate support across the urban spectrum. In Perez-Vasquez's study people with higher incomes and living in larger cities tend to assign higher WTP and WTA values. Such differences may have policy implications. In this sense, the contingent valuation methods (CVMs) could further inform stakeholder assessments, an initial step in any policy formulation exercise. The CVMs may be useful to account for the connectivity of particular UA sites with the rest of the urban space economy as these people implicitly consider such links in their valuation. In Perez-Vasquez's study the values depended on location, services, facilities and alternative options for the participants' leisure time; WTP also depended on the type of replacement development proposed.

Future research could break down overall values to show those associated with particular benefits and costs: locals and decision-makers might better see what and how much might be lost or gained through replacing UA with other uses and vice versa. More robust assessments of the value that both practitioners and local residents assign to UA, relative to other land-uses, also require applying the same CVMs to UA *and* to those other land-uses, and comparing the results. Values for specific land uses in a given setting could be ranked, including values for UA uses. If applied to the same land-uses but in different contexts (climate, employment, food security, open space), one might find that UA values take higher or lower rankings, depending on the urban context, group characteristics or city area. Results from such comparisons might surprise some urban decision-makers; they also could help to explain why, in some places, planned public UA has not thrived while in others, people have worked around planning constraints, physical and legal, to engage in some form of UA.

As with other methods, Perez-Vasquez's approach demonstrates that the usefulness of any particular method or technique is magnified when used in combination with others. As several studies in this volume clearly show, methods used in battery enable them to inform one another and complement each other for more comprehensive analysis and robust results.

In summary, new research can help us better understand the contexts where UA is or is not an important supplier of food to cities and the urban poor in particular. For better informed interventions, research can critique and improve the quality of data collected on different forms of UA by independent scientific surveys and, more so, by governmental census bureaus. To combat the survey fatigue of local informants, researchers must commit to follow up on initial baselines with supporting and informing concrete interventions, and this must be communicated appropriately to informants and potential beneficiaries; it is in most researchers' power to select those sites for their fieldwork that offer better potential for such interventions. A site assessment prior to their decision can be assisted by institutions and experts working in those areas. Research is also needed to assess the discourse and practices of the main UA stakeholders, particularly in government; this will help to identify divergences and consensuses, scenarios through which differences can be bridged, as well as action strategies that are workable for most stakeholders to make forms of UA more inclusive, productive and sustainable.

UA practised by the majority will not progress on the urban or municipal agenda unless producers themselves are better organized and represented: research is needed to draw lessons from experience, improve existing or create new organizations and partnerships. This is to enfranchise urban producers as legitimate stakeholders in agricultural and urban planning and management. With the rising role of food in social and cultural identities of an urban humanity, the contribution of UA to nurturing socio-biodiversity needs further attention. Finally, more work is needed to better quantify the social, economic and ecological benefits and costs of UA, and compare these to other resource uses in the city. The value that different population groups assign to UA, in different urban contexts and relative to other land or space-use options, is important information to assist decision-making for urban policy and planning.

Research on UA in the early 21st century has evolved considerably. Researchers are equipped with a much broader set of methods, are interacting with a much broader spectrum of local and international actors and informants, and are more committed to making public-funded research useful to the public good. Greater equity is critical to greater sustainability. New research on UA should continue to inform strategies and ground interventions to improve urban food security, livelihoods, environmental quality and overall social justice in our cities. And this can only take place through the kinds of partnerships exemplified in this volume. It is one good way in which seeds can be planted for an even richer crop of results to be harvested the next time around.

REFERENCES

Cruz, M. C. and Sanchez Medina, R. (2003) *Agriculture in the City: A Key to Sustainability in Havana, Cuba*, Ian Randle Publishers, Kingston, Jamaica and International Development Research Centre, Ottawa

Koc, M., MacRae, R., Mougeot, L. J. A. and Welsh, J. (eds) (1999) *For Hunger-Proof Cities: Sustainable Urban Food Systems*, International Development Research Centre, Ottawa

MDPESA (Municipal Development Partnership for Eastern and Southern Africa) (2003) *Report on Ministers' Conference on Urban and Peri-urban Agriculture in Eastern and Southern Africa: Prospects for Food Security and Growth*, MDPESA, Harare, Zimbabwe

Quon, S. (1999) 'Planning for urban agriculture: A review of tools and strategies for urban planners', *Cities Feeding People Report 28*, International Development Research Centre, Ottawa

Urban Agriculture Magazine (2001) Special issue on The Integration of Urban and Peri-urban Agriculture into Planning, no 4, July, Resource Centre for Urban Agriculture and Forestry (RUAF), Leusden

Index